Dedicated to my grandfather

Serjeant-Major William Beal (1892-   )
Bedfordshire Yeomanry   King's Liverpool Regiment
Ypres   Somme   Passchendaele   India   Ireland

and to my father

Lance-Corporal Joseph Thomas Groombridge (1907-1970)
Green Howards   7th Armoured Division   6th Australian Division
Bardia   Tobruk   Greece   Crete   Stalag 344

"Ah Dieu! que la guerre est jolie
Avec ses chants ses longs loisirs"

L'Adieu du Cavalier: Guillaume Apollinaire

神風

SUICIDE SQUADS

Axis and Allied Special Attack Weapons of World War II: their Development and their Missions

RICHARD O'NEILL

LANSDOWNE PRESS
SYDNEY · AUCKLAND · LONDON · NEW YORK

Published 1981 by
Salamander Books Ltd
Salamander House
27 Old Gloucester Street
London WC1N 3AF
United Kingdom

© Salamander Books Ltd 1981

ISBN 0 861 01098 1

Credits

Designer: Mark Holt

Illustrations & Maps
Kuo Kang Chen, Steve Cross,
Ian Steven, Nick Farmer
© Salamander Books Ltd

Photographs:
Full credits are given on page 296

Contents

Maps

Acknowledgements

This book could not have been written without the initial help and encouragement of Mr Ryohachi Ikeda, Deputy Chief Priest of Yasukuni Shrine, Kudan, Tokyo. In thanks to him, and in full accordance with my own belief, I respectfully urge the Government of Japan to restore state support to Yasukuni Shrine, where the men to whom Japan owes so great a debt are honoured.

Invaluable help was given by Mr Hideo Aita (former Lieutenant, Imperial Japanese Navy), who generously made available to me his operational history of Shinyo Squadron No 6. Among other veterans of the "Special Attack" units who provided information were several officers now serving with the Japanese Maritime Self-Defence Force. In accordance with naval custom, they prefer not to be named here. I make an exception, with his permission, of Commander Yoshio Masuda (former Lieutenant, IJN) of the Marine Science and Technology Centre, Yokosuka. For more than two years, in a correspondence that made great demands on his time and patience, Commander Masuda provided information based on his own experience and that of other veterans, as well as commenting on material I had gathered from other sources. His all too brief visit to me in London was a source of both pleasure and inspiration: I hope that one day we may together bow our heads at Yasukuni Shrine to honour the spirits of his fallen comrades.

Grateful acknowledgement is also made to the following individuals and organizations:
Mr Andrew Adams, Foreign Correspondents Club of Japan, Tokyo; Captain Alfredo Civetta and Commander S. Peroni, Italian Embassy, London; Mr N. J. Flanagan, Director, and the staff of the Australian War Memorial, Canberra; Miss Kyoko Funabashi; Mr Peter Hazelhurst; Herr H. Holzer, Deutsches Museum, Munich; Dr S. M. Instone; Captain Masayuki Koyama, JMSDF; Mr Bill Leary, US National Archives, Washington DC; Mr J. S. Lucas and the staff of the Department of Photographs, Imperial War Museum, London; the staff of the State Papers Room and Reading Room, British Library, London; Miss Phyllis Throssell and Captain E. J. Throssell; Ufficio Storico Della Marina Militare, Rome; the Librarian and staff of the War Studies Library, King's College, London; Colonel John Weeks.

I received invaluable help and encouragement from all at Salamander Books; especial thanks are due to Mark Holt for his patient and expert design work and to Malcolm Little and Ray Bonds.

The views expressed in this book are not necessarily shared by the individuals and organizations whose help is acknowledged here. Any mistakes or misinterpretations of fact are the responsibility of the author alone.

In conclusion, my gratitude and my love go to my wife, Doreen Ehrlich O'Neill, for her unfailing belief and support; and, for the pleasure of their company at all times, to my daughter Bekah and my son Danny.

Author's Preface

In this study of suicidal missions during World War II, I have concentrated upon those operations in which purpose-designed suicidal or semi-suicidal weapons were employed. Thus, although I attempt a comprehensive account of the development and deployment of such weapons as midget submarines, human torpedoes, explosive motorboats and *kamikaze* aircraft, I do not describe the hazardous missions of such special forces as the various Allied and Axis Commando, Ranger and Assault Pioneer units. Although dangerous in the extreme, their missions were not truly suicidal; in that they were not undertaken with the expectation, or the intention, of certain death. For this reason, I have not included details of such near-suicidal missions as the USAAF's "Doolittle Raid" on Tokyo; the raid of 617 Squadron, RAF, on the Möhne and Eder dams; the "Jaywick" and "Rimau" operations of LtCol Ivan Lyon's commandos in the Far East; or the exploits of pro- and anti-Soviet commandos on the Russian Front. For obvious reasons, I have made exceptions to this rule by describing in some detail the development and operations of British, Italian and German small submersibles, explosive boats and experimental aircraft having obvious affinities with similar weapons deployed suicidally by the Imperial Japanese Navy and Army.

Inevitably, Japanese weapons and operations occupy a major part of this book. I have followed the usage of all but the most specialized western sources in giving the names of Japanese individuals in western style, with given name preceding family name.

In the case of warships, I have included the designations "HMS", "HMAS", "USS", etc, only where the context makes such identification desirable. Similarly, I give the identification numbers of US Navy warships only when the context makes it necessary to establish the type of vessel—eg, CVE, escort carrier; DE, destroyer escort—or where more than one ship of the same name served during World War II; eg, USS *Laffey* (DD 459) and USS *Laffey* (DD 724).

In all cases, except where the context would render the practice otiose, imperial measurements are followed, in parentheses, by their metric equivalents. I have attempted always to indicate whether distances are given in nautical miles (nm) or statute miles: apologies are made for any inconsistencies caused by the necessity of reference to sources which fail to specify whether nautical or statute miles are quoted when dealing with naval subjects.

Richard O'Neill
London, 1981

"... and for the soul of man one flag above all the rest,
A spiritual woven signal for all nations, emblem
of man elate above death..."

Walt Whitman

Chapter One

The Samurai Spirit

Because much of this book deals with the operations during World War II of the "Special Attack" forces of the Imperial Japanese Army and Navy and their respective air arms, commonly known in the West as the *kamikaze*, it is necessary here to examine the ideals and beliefs that inspired the suicidal determination displayed by Japanese of all arms and ranks. It is possible to give only the briefest and most generalized account of the development of Japanese culture; yet such an account must be attempted if the reader is to have some answer to the questions most often asked concerning the kamikaze: "Why did they do it? How could they do it?"

The answer most frequently given by those Western writers who do not simply vilify the kamikaze as "fanatics", "barbarians" or even "sub-humans" is that the suicide squads were inspired by *bushido* ("the way of the warrior"), the code that governed the behaviour of the *samurai* (originally called *bushi-dan*, "warriors"; *samurai* means literally "one who is a servant"; ie, the retainer of a feudal lord) of traditional Japan. This answer is, indeed, substantially correct—but only if certain historical factors are taken into account. It must be realized that the 20th-century "samurai" and the "bushido" they followed differed significantly—and not only in point of time—from those of the formative, classical period of the warrior tradition.

Japan: the People and the Emperor
The long-preserved ethnic purity and intense national pride of the Japanese were a vital element in their maintenance of morale, of *Yamato-damashii* ("Japanese fighting spirit"), in the most adverse circumstances during World War II. Yet the racial origins of the Japanese people remain unresolved. Recent studies suggest that the Neolithic peoples of the Japanese islands, the Jomon (of whom the Ainu, now surviving in small communities in the extreme north, may be descendants), were largely supplanted by immigrants from northern China. These, from around the 3rd century BC, formed the basis of the Yayoi culture and thus of historic Japan, to which migratory Polynesian peoples may also have contributed. A true and indigenous civilization was certainly extant in Japan by the 6th century AD, when the Buddhist faith was imported from China. The first Imperial capital was established in southern Honshu in 710; first at Nara and then, from 794, at Heiankyo (modern Kyoto).

But the traditional Japanese version of these events—long accepted, and especially encouraged by the nationalistic State Shinto creed of the 20th century—is very different, and has a most important bearing on the main theme of this book. It is that Japan was the first-born of all the nations of Earth, the offspring of divine copulation. Dominion was granted to the storm god Susanowo, ancestor of the Japanese people. But because of his misbehaviour, Susanowo was replaced by Ninigi, grandson of the sun goddess Amaterasu, whose great grandson, Jimmu Tenno (*Tenno*, "Emperor") became *the first mortal yet still divine ruler of Japan*, establishing his capital in the Kyoto region in 660 BC. The present Emperor Hirohito, who was forced to renounce his god-head in January 1946 by the occupation authority (SCAP), is 124th in the direct line of descent from Emperor Jimmu.

Thus, while both Japanese people and Emperor are traditionally of divine descent, the Emperor's line is by far the greater. Nevertheless, for some 700 years—from around the beginning of the Heian Period (AD 1156) to the Meiji Restoration (1867-68)—the God-Emperor was virtually powerless. The *bakufu*, the central authority of the *shogun* ("great general"; a military overlord acting theoretically in the Imperial name), ruled Japan with the aid, or sometimes the opposition, of the *daimyo* ("great names"; the chiefs of the feudal clans) and their retainers, the samurai. Various clans sought to dominate the bakufu, frequently indulging in civil strife, while the Emperor remained a remote, unseen although always acknowledged presence, far removed from the ken of his people—and thus all the more convincingly credited with divine status in spite of his lack of "political" power.

The Samurai and the Bushido Code
A central government having been established by the 8th century, a system of provincial administration was necessary. Provincial officials enrolled mercenary war bands to help control their territories and thus, gradually, evolved the feudal pattern of daimyo and samurai (as in Europe, baron and man-at-arms). By the 11th-12th centuries, when the Taira and Minamoto clans waged a power struggle that ended in triumph for the Minamoto at the sea battle of Dannoura in 1185, and the subsequent installation as shogun of Yoritomo Minamoto, the samurai were an hereditary warrior caste (never constituting more than c.5-8 per cent of the total population) socially inferior only to the nobility—whose power, in any case, depended upon the loyalty of their samurai.

Loyalty to the Emperor, to the feudal lord, to the nation, *and to oneself*, was the cardinal virtue of bushido which, although not properly codified until the 17th-18th centuries in such works as the *Hagakure* ("Hidden Among the Leaves") of the samurai-monk Jocho Yamamoto, governed the conduct of samurai from the 13th century onward. The single most important influence on the development of bushido was Zen Buddhism (although another Chinese-derived system, Confucianism, exerted significant influence through its insistence on respect for traditional authority). First reaching Japan around the 8th century, Zen did not flourish until the Kamakura Period (c.1199-1333). The indigenous Japanese creed, Shinto, a somewhat amorphous, animistic system, contributed to bushido an insistence on "purity", on cleanliness of body and mind, and, in this and in its Manichaeanistic denial of the possibility of defining "good" and "evil" as absolutes—a denial, in effect, of the concept of "sin"—reinforced certain vital aspects of Zen.

It is impossible concisely to define Zen; especially because it has recently become tainted in the West by association with eccentric and libertarian cults and individuals. Very briefly: Zen teaches that *satori*, transcendental wisdom, may be attained through rigorous self-discipline; through meditation, asceticism, complete indifference to physical needs. The Zen adept is "right thinking": without ratiocination, by intuition alone, he acts immediately, decisively and correctly in all circumstances. Neither life nor death concern him:

thus, the samurai "lives so that he is always prepared to die"; or, in the words of *Hagakure*, "the way of the samurai is death".

The spiritual and *practical* appeal to a dedicated warrior of such a philosophy, with its emphasis on *immediate action which is inevitably correct*, is obvious. Let us remember that the professional fightingman who "lives by the book" is a type by no means limited to Japan.

Seppuku: the Origin and Practice of Ritual Suicide

The form of ritual suicide known as *seppuku* (a more dignified rendering of the term *hara-kiri*, "belly-slitting") was for centuries a *privilege* reserved by law for samurai. Traditionally, the first Japanese warrior to die by his own hand was Yorozu, a retainer of Moriya Mononobe. After the Mononobe clan's defeat by the Soga in AD 587, Yorozu, surrounded by enemies and having killed at least 30 of his adversaries, broke his bow, cast his sword into a river and stabbed himself in the throat with his dagger.

The first record of seppuku proper, however, is probably that in the 12th-century chronicle which tells how Tametomo Minamoto, defeated in an insurrection of 1170, ripped open his belly with his sword rather than face capture. Thus he set free his spirit; for in Japanese belief the abdomen is the source of the will and residence of the deepest emotions. When Yoshitsune Minamoto, foremost hero of Japanese chivalry, disembowelled himself to escape capture in 1189, seppuku was firmly established as the honourable end for a defeated warrior. (It was sometimes called *kusun-gobu*, "nine-and-one-half-inches", in reference to the short sword used in the act.) Other forms of suicide than disembowellment were regarded as far less honourable, although still preferable to surrender. "Don't survive shamefully as a prisoner; die, and thus escape ignominy", wrote General Hideki Tojo (who himself failed in an attempt at *teppo-bara*, suicide with a gun, at the war's end) in his *Instructions for the Military* during World War II.

Seppuku to avoid the disgrace of capture, called *setsujoku*, was not the only case in which suicide was the duty of the samurai. *Junshi* was suicide as a mark of respect on the death of one's lord: in 1912, General Maresuke Nogi, victor at Port Arthur in the Russo-Japanese War, died thus (with his wife) on the death of Emperor Meiji. *Kanshi* was suicide in protest against the action of a superior: in 1933, LtCdr Kusuhara of the Imperial Japanese Navy disembowelled himself when the government refused to grant funds for new battlecruisers. And seppuku might be a punishment, *ji-jin*: in 1867, xenophobic samurai who had attacked French sailors were ordered to perform *ji-jin* in the presence of the French Ambassador—who begged a pardon for the survivors after seeing 11 men die.

Samurai were instructed from childhood in the etiquette of seppuku. If circumstances permitted, it was to be performed in a specially-prepared enclosure before an invited audience. The samurai knelt on a white hassock on a white-edged *tatami* (reed mat), facing a small white table on which lay a short sword with its blade wrapped in white paper. Taking the blade by its middle in his right hand, the samurai made an incision in the left side of his abdomen, drew the blade to the right, and then made an upward cut. It was meritorious then to make another incision in the chest and a downward cut, allowing the entrails to spill out. Dying might take several hours, but it was usual for a close friend, the *kaishaku-nin*, to stand behind the victim and terminate his agony by decapitation at a given signal. In later times, it was permissible for the samurai to make only a token incision before decapitation. His wife might choose to die with him by *jigai*, stabbing herself in the throat with the dagger traditionally given as a wedding-present for this purpose.

Ritual suicide (committed by a number of senior officers in August 1945, as described in Chapter 6) persists in modern Japan. The most notable example in recent years was the seppuku of the great novelist Yukio Mishima who, on 25 November 1970, after haranguing men of the Army Self-Defence Force on modern Japan's decadence, slit his stomach and was beheaded (on the third attempt) by a fellow member of his ultra-nationalistic Shield Society. In March 1976, a light aircraft piloted by the actor Mitsuyasa Saeno made a kamikaze dive on the Tokyo residence of the industrialist Yoshio Kodama, in protest against the millionaire's alleged involvement in the "Lockheed scandal".

The Meiji Restoration and the "New Samurai"

From 1636 onward, by decree of the Tokugawa shogunate, Japan was closed to all foreigners (with the exception of a few Chinese and Dutch traders with concessions at Nagasaki) and the Japanese themselves were forbidden to travel abroad. The Christian religion, which had made considerable headway, was ruthlessly extirpated. For more than 200 years thereafter, the medieval society remained virtually unchanged. It was rigidly stratified: in order of precedence came the God-Emperor, the shogun, the daimyo and samurai, the peasants, the artisans, and, significantly in the lowest place as an expression of Japan's anti-materialism, the merchants.

Then, in 1853, the arrival of Commodore Perry's "black ships" of the US Navy brought the realization that Japan must either compete with the Western powers or face the political-economic colonization that was afflicting China and other Asian states. There began an amazingly swift, revolutionary period of development which, within some 50 years, transformed Japan into a modern industrialized nation, an emergent world power. The traumatic effect of this change, of its pace alone, cannot be overestimated.

The collapse of the old order was signalled in 1867-68 with the downfall of the Tokugawa shogunate and the restoration of the Emperor (although then, and subsequently, theoretically without "political" status) as the now apparent source of supreme power and focus of national loyalty and aspirations. Under Emperor Meiji (1852-1912), whose authority was exercised through the *genro* (a council of "elder statesmen"), Shinto became the national religion in 1868 — and by the 20th century State Shinto would become the vehicle of ultra-nationalism, until its disestablishment by SCAP in December 1945. The major tenet of State Shinto, like that of bushido, was absolute loyalty. Loyalty to the Emperor, divine head of the national family, at one with and indivisible from the concept of *Dai Nippon* ("Greater Japan").

We are concerned here only with the effect of the Meiji Restoration on Japan's so-called "militarism", culminating in the kamikaze. Paradoxically, one of Emperor Meiji's earlier acts, in 1873-76, was to abolish the samurai caste—and thus to make the greatest single contribution to the nationwide spread of the bushido ethic! For although some daimyo and samurai were to evolve into industrial magnates (the Mitsubishi company, for example, may be seen as a "clan" in much the same sense as the Minamoto of old), others would not lay aside their swords without protest.

The key event was the "Satsuma Rebellion" of 1887, led by Field Marshal Takamori Saigo, former commander of the Imperial Guard. Angered by what he saw as the excessive materialism of the new order and its insufficient emphasis on Imperial expansion (notably in Korea), Saigo led some 15,000 samurai into revolt against the conscript army, trained and organized in Western style, of the central government. At the Battle of Shiroyama, on 24 September 1877, the conscripts decisively defeated the samurai: Saigo, with his surviving followers, committed seppuku on the battlefield. But the result of Saigo's rebellion, defeat and death was not to discredit the conservative, traditional element in Japan—*but to imbue with the samurai spirit the new conscript forces of all ranks and classes*. In defeat, Saigo won a great victory for those virtues of which he had feared the loss and which he had sought to defend.

The Imperial Rescripts and Ultra-Nationalism
The feeling throughout Japan's fighting forces that "we are all samurai now" was even more firmly established by the *Imperial Rescript to Soldiers and Sailors* of 1882 and further reinforced by the *Rescript on Education* of 1890. The *Rescript* of 1882 embodies the famous precept that "duty is more weighty than a mountain; death is no heavier than a feather". The whole of modern Japan's military philosophy may be said to reside in that single statement.

Many parts of the *Rescript* would not seem out of place in a Western manual of military conduct, enjoining cleanliness, sobriety, deference to superiors, and so on. Its true importance lies in its implications, in the fact that, throughout, the concept of *chu*, the loyalty owed to the Emperor, is emphasized above that of *giri*, the duty to fulfil all other moral obligations. No man reading the *Rescript*, which all ranks were required to learn by heart and meditate upon daily, could doubt that duty to the Emperor and Japan (one and indivisible) outweighed all else. No act could be wrong if sincerely performed for the good of the Emperor and the Nation. The unfortunate, and to some Westerners inexcusable, excesses committed by Japanese troops during World War II must be considered in the light of this teaching, and of the similar teachings disseminated among the populace as a whole by the *Rescript on Education*.

The 20th century opened with proof, in the Russo-Japanese War, that *Yamato-damashii* could bring victory against an apparently more powerful Western nation. Now nationalism grew apace, fostered by State Shinto and by numerous ultra-nationalistic "secret societies" and, more importantly, military factions. Of the latter, the most influential was probably the *Kodo-ha* ("Imperial Way") group of senior officers (mostly Army) dedicated to the preservation of bushido virtues and to the establishment of the "Greater East Asia Co-Prosperity Sphere": Japanese hegemony in the European-dominated and -exploited areas of the Far East. But I disagree with those historians who cite Japan's greed for conquest and military glory as a major cause of the Pacific War; in my opinion, American policy from 1905 onward was aimed at a show-down with the United States' great Pacific rival, until, because of both racial provocation and economic warfare, Japan had no choice but to seem the aggressor.

Nevertheless, it cannot be denied that the rate of covert American aggression was matched by that of the increase of Japanese nationalism. From the earliest age, all Japanese were taught to go to any lengths to defend and preserve the *kokutai*; ie, the "national polity", the essential elements, from the Emperor to the most minor traditional usage, that made Japan unique among nations. It was for *kokutai* that the suicide squads, the kamikaze, fought and died.

In ending this brief attempt to explain the motivation of the kamikaze, I can do no better than to quote the statement concerning *kokutai* made by the irredentist LtCol Masahiko Takeshita to US interrogators after the war. He was asked why, when even the Allied terms for "unconditional surrender" tacitly agreed that Japan's "national polity" would not be drastically altered, he and others had wished to fight on to the death. Takeshita said (the italics are mine throughout):

"Although preservation of the national polity had been made [by Japan] the sole condition for surrender, disbandment of the armed forces and the occupation by foreign troops would mean that we would be compelled to change the national polity in whatever way the occupation forces desired. *Since such a unique national polity as we enjoyed was beyond the understanding of foreign nations*, there was little doubt that the occupation forces would eventually compel us to transform it as they wished. . . . . *It would be useless for the people to survive the war if the structure of the State itself were to be destroyed.*

"We did not believe that the entire people would be completely annihilated . . . [but] *even if the whole race were all but wiped out, its determination to preserve the national polity would be forever recorded in the annals of history, whereas a people who sacrificed will on the altar of physical existence could never rise again as a nation.*"

Chapter Two

The Midget Intruders

With the exception of the Imperial Japanese Navy's *Kairyu* ("Sea Dragon"), no midget submarine used in World War II was specifically designed as a suicide craft. However, the very nature of the midget submarine dictated its use in operations so hazardous as to be properly described as suicidal. It was a short-ranged, shock weapon, relying on the determination of its crew, from whom it demanded the acceptance of probable death as the price of operational efficiency. Unlike the fleet submarine, which made its attacks in the open sea, it was most often committed against defended anchorages whence, having revealed its presence at the moment of attack, it had small chance of escape. Although it offered the prospect of spectacular gain at small cost, its moral effect was equally important: throughout its history, the small submersible was often deployed—as in the American War of Independence; the War Between the States; and by the British Pacific Fleet in 1945—when politico-military considerations demanded a show of aggression from an under-strength force. Thus, from its inception, the function of the midget submarine was to carry out what the Japanese in World War II termed *tokko* ("special attack") operations—a euphemism for suicidal attack. A brief historical survey will serve to confirm this.

The American "Turtle"

The father of the "special attack" submersible was an American, David Bushnell (1742-1824). During the War of Independence, Bushnell designed and built the 2 ton (2.03 tonne) *Turtle*, a one-man craft in which screw propellers hand-cranked by the operator provided power for vertical and horizontal movement. Its wooden hull, some 6ft (1.8m) long and 4.5ft (1.3m) in beam, was provided with a turret-shaped conning tower with glass ports and contained enough air for about 30 minutes' submerged endurance. Instrumentation comprised a simple depth-gauge and a compass. With this frail but surprisingly efficient craft, Sgt Ezra Lee of Washington's army volunteered to

Bushnell's **Turtle** of 1776 had hand-cranked propellers and foot-operated pumps and flooding valves. The auger atop secured the detachable rear-mounted magazine to a ship's hull.

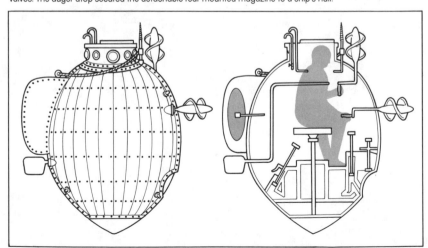

attack British blockading warships anchored in the East River above Staten Island, New York.

On the night of 5 September 1776, rowing boats towed the submersible upstream of the warships. Cast loose, Lee cranked furiously, reaching an estimated 3kt (3.45mph, 5.5kmh), to prevent the tide carrying him past his objective. At 0100, he came alongside the 64-gun ship-of-the-line HMS *Eagle,* secured *Turtle's* hatches, depressed a foot-operated lever that admitted water ballast, and submerged. Lee now attempted to screw into the warship's hull an externally-mounted auger from which a stout rope ran to a magazine containing 150lb (68kg) of gunpowder, mounted on *Turtle's* back. With the auger firmly seated, Lee would slip the magazine and crank *Turtle* away, with 30 minutes' grace before a clockwork time-fuze exploded the charge.

Failing to seat the auger in *Eagle's* copper sheathing, and manoeuvring to find an unprotected area, Lee inadvertently surfaced and was discovered. Cranking away, he was pursued by redcoats in a "twelve-oared barge" and, according to his own account, decided to make a truly suicidal end by "letting loose the magazine in hopes that if they should take me, they would likewise pick up the magazine and then we should all be blown up together". But the redcoats gave up the chase when the freed magazine exploded prematurely, and Lee was towed home by his compatriots.

Two more unsuccessful attempts on British warships were made by *Turtle* during the War of Independence, and it is believed that a second model of Bushnell's submersible was constructed for possible employment during the War of 1812, when semi-submersible rowing boats armed with spar-torpedoes also made an appearance in the American armoury. The US Navy had by this time turned down what might have been a more potent "special attack" weapon: Robert Fulton's 19 ton (19.3 tonne), copper-hulled, three-man submersible *Nautilus,* propelled by a hand-cranked screw and with a compressed-air supply giving a submerged endurance of up to four hours. Finally constructed for Napoleon's navy, *Nautilus* ran fairly successful trials but never saw action.

The Confederate Submersibles
In 1863, hard-pressed by the Federal blockade, the Confederate States Navy began to make use of "special attack" submersibles. The first to see action were semi-submersibles called *Davids* to emphasize their giant-killing role. The *David* was a small, cigar-shaped steam-boat with a four-man crew. It was armed with a spar-torpedo—a 20ft (6m) pole projecting from the bow and ending in a copper canister containing 134lb (61kg) of gunpowder, fired by a chemical impact fuze. Intended for night operations, the *David* could be trimmed down for attack until only her funnel and superstructure were above water. On the night of 5 October 1863, a *David* commanded by Cdr W.T. Glassell, CSN, survived an attack in which she severely damaged the Federal ironclad *New Ironsides* off Charleston.

The Confederate States Army now took a hand with a true submersible—the fifth in a series built at Mobile, Alabama, by Horace

A. Hunley. This 19 ton (19.3 tonne) craft was an iron tube some 30ft (9m) long and 5ft (1.5m) in beam, propelled by a stern-mounted screw cranked by eight men. It had a squat conning tower at either end as the commander's station, with hydroplane and rudder controls, and was armed first with a towed explosive charge and then with a 134lb (61kg) spar-torpedo with a barbed end. The craft normally ran awash but was theoretically capable of submerging for up to two hours. Simply to crew this submersible was suicidal: it was totally unstable and sank four times during trials, killing 33 men — including Hunley himself. The inventor was posthumously honoured by having the first operational model bear his name.

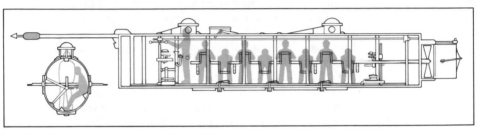

CSS **Hunley**, the "special attack" submersible deployed by the Confederate States Army in 1864.

CSS *Hunley* slipped out of Charleston on the evening of 17 February 1864 to strike at the patrolling USS *Housatonic*. Lt George E. Dixon, CSA, *Hunley*'s commander, intended to drive home the barb of his spar-torpedo below the waterline of the 20-gun sloop. He would then back water, unreeling a lanyard that would fire the charge when *Hunley* was at a safe distance. The ramming attack succeeded and *Housatonic* swiftly sank, taking down with her five of her crew — and the nine men of *Hunley*, which was dragged down with her victim. In spite of the obviously suicidal nature of such weapons it was found, when the South's shipyards fell to Federal troops, that the Confederacy had implemented an extensive building programme for "special attack" craft.

Russian Midgets—and the "Fenian Ram"

The value of the small submersible in anti-blockade operations had been demonstrated in Europe as early as 1850-51, when the mere rumour of Wilhelm Bauer's *Brandtaucher* was sufficient to cause a temporary relaxation of the Danish blockade of Kiel. *Brandtaucher,* a slab-sided iron coffin some 26ft (7.9m) long, displacing 38.5 tons (39.1 tonnes), and hand-cranked by two men, was armed with crude "limpet" charges which the crew were to fix to enemy hulls with leather "gloves" protruding from the craft's hull.

Brandtaucher sank on trials and Bauer moved to Russia, where his later designs may have influenced the inventor Alexandrowski, whose submersible of 1868 utilized an engine driven by compressed air. Stepan Drzewiecki's *Podascophe*, built at St Petersburg in 1876, returned to man-power for propulsion; but this 16ft (4.9m), two-man boat incorporated such notable features as a periscope, an adjustable screw and a caustic-soda air purifier.

Podascophe was armed with mines which were to be carried on the casing and released when the submersible lay beneath enemy ships. The Tsar's navy ordered 52 boats of Drzewiecki's design, but their fate is obscure. However, in September 1904 the Russian Navy is said to have contemplated a suicidal attack on Japanese warships blockading Port Arthur, with a two-man submersible in which an automobile engine replaced the bicycle-type pedals of Drzewiecki's midgets. In 1902-03 the Russians had bought five examples of the American inventor Simon Lake's *Protector* (which cannot be classified as a midget) and were experimenting with a Spanish-designed, German-built, 17 ton (17.3 tonne) midget called *Forelj*, which they planned to use against an anticipated Japanese attack on Vladivostock.

One other abortive design for an early "special attack" midget deserves mention, since it was the work of the chief begetter of the modern fleet submarine, John Philip Holland (1840-1914). Holland, Irish-born and a violent Anglophobe, built his early submersibles with private backing after his designs had been rejected by the US Navy. His third model was built for operations against the Royal Navy: the Fenian Society, an organisation of Irish-American patriots, financed the *Fenian Ram*, a 19 ton (19.3 tonne), 33ft (10m) submersible powered by a 15hp internal combustion engine with a compressed-air unit for submerged running. It mounted a 9in (229mm) compressed-air underwater cannon, an impractical weapon which the Fenians hoped to use against British warships; possibly in "special attacks" in Canadian waters.

Fenian Ram was launched in 1881; but in 1884, losing patience with Holland's insistence on exhaustive trials, the Fenians hijacked the submersible in the Hudson River. Holland thereupon washed his hands of the project and, plagued by mechanical failures in the hands of amateurs, *Fenian Ram* ended as a derelict on the beach at New Haven, Connecticut. But Holland went on to design successful submarines which, around the turn of the century, entered service with the navies of the USA, Britain, Russia—and Japan.

Japanese Midget Submarines

The Imperial Japanese Navy purchased its first submarines, five *Holland Xs*, from the Electric Boat Company, Quincy, Massachusetts, in 1904-05; at the same time laying down two similar boats at the Kawasaki yard, Kobe. Although the latter were diminutive craft—of 57 tons (58 tonnes) and 78 tons (79.2 tonnes)—Japan thereafter manifested little interest in midget designs until the 1930s; development in midget submersibles being left largely to the Italian and British navies.

The genesis of the IJN's midget submarines of World War II is somewhat obscure; some accounts ascribe the seminal designs to private individuals. Credit is sometimes given to a retired naval officer, Captain Noriyoshi Yokou, a Russo-Japanese War veteran, who followed up a plan for "human torpedoes" dating from that conflict. Yokou's design, it is said, was refused by the Naval General Staff in 1933 because of its obviously suicidal nature. One Japanese naval historian credits a civilian called Nishimura with an influential role.

Nishimura's boat was built by Mitsubishi in the mid-1930s and was a one- or two-man craft displacing c.20 tons (20.3 tonnes), propelled at a maximum submerged speed of c.4.5 kts (5.2mph, 8.3kmh) by a 16hp electric motor. It was unarmed and seems to have been intended primarily for underwater exploration: in February 1939, when the fleet submarine *I-63* was sunk in collision in Bungo Strait, Nishimura-type submersibles were employed to locate the wreck.

While the designs of Yokou and Nishimura may have exerted some influence, it is probable that the greatest credit should be given to a team of naval officers under the overall direction of Capt Kaneharu Kishimoto. This officer put forward a plan for the development of what was to become the *Type A* midget in 1933, and work was approved by the Naval General Staff — on the understanding that the submarine was *not* to be a suicide weapon. This raises the interesting question of whether Capt Kishimoto's original proposal was for what he regarded as a suicide boat. Work began at Kure Naval Yard in 1934.

From the first, the project was shrouded in secrecy: at various stages of their development the midgets were codenamed *A-Hyoteki* ("A-Target"); *H-* or *A-Kanamono* ("Type H or A Metal Fittings"); *Maru-Ichi; Go-Sen;* and *Bakugeki-Hyoteki* ("Anti-submarine Bombing Target"). In 1938, after several design stages, there emerged a production model designated *Ko-Gata* ("Type A").

The Type A Midget Submarine

The 1934 prototypes had had no conning tower and no armament, being purely experimental vehicles. Two improved models, *Ha 1* and

JAPANESE MIDGET SUBMARINES					
Type:	"TYPE A" (KO-GATA)	"TYPE C" (HEI-GATA)	"TYPE D" (KORYU)	KAIRYU	U-KANAMONO
Submerged displacement:	46 tons (46.74 tonnes)	49.8 tons (50.6 tonnes)	59.7 tons (60.6 tonnes)	19.25 tons (19.6 tonnes)	15 tons (15.2 tonnes)
Length: overall:	78.5ft (23.9m)	81.75ft (24.9m)	86ft (26.2m)	56.75ft (17.3m)	46ft (14m)
Beam:	6ft (1.8m)	6ft (1.8m)	6.7ft (2.04m)	4.5ft (1.37m) (less fins)	6.5ft (1.98m)
Draught:	6ft (1.8m)	6ft (1.8m)	6.7ft (2.04m)	4.5ft (1.37m)	6.5ft (1.98m)
Machinery:	electric motor =600hp	1 – shaft diesel =40bhp electric motor =600shp	1 – shaft diesel =150bhp electric motor =500shp	1 – shaft petrol =85hp electric motor =80hp	1 – shaft compressed-air torpedo motor
Max speed surfaced: submerged:	23kt 19kt	6.5kt 18.5kt	8kt 15kt	7.5kt 10kt	3kt (awash)
Range surfaced: submerged:	80nm @ 2kt 20nm @ 19kt	300-350nm @ 6kt 120nm @ 4kt 18nm @ 18.5kt	1,000nm @ 8kt 320nm @ 15kt	450nm @ 5kt 36nm @ 3kt	not known (low)
Armament:	2x17.7in (450mm) TT	2x17.7in (450mm) TT	2x17.7in (450mm) TT or bow-mounted explosive	2x17.7in (450mm) torpedoes or 1,320lb (600kg) explosive charge	1x17.7in (450mm) TT
Crew:	2	3	5	2	2
Number completed:	62	15	115	215	14

Ha 2, were launched in 1936; these had small conning towers and two superimposed 17.7in (450mm) bow torpedo tubes. A major fault of these boats, as of later Type As, was the limited range and endurance concomitant with having a single-shaft 600hp electric motor, without self-charging capacity, as the sole means of propulsion.

Although capable of a surfaced speed of 23kt (26.5mph, 42.5kmh), the two-man Type A had a surface combat radius of only 80nm (92 miles, 148km) at no more than 2kt (2.3mph, 3.7kmh). The high submerged speed of 19kt (22mph, 35kmh) could be maintained over a combat radius of only 20nm (23 miles, 37km). However, at this time Japanese doctrine envisaged a "decisive battle" fought in home waters, where Japan would have the necessary surface and air superiority to allow midget submarines to operate efficiently when

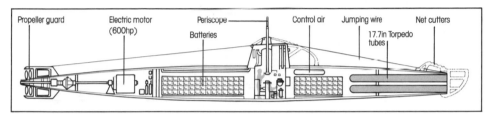

Later **Type A** midget submarine, with capped tubes, net-cutters, jumping-wires and propeller-guards.

launched close to their targets from surface ships or fleet submarines.

Fortytwo Type As (numbered *Ha 3* to *Ha 44*) were ordered in 1939-40 and built at a specially-established branch of Kure NY at Ourazaki. A further 15 units (*Ha 46* to *Ha 52; Ha 54* to *Ha 61*) were built at Ourazaki in 1941-42. These later Type As incorporated several improvements: the torpedo tubes, open to the sea in earlier models, were capped; and jumping-wires, propeller-guards and serrated steel net-cutters were fitted, slightly reducing the maximum submerged speed of the submarines thus equipped.

Mother Ships for Midgets

Notwithstanding the role they would eventually play, the Type As were not at first intended to be used against enemy bases. It was planned that in the "decisive battle" they would be carried on mother ships with the main battle fleet and released to make surprise attacks during a general engagement.

To this end, the seaplane tenders (really "seaplane carriers", since they were equipped to carry and catapult-launch up to 24 aircraft) *Chitose* and *Chiyoda*, completed in 1938, were constructed so that they could be easily converted to carry and launch midget submarines. *Mizuho,* completed in 1939, although classified as a seaplane tender, was designed primarily as a midget submarine carrier. *Nisshin,* designed as a combination of seaplane tender and minelayer, was stripped of her minelaying gear soon after completion in 1942 and refitted to carry and launch 12 midgets; and the supply and repair ship *Chogei* probably underwent a similar refit in 1943.

For trials in 1939, *Chitose's* aircraft-handling capacity was reduced to 12 seaplanes and a number of Type A midget submarines were housed in her lower-deck storage hangar. The hangar deck had been converted to give a fore-to-aft incline towards the hinged steel doors of a large stern hatch, through which the Type As, moved along the rails normally used for handling aircraft, were launched. *Chiyoda* was similarly converted in 1941. Both ships could carry up to 12 Type As which, in favourable seas and with skilled handlers, could all be launched, two at a time, inside 17 minutes.

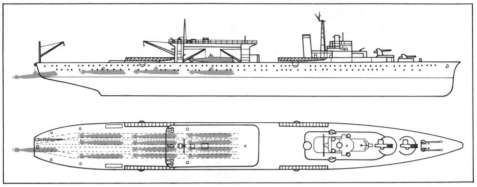

In 1939-42, the 11,023-ton seaplane tenders/carriers **Chitose** and **Chiyoda** were temporarily refitted to carry up to 12 **Type A** midgets, launched along rails through a large stern hatch.

By 1940, however, there had been a significant change in the IJN's doctrine concerning midget submarines. Instead of operations with the main battle fleet, increasing emphasis was placed on the midgets' ability to penetrate defended anchorages. But the Type As were short-ranged — and a mother ship would obviously be at great risk when approaching an enemy base. Therefore, the five 2,554/3,561 ton (2595/3618 tonne) Type C1 submarines of the I-16 class — *I-16, I-18, I-20, I-22* and *I-24* — completed between March 1940 and October 1941, were each equipped to carry a Type A in chocks situated on the casing aft the conning tower. These large submarines had an action radius of 14,000nm (16,100 miles, 25,900km) at 16kt (18.4mph, 29.6kmh) surfaced and 60nm (69 miles, 111km) at 3kt (3.45mph, 5.5kmh) submerged. By early 1942, two Type B1 boats (of similar dimensions to the Type C1, but with a submerged radius one-third greater) — *I-27* and *I-28* — originally designed to carry and launch a reconnaissance seaplane, had been refitted to carry Type As. At the same time, *Chitose* and *Chiyoda* were reconverted to become small, conventional aircraft carriers.

Type B and Type C Midgets

As will be seen, the major operations in which the Type A midgets were deployed were truly suicidal. A major factor militating against their chance of survival was their limited range — and the experimental Type B design aimed to remedy this deficiency. Completed in February 1943, *Ha 45*, the only Type B *(Otsu-Gata)* boat, was a little larger than the Type A (see Table, page 22). As well as a 600shp electric motor it had a single-shaft 40bhp/25kw diesel which would both propel the submarine on the surface (at a much reduced speed)

Above: Naval cadets at Etajima begin the day by bowing towards the Imperial Palace. Veneration for Japan's traditional values would inspire many volunteers for "special attack" duties.

Left: A living god honours his country's guardian spirits, October 1940. Emperor Hirohito leaves Yasukuni Shrine, Tokyo, where the souls of those who die in battle meet as demi-gods.

Below: The "human bombs" of the Sino-Japanese conflict, who gave their lives to destroy an obstacle with a "Bangalore Torpedo", were commemorated as an example to Japan's youth.

Above: Pearl Harbor, 7 December 1941 – the air attack on "Battleship Row" begins. Torpedo tracks streak the water and **West Virginia**, third in line from the left, is already listing.

Below: Salvaged at Pearl Harbor after the war and returned to Japan, this **Type A** midget submarine is now preserved at Etajima Naval Academy by the Maritime Self-Defence Force.

Bottom: Ensign Kazuo Sakamaki's **Type A** aground on the north coast of Oahu. Sakamaki swam ashore to become the first Japanese PoW of the war; his crewman, PO Kyoji Inagaki, was drowned.

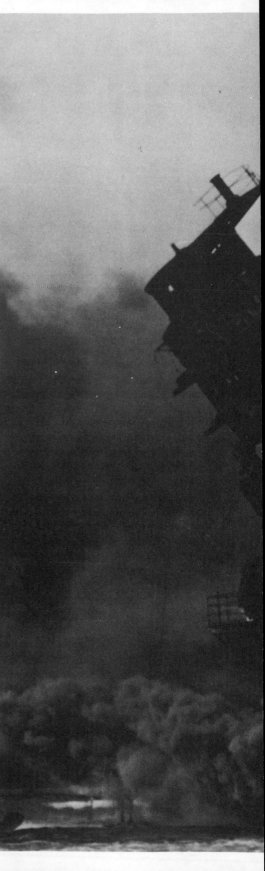

Left: USS **Arizona** (BB 39) on fire and listing. To the fury of Japanese airmen, credit for her sinking was given by the propaganda machine to SubLt Masaharu Yokoyama's **Type A** midget submarine.

Below: Found in Sakamaki's **Type A**, this chart showing the course he had hoped to take gave rise to a belief that he had penetrated Pearl Harbor well in advance of the air strikes.

Top: Nineteen seamen died in the former harbour ferry **Kuttabul**, torpedoed by a **Type A** midget submarine in Sydney Harbour, 31 May 1942.

Above: A **Type A** sunk during the raid on Sydney Harbour is salvaged. There was criticism in Australia of the decision to bury its crew's remains with full military honours.

Left: Scuttled off Guadalcanal in November 1942, and raised by USN "Seabees", a **Type A** is beached near the hulk of the transport **Yamazuki Maru**. Note the midget's net-cutter, jumping-wire, and two torpedoes still in the open tubes.

Above left: A bomb from a US carrier aircraft detonates near the IJN's midget submarine and explosive motorboat base at Unten, Okinawa, during air strikes made in October 1944.

Above centre: This nearly-completed **Kairyu** midget submarine (note fins with inset diving rudders beneath conning tower and astern) was found by US occupation forces at Yokosuka.

Above: A **Type D** (**Koryu**) five-man submarine under construction. Some of these boats had their two 17.7in (450mm) bow torpedo tubes replaced by explosive charges for suicidal ramming attacks.

Left: The **Type C** three-man midget submarine **Ha 69** in its launching cradle on the "Type 1" fast transport/landing ship **T 5**, August 1944. It was launched on rollers down a stern ramp.

Below: **Koryu** await completion in a pen at Kure Navy Yard at the war's end. Parts were mass-produced in dispersed workshops and were then trucked to the dockside for final assembly.

Below: The British "X-5" class midget **X-25** runs on the surface. Note the stepped casing: in "XE" boats the casing extended flush to the bow, giving added interior accommodation.

Bottom: Note the large air-induction pipe on **X-25**. With a special valve fitted, this could function as a "Schnorkel" (Snort), allowing limited use of the diesel when submerged.

Above: A German **Biber** one-man submarine is lowered to the water. One of its two 21in (533mm) electric torpedoes can be seen in its semi-recessed position on the port side of the hull.

Left: Korvettenkapitän Hans Bartels was chiefly responsible for the design of the **Biber**, used semi-suicidally by the German Navy's **Kleinkampf-verbände** ("Small Battle Units" or "K-Force").

Below: Clinging to his boat's exhaust pipe, a **Biber** pilot inspects the icy waters of Rotterdam, December 1944. Note trailing hose of breathing gear, and armour-glass ports in conning tower.

Above: A British ship's boat approaches a German **Biber** midget submarine lying on the surface after a night sortie in the English Channel.
Above right: The **Biber** is secured. Its pilot is dead or dying, poisoned by fumes from the automobile engine fitted for surface running.

Right: En route by road, on a special trailer, to its launching base on the Channel, this **Biber** was abandoned after its convoy was shot up by Allied fighter-bombers.

Below: A **Biber**'s periscope is camouflaged with foliage before its sortie along the Waal River, eastern Holland, to strike at the Nijmegen road bridge, 12-13 January 1945.

Above: Although considerably larger than the **Biber**, the **Molch** was also a one-man boat. Powered by an electric motor, it was safer to operate and had a greater submerged range.

Right: The "Type XXVIIB" U-boat, the two-man **Seehund**, was perhaps the best midget submarine of World War II. In almost all but armament, it resembled a miniaturized fleet submarine.

Below: Seehund midgets on the assembly line in the giant bomb-proof "Konrad" shelter at Germania Werft, Kiel, May 1945. Prefabricated sections were trucked to shelters like these for assembly.

and recharge the batteries of the electric motor. It carried a third crewman as engineer.

Trials of *Ha 45* resulted, later in 1943, in an order for 15 Type C *(Hei-Gata)* midgets—*Ha 62* to *Ha 76*—to be built at Ourazaki. These three-man boats differed from the Type B only in that they carried a slightly larger fuel supply and that the time needed to recharge batteries (18 hours in the Type B) was a little reduced. Armed with two 17.7in (450mm) bow torpedo tubes, the Type C had a maximum surface speed of 6.5kt (7.5mph, 12kmh) and an action radius of

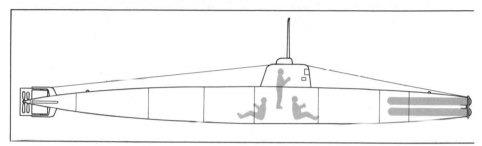

The **Type C**, like the **Koryu** (below), was designed to be carried and launched by a "Type 1" ship.

300-350nm (345-402 miles, 555-647km); submerged, its action radius was 120nm (138 miles, 185km) at 4kt (4.6mph, 7.4kmh) or c.18nm (21 miles, 33km) at a maximum 18.5kt (21.3mph, 34kmh). A few Type Cs were constructed with a conning tower extension and two periscopes for training duties.

The Type D Koryu

The Type A midget, although not designed as a suicide weapon, was used as such. The Type C, used mainly for local defence at bases in the Philippines, where eight were lost in action in 1944-45, was never used suicidally; although it was deployed, with other midgets, for the final, suicidal defence of the home islands in mid-1945. However, with the Type D *(Tei-Gata),* usually called the *Koryu* ("Scaly Dragon"), the IJN moved towards a purpose-designed suicide submarine. Plans for this submarine were completed early in 1944, when the *kaiten* manned-torpedo (see Chapter 5) was also accepted by the IJN.

Although not very much larger than the Type C, the koryu carried a crew of five. Its diesel unit was uprated to 150bhp/100kw to give a slightly higher surface speed and, more important, cut the time

Some five-man **Type D** (**Koryu**) submarines deployed for defence of the home islands in 1945 had their bow torpedo tubes replaced by explosive charges for suicidal ramming attacks.

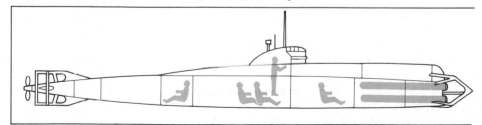

needed for recharging batteries to eight hours. However, the extra crew space necessitated a reduction in the size of the electric motor, cutting the maximum submerged speed to around 15kt (17.25mph, 28kmh). The original design was modified so that the koryu could be prefabricated in five sections; builders in a number of yards set up workshops for the mass production of parts which could be transported in trucks for assembly at the dockside. It was planned to produce 540 koryu by September 1945 and some 180 every month thereafter, but US bombing and material shortages so disrupted the programme that only 115 had been completed (with 496 under construction) by the war's end.

With a maximum surface action radius of 1,000nm (1150 miles, 1850km) at 8kt (9.2mph, 14.8kmh) and a submerged radius of 320nm (368 miles, 592km) at a maximum 16kt (18.4mph, 29.6kmh), the koryu might have proved extremely effective if deployed, as was planned, in large numbers at bases throughout the Philippines and at Okinawa. But by the time the first of the series, *Ha 77*, was completed in January 1945, it was obvious that its major function would be home defence. The koryu could be deployed aboard the 21 "Type 1" fast transports/ landing ships completed in 1944-45, which had launching rails for two Type Cs, two koryu or six kaiten manned-torpedoes—but for home defence they would be launched from the shore, on rails or by crane. In this role, some koryu had their two 17.7in (450mm) bow torpedo tubes replaced by an explosive charge for suicidal ramming attacks. Some koryu, fitted with a long conning tower and two periscopes, were used in the training programme for kaiten pilots.

The Kairyu Suicide Submarine

The design of the *Kairyu* ("Sea Dragon") stemmed from modifications made to a Type A midget in late 1943. In this experimental boat, codenamed *S-Kanamono* ("S-type Metal Fittings"), lateral fins with diving rudders inset into their trailing edges were fitted to the hull below the conning tower and aft to increase stability. A second model, again a modified Type A, was produced in 1944 and served as a basis for the production at Yokosuka Naval Repair Yard of a much smaller, "winged" submarine which had affinities both with the kaiten manned-torpedo and the German *Biber* (see page 66).

Like the koryu, the two-man kairyu was originally intended for local defence in the Philippines and at Okinawa and was eventually seen as a suicide weapon for the defence of the home islands. It was, as built, something of an improvization, intended to be mass-produced in three sections and assembled at the dockside. It was driven on the surface by a single-shaft, 85hp Isuzu automobile engine, giving a surface radius of 450nm (517 miles, 832km) at 5kt (5.75mph, 9.25kmh), with a maximum speed of 7.5kt (8.6mph, 13.9kmh). An 80hp electric motor gave a maximum submerged speed of 10kt (11.5mph, 18.5kmh) and a radius of 36nm (41 miles, 67km) at 3kt (3.45mph, 5.5kmh).

Completed kairyu varied slightly in dimensions and performance, since non-standard automobile engines were sometimes fitted, and in armament. The midget was originally intended to carry two 17.7in (450mm) torpedoes underslung in dropping gear, but a torpedo

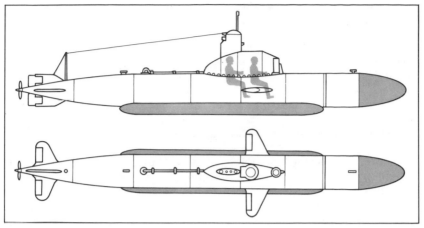

The **Kairyu** was armed with two underslung torpedoes and/or a 1,320lb (600kg) explosive warhead.

shortage—added to Japan's increasing determination to make a suicidal stand—meant that most completed kairyu carried a 1,320lb (600kg) explosive warhead for ramming attack. Its low speed suggests that its success in this role would have been limited. In fact, it is probable that no kairyu became operational: the construction programme called for some 760 units by September 1945, but by the war's end only about 215 had been completed (almost all at Yokosuka NY, where they were found after the surrender).

Experimental Midget Submarines

Besides the midget submarines described above, Japanese designers produced a number of experimental models which did not achieve operational status. Had they done so, they would have been deployed for the final defence of Japan—as suicidal weapons.

The only model to go into production—about 14 were said to be on hand at Kure in August 1945—was the boat known only by the codename of *U-Kanamono* ("U-Type Metal Fittings"). This crude weapon was strongly reminiscent of the Confederate semi-submersibles of the War Between the States: it was an awash-boat controlled by a two-man crew housed in a squat turret on a cigar-shaped hull, some 46ft (14m) long and 6.5ft (1.98m) in beam. Displacing c.15 tons (15.24 tonnes), it was powered by a single-shaft compressed-air torpedo motor, giving a maximum speed of only c.3kt (3.45mph, 5.5kmh) and a very limited action radius. Its armament consisted of one 17.7in (450mm) bow torpedo tube.

U-Kanamono was an awash-boat of crude design, mounting a single torpedo tube at the bow.

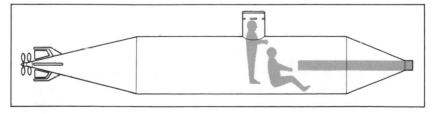

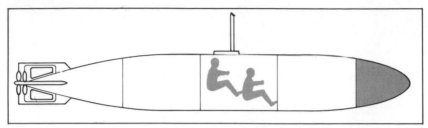

The experimental **Shinkai** carried a detachable warhead of 2,000lb equipped with magnetic clamps.

The smallest of Japan's midgets, the two-man, 11.5 ton (11.7 tonne) *Shinkai* ("Sea Vibrator"), was intended for suicidal expeditions into Allied anchorages in operations somewhat resembling those of the Italian "Pig" and British "Chariot" (see Chapter 5). It was a shallow-draught (3.9ft, 1.2m) submersible armed with a detachable, magnetic, 2,000lb (907kg) warhead, to be affixed to the hull of an enemy ship. The only unit built, codenamed *9-Kanamono* ("Type 9 Metal Fittings") and completed at Ourazaki in August 1944, was powered by a 20shp electric motor giving a maximum 9kt (10.3mph, 16.6kmh) submerged. The 41ft (12.5m) craft was both unstable and plagued by mechanical failure.

Also intended for attacks on Allied anchorages was the Type C variant known as *M-Kanamono* ("Type M Metal Fittings"), built at Ourazaki in late 1944. Very little larger than the Type C, and with the same engines, it had no torpedo tubes and instead carried four mines. The single unit completed is said to have been equipped with tracks for crawling along the sea bottom.

The last of the experimental midgets was the *Maru-Se* ("SE boat"), of which one prototype was built by Kawasaki in 1944 for the Imperial Japanese Army. This craft, of which few details survive, was powered by a Walter high-test peroxide motor, a German-developed unit similar to the hydrogen-peroxide/hydrazine engine used in the experimental *Kaiten II* (see Chapter 5). This gave a submerged speed of c.15-20kt (17-23mph, 28-37kmh). It was to be armed with two electrically-driven torpedoes, then under development.

Japanese Midget Submarine Operations

At 0645 (Honolulu Time) on 7 December 1941, Boatswain's Mate A. Art fired No 1 gun of the old destroyer USS *Ward* (DD 139). His target was the conning tower of a Japanese midget submarine. The shot, which missed, was the first fired by the US Navy in the Pacific War.

The Japanese attack on the US Pacific Fleet's base at Pearl Harbor, Hawaii, has often been described; and this account is concerned only with the part played in it by Type A midget submarines. However, since many Japanese writers deny that the midgets were sent on a *suicide* mission, a little must be said of the preliminary planning for the attack.

A surprise attack on Pearl Harbor had featured in both Japanese and American naval thinking for some years: US fleet exercises in the 1930s had taken into account the possibility of such an attack; and a Japanese historian has claimed that detailed planning in Japan, incorporating a scale model of Pearl Harbor, was begun as early as 1928. However, it is generally accepted that the Japanese plan dated from 1940-41 and that its main architects were Fleet Admiral Isoroku Yamamoto, C-in-C Combined Fleet, and Rear-Admiral Takijiro Onishi, then Chief of Staff of the 11th (Naval) Air Force (and later the "father" of the kamikaze air squadrons).

In mid-1941, a group of junior officers headed by Lt Naoji Iwasa, who had been chief test pilot during the development of the Type A, began to press for the employment of the midget submarines in the attack on Pearl Harbor. They were strongly supported by Capt Kaku Harada who, as commander of Chiyoda, had formed a favourable estimate of the Type A's capabilities, and by LtCdr Ryunosuke Arizumi, a submarine officer on the Naval General Staff. It was assumed that, following the air strikes on Pearl Harbor, the surviving units of the US Pacific Fleet would make a run for the open sea. To intercept the fleeing warships, an "Advance Force" of some 25 fleet submarines was to be deployed—and Iwasa and his group suggested that some of these fleet submarines should carry Type A midgets. These would be launched off Pearl Harbor before the attack, penetrate the anchorage, and attack in the aftermath of the air strikes—if possible, sinking warships in such a position as to block the harbour entrance. (This is the Japanese version: the US Navy's historian believes that midget submarines figured in the Pearl Harbor plan from the beginning, and that crews were specifically trained for the operation for at least one year beforehand.)

Admiral Yamamoto most certainly considered that such a mission would be suicidal. His recorded comment was: "If they enter the anchorage, it is certain that they cannot return". Yet he was persuaded to agree to the plan: and it may be supposed, in view of his later wholehearted espousal of suicide tactics, that Onishi was largely responsible for this. Capt Masayuki Koyama, an instructor at the Kure base of the IJN's Midget Submarine Unit from October 1943 to August 1945, told the author that the midget submarine was not (in 1941) regarded as a suicide weapon, and that "Yamamoto gave permission for these midget submarine operations only on condition that the midgets could be recovered". But, Capt Koyama added, "for all practical purposes, I suppose that the crews of the midget submarines suspected that they could not make their escape". It is notable, in view of the accounts given elsewhere in this book of the selection of personnel for suicidal missions, that none of the Type A crewmen—with the exception of Lt Iwasa—was a volunteer. All had been carefully screened for physical and emotional suitability and then posted to midget submarine duty early in 1941. However, it is possible to see the naval command's tacit acceptance of the suicidal nature of their duties in the fact that, as was the case with later volunteers for kamikaze missions, only men without major family responsibilities were thus posted.

The recorded behaviour of the midgets' crews makes it obvious that, whatever the "official" view, the men concerned regarded their mission as suicidal. The official name given to the midget submarine force is also significant: it was the "Special Naval Attack Unit"—and "special attack" (*tokko* or *toku*, an abbreviated form of *Tokubetsu Kogekitai*, "Special Attack Force") was the most frequent Japanese euphemism for suicide attack.

Date: **7 December 1941**
Place: **Pearl Harbor, Oahu, Hawaii**
Attack by: **Japanese Type A midget submarines**
Target: **US Pacific Fleet**

The Special Naval Attack Unit sailed from Kure on the evening of 18 November 1941. Each of its five Type C1 submarines—*I-16*, *I-18*, *I-20*, *I-22* and *I-24*—carried a Type A midget secured to the casing aft the conning tower with four large clamps. In overall command was Capt Hanku Sasaki. The full roll of the Type A crews was: *I-16:* SubLt Masaharu Yokoyama and PO Teiji Ueda; *I-18:* SubLt Shigemi Haruno and PO Harunori Yokoyama; *I-20:* Ens Akira Hiroo and PO Yoshio Katayama; *I-22:* Lt Naoji Iwasa and PO Naoharu Sasaki; *I-24:* Ens Kazuo Sakamaki and PO Kiyoji Inagaki.

Usually running submerged by day, especially when within range of US air patrols from Wake Island, and surfacing in the evening so that the midgets' crews could check their weapons, the submarines maintained a loose formation about 20nm (23 miles, 37km) apart.

By 5 December, the IJN had thrown a submarine cordon around Pearl Harbor. The main force of some 20 fleet submarines, sailing a few days earlier than the midget carriers, had taken up patrol positions between 9 and 100nm (10-115 miles, 17-185km) from the US base. The five submarines of the Special Attack Unit made landfall off Oahu on the evening of 6 December and surfaced at c.2300 some 8nm (9 miles, 15km) west of Pearl Harbor, close enough to see the neon lights of Waikiki beach. The midgets' crews made neat packages of their personal effects for return to their families (including fingernail parings and a lock of hair for the family altar), wrote farewell letters, and put on their uniforms—a leather jerkin, a cotton *fundoshi* (breech-clout) and a white *hachimaki* (head-band). Some followed an ancient custom of the samurai when facing death and anointed their bodies with perfumed oil.

The midgets were to be launched at c.0300 and were ordered to penetrate Pearl Harbor and attack at will at any time after the first air strike (timed for c.0800, immediately *after* the war declaration was delivered by Japan's representatives in Washington). While final checks were being made on the Type As, the aircraft carriers of Vice-Admiral Chuichi Nagumo's task force were approaching the position some 230nm (264 miles, 425km) north of Oahu from which the first strike of 183 aircraft would be launched at 0600. Final intelligence reports had told Nagumo that the prime targets, the US Pacific Fleet's three aircraft carriers, were *not* in Pearl Harbor. Present, however, were eight of the fleet's nine battleships, 12 cruisers, 41 destroyers, 5 submarines and 40 minor warships.

At c.0300 the midgets' mother boats submerged, the clamps were released, and the Type As moved away under the power of their electric motors. Aboard *I-24* (LtCdr Hiroshi Hanabusa) there was trouble: the final check by the Type A's commander, Ens Kazuo Sakamaki, had revealed that the midget's gyrocompass was unserviceable. His crewman, PO Kyoji Inagaki, and a technician worked frantically on the defective equipment—but when Sakamaki's Type A was at last launched, at c.0530, the gyrocompass was still not working. By this time, the other midgets were approaching the nets guarding the Pearl Harbor channel entrance. The mother boats took station some 10nm (11 miles, 18km) off the entrance, hoping to torpedo any US warships running from the harbour.

The Unattainable Rendezvous

Official provision had been made for the mother boats to surface after dusk on 7 December to pick up the crews of the surviving midgets and scuttle their boats. The rendezvous was some 7nm (8 miles, 13km) west of Lanai Island. A glance at a map will show that this order reflected the truly suicidal nature of the mission: Lanai lies some 70nm (80 miles, 129km) ESE of Pearl Harbor. Thus, there was no chance of the Type As, with their maximum *surfaced* radius of only 80nm (92 miles, 148km), making the rendezvous after the expenditure of battery power in the attack itself—and no chance of the midgets' crews reaching the rendezvous after abandoning their craft. Even if the mother boats intended to meet off Lanai and then stand in towards Pearl Harbor, it is unlikely that they could have hoped for a successful rendezvous with the midgets at sea in the face of enemy air activity to be expected in the aftermath of the attack.

The narrow Pearl Harbor entrance channel was protected by a double gate of anti-submarine netting, and the midgets' best chance of passing this was to follow submerged in the wake of a US ship. The Japanese had good intelligence of the Pacific Fleet's routine, and knew that an early-morning sweep outside the gate was made by coastal minesweepers, which then returned through the gate under the eyes of a patrolling destroyer.

At 0342, the minesweeper *Condor* sighted the periscope of a submarine about 1,000yds (914m) from the channel entrance. Knowing that no US submarines should be in the area, *Condor* signalled the estimated course and speed of the intruder to the destroyer *Ward,* patrolling the entrance. *Ward* went to general quarters for about one hour, searching without result for the mine-sweeper's contact. Meanwhile *Condor* returned to harbour: the gate was opened for her at 0458, and at 0508 she was followed in by the minesweeper *Crossbill.* The gate should now have been closed, but because the transport *Antares* and the tug *Keosanqua* were shortly to meet there to bring in a barge, it was left open. It was probably at this time that at least two Type As gained entrance.

The First Shots

A third Type A, thought to have been that of Lt Iwasa, was less fortunate. At 0630, as *Antares* approached the gate, *Ward's* lookouts, alert from their earlier search, spotted a dark object in the water between the transport and the towed barge. *Ward's* OOD at first identified it as a buoy, but soon decided that it was a small conning tower. A patrolling PBY Catalina flying-boat dropped smoke markers

43

on the suspicious contact and *Ward's* commander, Lt William W. Outerbridge, ordered his guns manned. At 0645 *Ward* opened fire at 100yds (91m) range. The first round missed, but as *Ward* closed to 50yds (46m) a shell from No 3 gun struck home. Moments later, the destroyer had overrun the target, leaving the semi-submerged midget wallowing in her wake. Four depthcharges rolled from *Ward's* stern racks; more depth bombs were delivered by the PBY.

The IJN's first loss of the Pacific War sank in 1,200ft (365m) of water—and at 0654 Outerbridge (who had not reported *Ward's* earlier search) signalled to 14th Naval District HQ:

WE HAVE ATTACKED FIRED UPON AND DROPPED DEPTH CHARGES UPON SUBMARINE OPERATING IN DEFENSIVE SEA AREA

It was typical of the American reaction to the first indications of the surprise attack that no earlier report was made; that *Ward's* message was not decoded for the duty officer until 0715; that a similar report from the PBY was not decoded until 0741; and that the ready duty destroyer *Monaghan* was not ordered to investigate *Ward's* contact until 0751—only four minutes before the first bombs from Japanese carrier aircraft fell on the Naval Air Station at Ford Island.

From this point in the action, it is difficult to trace in detail the movements of the Type As that penetrated either the entrance channel or Pearl Harbor itself. Only one, the late starter crewed by Ens Sakamaki and PO Inagaki, can be followed with any certainty.

The Fate of Sakamaki

Sakamaki had managed to bring his Type A to the entrance channel but, without a compass, was unable to make a submerged approach. At c.0815, surfacing to take bearings, he was sighted by a destroyer, made an emergency dive, and piled up on Tripod Reef, exposing his conning tower. The destroyer—USS *Helm*, first vessel underway from Pearl Harbor following the initial air strike—opened fire on the half-submerged midget as she passed it at flank speed. Near-missed, the Type A slid from the reef and disappeared. *Helm* had not made a kill: with one torpedo tube buckled and choking gas seeping from his batteries, Sakamaki took his midget south and east in a painful voyage around Oahu. All morning, the two Japanese sailors fought to bring their craft under control and return to the battle area; but by 1400, having wrecked his second torpedo tube on a reef, Sakamaki decided to head for the rendezvous point at Lanai. This was a faint hope: that evening the Type A grounded irrevocably some 200yds (183m) offshore on the northern coast of Oahu. Attempting to swim ashore, PO Inagaki was drowned; Sakamaki reached the beach and collapsed—recovering to find himself the first Japanese POW of the war, the only Type A crewman to survive Pearl Harbor.

A chart of Pearl Harbor found in Sakamaki's wrecked submarine (which was later exhibited throughout the USA in a War Bonds drive) gave rise to a short-lived belief that he had actually penetrated the anchorage—some hours or even days before the air strikes—and had circumnavigated Ford Island, noting the positions of US warships. In

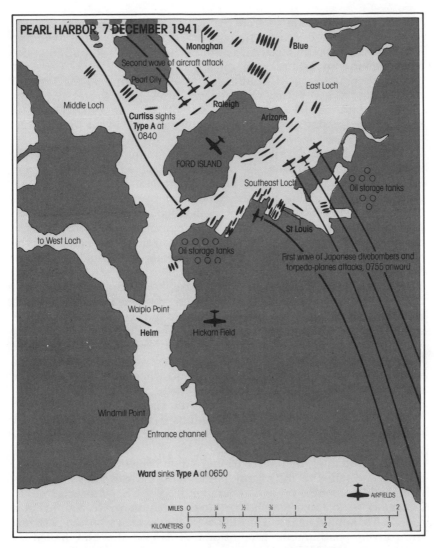

PEARL HARBOR, 7 DECEMBER 1941

Monaghan

Blue

Second wave of aircraft attack

Pearl City

East Loch

Middle Loch

Raleigh

Curtiss sights
Type A at
0840

Arizona

FORD ISLAND

Oil storage tanks

Southeast Loch

to West Loch

Oil storage tanks

St Louis

First wave of Japanese divebombers and
torpedo-planes attacks, 0755 onward

Waipio Point

Helm

Hickam Field

Windmill Point

Entrance channel

Ward sinks Type A at 0650

AIRFIELDS

MILES 0   ¼   ½   ¾   1   2

KILOMETERS 0   ½   1   2   3

The attack on Pearl Harbor, 7 December 1941. USN warships are shown at the berths they
occupied immediately before the first wave of Japanese aircraft struck at 0755 hours.

fact, the chart showed the course Sakamaki had hoped to take and,
further evidence of wishful thinking, showed the aircraft carrier
Saratoga in the berth where Japanese pre-war intelligence had
reported her.

The End of the Midgets

Soon after *Helm's* brush with Sakamaki, one of the remaining Type
As, that of SubLt Yokoyama, made its attack inside the anchorage.
The midget surfaced in East Loch just northeast of Ford Island at
c.0834 and was first sighted about 700yds (640m) from the seaplane
tender *Curtiss*. Hoisting a warning signal that brought *Monaghan* to
her support, *Curtiss* opened fire, claiming two 5in (127mm) hits. This

45

did not prevent the midget from firing a torpedo that passed between *Curtiss* and the light cruiser *Raleigh* and detonated against a dock at Pearl City. *Monaghan* raced in, avoiding the midget's second torpedo, which again ran ashore, and missed with 5in (127mm) fire that damaged a crane barge. But at 0843 *Monaghan* rammed the Type A, completing its destruction with depthcharges. (The wreckage of this craft was later raised and, the remains of Yokoyama and PO Ueda having been granted a military funeral, was buried in the foundations of a new breakwater.)

Within the next 90 minutes, submarine sinkings were claimed by several US warships. *Monaghan* is sometimes credited with a second kill, as is the destroyer *Blue*, but it seems probable that only one Type A was sunk at this time and that credit is properly given to the light cruiser *St Louis*. Steaming into the harbour entrance at c.1000, *St Louis* was menaced by two torpedoes apparently fired from outside the gate. Dodging at 20kt (23mph, 37kmh) in the narrow channel, the cruiser avoided the torpedoes, sighted the midget that had fired them, opened fire and probably destroyed it.

From a comparison of various accounts, it appears that the last of the five Type As penetrated the anchorage, remained undetected, and was scuttled (no trace having ever been found) to become its crew's coffin some time on the evening of 7 December. Cdr Naḳaoka, skipper of the fleet submarine *I-68* (later renumbered *I-168*) reported that while lying close in to Pearl Harbor at c.1850 hours, he received a radio signal from one of the midget submarines; it said simply: "I have succeeded". This was interpreted by the Japanese propaganda machine to mean that the pilot, at that time identified as SubLt Yokoyama, had torpedoed the battleship *Arizona* (in fact, sunk by multiple bomb and torpedo hits in the first air strike, exploding in a conflagration that killed 1,177 men).

Perhaps because the conventional submarines deployed at Pearl Harbor had failed to inflict any damage on US warships—and one, *I-70,* had been sunk by a divebomber from USS *Enterprise* on 10 December—the Japanese high command was happy to claim that a Type A had sunk *Arizona*. The nine Type A crewmen who had perished were given posthumous promotions of two ranks and hailed as deathless heroes. JNAF pilots were furious; particularly when similar promotion was denied to the crews of the 29 aircraft lost in the attack. The supposed success of the Type As led to demands from junior submarine officers for more daring and glorious missions to be allocated to these frail and vulnerable craft. On the other hand, the poor performance of the fleet submarines contributed to a general devaluation of this arm in Japanese military thinking: Sixth Fleet (the submarine fleet) was thereafter too often deployed for supply runs to island garrisons, rather than for aggressive patrols.

In March 1942—on the express order of Admiral Yamamoto according to a Japanese account—plans were made for two near-simultaneous, suicidal operations by midget submarines. The raids had a dual function: practical, to inhibit the Allied buildup at important bases in the Pacific and Indian Oceans; and moral, to impress on the Allies the determination and ability of the IJN to strike at any cost at near-impregnable targets. A special Sixth Fleet unit, the 8th Submarine Squadron commanded by Rear-Admiral N. Ishizaki, was set up to carry out these operations.

Date: **29-30 May 1942**
Place: **Diégo-Suarez Bay, Madagascar**
Attack by: **Japanese Type A midget submarines**
Target: **British warships at anchor**

On 30 April 1942, Admiral Ishizaki sailed from Penang, northwest Malaya, in *I-10*, a Type A1 boat designed to function as the headquarters of a submarine pack and carrying a Yokosuka E14Y1 ("Glen") reconnaissance seaplane. With *I-10* sailed *I-16*, *I-18* and *I-20*, each carrying a Type A midget. On 5 May they refueled at sea from the armed merchant cruiser *Hokoku Maru,* in preparation for a cruise off southern Africa in search of suitable targets for the Type As. At dusk on 20 May, *I-10's* aircraft scouted Durban,and on succeeding nights made similar fruitless searches for major warships at East London, Port Elizabeth and Simonstown. Farther north, a seaplane from *I-30* hunted for heavy units of the British Eastern Fleet at Aden, Djibouti, Zanzibar, Dar-es-Salaam and Mombasa.

In November 1941, under German pressure, Laval's Vichy French government had agreed in principle to Japanese occupation of the island of Madagascar, off the east coast of Africa. Although there was little chance of a fullscale Japanese takeover of the huge (227,602 sq mile, 589,489 sq km) island, the Allies could not ignore the threat to the Indian Ocean supply routes that a Japanese presence at the well-equipped French base of Diégo-Suarez, at the island's northern tip, would pose. Thus, on 5 May 1942, the British launched "Operation Ironclad", an amphibious attack on Diégo-Suarez against determined but short-lived Vichy French opposition. By the end of May the base had been secured and most of the invasion fleet's warships had dispersed. There remained, however, a force consisting of the battle-ship HMS *Ramillies,* three destroyers and two corvettes.

At 2230 on 29 May, *I-10's* seaplane flew over Diégo-Suarez Bay and returned to report "one 'Queen Elizabeth' class battleship and one cruiser at anchor". The reconnaissance flight was spotted by the British, who suspected that it was a French plane scouting for Vichy French submarines believed to be still active in the area. At 0500 next morning, the most likely time for a submarine attack, *Ramillies* weighed anchor and kept moving around the bay until full light, while Fleet Air Arm aircraft flew anti-submarine patrols.

Admiral Ishizaki's midgets were launched at dusk on 29 May. The Type A carried by *I-18* proved to be unserviceable, so the attack was to be made by midgets from *I-16* (crewed by Ens Katsusuke Iwase and PO Kozo Takada) and *I-20* (Lt Saburo Akeida and PO Masami Takemoto). Like Iwasa, lost at Pearl Harbor, Lt Akeida had been a test pilot during the development of the Type A and was a volunteer for operational duty with the weapon.

It was obvious that the midgets had no chance of returning: launched 10nm (11 miles, 18km) out to sea, they were expected to pass undetected through the 1,300yd (1190m) wide Oronjia Passage and

47

navigate a channel some 8nm (9 miles, 15km) long, notorious for reefs, rocks and treacherous currents, before reaching the main anchorage at Antisirane. After making their attacks, the crews were ordered to scuttle their craft and return to the parent boats as best they could — presumably by making their way overland to a coastal rendezvous specified in advance.

It is believed that only one Type A penetrated the anchorage, the other having been lost without trace on the voyage in. The first indication the Royal Navy received of an intruder came at 2025 on 30 May, when a torpedo struck *Ramillies* on the port bulge forward of 'A' turret, causing extensive damage in the forepart of the battleship. A short time later, another torpedo struck the tanker *British Loyalty* (6,993 tons, 7105 tonnes), which sank almost immediately. The British corvettes immediately got under way and combed the bay throughout the night, making frequent depthcharge attacks. Although no confirmed contact was made, the Type A was probably damaged, for by morning it had been abandoned by its crew and had drifted on to a reef, where it was discovered in a wrecked condition some two weeks later.

Ramillies, with a 900 sq ft (84 sq m) hole torn in her bulge and a 320 sq ft (30 sq m) rent in her outer bottom, rapidly took water in her forward magazines and compartments and began to settle by the bow. Rapid discharge of oil fuel and offloading of ammunition restored her trim and, with her main machinery undamaged, she was able to steam for repair to Durban, where she remained out of action for nearly one year. *British Loyalty* had settled in shallow water and was raised and repaired. It was at first thought that the attack had been made by a Vichy French submarine, but a few nights later the two Japanese crewmen were cornered ashore by a Commando patrol and, refusing to surrender, were shot dead. Had the attacker been identified at once as a Japanese midget submarine, and an immediate report sent to other Allied bases, Allied naval units might have been spared a severe shock less than one day later, when the Type As struck at Sydney, Australia.

Date: **31 May-1 June 1942**
Place: **Sydney Harbour, Australia**
Attack by: **Japanese Type A midget submarines**
Target: **USN, RAN, RIN and RNN warships**

While Admiral Ishizaki's raiding group scouted for targets off southeast Africa, a similar group commanded by Capt Hanku Sasaki, overall commander of the Pearl Harbor midgets, prepared to make a surprise attack in Australian waters. Sasaki's group consisted of the aircraft-carrying submarines *I-21* and *I-29* and the Type A carriers *I-22, I-24, I-27* and *I-28.* The four latter were called from patrol duties off Port Moresby, New Guinea, on 11 May and ordered to the IJN's base at Truk atoll in the eastern Carolines to take aboard Type As and their crews. Meanwhile, *I-21* and *I-29* made aerial reconnaissance of major anchorages at Suva in Fiji, Auckland in New Zealand, and on the east coast of Australia, in search of large Allied warships refitting after the Battle of the Coral Sea (5-8 May).

On 17 May, on the last leg of her voyage to Truk, *I-28* was running on the surface SSE of the atoll when she was sighted by the US submarine *Tautog* (Cdr J.H. Willingham). A torpedo hit crippled the Japanese submarine, which managed a brief and unavailing burst of gunfire before a second torpedo hit under the conning tower sent her down with all hands. But *I-22* (Cdr Kiyotake Ageta), *I-24* (Cdr Hiroshi Hanabusa) and *I-27* (Cdr Iwao Yoshimura) all arrived safely at Truk and sailed again with Type As aboard on c.20 May. By 29 May they had made rendezvous with *I-21* and *I-29* some 40nm (46 miles, 74km) ESE of Sydney, where reconnaissance flights on 20-23 May had reported the presence of major warships.

In fact, the only major Allied units in Sydney Harbour (Port Jackson) were the heavy cruisers USS *Chicago* (CA 29) and HMAS *Canberra* and the old light cruiser HMAS *Adelaide*. With them were the destroyer tender USS *Dobbin*, the destroyer USS *Perkins* (DD 377), the minelayer HMAS *Bungaree,* the armed merchant cruisers HMAS *Kanimbla* and *Westralia*, the corvettes HMAS *Whyalla*, HMAS *Geelong* and HMIS *Bombay,* the old Dutch submarine *K.IX*, and the depot ship HMAS *Kuttabul*. (For their respective positions, see map on this page). The harbour defence force—all Australian ships—consisted of the anti-submarine vessels *Bingera* and *Yandra,* two minesweepers, six channel patrol boats and four unarmed auxiliary patrol boats.

Although the probable presence of at least one unidentified submarine off Sydney had been reported by RNZAF aircraft on 26 and 29 May, no specific measures against submarine attack had been taken. Of the permanent anti-submarine installations, the outer

Japanese **Type A** midget submarines raid Sydney Harbour, Australia, 31 May-1 June 1942. Allied warships are shown at the berths they occupied immediately before the attack, at c.2200 hours.

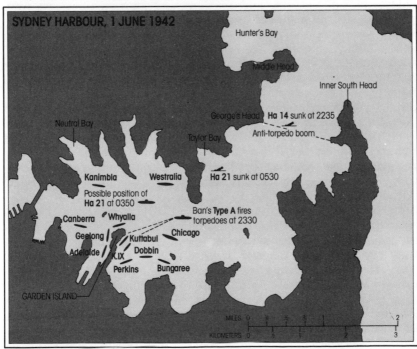

49

magnetic indicator loop at the Heads (the points flanking the harbour's 1.5-mile wide outer entrance) was unserviceable, and the anti-torpedo boom at the 1,500yd (1370m) wide inner entrance was only partially completed and had gaps at both ends. Around the 12-mile (19km) long harbour a "brown-out" was in force, but repair shops on Garden Island were brightly lit, silhouetting the warships in Man-of-War anchorage to the east.

Even the sighting of a reconnaissance plane over the harbour early on 30 May failed to rouse the defences. Lt Susumo Ito's "Glen" seaplane was catapulted from *I-21* at c.0300, some 30nm (35 miles, 56km) northeast of Sydney, and at 0420 flew over the inner harbour at 600ft (180m), circling twice over *Chicago*. The cruiser's duty officer identified the Japanese monoplane as a Curtiss SOC Seagull biplane "from an American cruiser", and apart from brief patrols by RAAF fighters no special precautions were taken. Ito's aircraft was lost when he landed in rough water near *I-21*, but he and his observer survived to report "battleships and cruisers" at Sydney.

Crossing the Loop

At dusk (c.1630) on 31 May, some 7nm (8 miles, 13km) east of Sydney Heads, the Japanese fleet submarines launched their Type As: *Ha 21* (Lt Matsuo Keiyu and PO Takeshi Omori) from *I-22;* an unidentified midget (SubLt Katsuhisa Ban and PO Mamoru Ashibe) from *I-24;* and *Ha 14* (Lt Kenshi Chuman and PO Masao Takenaka) from *I-27*.

To reach their objective, the midgets would have to travel some 20nm (23 miles, 37km) through heavily-defended waters; their attack would stir up a hornets' nest of air and surface activity; it was obvious that none would return. For their one-way journey, the crews were provided with excellent charts and aerial photographs, and (possibly as a "token" of the chance of survival) rations enough for one week—including staples like dried fish and pickled plums as well as such luxuries as chocolate and whisky.

As night closed down, the Type As were able to take navigational fixes from the lights on the Sydney Heads, entering the harbour approaches in darkness. Subsequent examination of the magnetic loop log revealed that *Ha 14* was the first to enter the outer harbour, at 2000, although its "signature" was not then distinguished from that of other harbour traffic. This was *Ha 14's* last piece of luck: by 2015 the midget had become entangled in the western section of the anti-torpedo boom, where it was spotted by a watchman in a rowing boat. Although reaction was leisurely—the channel patrol boat *Yarroma* did not arrive until c.2130—Lt Chuman and PO Takenaka failed to free their craft. At 2235, as *Yarroma* opened fire with her two Vickers machine guns and prepared to drop her four depthcharges, Chuman fired a demolition charge that destroyed *Ha 14* and its crew.

Lt Ban's Type A had already crossed the loop, at 2148, and was making its run-in of c.6nm (7 miles, 11km) to the "battleship" at Man-of-War anchorage. A general alarm was raised in Sydney Harbour at 2227, but the order to darken all ships did not come until 2314, and dockside lights were not doused until 2325. Thus, the harbour was still well lit at c.2257, when Ban's Type A surfaced about

500yds (457m) off *Chicago's* starboard quarter, where it was sighted and caught in the cruiser's searchlight. *Chicago* opened fire, first with light weapons and then with her 5in (127mm) — some of the shells from the latter fell ashore, damaging buildings but *not,* as popular legend had it, killing a lion in Sydney Zoo. The Type A submerged and made off towards the north shore. *Perkins* (with defective sonar gear) made a brief patrol with the Australian corvettes *Geelong* and *Whyalla,* but was ordered to anchor by Capt H.D. Bode of *Chicago,* who probably believed that he had destroyed the intruder.

In fact, the Type A was unharmed, and at c.2310 Ban surfaced again to the northeast of Garden Island, whose dock lights illuminated *Chicago's* berth. But before he could fire his torpedoes he was sighted and fired on by *Geelong;* and by the time he was ready to attack, at 2330, the dock lights had at last been switched off. Ban fired both tubes: one, a dud, ran ashore on Garden Island; the second narrowly missed *Chicago,* passed beneath the Dutch submarine *K.IX,* and exploded under the old harbour ferry *Kuttabul,* a naval barracks ship, killing 19 and wounding 10 of the seamen billeted aboard. *Perkins,* the corvettes and harbour defence craft immediately began intensive patrols — but again Ban was able to slip away, heading back towards the harbour entrance. A signature on the loop at 0158 is believed to have been that of Ban's boat making its exit — but what became of the Type A after that is unknown, for it was never seen again.

The Hunt in Taylor Bay

The remaining midget, Lt Keiyu's *Ha 21,* was detected on its inward journey, at c.2250, before reaching the loop, by the unarmed patrol boat *Lauriana* and the anti-submarine vessel *Yandra.* The latter attempted to ram the midget, lost contact temporarily, and at 2307 dropped six depthcharges. Shaken, but with his boat still intact, Keiyu apparently decided to lie low for a while in the harbour approaches. By 0300 ᵉhe was again attempting to penetrate the harbour, when the outward-bound *Chicago* reported a periscope close aboard in the loop area. It is difficult to trace Keiyu's subsequent movements, for by this time the harbour was in uproar, with reports of contacts and periscope sightings from all quarters. It is possible that the contact fired upon by *Kanimbla* at 0350, from Neutral Bay, represented *Ha 21's* deep penetration of the anchorage. By c.0530, *Ha 21* was again outward bound, to be located and subjected to a three-hour hunt in Taylor Bay by *Yarroma* and the patrol boats *Sea Mist* and *Steady Hour.* Repeated depthcharge attacks were made — but when *Ha 21* was located by a diver later that day it was found that the Type A's motor was still running and that Keiyu and Omori had committed suicide with their pistols after scuttling their boat. *Ha 21's* torpedoes were still in their tubes, which had been fouled by the midget submarine's bow-mounted net-cutter.

Ha 14 and *Ha 21* were salvaged and cannibalized to build a single midget, which was toured through Australia to raise money for the Naval Relief Fund. The Japanese crews' remains were cremated and given a funeral with full military honours — a proceeding which attracted some criticism, especially because the fleet submarines that had launched the midgets shelled the Sydney suburbs and the Newcastle industrial plant before heading homeward. But although Japanese propaganda claimed that the operation had resulted in the sinking of the battleship HMS *Warspite,* the Sydney raid represented the last major suicidal operation of the Type A midgets. Thereafter their operations were sporadic and, although not openly suicidal, hazardous enough to warrant a brief summary here.

Midway and the Aleutians

In the same week as the Diégo-Suarez and Sydney raids, the Midway invasion fleet sailed from Japan—to experience the IJN's first major defeat, on 4-6 June in the Battle of Midway. With Admiral Yamamoto's Main Force were the seaplane tenders *Chiyoda* and *Nisshin,* each carrying 6-12 Type As with which it was intended to set up a base at Kure atoll, from which the midgets would sortie against an Allied counter-invasion force. Defeat at Midway frustrated this plan.

A midget submarine base was established at Kiska in the Aleutians—the 1,000 mile (1600km) long island chain off southeast Alaska, where major islands were occupied by the Japanese from June 1942 to August 1943. About one dozen fleet submarines were available to carry the Type As into action—but the stormy waters of the North Pacific and Bering Sea proved hazardous even for the operations of the big I-boats. The Type As were never taken to sea, and a number were destroyed in the USAF's low-level strikes on Kiska. When the island was reoccupied by US forces, several midgets destroyed by demolition charges were found ashore, some mounted on rail-trolleys for launching from the beach.

Guadalcanal: Type As and "Cargo Pipes"

Allied reports of midget submarine activity in the Solomon Islands in 1942-43 were frequent; but many were inspired not by aggressive Type As but by the supply method adopted by the Japanese for the Guadalcanal garrison. Fleet submarines carried "cargo pipes" *(Tokugata Unka-To)* of various kinds, the most common being 77ft (23.5m), 44 ton (45 tonne), one- or two-man submersibles, somewhat resembling the Type A but unarmed and propelled by a compressed-air torpedo motor. Launched offshore from a submerged fleet boat, these craft were capable of one trip of c.4,000yds (3660m) at c.3kt (3.5mph, 5.5kmh), carrying 8-10 tons (8.13-10.2 tonnes) of cargo.

In November-December 1942, the fleet submarines *I-16* and *I-20* sortied twice from Truk to launch Type As against US shipping off Guadalcanal. The midgets' crews were ordered to scuttle their boats and join the Japanese garrison ashore after making their attacks. At least two Type As were lost in these operations, and although the Japanese claimed to have sunk a destroyer and four transports, only one success can be traced.

On the morning of 28 November 1942, *Ha 10,* launched from *I-16,* penetrated a screen of five destroyers at Lunga Point, north Guadalcanal, and torpedoed the 6,200-ton (6300-tonne) cargo ship USS *Alchiba,* loaded with aviation gasoline and ordnance. With her forepart in flames, *Alchiba* was run on to the beach and saved only after four days' firefighting. What became of *Ha 10's* crew is not known; but when their boat was salvaged in June 1943 it was found to be equipped with a cage-like shield around its propeller—a counter to the small-meshed anti-submarine netting that had been introduced to protect US anchorages after the Diégo-Suarez and Sydney raids. British bases were similarly protected—and as late as March 1944 a British submarine skipper based at Trincomalee, Ceylon (now Sri Lanka), remarked that swimming in the harbour was hazardous because, every time the gate in the boom was opened, launches dropped small depthcharges as a precaution against marauding midgets penetrating the major British base.

By that time, however, the IJN's midget submarines were largely relegated to a training role for the pilots of *kaiten* manned-torpedoes; although a number were deployed for local defence at bases outside the home islands. Several Type As, along with some Type C and Type D (Koryu) boats, were deployed at Okinawa and in the Philippines.

Type As at Okinawa

Late in August 1944, 11 Type As were transported to Okinawa, where they were based at Unten, on the northwest shore of the wide bay that indents the island's northern coast, along with four squadrons of explosive motorboats (see Chapter 3). On 10 October, Vice-Admiral Mitscher's nine aircraft carriers launched 1,396 sorties in the first pre-invasion strikes at Okinawa. Unten suffered heavily: two Type As of the "Dragon Squadron" were destroyed, along with their depot ship, the 5,160-ton (5243-tonne) *Jingei.*

By late March 1945, the number of serviceable Type As at Unten had been reduced to six by US bombing. Three of these boats sortied late on the evening of 25 March to strike at Admiral Deyo's Task Force 54, the Okinawa bombardment force. One only returned to base, claiming two hits on "an enemy battleship": on the Allied side, the only record is of torpedo tracks sighted, and avoided, by the cruisers USS *Wichita, St Louis* and *Biloxi* at c.0940-1040 on the morning of 26 March: the torpedoes may have come from midgets.

Although a few more sorties were made, and unconfirmed successes claimed, Unten continued to suffer attrition from pre- and post-invasion air strikes. On 6 April, as US ground forces advanced on Unten, the base personnel destroyed the one remaining serviceable boat and, with some 3,000 more of Rear-Admiral Minoru Ota's command, prepared to fight to the death as infantry with LtGen Mitsuri Ushijima's 32nd Army.

Midget Submarines in the Philippines

In the Philippines, a force originally consisting of 10 midget submarines was based on Cebu Island for operations against Allied invasion shipping in the Sulu and Mindanao Seas. In command was Rear-Admiral Kaku Harada, the former captain of *Chiyoda*, who had so strongly supported the commitment of the Type As at Pearl Harbor in spite of Yamamoto's misgivings.

A sortie by Harada's boats on the afternoon of 5 January 1945—a sacrificial attack on a US Task Group—came close to claiming a notable victim. An account given to the author by a former IJN officer suggests that one Type C boat *(Ha 69)* and two Type D Koryu *(Ha 81 and Ha 82)* made this attack—which would suggest that the Type Ds were in production before the generally-accepted date of January 1945. It is possible, if not probable, that all three boats were Type Cs.

The three midget submarines sortied from Cebu and, at c.1500, in the 11-mile (18km) wide strait between Negros and Siquijor islands, encountered a strong US force: the headquarters ship *Wasatch,* light cruisers *Boise, Phoenix, Montpelier* and *Denver,* and nine destroyers. Aboard *Wasatch* were Admiral Thomas C. Kinkaid, commander 7th Fleet, and LtGen Walter Krueger, commander 6th Army—and aboard *Boise* was General Douglas MacArthur, soon to be Allied Supreme Commander in the Pacific. Whether or not the Japanese crews knew the potential value of their target, they attacked without hesitation.

At c.1508, destroyer *Nicholas* spotted torpedo tracks. A message went over the TBS to *Phoenix,* which in turn warned *Boise.* While MacArthur watched from the bridge—"calmly puffing on his corncob (pipe)", according to an aide—Capt Willard M. Downes narrowly avoided the torpedoes by altering course hard to starboard at flank speed. Now *Nicholas* and the destroyer *Taylor* closed in on the attacker, *Ha 82,* which had surfaced after firing, while a CAP plane dropped a depth bomb. *Taylor* made the kill: Cdr Nicholas J. Frank, Jr, rammed the midget amidships, splitting it apart. Nothing was seen of its two companions, which may have returned safely to base.

As well as the Cebu force, a few midget submarines of Types A and C, operational in the same sea area, were based at Dumaguete, southeast Negros; on Basilan Island, just southwest of Mindanao; and at Davao, on the broad gulf in southeast Mindanao. A Japanese account claims that these midgets sank 14 ships—including two cruisers and five destroyers—between 8 December 1944 and 21 March 1945; but this claim cannot be substantiated. By the end of March 1945, the US advance had forced the abandonment of the bases and the redeployment of their personnel as infantry.

The final sorties of the midget submarine force in the Philippines appear to have been made from the Cebu base on 26-27 March, during the invasion of the island, when the destroyers USS *Conyngham* and *Flusser* and the APD *Newman,* of Capt Albert T. Sprague's Task Group 78.2, claimed the destruction of at least two midgets.

Thereafter, the IJN's midget submarines were deployed in the home islands for suicidal operations against the expected invasion armada (see Chapter 6).

ITALIAN MIDGET SUBMARINES

Although the presence of midget submarines on both sides was rumoured during the Russo-Japanese War, the Italian Navy may claim to have been the first to deploy midgets in 20th-century warfare. During World War I, a few small submersibles of c.16 tons (16.25 tonnes) surfaced displacement were constructed and, having proved unsuitable for operations outside sheltered waters, were used for harbour defence in the Adriatic. These pioneer designs were dusted off in the mid-1930s when, at the time of Mussolini's venture into

ITALIAN MIDGET SUBMARINES				
Type:	C.A.1	C.A.2 (1941 conversion)	C.A.3/C.A.4	C.B.
Submerged displacement:	16.4 tons (16.7 tonnes)	14 tons (14.2 tonnes)	14 tons (14.2 tonnes)	45 tons (45.72 tonnes)
Length overall:	32.8ft (10m)	32.8ft (10m)	34.3ft (10.47m)	49.2ft (14.99m)
Beam:	6.43ft (1.96m)	6.43ft (1.96m)	6.2ft (1.9m)	9.84ft (3m)
Draught:	5.25ft (1.6m)	5.25ft (1.6m)	6ft (1.83m)	6.9ft (2.1m)
Machinery:	1 – shaft diesel=60hp electric motor=25hp	electric motor=21hp	electric motor=21hp	1 – shaft diesel=90hp electric motor=100hp
Max speed surfaced: submerged:	6.5kt 5kt	7kt 6kt	7kt 6kt	7.5kt 7kt
Range surfaced: submerged:	700nm @ 4kt 57nm @ 3kt	not known 70nm @ 2kt	not known 70nm @ 2kt	1,400nm @ 5kt 50nm @ 3kt
Armament:	2x17in (450mm) TT	2x17.7in (450mm) TT or 8x220lb (100kg) explosive charges	20x4.4lb (2kg) "limpet" mines	2x17.7in (450mm) TT or 2 mines
Crew:	2	3	3	4
Number completed:	1	1	2	22

Abyssinia (now Ethiopia), conflict with Great Britain temporarily threatened. A weapon for clandestine penetration of such British Mediterranean bases as Malta, Gibraltar and Alexandria was advocated by many Italian officers, with Cdr Angelo Belloni, a leading spirit in the training of volunteers for the *Decima Flottiglia MAS* (10th Light Flotilla), the Italian Navy's "special attack weapons" unit, prominent among them.

In the event, the *Maiale* ("Pig") manned-torpedo (see Chapter 5) was to be the major penetration weapon; but in the pre-war years it was planned that midget submarines should penetrate enemy bases, either to carry out torpedo attacks or to release frogmen to place explosive charges. In conditions of strict secrecy, the Italian Navy constructed and had operational by April 1938 the midget submarines *C.A.1* and *C.A.2* (*C= Costiero-tipo*, "coastal-type"), built by Caproni, Taliedo of Milan.

In their original form, *C.A.1* and *C.A.2* were two-man boats displacing 13.5 tons (13.7 tonnes) surfaced; 32.8ft (10m) long overall; 6.43ft (1.96m) in beam; and drawing 5.25ft (1.6m). On the surface, a single-shaft 60hp MAN diesel gave a maximum speed of 6.5kt (7.5mph, 12kmh) and a range of 700nm (805 miles, 1295km) at 4kt (4.6mph, 7.4kmh). Submerged, a 25hp Marelli electric motor gave a maximum 5kt (5.75mph, 9.25kmh) and a range of 57nm (65.5 miles, 105km) at 3kt (3.45mph, 5.5kmh). Armament consisted of two 17.7in (450mm) torpedoes in external dropping gear.

Trials soon showed that *C.A.1* and *C.A.2* were not capable of operations involving sea passages of any distance. Nor was there much chance of the midgets surviving independent missions in the clear, shallow, inshore waters of the aircraft-dominated Mediterranean. In 1941, it was decided that the midgets must be carried to their target areas on mother boats and released under cover of darkness to penetrate defended anchorages and lay explosive charges. The diesel units were removed from both midgets, as were the torpedo racks. This reduced displacement to 12 tons (12.2 tonnes) surfaced and 14 tons (14.2 tonnes) submerged; increased maximum submerged speed to 6kt (6.9mph, 11kmh) and submerged range to 70nm (80.5 miles, 129km) at 2kt (2.3mph, 3.7kmh); and permitted a crew of three to be carried; at least one a trained "frogman".

Date: **December 1943**
Place: **Hudson River, New York, USA**
Attack by: **Italian midget submarine "C.A.2"**
Target: **Shipping at anchor and dock installations**

Urged on by the German high command, who stressed the moral effect on the Allies of increased Italian naval effort in the Atlantic, Cdr Prince Junio Valerio Borghese, commanding the 10th Light Flotilla, planned spectacular and potentially suicidal missions for the Italian midgets: attacks on the British base at Freetown, Sierra Leone, on the west coast of Africa—and on harbours along the east coast of the United States. The Freetown plan, for which *C.A.1* was allocated, was abandoned when it was decided that British defensive measures allowed no chance of success; but the operation against the USA, with New York specified as the target for maximum psychological effect, reached an advanced planning stage.

In mid-1942, in preparation for the New York raid, *C.A.2* was transported overland to Bordeaux, where "Betasom", headquarters for Italian submarines operating in the Atlantic, was commanded by Capt Enzo Grossi. There, too, came the Marconi-class submarine *Leonardo da Vinci* of 1,190/1,489 tons (1209/1513 tonnes), selected as

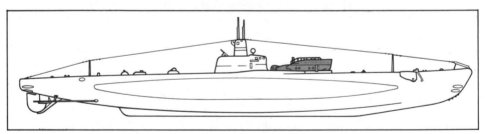

A "Kangaroo" with its "Baby": an Italian **C.A.** type midget rests in its "pouch" on the forward casing of a "Marconi" class submarine from which the 3.9in gun has been removed.

the midget's carrier. Under the direction of Cdr Borghese and SubLt Massano, Italian workshops at Bordeaux under Major (naval rank) Fenu removed *Da Vinci's* 3.9in (100mm) gun and in its place, just forward of the conning-tower, constructed a semi-recessed "pouch" with retaining shackles for *C.A.2*. This arrangement led to the mother boat being designated the *Canguro* ("Kangaroo"). Sea trials under Borghese's command proved to his satisfaction that the midget could be launched from the submerged Kangaroo and could be recovered when the mother boat surfaced beneath it. The latter point was important in avoiding any indication that the projected mission was regarded as suicidal: just so had the IJN made "official" plans to recover its midgets after Pearl Harbor.

According to Borghese, the Kangaroo (not *Da Vinci*, which was sunk by British warships off the Azores in May 1943) would launch its midget while submerged off New York Bay. *C.A.2* (or, in the later stages of the operational planning, the near-identical *C.A.3* or *C.A.4*) would make its way by night into the crowded harbour at the mouth of the Hudson. Two of the three crewmen, in frogmen's gear, would leave the boat to plant time-fuzed explosive charges—eight 220lb (100kg) charges and twenty 4.4lb (2kg) "limpets" were carried—under ships and against dock installations. Then *C.A.2* would slip downriver to make rendezvous at sea with the Kangaroo.

The suicidal nature of the plan is obvious. Borghese made the airy assumption that New York's harbour defences "against such a surprise attack presumably didn't exist"—although the "happy time" enjoyed by German U-boats off the American east coast in the earlier part of 1942 had resulted in much-improved anti-submarine patrolling. The Kangaroo would have to surface in American coastal waters to allow the midget's crew to enter their craft, since they had no means of access from the mother boat; and it would have to surface again offshore, in the aftermath of the attack, to retrieve the midget. Finally, it was estimated that the midget itself, with a submerged capability— for *C.A.2*, *C.A.3* or *C.A.4*—of no more than 70nm (80.5 miles, 129km), might need to remain in the Hudson for up to two days. Yet, according to Borghese, only Italy's collapse in September 1943 prevented the mission from being carried out, as planned, in December of that year.

As well as the four *C.A.*-type boats, the Italian Navy built 22 midgets of *C.B.*-type (some of them completed under the Italian Fascist Republic in 1943-44). These four-man boats of 36/45 tons (36.6/45.7 tonnes) were not used for "special attack" missions but for conventional torpedo operations. In this role, they had some success in the Black Sea, where a six-strong flotilla operating from the Romanian port of Constanta is credited in Italian and German records (at variance with other sources) with sinking the Soviet submarines *Shch. 208*, in June 1942, and *Shch. 207* in August 1943.

BRITISH MIDGET SUBMARINES

Britain was not far behind Italy in the development of midget submarines—and might have been in advance. As early as 1909-12, Lt Godfrey Herbert, RN, designed the *Devastator*, a one-man submersible which set the later style of British boats in being armed with a detachable explosive warhead. Submitted to the Admiralty in 1912, the boat was then (as later, during World War I) refused on the grounds that the operator's survival could not be guaranteed; ie, that it was a suicidal weapon. However, it attracted the attention of Capt Max Horton, a submarine "ace" of World War I, who contributed suggestions for its improvement and was, according to his biographer, prepared to accept the fact that "the crew would have to be expendable". Early in World War II, Admiral Sir Max Horton, as Flag Officer, Submarines, was to be a strong advocate of the development and deployment of British midgets.

Herbert's design was not the only one to influence the British midgets of World War II. In 1915, Robert H. Davis of the Siebe, Gorman company patented a three-man boat incorporating an "escape" compartment. And in 1924, Max Horton himself put forward plans for three types: the *A Type*, based largely on Herbert's designs; the two-man *B Type*, with a detachable compartment containing both warhead and main engines; and the *C Type*, armed with a single torpedo slung beneath the main hull. Although the *C Type* met with some interest, none was adopted: the midgets were once again adjudged to be at best semi-suicidal craft.

All these design strands were woven together in 1939-40, when Admiral Horton learned that a private yard near Southampton was constructing a midget incorporating many features of earlier designs, including the Davis escape apparatus, to the plans of a retired submariner of World War I, Cdr Cromwell H. Varley. In spite of some opposition, Horton and Cdr Herbert (the same officer who had begun his own midget design in 1909) had Varley's craft evaluated and subsequently improved by the Directorate of Naval Construction. It was to become the "X-craft".

Characteristics of the "X-craft"

The prototype X-craft, the two-man *X-3* and *X-4*, were built from early 1942 onward, and these experimental submersibles were quickly followed by the operational "X-5" class of 12 boats, which were to be the midgets that carried out missions in European waters. Without explosive charges (see below) an "X-5" midget displaced 27/30 tons (27.4/30.5 tonnes) and was 5.9ft (1.8m) in beam. The craft was 51.25ft (15.7m) long overall and 7.5ft (2.3m) in draught. A single-shaft 42hp

BRITISH MIDGET SUBMARINES			
Type:	"X-5" CLASS	"XE" CLASS	WELMAN
Submerged displacement:	30 tons (30.48 tonnes)	33.5 tons (34 tonnes)	2.05 tons (2.08 tonnes)
Length overall:	51.25ft (15.7m)	53.25ft (16.2m)	16.8ft (4.3m)
Beam:	5.9ft (1.8m)	5.75ft (1.75m)	3.5ft (1.1m)
Draught:	7.5ft (2.3m)	5.75ft (1.75m)	5.75ft (1.75m)
Machinery:	1 – shaft diesel=42hp electric motor=30hp	1 – shaft diesel=42hp electric motor=30hp	1 – shaft electric motor=2.5hp
Max speed surfaced: submerged:	6.5kt (with charges) 5.5kt (with charges)	6.5kt (with charges) 5.5kt (with charges)	3kt 2kt
Range surfaced: submerged:	1,860nm @ 4kt (without charges) 1,320nm @ 4kt (with charges) 80 hours @ 2kt	slightly greater than "X-5" class	not known 20 hours @ 1.7kt
Armament:	2 side charges of 4,400lb (1996kg) each	2 side charges of 4,400lb (1996kg) each	1 x 560lb (254kg) explosive charge, magnetic
Crew:	4	4 or 5	1
Number completed:	12	11	very few
Note: Dimensions are for boats without charges.			

Gardner diesel gave a maximum surfaced speed of 6.5kt (7.5mph, 12kmh), and a 30hp electric motor a maximum submerged speed of 5.5kt (6.3mph, 10kmh)—with explosive charges, in both cases. Maximum surfaced range was 1,320nm (1,518 miles, 2442km) with charges or 1,860nm (2,139 miles, 3441km) without charges—at 4kt (4.6mph, 7.4kmh), in both cases. The craft carried a crew of four, one of them a trained diver.

The boat was divided into four main compartments. Forward was the "wet-and-dry" compartment, with a hatch from which the diver could leave the craft, to place demolition charges or to deal with underwater obstacles, and return when his task was completed. Also forward was the battery compartment, with the control room amidships and the engine room aft. Armament reflected the role for which the boats were chiefly intended: attacks on major warships at anchor. Unlike the torpedo-armed Japanese, Italian and German midgets (but

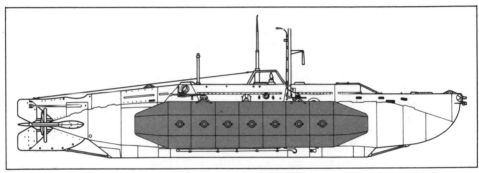

British midget of "X-5" class: note 4,400lb detachable side-charge shaped to its outline.

like the Italian "Pig" and British "Chariot" described in Chapter 5) the X-craft carried only detachable explosive charges. On each side of the boat, slung in a steel frame and streamlined to the boat's outline, was a 4,400lb (1993kg) charge of Torpex. Released from within the X-craft, the charges sank beneath a target to become lethal mines, with clockwork fuzes running up to 36 hours.

Although the X-craft were stout boats of remarkable range and endurance— capable of diving safely to more than 300ft (91m), with a submerged endurance of 80 hours at 2kt (2.3mph, 3.7kmh), although with the necessity of rising to ventilate every 12 hours—their seaworthiness was limited by instability in rough weather and by the effect on their crews of long periods in such confined spaces. Thus, they were normally towed to the target area by fleet submarines, while manned by a passage crew; an operational crew travelled out on the mother boat and took over the midget for the attack.

Considering their efficiency, the X-craft were under-used; and some would ascribe this to the Admiralty's equivocal attitude to what was still felt to be a semi-suicidal weapon. The major missions described briefly below will give the reader some opportunity of deciding for himself just how "suicidal" the X-craft were in comparison with the Japanese, Italian and German midgets. Meanwhile, it should be noted that X-craft also performed valuable services in such roles as reconnaissance of invasion beaches and the landing of clandestine agents. (Six boats of the "XT-class" were commissioned as training vehicles between June 1943 and March 1944; these were similar in most respects to the "X-5" boats, but were not fitted out for operational use; 12 were ordered but not built.)

Date: **22 September 1943**
Place: **Altafjord, northern Norway**
Attack by: **British X-craft**
Target: **German battleship "Tirpitz", at anchor**

From late 1940, when she was fitting out at Wilhelmshaven, until November 1944, when she was sunk in Norwegian waters, the German battleship *Tirpitz* (52,600 tons, 53,442 tonnes, full load; eight 15in, 381mm, guns) was a major target of Allied air attack. Although her sorties from Norwegian hideouts were infrequent, she constituted an ever-present theat to Allied convoys to Russia; a fleet-in-being in herself. Up to October 1942 she was subjected to six raids while at anchor by Bomber Command: no damage was done to the battleship, but 12 aircraft were lost to the heavy anti-aircraft defences that ringed her anchorages.

On 16 February 1943, Winston Churchill, ever an enthusiastic advocate of "special attack" operations, minuted his service chiefs:

"Have you given up all plans of doing anything to *Tirpitz* . . .? We heard a lot of talk about it five months ago [ie, at the time of the abortive manned-torpedo raid mentioned in Chapter 5] . . . It seems very discreditable that the Italians should show themselves so much better in attacking ships in harbour than we do . . . It is a terrible thing that this prize should be waiting, and no one able to think of a way of winning it."

In fact plans were already hatching to win this mammoth prize by the use of X-craft.

Intelligence from Norwegian agents, aerial reconnaissance and "Ultra" had built up a comprehensive picture of *Tirpitz's* lair in Kaafjord, a narrow arm of the upper reach of the 20-mile (32km) long Altafjord, northern Norway. Nearby were the berths of the battle-cruiser *Scharnhorst* and heavy cruiser *Lützow,* so simultaneous attacks were planned on both these units. Shore defences were intense; Kaafjord was partly closed by anti-submarine netting; *Tirpitz's* berth was completely enclosed by netting; and launches with listening gear were on constant patrol.

Some 1,200 miles (1930km) from the target area lay the base of the X-craft; at Loch Cairnbawn, northern Scotland, where training for the mission, with the battleship HMS *Malaya* acting as target, began in June 1943. At least one officer was lost during training. The first six "X-5" midgets to be completed, numbered *X-5* to *X-10,* were assigned to "Operation Source", along with six fleet submarines as mother boats. It was calculated that the voyage to the target area, with each mother boat towing its midget on a hemp or nylon cable with telephone-link wiring at its core, would take eight days.

The boats of "Operation Source" sailed from Loch Cairnbawn on 11-12 September: HMS *Truculent,* towing *X-6,* and *Syrtis,* towing *X-9,*

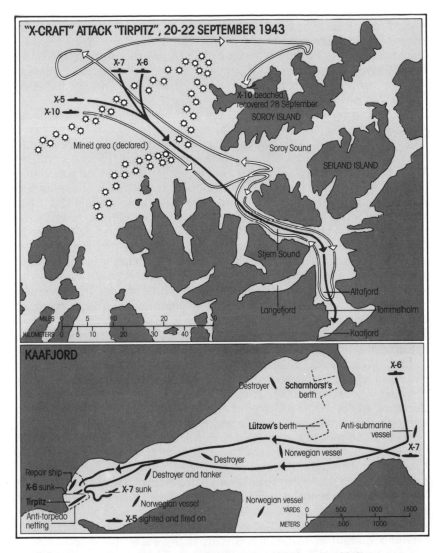

Upper chart: Courses set by X-craft into (and out of, **X-10**) Altafjord, 20-21 September 1943.
Lower chart: X-6 and X-7 attack **Tirpitz** in Kaafjord, 0350-0812 hours, 22 September 1943.

at 1600 hours; *Thrasher* with *X-5* at 1800; *Seanymph* with *X-8* at 2000; *Stubborn* with *X-7* at 2200; and *Sceptre* with *X-10* at 1300 on 12 September. Proceeding on courses at least 20 miles (32km) apart, the boats made for the midgets' jumping-off point at Soroy Island, some 11 miles (18km) off the Norwegian coast and almost 100 miles (160km) from Kaafjord. Having slipped their tows there, *X-5, X-6* and *X-7* were to strike at *Tirpitz; X-8* at *Lützow;* and *X-9* and *X-10* at *Scharnhorst.*

By day, the mother boats and their charges travelled submerged, the midgets surfacing for some 15 minutes at six-hourly intervals to ventilate, and at night the mother boats ran surfaced to recharge their batteries. The strain on the tow-ropes was great and on the night of 15-16 September, in a heavy sea, the tow between *Syrtis* and *X-9* parted. In spite of a two-day search by *Syrtis,* the midget and its three-man passage crew were lost. *X-8* broke free from *Seanymph* on the same night; she was recovered, but began to manifest alarming instability. Her passage skipper was forced to jettison explosive charges, one of which exploded prematurely and damaged *X-8* so badly that she had to be scuttled.

By first light on 20 September, the four remaining X-craft were on station with operational crews aboard, ready to slip their tows. Between 1830 and 2000 that evening, all four left their mother boats for the 24-hour run in: on the surface across a declared minefield and then submerged through Soroy Sound and Stjern Sound and along Altafjord to a rendezvous off Tommelholm Island, near the mouth of Kaafjord. *Scharnhorst* was now to be *X-10's* target, while the other three were to strike at *Tirpitz.* (In fact, both *Scharnhorst* and *Lützow* were away from their berths.) The attacks were to begin at 0100 on 22 September, and to avoid any X-craft being destroyed by charges laid by another, the attack periods and the timing of fuzes were limited to times specified in advance.

X-10 was soon in trouble. Water seeping into her electrical circuits put periscope and gyrocompass out of commission and, in spite of tremendous efforts at repair made by Lt K. Hudspeth, RANVR, and his crew as she skulked off Tommelholm, *X-10* would take no part in the attack on the German battleship.

In *X-6,* Lt Donald Cameron, RNR, was also having trouble with a near-useless periscope and with a flooded starboard charge that gave his boat a pronounced list. Almost blind when submerged, Cameron dared to negotiate the boom at the Kaafjord entrance by slipping through awash, at c.0500, in the wake of a coaster. Submerged again, Cameron and his crew struggled to repair the periscope as *X-6* inched "by guess and by God" up the two-mile-long fjord to *Tirpitz's* berth, blundering through a maze of anchored shipping: three German destroyers, a repair ship, a tanker and two Norwegian warships. Soon after 0700, Cameron brought his craft safely through a gap in the battleship's anti-torpedo netting. Then, with the target little more than 100yds (91m) away, *X-6* grounded and bobbed to the surface. A German lookout identified the disturbance as a porpoise!

Such luck could not last: at c.0712 the midget fouled more netting and surfaced again, now only about 75yds (70m) to port of *Tirpitz.* German sailors cut loose with small arms (the battleship's armament would not bear) and grenades. Calmly, Cameron brought *X-6* alongside the battleship, released his side charges, opened the Kingston valves to flood his boat, and joined his crew on the casing with hands held high. The British submariners were taken aboard *Tirpitz,* where Kapitän Hans Meyer immediately began preparing to move his ship, suspecting that a charge had been laid or that other midgets were lurking, possibly armed with torpedoes.

As well as the charges dropped by *X-6,* the fuzes on four tons of explosive were already running beneath *Tirpitz. X-7,* commanded by Lt Godfrey Place, RN, had entered Kaafjord without difficulty at 0350, but had first become entangled in the netting around *Lützow's* empty berth and then, after an hour-long struggle for freedom, in

Tirpitz's netting. Breaking free once more, Place approached the battleship at a depth of 40ft (12m), scraped along her side, dropped one charge below the keel forward, and moved along the battleship's 822ft (251m) length to release a second charge near her stern. Almost as he placed his charges, Place heard the din of grenades exploding around Cameron's *X-6.*

Now Place attempted to take *X-7* out of Kaafjord, but his struggles with netting had rendered his compass unserviceable. *X-7* surfaced, was spotted, and was raked with small arms fire before diving to the bottom of the fjord. Groping along, she encountered netting yet again. At 0812, massive explosions beneath *Tirpitz* marked the success of the midget's mission. The shock-waves tore *X-7* clear of the netting, but damaged her so badly that, as German destroyers began to plaster the fjord with depth charges, Place was forced to surface and surrender as *X-7* sank beneath him. Two of his crew died in the sinking X-craft.

Tirpitz was hard hit. The near-simultaneous explosion of the charges lifted the battleship from the water and slammed her back with a gashed and distorted hull, machinery jarred from its mountings, and two main turrets lifted off their roller-bearing rings. The port rudder and all three propeller shafts were unserviceable. One man was dead and 50 injured. (*Tirpitz* remained out of action until March 1944, and was never again fully operational. Continuing to lie in Kaafjord, she was attacked and damaged several times by aircraft of the RAF and Fleet Air Arm. On 12 November 1944, having moved to Tromso, she was sunk by RAF Lancasters of 617 Squadron, the "Dam Busters", with 12,000lb, 5436kg, "Tallboy" bombs.)

It remains uncertain whether the damage to *Tirpitz* on 22 September was caused by the charges of two or three X-craft. *X-5* (Lt Henty-Creer, RNVR) was sighted in Kaafjord after the explosion, at 0843, was taken under fire by heavy and light AA guns, and was claimed sunk. It was thought that, having missed the first specified "attack period", she had waited in the fjord to lay charges after those of her consorts had detonated. However, Norwegian observers reported sighting a midget heading out of Altafjord on the day after the attack; thus suggesting that *X-5* had planted her charges and escaped, only to be lost with all hands on the way to her rendezvous with her mother boat. Certainly, a British diving team that explored Kaafjord in 1976 failed to find any trace of *X-5.*

The crippled *X-10* was the only X-craft to return to the rendezvous—and on the homeward tow the threat of foul weather caused the Admiralty to order her scuttling. Thus, in "Operation Source", all six X-craft were lost; nine men were killed (three in *X-9* on passage; two in *X-7;* four in *X-5*); and six survived as prisoners. Rear-Admiral Barry, who had succeeded Horton as Flag Officer, Submarines, characterized the mission as "one of the most courageous acts of all time".

Pacific Operations: XE-Craft
The Royal Navy's "XE-class" midgets were developed from the X-craft specifically for service in the Pacific. Between December 1943 and April 1945, 12 boats of this class were building, although only six were put into commission. With consideration for the climate in which they

were to work, these boats were air conditioned. Each was fitted with a tripod-mounting beneath the hull, providing stabilising "legs" when bottomed. In exterior dimensions, they differed hardly at all from the "X-5" boats, although an extension of the casing forward allowed a five-man crew to be shipped if necessary.

The XE-craft, on the depot ship HMS *Bonaventure,* arrived in the Pacific theatre at Brunei Bay, northwest Borneo, in July 1945. In these waters the US Navy was the dominant Allied partner and Fleet Admiral Chester W. Nimitz had already made it clear that he was opposed to the deployment of the British boats—probably because the American commander at first believed that they had an endurance no greater than that of the Japanese *Type As,* whose operations Nimitz, for one, certainly regarded as suicidal. However, Rear-Admiral James Fife, commanding US submarines in the Southwest Pacific, was a supporter of the British effort.

On 30-31 July 1945, therefore, XE-craft were deployed on three near-simultaneous missions. In attacks on Japanese communication links, *XE-4* (Lt M.H. Shean, RANVR) cut the submarine telegraph cable off Saigon, Indochina, and *XE-5* (Lt H.P. Westmacott, RN) cut the cable in the Lamma Channel, Hong Kong—after the two divers carried in *XE-5* had experienced great difficulty working in deep mud some 40ft (12m) down.

In the third operation, *XE-1* (Lt J.E. Smart, RNVR) and *XE-3* (Lt I.E. Fraser, RNR) were towed to a point some 40 miles (64km) off Singapore by the submarines HMS *Spark* and *Stygian.* They were cast loose to strike at the Japanese cruisers *Takao* and *Myoko,* which lay at anchor in the narrow Johore Strait. In the event, both XE-craft deposited explosive charges beneath *Takao* (in this operation, one 4,400lb, 1993kg, side charge and a number of smaller "limpet" charges were carried), which was badly damaged. Both midgets returned safely to their mother boats. Like Cameron and Place of the *Tirpitz* mission, Lt Fraser of *XE-3* and his diver Leading Seaman James Magennis—who had fixed limpets to *Takao* and then had left the midget yet again to clear an obstruction that had trapped the XE-craft beneath the cruiser—were awarded the Victoria Cross.

The Welman Midget Submarine

A third British-developed midget deserves mention: the Welman (sometimes spelt "Wellman") one-man submersible, a type falling somewhere between a true midget submarine and a manned-torpedo. This tiny craft, designed by an Army officer, had a surfaced displacement of only 4,600lb (2084kg); it was 16.8ft (5.1m) long without its detachable warhead, 3.5ft (1.07m) in beam, and drew a maximum 5.75ft (1.75m). A 2.5hp electric motor gave it a maximum submerged speed of around 3kt (3.45mph, 5.5kmh), with an endurance of up to 20 hours at 1.7kt (1.9mph, 3.1kmh). It was said to be able to dive safely to c.300ft (91m), but was intended to operate at no more than 75ft (23m).

Seated in a cramped cockpit beneath a turret-like conning tower with armoured-glass portholes, the operator navigated by sight rather than by instruments (although rudimentary instruments were fitted),

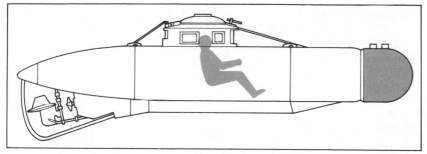

The British "Welman" midget, with a 560lb (254kg) warhead equipped with magnetic clamps.

trimming his boat with hand- and foot-pumps and steering by means of a control column. At the Welman's bow was mounted a 560lb (254kg) explosive charge, which was released from within to clamp magnetically on to the target. The Welman was intended to be carried to its operational area aboard a submarine, MTB or destroyer.

During 1943, Norwegian volunteers and members of the British Army's Special Boat Section were in training with Welmans on Scottish lochs. Later that year, although Royal Navy officers deprecated their employment, Norwegian-crewed Welmans dropped from MTBs were used in at least four attempts to penetrate the German-held port of Bergen, southwest Norway. Their target was the huge Laksevaag floating dock, a vital installation for Bergen-based U-boats, but all attempts failed, although the Welman operators survived. (The dock was eventually put out of action by charges laid by *X-24,* commanded by Lt H.P. Westmacott, RN, on 11 September 1944; the same midget had penetrated Bergen on 14 April 1944, under Lt M.H. Shean, RANVR, sinking the German blockade-runner *Barenfels* (7,569 tons; 7690 tonnes) with explosive charges.

GERMAN MIDGET SUBMARINES

It should be noted that although many sources refer to all submersibles of the *Kleinkampfverbände* ("Small Battle Units" or "K-Force") as "midget submarines", the *Neger, Marder* and *Hai* were properly manned-torpedoes and are thus dealt with in Chapter 5. A brief account of the formation of the K-Force is given in Chapter 3, where the operations of *Linsen* explosive boats are described.

The *Kriegsmarine* came late into the field of midget submarines. In the early war years, effort was concentrated on the four-man *V.80,* which was built solely as a test-bed for the Walter turbine and which, being 85.25ft (26m) long and displacing 71/80 tons (72.1/81.3 tonnes), cannot properly be described as a midget. Advocates of "special attack" submersibles for coastal defence — notably the Lübeck industrialist Heinrich Dräger and Kapitänleutnant Hans Bartels — were ignored during the years of Germany's triumphs. By late 1943, however, the possibility of an Allied cross-Channel invasion had led to the formation of the K-Force and to the design of the first "special weapons" for use against transports — the manned-torpedoes.

These were soon followed by the *Biber* ("Beaver") midget submarine. The now Korvettenkapitän Bartels was chiefly responsible for

GERMAN MIDGET SUBMARINES				
Type:	TYPE XXVIIA "HECHT"	TYPE XXVIIB "SEEHUND"	"BIBER"	"MOLCH"
Submerged displacement:	12 tons (12.19 tonnes)	14.7 tons (14.94 tonnes)	6.5 tons (6.6 tonnes)	11 tons (11.2 tonnes)
Length overall:	34ft (10.4m)	39ft (11.9m)	29.5ft (9m)	35.4ft (10.8m)
Beam:	5.5ft (1.68m)	5.5ft (1.68m)	5.25ft (1.6m)	5.97ft (1.82m)
Draught:	5ft (1.52m)	5ft (1.52m)	4.5ft (1.37m)	5.97ft (1.82m)
Machinery:	1–shaft electric motor=13shp	1–shaft diesel=60hp electric motor=25hp	1–shaft petrol=32hp electric torpedo motor=13hp	1–shaft electric motor=13.9hp
Max speed surfaced: submerged:	5.6kt 6kt	7.75kt 6kt	6.5kt 5.3kt	4.3kt 5kt
Range surfaced: submerged:	78nm @ 3kt 40nm @ 6kt or 69nm @ 4kt with additional battery	300nm @ 7kt or 500nm @ 7kt with external fuel tanks 63nm @ 3kt	130nm @ 6kt 8.6nm @ 5kt	50nm @ 4kt 40nm @ 5kt
Armament:	1x21in (533mm) torpedo underslung or 1 mine	2x21in (533mm) torpedoes underslung	2x21in (533mm) torpedoes underslung	2x21in (533mm) G7t torpedoes underslung
Crew:	3	2	1	1
Number completed:	3	285	324	363

its design, which is believed to have been influenced by a British Welman midget captured intact at Bergen. Bartels presented his plans to Flenderwerke, Lübeck, on 4 February 1944, and within six weeks was himself running trials in the prototype, nicknamed "Adam". Inspected and approved by Grossadmiral Dönitz, the Biber was taken into service on 29 March. (It has been alleged by a German historian that towards the end of the war, Dönitz, who had lost two sons in the U-boat service, gave orders that the German midgets were to be used in "suicide missions"; and it is noted elsewhere that the men of the K-Force themselves regarded their actions as suicidal.)

Characteristics of Biber and Molch

The Biber was a one-man boat displacing only 6.5 tons (6.6 tonnes). It was 29.5ft (9m) long, 5.25ft (1.6m) in beam, and of 4.5ft (1.37m) draught. On the surface a 32hp Opel-Blitz automobile engine gave a maximum speed of 6.5kt (7.5mph, 12kmh); submerged, a 13hp electric torpedo motor gave a maximum 5.3kt (6mph, 9.8kmh). Fitted in default of a suitable diesel unit being available, the gasoline engine made the Biber a potential death-trap: the operator risked death from carbon-monoxide poisoning if he ran with his hatch closed for more than c.45 minutes, and although pilots were provided with breathing gear and a 20-hour supply of oxygen, many succumbed. (Among them was the pilot of the Biber which is now displayed in the Imperial War Museum, London; his craft was found drifting in the Channel on 29 December 1944.) Surfaced endurance was 130nm (149 miles, 240km) at 6kt (7mph, 11kmh)—although to remain long on the surface in the aircraft-dominated narrow seas was to risk another kind of death than

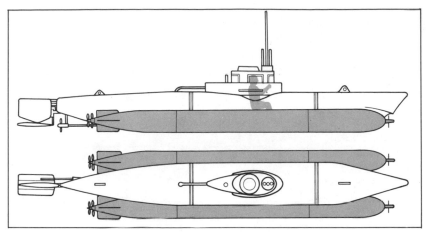

German **Biber** midget submarine, with two 21in (533mm) torpedoes semi-recessed beneath its hull.

poisoning—and submerged endurance was no more than 8.6nm (9.9 miles, 16km) at 5kt (5.75mph, 9.25kmh).

From these details, it may be judged that the Biber was truly a suicidal craft. Its pilot, fortified by a special ration of chocolate containing caffeine and other stimulants, sat with his head protruding into a 28in (711mm) high conning tower with armoured-glass ports, surmounted by a 48in (1219mm) periscope. He navigated largely by sight, with the aid of a wrist compass. Although fairly manoeuvrable on the surface, the Biber could not maintain a consistent depth when submerged: it was stable only on the surface, in a fairly calm sea, or when bottomed, with a safe depth of c.100ft (30m). Thus, its voyages and its attacks were both made while awash. Armament consisted of two 21in (533mm) G7e electric wakeless torpedoes, slung in dropping gear recessed on either side of the hull. Alternatively, two mines could be carried; and as clandestine minelayers, Bibers proved effective against Allied shipping in the Scheldt area and might well have justified themselves if restricted to this role.

Not unlike the Biber, but intended for operations in coastal waters only, was the *Molch* ("Salamander"). Larger than the Biber—displacing 11 tons (11.2 tonnes) and 35.4ft (10.8m) long—it was powered only by a single-shaft electric torpedo motor, giving a maximum 4.3kt (5mph, 8km) surfaced and 5kt (5.75mph, 9.25kmh) submerged. Although this single power unit limited surfaced range to 50nm (57.5 miles, 92.5km) at 4kt (4.6mph, 7.4kmh), it removed the danger of poisoning the operator, housed beneath a plexi-glass dome aft, and allowed the boat to operate submerged (to a safe depth of c.80ft, 24m) to a range of 40nm (46 miles, 74km). Like the Biber, the Molch carried two underslung torpedoes.

Biber and Molch in Action

A total of 324 Bibers and 363 Molche was built between March 1944 and the war's end; but since they were committed to battle piecemeal from bases on the Channel and North Sea, both in packs up to 30 strong and in individual sorties, it is not possible here to give more

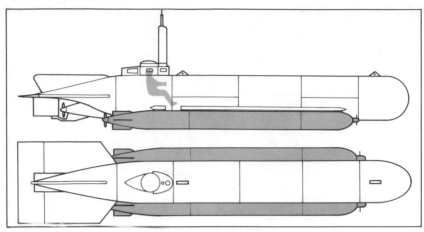

German **Molch** midget submarine; larger but shorter-ranged – and less hazardous – than the **Biber**.

than a brief account of their operations overall. Some unusual missions are, however, described in more detail. Molche, it may be noted, were also used in very small numbers in the Mediterranean, without success.

Allied records make little distinction between the two types, but are unanimous in declaring that neither type scored any successes with torpedoes. British official figures show that in the period January-May 1945, Bibers and Molche operating from Rotterdam made 102 sorties and suffered 70 losses (a German authority estimates the loss rate of Bibers alone at 60-70 per cent). In that period, seven small Allied craft were sunk and two damaged by *mines* laid by the midgets. And according to the same source, 52 Bibers had been destroyed (again, without any operational success) in the period August-December 1944, the majority caught on the surface by Allied fighter-bombers.

The Biber's operational debut was made on the night of 29-30 August 1944, by the boats of K-Flotilla 261. Of 20 Bibers brought by truck to Fécamp, near Le Havre, 18 were able to sortie. A heavy Channel chop and a Force 5 gale tested the pilots to the uttermost, and although all returned safely their claims to have sunk a 7,000-ton "Liberty" ship and a large landing ship cannot be substantiated. Further, all the Bibers were destroyed by their crews next day at the order of the local Army commander, who was not certain that they could be safely evacuated from the Le Havre area.

Date: **12-13 January 1945**
Place: **Nijmegen, eastern Holland**
Attack by: **"Biber" midget submarines**
Target: **Waal River road bridge**

Ever since its seizure by the US 82nd Airborne Division in September 1944, the Germans had made determined attempts to destroy the road bridge over the Waal River at Nijmegen. A daring raid by frogmen of the K-Force had damaged the railway bridge — and had resulted in the strengthening of the British defences of the road link, notably by rigging four net-and-boom barriers across the Waal upstream from the bridge. At Emmerich, some 30 miles (48km) farther upstream, beyond the confluence of the Waal with the Rhine, the Germans planned a riverine attack by Bibers.

On the night of 12-13 January 1945, from the German lines only a few miles above Nijmegen, 240 mines were floated downstream in timed waves of 60 each to detonate against the net-and-boom barriers. These were followed by 20 Bibers, their torpedoes fitted with grapnels which, it was hoped, would hold them to the nets for maximum effect. Since Allied troops held both banks of the Waal above the bridge, and because the Bibers must run very nearly awash, the midgets' stubby periscopes were camouflaged to resemble clumps of drifting foliage. But by the time the Bibers reached their torpedo-launching position above the first line of netting, the explosion of those mines that had reached the target had alerted the defenders, who raked the river with artillery and automatic fire. The Bibers' losses are not known, but were presumably heavy.

As the surviving boats withdrew after firing their torpedoes, four more Bibers approached. Each towed a large tree-trunk, beneath which was a 6,600lb (2990kg) explosive charge supported by flotation chambers. These massive mines were to be towed to within 1,000yds (914m) of the bridge—around a wide bend in the Waal, where the trunks would probably have gone ashore if floating free—and released at dawn. As the trunks floated beneath the bridge, the change of light would cause photo-electric cells built into the upper sides of the trunks to trigger the firing circuits of the charges.

The Bibers launched their floating missiles successfully, but by this time Allied fire from the banks had risen to a crescendo. Before the sluggish logs could reach their goal, they were detonated by artillery fire. In any case, the earlier floating mines and torpedoes had breached only three of the net-and-boom lines: the fourth still held.

Arctic, Egypt—and Accidents

The most ambitious plans made for the utilization of the Bibers proved abortive. One, strikingly similar to the operations of the Japanese midget submarines described above, was for a raid on Allied escort warships for the Russian convoys while at anchor in Kola Inlet, near Murmansk, on the Barents Sea. Training for this mission was begun by Bibers of K-Flotilla 265 at Harstadt, Norway, in November 1944. Three "mother" boats—the "Type VIIC" U-boats *U.295, U.716* and *U.739*—were equipped with deck clamps to carry two Bibers apiece. They were to free the midgets, by releasing the clamps and submerging beneath them, some 40 miles (64km) off the target area, in mid-afternoon. The Bibers would spend some 12 hours in penetrating Kola Inlet and choosing targets, launching torpedo attacks in the early morning dark. After the attack, they would be guided by acoustic signals to the mother boats, now lying some 4 miles (6.5km) offshore, which would take off the Bibers' pilots and scuttle their craft.

The three U-boats with midgets aboard left Harstadt on 5 January 1945. The attack was scheduled for 8 January, when it was believed that the Soviet battleship *Archangelsk* (the former HMS *Royal Sovereign*) and other heavy units would be in Kola Inlet. The generally poor construction of the Bibers proved the mission's undoing: the continual vibration of the U-boats' diesels in high-speed surface running started leaks in the Bibers' fuel pipes and, although great efforts were made to patch them up, evidence of more serious structural damage caused the abandonment of the enterprise.

An even more suicidal plan was to load a Biber aboard a Blohm und Voss Bv 222 flying-boat, one of the very few of these six-engined giants to be operational. The aircraft was to land on one of the lakes along the Suez Canal and lower the Biber into the water. The midget would penetrate the Canal itself and attempt to block it by torpedoing a large ship. Thereafter, the Biber's pilot was to scuttle his boat and, presumably, surrender his person. It is difficult to say how seriously this wild scheme was considered.

As well as its truly suicidal loss rate, two serious accidents contributed to the phasing out of the Biber in favour of the *Seehund* (see below) from February-March 1945. When operating against Allied shipping in the Scheldt area, Bibers were towed by harbour tugs from their pens in Rotterdam to the Hellevoetsluis lock on the Haringvliet, at the head of the Waal-Maas estuary. There they received a final combat check before sortieing. Early in January 1945, a mechanic thus engaged inadvertently fired a Biber's torpedoes: in the confines of the lock, the greater part of a flotilla of 30 Bibers was destroyed by the explosion and shock waves. On 6 March 1945, a similar accident wrecked another full flotilla, this time killing or disabling most of its pilots as well.

The Seehund

If the hastily-designed, poorly-constructed, petrol-engined Biber was the worst midget submarine of World War II, the Kriegsmarine's "Type XXVIIB" U-boat *Seehund* ("Seal") might claim to be the best. Its very success virtually removes it from the scope of this book: since its losses ran no higher than 10 per cent, according to a reliable German source, it cannot properly be described as suicidal. A brief account is, however, desirable.

The improvizational Biber was little more sophisticated than the awash-boats of the Confederacy in the War Between the States: the purpose-designed Seehund, although short-ranged, had some points that conventional U-boats' crews may have envied: its characteristics

German "Type XXVIIB" U-boat, the **Seehund**: a safe and comparatively effective midget submarine.

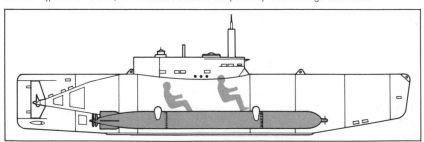

were, in fact, those of a miniaturized fleet submarine. A two-man boat displacing only 14.7 tons (14.9 tonnes) and 39ft (11.9m) long, it handled well on the surface, where a 60hp single-shaft Büssing diesel gave a maximum 7.75kt (9mph, 14.3kmh), and was small enough to be virtually undetectable by sight or radar. Even if spotted and attacked, it had a good chance of survival: it was capable of full submergence within 3-5 seconds (the pilot simply trimmed his diving planes and dived with his diesel at full power) and was light enough to "ride" the shock-waves of depthcharge detonations. However, its submerged speed and range, on a 25hp AEG electric motor, were lower than desirable: a maximum 6kt (7mph, 11kmh) and an endurance of 63nm (72 miles, 117km) at 3kt (3.5mph, 5.5kmh). Only in its armament of two 21in (533mm) torpedoes on external dropping gear did the Seehund resemble the Biber.

A total of 285 Seehunde was built at Kiel, Elbing and Ulm before the war's end, many being assembled in bomb-proof shelters to which prefabricated parts were delivered by road, and close on 100 were captured incomplete in May 1945. Completed units bore numbers between *U.5001* and *U.6252*. Most operated from Ijmuiden, where some 30-40 were normally on hand, slipping out in small groups from the North Sea Canal to hunt in the narrow Strait of Dover.

After a disastrous debut on the night of 31 December-1 January 1945, when 16 out of 18 Seehunde heading for the Scheldt were lost in a storm, these midgets built up a useful combat record. According to British official figures (which indicate a loss of 35 Seehunde in 142 sorties for the period; the number of sorties seems entirely too low), in January-May 1945, torpedoes fired by Seehunde sank nine Allied ships totalling 18,451 tons (18,746 tonnes) and damaged three more totalling 18,384 tons (18,678 tonnes). These figures are possibly an under-estimate: the K-Force's German historian claims a total of some 120,000 tons (121,920 tonnes) sunk by Seehunde in February-April 1945—but this figure is surely too high.

The most notable victim of the Seehunde was the Free French frigate *La Combattante* (formerly the "Hunt-class" destroyer HMS *Haldon*), sunk in the North Sea on the night of 23 February 1945 by a single torpedo fired from a range of c.850yds (777m) by a Seehund commanded by Leutnant zur See Klaus Sparbrodt. Of more significance overall was the midgets' achievement in forcing the Allies to deploy an estimated 500 escorts and more than 1,000 aircraft to counter the threat of the small intruders.

Experimental German Midgets

The earliest of the experimental midgets (ie, those craft which did not achieve operational status) was the "Type XXVIIA" U-boat named *Hecht* ("Pike"), developed by the Naval Construction Bureau in the first half of 1944. A three-man boat, it almost exactly resembled the Molch in design and performance and may, in fact, be merely a variation of that type. It differed in armament: Hecht was designed to carry a detachable warhead. By the time it approached production, the requirement had been changed: Hecht was now to have a detachable bow compartment capable of housing three frogmen, with an infla-

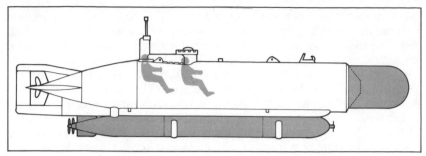

German "Type XXVIIA" U-boat, **Hecht**, closely resembled **Molch** but carried a detachable warhead.

table boat, for penetration missions against enemy harbours. A total of 53 boats was built at Kiel, but in the event they were limited to training duties for crewmen of operational types.

In July 1944, at the insistence of the K-Force CinC Vice-Admiral Hellmuth Heye, *Versuchskommando 456* ("Experimental Command 456") was formed for research and development of underwater weapons. An early result of its work was the *Delphin* ("Dolphin") project. Delphin I (or *Kleine Delphin*, "Little Dolphin") was most certainly, in one of its variants, a suicide weapon with a built-in warhead, much resembling the Japanese *Kaiten*. A one-man, 2.75 ton

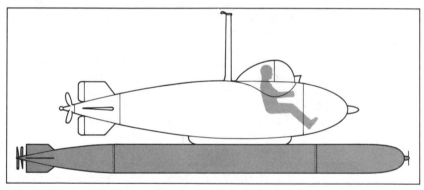

Kleine Delphin, shown with underslung torpedo, might also be fitted with an integral warhead.

(2.8 tonne) boat, it was only 16.75ft (5.1m) long. It was to be powered by an 80hp Opel-Kapitän gasoline engine running on a closed cycle—ie, on its own exhaust gases, catalysed and reconstituted by liquid oxygen—which would give a submerged speed comparable to the 30-40kt (34-46mph, 55-74kmh) of the similarly-powered Kaiten. (Although there was some exchange of information on "special attack" weapons between Germany and Japan, it is not possible to say whether Delphin I was directly inspired by the Kaiten.) It was also to operate in the same way as the Kaiten: the pilot would aim his craft at an enemy ship and, in theory, "eject" before impact.

Although the prototype Delphin I was, in fact, powered only by a 24hp electric motor, its "tear-drop" hull configuration enabled it to reach a submerged speed of 17kt (19.5mph, 31.5kmh). But slinging a conventional torpedo beneath it—for less suicidal use than the internal warhead—reduced maximum speed to no more than 5kt (5.75mph, 9.25kmh); and some thought was given to arming the boat with a pole-towed torpedo or mine, thus preserving the hull's hydrodynamic advantages. The accidental sinking of the prototype in January 1945 effectively ended the programme.

Delphin II (or *Grosse Delphin*, "Big Dolphin") was a more conventional midget. The single prototype, displacing 7.38 tons (7.5 tonnes) and 28.5ft (8.7m) long, was to be powered by a closed-circuit 60hp Daimler Benz diesel, giving some 18kt (21mph, 33kmh) submerged, and armed with two torpedoes or mines in dropping gear. Tests were also made with closed-circuit engines for modified two-man Bibers, but these were abandoned in favour of experiments with a closed-circuit Seehund; neither scheme proved fruitful.

Seeteufel ("Sea Devil"), also called *Elefant* ("Elephant"), was a 19.7 ton (20 tonne), two-man craft which was intended to be able to launch itself from or land upon any suitable beach. An 80hp gasoline engine (in the single prototype; a 250hp unit was planned for production models) driving caterpillar tracks beneath the hull gave it a land speed of 6.2mph (10kmh) and a water speed, surfaced, driving a single shaft, of 8kt (9.2mph, 15kmh), with about the same speed submerged coming from an electric motor. The sea armament of two torpedoes or mines underslung was supplemented by a machine gun and flame-thrower for land use. Trials were reasonably satisfactory, and this amphibian was ordered into production shortly before the war's end.

The most ambitious experimental programme was aimed at an "underwater fighter aircraft", named *Schwertal* ("Grampus"). This torpedo-shaped, two-man craft had stubby "wings" forward and at the

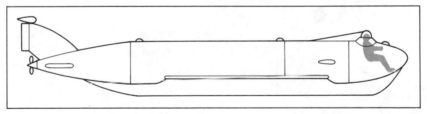

Prototype design for **Schwertal**: a 30kt (submerged) super-manoeuvrable midget submersible.

tail. It was to be powered by an 800hp closed-circuit Walter turbine, using hydrogen peroxide (Ingolin) as a catalyst, which was expected to give a submerged speed of some 30kt (34mph, 55kmh) and a range of 500nm (575 miles, 925km) at 10kt (11.5mph, 18.5kmh). Displacing 14.5 tons (14.7 tonnes) and 37ft (11.3m) long, the super-manoeuvrable hunter-killer was to be armed with underslung rocket-torpedoes and would mount rocket-launchers and flame-throwers for surface use. British experts who examined the single prototype, discovered sunk in Lake Plön at the Walter works in July 1945, seem not to have been impressed. Schwertal II, a paper project only, incorporated hydrodynamic improvements. It was suggested as the basis for the *Manta* ("Manta-ray"), in which two operators in a central housing between two Schwertal II units would use their craft as a 50kt (57mph, 92kmh) surface skimmer or a 30kt (34mph, 55kmh) midget submarine.

"Boundless as the dome of the sky above
Is what we owe to our Emperor;
Fathomless as the deep sea below
Is what we owe to our country.
Now is the time to repay what we owe"

Commander Takeo Hirose, I J N, Port Arthur, 1904

Chapter Three

Ocean Shakers

Like the midget submarine and the manned torpedo, the explosive motorboat (EMB) of World War II was a shock weapon that offered to naval planners the prospect of spectacular gain at little cost. And as in the case of the midget submarine and manned torpedo, that cost was all too often the life of the EMB's pilot. Only the Imperial Japanese Army and Navy built and deployed EMBs as part of an overtly suicidal effort; but, as the following account will show, the EMBs of the Italian and German navies at times carried out what may properly be called suicide missions. Because of its nature, the EMB at all times demanded suicidal bravery from its crew.

EMBs of World War I

A Japanese naval historian has stated that inspiration for the IJN's *shinyo* ("ocean shaker") EMB of c.1943 came from a World-War-I weapon: the *Fernlenkbooten* (FL, "remote-controlled boats") developed by the Imperial German Navy in 1915-17. The FL itself may have been partly derived from an even earlier model, the *Küstenbrander* explosive boat designed by an Austrian naval officer, Fregattenkapitän Giovanni de Luppis, in the 1860s. This small craft, guided from a distance by lines attached to its rudder, was not in itself a viable weapon, but it is said to have aided Robert Whitehead in his development of the locomotive torpedo.

The German FL of World War I displaced 6 tons (6.1 tonnes), was 42.75ft (13m) long, and carried in its bow a 1,750lb (793kg) impact-fuzed explosive charge. The FL's crew aimed the boat at its target, armed the charge, and jumped overboard to be picked up by a following launch. The unmanned craft was then kept on course at a maximum 30kt (34mph, 55kmh), by direct-wire guidance from a director station aboard a picket ship, aided by a spotter seaplane. About 12 FLs were built by Lürssen, but their only success appears to have been a hit on the monitor HMS *Erebus*, which put her out of action for a fortnight, in October 1916. The Royal Navy thereupon experimented with similar craft, and in July 1918 five CMBs (Coastal Motor Boats) were converted to DCBs (Distant Controlled Boats), which operated in much the same way as the FLs.

The true pioneers of manned EMBs, as distinct from remote-controlled craft, were the men of the Royal Italian Navy. Some accounts of Italian operations suggest that the country's interest in EMBs also began with a World-War-I craft, the *Grillo* ("Cricket"). In fact, the *Grillo* was called a *barchino saltatore* ("jumping boat") and, as a weapon, fell somewhere between a conventional motor torpedo boat and the *Maiale* ("Pig") manned torpedo described in Chapter 5. Designed by the Italian Navy's Instructor-General Pruneri, it was a four-man, 8 ton (8.13 tonne), 52.5ft (16m) long craft, powered by two 10hp electric motors giving a maximum 4kt (4.6mph, 7.4kmh), and armed with two 17.7in (450mm) torpedoes in dropping gear aft. Caterpillar tracks ran around both sides of the hull in a layout similar to that of the early tanks, and with this aid it was hoped that the four examples built might clamber over the net-and-boom defences of Pola harbour to torpedo Austrian warships. An attempt was made on the night of 13 May 1918, when a *Grillo* commanded by

LtCdr Antonio Pellegrini was sighted and fired upon by the Austrian battleship *Radetzky* while negotiating the defences. After scuttling their craft, the Italian raiders were taken prisoner.

The Tenth Light Flotilla

Between the wars, the Italian Navy continued to display interest in small-boat warfare and, in 1936, formed the unit which was to become famous as the *Decima Flottiglia MAS* (10th Light Flotilla) specifically for operations of this type. At about the same time, General Duke Amadeo of Aosta of the Italian Air Force and his brother, Admiral Duke Aimone of Spoleto, conceived the project of mounting small explosive boats between the floats of obsolescent Savoia-Marchetti S.55 flyingboats. The boats were to be released at close range for mass attacks on enemy naval bases immediately after the beginning of hostilities. The prototype, a flimsy wood-and-canvas craft with a small, bow-mounted, impact-fuzed explosive charge, was designed by the engineer Guido Cattaneo and by Cdr Mario Giorgini. The project was thereafter allowed to languish until the appointment to the command of the Italian Navy's light forces, in 1938, of Cdr Paolo Aloisi. While the training of personnel continued under Aloisi's direction, Cattaneo and the Baglietto yard at Varazze worked to produce an ingenious and effective EMB that was available for use by the time of Italy's entry into the war on 10 June 1940.

MTM: the Italian Navy's Explosive Motorboat

The basic EMB employed by the 10th Light Flotilla during World War II was the MTM *(Motoscafi da Turismo modificati,* "modified tourist motorboat"); these were commonly known as *barchini esplosivi* ("explosive boats") or simply *barchini.* (An authoritative Italian source refers to the MTMs as "E-boats": I have avoided this usage in order not to confuse the MTM with the German MTB to which this name is most often applied.)

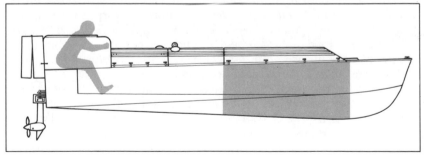

Italian **MTM** explosive motorboat, with folding life-raft aft and 660lb (300kg) warhead forward.

The one-man, 17ft (5.2m) MTM displaced 1.5 tons (1.52 tonnes) and was powered by an Alfa Romco 2500 internal combustion engine of 95bhp. It had a maximum speed of 34kt (39.1mph, 62.9kmh) and an action radius of some 60nm (69 miles, 111km) at high speed or a total endurance of some five hours. Its propeller and rudder were mounted as a single outboard unit which could be lifted by the pilot in order to cross defensive netting. It was armed with a 660lb (300kg) bow-mounted explosive charge.

Having reached an attacking position, the MTM's pilot, who wore a frogman's suit and was housed in a partly shielded cockpit at the stern, set his boat on a collision course, locked the rudder, increased to maximum speed and then, when less than 100yds (90m) from his target, tripped a lever that freed the wooden back-rest of his cockpit, before himself taking to the water. In the few seconds between his ditching and the MTM's impact with the target, the pilot scrambled on to his wooden life-raft in order to escape the shock-wave caused by the explosion of the boat's warhead.

When the umanned boat struck the target, small impact-fuzed charges set centrally around its hull broke the MTM apart. When its fore-part had sunk to a depth pre-set according to the estimated draught of the target ship, hydrostatic pressure triggered the main charge. In theory, therefore, the MTM was not a suicide weapon. Nevertheless, such a complex detonation system was obviously liable to malfunction and for this reason, as well as to ensure that his boat actually struck its target, the MTM pilot was often tempted to set his fuze to explode on impact and to stay with his craft until it was too late to save himself. As the brief account of MTM operations given below shows, pilots were on occasion asked, or ordered, to sacrifice themselves in order to ensure success.

MTMs were generally carried to their operational areas aboard warships specially equipped for such duties with deck clamps for transport and electrically-powered hoists for launching. When thus equipped, the 970-ton (986 tonne) Sella-class destroyers *Francesco Crispi* and *Quintino Sella* proved capable in trials of launching six MTM apiece within 35 seconds.

A smaller version of the MTM, the MTR, was designed to be carried to its attack zone in a metal cylinder (the same cylinder designed to house the Pig manned torpedo) on the hull of a submarine. Also operated by the 10th Light Flotilla were the MTSM *(Motoscafi da Turismo, Siluranti, Modificati,* "tourist motorboat, torpedo, modified") and its later development the SMA *(Silurante, Modificato, Allargato,* "torpedo, modified, enlarged boat"). These were not EMBs but small MTBs, somewhat resembling the British CMBs of World War I, and they do not fall within the scope of this book.

In view of the remarks made elsewhere in this book concerning Japanese criteria for selecting personnel for suicidal duties, it is worth noting a major aspect of Italian selection procedure. At the Training Centre for Sea Pioneers, San Leopoldo, Livorno, established in September 1940 to train crews for assault craft duties, the emotional stability and general moral character of the volunteers was considered to be even more important than their physical aptitude for such work.

Soon after Italy's entry into the war, command of what by now had become the 10th Light Flotilla was assumed by Commander Vittorio Moccagatta. The Flotilla's "surface division", responsible for EMB operations, was headed by LtCdr Giorgio Giobbe. The Pigs (the manned torpedoes whose operations are briefly described in Chapter 5) were soon in action; the operational debut of the MTM explosive boats was, however, delayed to await a suitable target. A favourable opportunity came early in 1941, with the increasing buildup of Allied shipping off Greece and, particularly, in the anchorage of Crete.

Date: **26 March 1941**
Place: **Suda Bay, Crete**
Attack by: **MTM boats of the Italian 10th Light Flotilla**
Target: **Allied warships and transports at anchor**

During early 1941, close aerial surveillance was maintained on Suda Bay, the Allied fleet anchorage in northwest Crete; while at Parteni Bay on the Dodecanese island of Leros the 10th Light Flotilla waited to sortie. Twice, in January and again in February, the *Francesco Crispi* and *Quintino Sella* sailed with MTMs aboard — and twice the mission was aborted because air reconnaissance reported a lack of suitable targets. Nevertheless, in spite of British air raids that inflicted casualties on the unit, the Flotilla's morale remained high. On 25 March, the two destroyers lay at Astypalaia Island in the Dodecanese, with MTMs aboard. Weather conditions were good — sea calm and moon dark — and reconnaissance reported a large cruiser, two destroyers and at least 12 transports in Suda Bay. Immediately after an air raid that caused slight damage to *Crispi*, a sortie was ordered. Each destroyer carried three MTMs, the boat unit being commanded by Lt Luigi Faggioni.

The MTMs were launched some 9nm (10.3 miles, 17km) off the entrance to Suda Bay at 2330 on 25 March. Sailing in formation, the small craft reached the mouth of the 6 mile (10km) long Bay before 0100 on 26 March and moved into the narrow inlet leading to the anchorage. Barring their way were three buoy-and-net booms, covered by artillery batteries ashore and periodically swept by searchlights. By 0445 the shallow-draught boats had successfully negotiated all three barriers undetected. Gathering his force together, Lt Faggioni ordered them to stop engines and await the light of dawn before making their attacks. They lay so close to the Allied ships that the sounds of reveille aboard could be clearly heard at 0500, when, under minimum power, the MTMs of SubLt Angelo Cabrini and CPO Tullio Tedeschi moved to within about 300yds (275m) of the major objective, the 8,250-ton (8382-tonne) cruiser HMS *York*.

At 0530, as the light rapidly improved, Cabrini and Tedeschi opened their throttles and headed at maximum speed, side by side, towards *York*. The attack went according to the book: ditching some 90yds (82m) short of the target, both pilots were safe aboard their life-rafts when their boats struck the 575ft (175m) long cruiser. With a gaping wound in her side, *York* began to list almost immediately, while gunners aboard and ashore opened up at the invisible "low-flying aircraft" which were presumed to be attacking. (Lt Faggioni, taken from the water and made prisoner, was immediately asked what had happened to his aircraft.)

Meanwhile, CPO Lino Beccati had scored a crippling hit on the Norwegian tanker *Pericles* (8,324 tons, 8457 tonnes), while the MTMs of Master Gunner Alessio De Vito and Sergeant Gunner Emilio Barberi narrowly missed other transports. Lt Faggioni himself had held back,

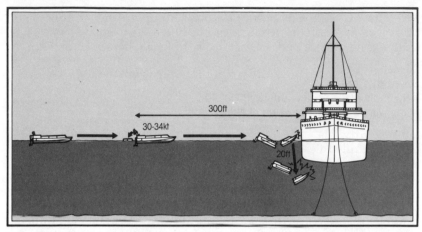

Final stage of **MTM** attack. The pilot sets his boat on course, locks the rudder, increases to maximum speed, frees his life-raft and ditches when within 300ft (90m) of the target. When the **MTM** strikes, small impact-fuzed charges break it apart and the explosive-laden forepart sinks until the main charge is detonated by hydrostatic pressure beneath the target ship's hull.

intending to make a run on *York* if necessary: seeing the cruiser hard hit, he picked a nearby warship (thought to be the cruiser HMS *Coventry*) as his target, but missed. All the Italian pilots survived to be taken prisoner. *York* was towed inshore and settled on the bottom, where German aerial bombing soon rendered her a constructive total loss. (Italian sources claim that no further damage was inflicted by German aircraft, and that British demolition charges completed the work the 10th Light Flotilla had begun.) *Pericles* broke in two and sank when an effort was made to tow her to Alexandria for repair.

Date: **26 July 1941**
Place: **Grand Harbour, Valletta, Malta**
Attack by: **Italian MTM boats and Maiali torpedoes**
Target: **Allied warships and transports at anchor**

The MTM pilots who had made the hazardous and successful attack at Suda Bay had all survived, but the last major operation in which MTMs were deployed (their role subsequently being taken over by the small, torpedo-armed MTSM and SMA boats mentioned above) proved to be a true suicide mission—both in execution and, it may be suspected, in planning. At Suda Bay, the frail explosive boats had been pitted against an unprepared enemy and improvised defences at a location that had been thoroughly reconnoitred. This was not the case with the newly-chosen target: after MTMs had been launched to make seaborne reconnaissance of such Allied anchorages as Porto Edda (Sarandë) in southern Albania, and Corfu, the choice fell on the Allies' Mediterranean bastion—Malta. In spite of its formidable defences and the lack of intelligence concerning them, Grand Harbour at Valletta was designated the target.

It must have been obvious at the planning stage that self-sacrifice would be unavoidable if the attackers were to penetrate the anchorage and that, even if the penetration were made, there would be little chance of survival for the crews of small boats under concentrated fire in the narrow, crowded harbour. This was certainly realized by *Maggiore Genio Navale* (Major, naval rank) Teseo Tesei, co-inventor of the Pig, who maintained that the attack should be made simply as a demonstration of Italian gallantry and determination, as an inspiration to "our sons and Italy's future generations". Tesei, who had already been told that his exploits in Pigs had overstrained his heart and that he faced death if he did not retire from operations, wrote a farewell letter shortly before the Malta mission in which he stated his intention of "winning the highest of all honours, that of giving my life for the King and the honour of the Flag." Tesei's determination was matched by that of Cdr Moccagatta and, faced with such enthusiasm, Admirals de Courten and Campioni of the Naval Chiefs of Staff gave somewhat grudging approval to the mission. It will be noted that, as in Japan, the employment of suicidal weapons and tactics was, at first, more enthusiastically advocated by junior officers than by their superiors; ie, by the men who would be intimately concerned with the operation of such weapons.

After a further series of seaborne reconnaissances, it was decided to mount the attack on Malta on the night of 27-28 June. Late on 27 June, a small task force of MTMs towed by MTBs sailed from Augusta, eastern Sicily, where training had been underway since April. Foul weather forced a return to base. Two nights later, Moccagatta's force tried again: this time, engine failure on two MTMs resulted in a further postponement—until the corresponding dark of the moon in July. Profiting from experience, Moccagatta now changed the composition of his task force: instead of being towed to the operational area, the MTMs would be carried aboard the fast sloop *Diana* (1,764 tons, 1792 tonnes; originally built as Mussolini's official yacht) and would be led into the attack by an MTSM and, at the insistence of Major Tesei, by two Pigs. The human torpedoes would, in fact, spearhead the attack: one would blow a hole in the net defences of Grand Harbour; the other would make a diversionary raid on the Royal Navy's submarine base at Marsa-Muscetto, in the western arm of Valletta harbour. An air raid was timed to coincide with the surface attack and was expected fully to occupy the harbour batteries.

Moccagatta's force sailed from Augusta at sunset on 25 July. Aboard *Diana* (LtCdr Mario Di Muro) were nine MTMs; an MTSM, in which LtCdr Giobbe would direct the attack; and a small, electric-powered (and therefore silent-running) motorboat which would carry the two Pigs to their launching point. The Pigs were carried from Augusta on the 20-ton (20.3 tonne) motor torpedo boats *MAS 451* (SubLt Giorgio Sciolette) and *MAS 452* (Lt G. Batta Parodi). The Pig crews were Major Tesei with CPO Alcide Pedretti and Lt Franco Costa with Sgt Luigi Barla. Thus, the commander of 10th Light Flotilla (Moccagatta, aboard *MAS 452*) and all his principal officers intended to play an active part in the desperate enterprise; even the Flotilla's chief medical officer, Captain Surgeon Bruno Falcomatà volunteered as a member of *MAS 452's* crew. Although the mission had not been planned to take advantage of the fact, Valletta now offered an excellent selection of targets, for the transports of the hard-fought "Substance" convoy had entered Grand Harbour on 24 July.

Gallant Failure at Valletta

Nine MTMs were launched from *Diana* some 20nm (23 miles, 37km) off Malta at some time before midnight on 25 July. One sank immediately. The remaining eight, with the electric launch carrying the Pigs, headed inshore, escorted by the MTSM and the two MTBs. By 0300 on 26 July, the electric launch was within 1,100yds (1000m) of the entrance to Grand Harbour, at which point the Pigs were to launch. Engine failure on the Pig of Costa and Barla delayed the launching time by at least one hour (en route to their target, Marsa-Muscetto, the engine failed again and, unable to complete their mission, the two men were later taken prisoner). Tesei and Pedretti had the vital task of destroying the steel-plate-and-mesh anti-torpedo net, suspended from a two-span bridge, that guarded the narrow passage leading into Grand Harbour below Fort St Elmo. In spite of the delay in launching, Tesei made it clear that he intended to destroy the net at the appointed time (0430)—even if, as seemed likely, this entailed the self-destruction of himself and Pedretti. Meanwhile, Giobbe told the MTM pilots that if, following up Tesei, they found the barrier still intact, the leaders must sacrifice themselves in order to ensure that at least one boat penetrated the harbour and reached Allied shipping.

But by the time the Pigs were on the way, the harbour defence force was on the alert. *Diana's* arrival and departure had been logged by surface radar and, because the diversionary raids by Italian aircraft were sporadic and ill-timed, the small boats' engines had been heard. Even so, the Pig crewed by Tesei and Pedretti was able to reach the St Elmo bridge where, at 0425, true to his word, Tesei detonated the warhead of his torpedo immediately, sacrificing himself and Pedretti —but failing to breach the net. To seaward, hearing the explosion, Giobbe ordered the MTMs in to the attack.

In the first light of dawn, the MTMs hurled themselves at the still-intact barrier. In the leading boat, SubLt Roberto Frassetto flung himself clear just before the impact: his MTM struck the netting but failed to detonate. Following him, SubLt Aristide Carabelli remained at the helm until the last, perishing in a massive explosion that seriously wounded the swimming Frassetto, breached the netting— and brought down one of the bridge spans, rendering the boat channel impassable. As SubLt Carlo Bosio led in the remaining boats, their path was illuminated by searchlights, and 6-pounder batteries, Bofors AA guns and machine guns opened up from the shore. Caught in the blocked channel under a savage crossfire, the MTMs were soon sunk; Bosio was killed and the surviving pilots, all wounded, were captured.

As the light improved, some 30 Hawker Hurricanes joined the battle and, although opposed by 10 Macchi C.200 Saetta fighters (which succeeded in shooting down one Hurricane, but lost three of their number) located and attacked the two MTBs and the two smaller motorboats which had been standing by to take off any surviving MTM and Pig crewmen. *MAS 451*, raked by cannon fire from the Hurricanes, blew up and sank, killing four of her 13-strong crew. The electric launch was also sunk, and aboard *MAS 452*, Moccagatta, Giobbe, Falcomatà, Parodi and four other men were killed by gunfire. Abandoning *MAS 452*, 11 survivors succeeded in reaching *Diana*.

Fifteen men had been killed, among them the senior officers of the 10th Light Flotilla, and 18 captured in the gallant but ineffective action.

Abortive Missions with MTR boats

Thereafter, the MTMs played little part in the 10th Light Flotilla's activities. However, as described later in this chapter, the explosive boat concept was adopted by the German Navy and Cdr J. Valerio Borghese (who succeeded Moccagatta in command), remaining faithful to the Axis cause even after Italy's surrender, passed on his experience to German volunteers.

Before Italy's collapse, however, two abortive missions were launched with the smaller MTR explosive boats. In mid-1943, following the Allied invasion of Sicily, it was planned to attack shipping in Syracuse harbour with MTRs. The submarine *Ambra* (LtCdr Renato Ferrini), carrying three MTRs in the deck cylinders originally designed for the transportation of Pigs, stood off Syracuse on the night of 25 July 1943. But the activities of German U-boats had put the harbour defences on full alert: picked up on the radars of patrolling aircraft, *Ambra* was

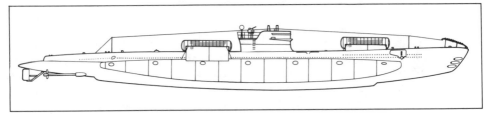

Watertight metal cylinders (one forward; two side-by-side aft) were fitted to the Italian submarine **Scirè** to transport **MTR** (smaller **MTM**) explosive boats or **Maiali** manned-torpedoes.

bombed, depthcharged, and forced to retire with heavy damage, including the crushing of the MTRs' cylinders.

A similar mission was planned for 2 October 1943, when the submarine *Murena* (Cdr Longanesi), equipped with four transportation cylinders, was to launch four MTRs on the Spanish side of Algeciras Bay. The boats were to make their way along the neutral shore and, at 1100 hours, carry out a suicidal daylight attack on merchant shipping at Gibraltar. In the resultant confusion, it was hoped, a Pig launched from the secret base aboard the *Olterra* (see Chapter 5) would penetrate the military harbour and attack the largest warship in sight. The operation was forestalled by Italy's surrender on 8 September 1943.

JAPANESE EXPLOSIVE MOTORBOATS

In March 1944, the Imperial Japanese Army's Warship Research Institute at Himeji, near Kobe, was directed to devote considerable effort to the development of "special (attack) boats"; in other words, suicide boats. One month later, the Imperial Japanese Navy issued a similar directive concerning suicide weapons of all kinds to its departments of warship and aircraft production. It is certain, however, that the employment of suicide weapons had been under consideration since at least mid-1943, and that the activities of early 1944 merely represented official sanction for such weapons; for the first suicide boat units of both Army and Navy were being deployed for operations as early as August-September 1944. Thus, as in the case of the kaiten torpedo and the ohka piloted-bomb, the design and construction of a suicide weapon considerably predated "official" references to it.

The Army's Suicide Boats

The Army's interest in EMBs was provoked by the inability of its aircraft, in the face of Allied air superiority, to strike effectively at the most vulnerable element of the Allied amphibious landing forces — the landing ships. Seeking a method of attacking at night and hitting the transports while they lay off the beaches, the IJA adopted the concept of the *maru-ni* ("capacious boat") units. The name reflected a reluctance to be openly committed to a suicidal weapon; the term *renraku-tei* ("communications boat") was also used. (The Navy displayed less reluctance to acknowledge the weapon's true nature, calling its EMBs *shinyo*, "ocean-shakers" or "sea-quake" boats.)

But the Army's commitment to suicide tactics became increasingly overt after the fall of Saipan in June 1944, when Imperial General HQ issued a directive called *Essentials of Island Defence*. This stressed the importance of attacking invasion shipping during the approach to the beaches and the unloading phase. The Army Air Force was ordered to concentrate its attacks on transports, ignoring escorts, and to employ low-level "skip-bombing" techniques and, if necessary, suicide dives. Suicidal surface craft were to strike at transports at anchor. The Navy's need for suicide boats, on the other hand, stemmed largely from its pre-war neglect of conventional MTB development and its inability, in wartime conditions, to produce small, fast attack craft comparable to the US Navy's PT-boats.

The Maru-ni Explosive Boat

The Army's maru-ni was a one- or two-man boat of wooden construction, a little over 18ft (5.4m) long and displacing about 1.6 tons (see data table on page 87 for full details). Power was provided by a rebuilt automobile engine, an 80shp unit giving a maximum speed of 25-30kt (28-35mph, 46-56kmh). Its armament consisted of one 441lb (200kg) depthcharge (or sometimes two smaller charges) held on dropping gear at the stern.

Theoretically, the maru-ni was not a suicide boat. An Army manual stated that the recommended method of attack was to make a high-speed run on the target; release the depthcharge, fuzed to detonate in about 4 seconds, alongside; and then head away before the explosion. In practice, the pilot obviously had little chance of surviving the attack and, according to the testimony of former members of EMB units, most pilots elected to ensure a hit by making ramming attacks.

The Army made an attempt to produce a truly high-speed attack craft by fitting the Type N-1 maru-ni with booster rockets which could be cut in on the last few hundred yards to the target. In experiments made at Ujima, Hiroshima, late in 1944, rocket-assisted boats achieved speeds of 50-60kt (57-69mph, 92-111kmh) over short distances. However, since only two or three such boats were built, it is obvious that they were deemed unsuitable for operational use.

Above: An **MTM** pilot of the Italian Navy's **Decima Flottiglia MAS** (10th Light Flotilla), a "special attack" unit, steers his explosive motorboat towards a target during training.

Left: The fishing-boat **Cefalo** carries **MTM**s slung on davits. Destroyers or, for the attack on Valletta, Malta, Mussolini's yacht **Diana**, usually carried **MTM**s to the operational area.

Below: **MTM**s at operational readiness, in dark paintwork and with shielded cockpits. Note the "bumper" around the bow of the rear boat, to trigger explosive bolts or impact-fuzed charges.

Left: The final stage of an **MTM** attack during training. The pilot has freed his wooden life raft (visible aft the cockpit in the photographs on the previous page) and has ditched. With less than 100yds (90m) to go, the **MTM** heads for its target at around 34kt (39mph, 63kmh).

Below: The 8,250-ton British cruiser HMS **York** was struck by two **MTM**s in Suda Bay, Crete, during a dawn attack on 26 March 1941, when a tanker was also sunk. Badly damaged by their 600lb (300kg) warheads, **York** was towed inshore and settled on the bottom, where German divebombers completed her destruction.

Above: An American officer takes a joyride in a captured **Maru-ni** motorboat of the Imperial Japanese Navy. Note brackets and ramp of depthcharge dropping-gear aft the cockpit.

Far left: "Type 1/Improved 4" **Shinyo** explosive motorboats of the Imperial Japanese Navy, found on Kerama Retto. Note the anti-boom devices fitted forward and the slides for two 4.7in (119mm) RAK-12 rocket guns astern.

Left: Captured **Shinyo** under guard at Motobu peninsula, Okinawa. Chalked on the bow of the boat in the foreground is the warning: "Danger – these boats are booby trapped"!

Below: A "Type 1" **Shinyo** captured on Okinawa is mounted on a wheeled trolley which can be run along rails to the water for launching.

Right: On 7 April 1945, as the super-battleship **Yamato** and her escorts raced south on a suicide run to Okinawa, some 280 US carrier aircraft struck. Here, already afire, **Yamato** is struck by a bomb aft, while a near-miss raised a great plume of water off the port side.

Far right: Trailing smoke but not yet crippled by torpedoes, **Yamato**, and one of her escorting destroyers (**right**), plough onward as US aircraft circle before yet another attacking run.

Below: The biggest, most heavily-armed and -armoured battleship ever built, HIJMS **Yamato** runs high-speed trials in October 1941. Displacing 72,809 tons full load, **Yamato** mounted nine 18.1in (460mm) guns.

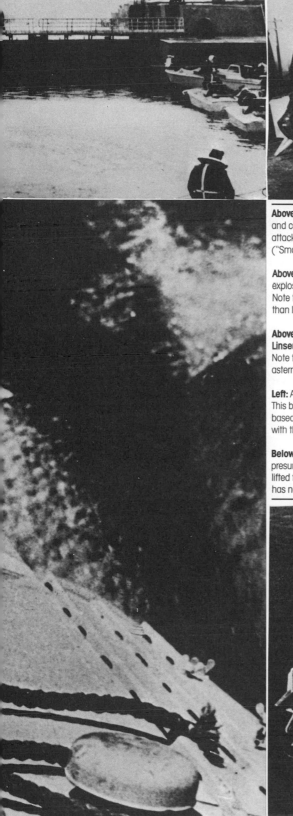

Above left: Vice-Admiral Hellmuth Heye, creator and commander of the German Navy's "special attack" force, the **Kleinkampfmittel Verband** ("Small Battle Force"), awards a medal.

Above centre: A group of **Linsen,** German explosive motorboats, in Holland, late 1944. Note that the pilots have life-jackets, rather than life-rafts mounted on their boats.

Above: Mechanics check out newly-delivered **Linsen** at a North Sea base in January 1945. Note the shielded recognition light mounted astern on the boat in the foreground.

Left: A **Linse** pilot in training, September 1944. This boat appears to be of the earlier type, based on the Italian **MTM**; compare its cockpit with those of the boats seen above (centre).

Below: With its detachable life-raft missing, presumably after a training run, a **Linse** is lifted from the water. The training boat has no "bumper" detonator around the bow.

Above: Vice-Admiral Takijiro Onishi formed the first "official" **kamikaze** suicide unit at Mabalacat, Luzon, on 19 October 1944.

Above centre: Admiral Onishi offers a flask of **sake** for a ceremonial toast by **kamikaze** pilots.

Far right: Kamikaze attack on Task Force 38 off Luzon, Philippines, on 25 November 1944. (**Top**) The 5in (127mm) AA guns of the heavy carrier USS **Essex** are trained skyward as a Yokosuka D4Y2 "Judy" divebomber, already hit, heads towards her. (**Centre**) The "Judy" smashes down on the flight deck forward, killing 15 men. (**Bottom**) Although **Essex** appears to be hard hit, aircraft were again being operated normally within 30 minutes of the **kamikaze** strike.

Right: A senior lieutenant of the IJNAF salutes as he receives his orders for a **kamikaze** sortie.

Below: A **kamikaze** pilot's **hachimaki**, the headband traditionally worn by a **samurai** when going into battle, is tied on by a comrade.

Above: The flight deck of USS **Belleau Wood** (CVL 24) blazes after the impact of a bomb-laden Zero, which killed 92 men, on 30 October 1944.

Left: A ''Judy'' dives on the light cruiser USS **Columbia** off Lingayen, 6 January 1945. This is possibly a Yokosuka D4Y4, specially-equipped for suicide attack with a 1,764lb (800kg) bomb and RATOG rockets to boost terminal diving speed.

Below: A kamikaze makes a bow-on approach to the heavy cruiser USS **Louisville,** 5 January 1945. Its spectacular impact **(Bottom)** killed one man, injured 59, and caused only moderate damage.

The Shinyo Explosive Boat

Most accounts by western writers of Japan's special attack forces make little mention of the EMBs, and often fail to differentiate between the maru-ni of the Army and the Navy's shinyo. In fact, although the dimensions and performance of the boats was much alike, there were significant differences in armament.

The Type 1 shinyo (see data Table on page 87 for details of all types) was a one-man boat built largely of plywood, although a few were of metal construction. It was 19.7ft (6m) long and displaced 1.35 tons (1.37 tonnes). It was powered by a 67bhp internal combustion engine, supposedly giving a maximum speed of 26kt (30mph, 48kmh) and an action radius of 105nm (121 miles, 194km) at high speed. In fact, the use of reconditioned automobile engines meant that the shinyo's power units were notoriously unreliable: the former commander of a shinyo squadron states that none of his Type 1 boats was capable of

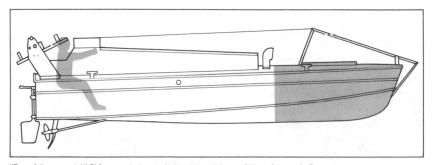

"Type 1/Improved 4" **Shinyo** motorboat of IJN, with anti-boom fittings fore and aft.

more than 23kt (26.5mph, 42.5kmh) unladen, or more than 18kt (21mph, 33kmh) when carrying a warhead.

The shinyo's warhead consisted of a 551-661lb (250-300kg) explosive charge. This was usually rigged to explode only on impact, when the crushing of the boat's bows completed a simple electrical circuit. On later boats, a trigger or switch in the cockpit could be used to detonate the charge, thus in effect turning the pilot into a human bomb. Most shinyo built after January 1945 incorporated two RAK-12 rocket-guns, crude wooden projectors mounted on either side of the cockpit. Each discharged a single 4.7in (119mm) projectile weighing 49.5lb (22.4kg). These were intended to be fired at close range, liberating a shot-gun scatter of metal slugs that would be effective against the target ship's 40mm and 20mm gunners in their lightly-protected or exposed positions.

One boat in each squadron of 40-50 shinyo was to be crewed by two men — the squadron commander and his pilot. It was intended that in a mass sortie the commander should bring up the rear, observing the attacks made by his men and, if possible, assisting them with covering fire from a machine-gun on a swivel mounting just forward of his cockpit. (The 13.2mm Type 93 heavy machine gun was specified, to be mounted on the Type 1/Improved 4 and the larger Type 5 boats.) Having seen all his men strike home, the commander would then order the pilot of his own boat to attack and both men would perish together.

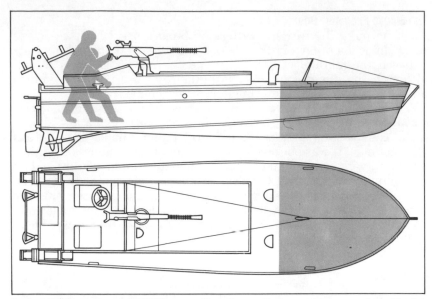

One boat in each squadron of 40-50 **Shinyo** was a "Type 5", crewed by the squadron commander and his pilot. During a mass attack, the commander attempted to assist his men with covering fire from the swivel-mounted 13.2mm MG, before closing in on his own ramming mission.

The First Suicide Boat Squadrons

By the summer of 1944, both the Army and Navy had formed and were beginning to deploy suicide boat squadrons. The former commander of one of the IJN's first EMB squadrons related his own experience to the author. In August 1944, having expressed his willingness to undertake hazardous duty (its exact nature apparently unspecified, although he was in no doubt that he was volunteering for suicidal operations), he was posted to Yokosuka Naval Base and found on arrival that he had been given command of Shinyo Squadron No 6 (SS 6). The Squadron—48 shinyo and some 200 men—had already been formed. The shinyo pilots, some 50 officers and petty officers, were volunteers for special duty; the supporting personnel had simply been assigned in the usual way.

The early shinyo squadrons and maru-ni seem all to have been made up in this way; that is, with volunteer pilots who had been made aware that their duties would be "special", ie, suicidal; and it must be remembered that the *Imperial Rescript* concerning military conduct, the expression of the Emperor's will, assumed that Japanese service-men were prepared to sacrifice their lives at any moment should their duty demand it. In any case, all EMB personnel seem to have accepted their postings with equanimity.

Although a three-month training period in small-boat handling, mechanics and attack techniques was prescribed for EMB units, the early squadrons were expected to fit their training schedules into a series of rapid deployments necessitated by the urgent need for their services for the defence of the Philippines, Okinawa, Formosa and Hainan Island. In September 1944, Shinyo Squadrons 1-5 were sent to Chichijima and Hahajima in the Bonin Islands, while Squadrons 6-13

EXPLOSIVE MOTORBOATS OF THE IMPERIAL JAPANESE NAVY & ARMY						
Type:	SHINYO TYPE 1 (NAVY)	SHINYO TYPE 1 IMPROVED 1 (NAVY)	SHINYO TYPE 1 IMPROVED 4 (NAVY)	SHINYO TYPE 5 (NAVY)	MARU-NI TYPE N-1 (ARMY)	K-GATA-TAI TYPE K (ARMY)
Hull:	Steel or wooden	Wooden	Wooden	Wooden	Wooden	Wooden
Displacement:	1.35 tons (1.37mt)	as Type 1	1.4 tons (1.42mt)	2.15 tons (2.18mt)	1.6 tons (1.63mt)	1.2 tons (1.22mt)
Length overall:	19.7ft (6m)	16.7ft (5.1m)	17.7ft (5.4m)	21.3ft (6.5m)	18.37ft (5.6m)	18.04ft (5.5m)
Beam:	5.5ft (1.67m)	as Type 1	as Type 1	6.1ft (1.86m)	5.6ft (1.7m)	5.25ft (1.6m)
Draught (full load):	2.6ft (0.785m)	as Type 1	as Type 1	as Type 1	2ft (0.6m)	2ft (0.6m)
Machinery:	1 automobile engine 67bhp=26kt	as Type 1	1 automobile engine 62bhp=20kt	2 automobile engines 134bhp=28kt	1 automobile engine 80shp=25kt	as Type N-1 80shp=30kt
Action radius:	105nm @ 26kt 125nm @ 18kt	as Type 1	125nm @ 20kt 130nm @ 12kt	115nm @ 28kt 125nm @ 18kt	not known (less than shinyo)	not known (less than shinyo)
Armament:	2x4.7in RAK-12 rocket guns with two shells (on some boats only)	as Type 1 (on all boats)	2x4.7in RAK-12 rocket guns with two shells; 1x13mm MG (on some boats)	as Type 1/ Improved 4 but with MG on all boats	personal weapon(s) of crew	as Type N-1
Explosives:	bow-mounted charge of 551lb (250kg) or 661lb (300kg)	bow-mounted charge of 551lb (250kg)	as Type 1/ Improved 1	as Type 1/ Improved 1	1x441lb (200kg) depth charge on dropping gear at stern	as Type N-1
Crew:	1	1	1 or 2	2	1 or 2	1 or 2

Note: These are "official" data; there were many variations in size, machinery, radius and armament/explosives.

were ordered to the Philippines. Thus, it is obvious that even before the "official" inception of EMB training (in October-November 1944), some 650 pilots and 2,500 support personnel were available for the Navy's shinyo squadrons alone; while the scale of maru-ni deployment in the Philippines at this time suggests that the Army's numbers were at least as great.

The semi-secrecy with which the early squadrons were formed led to problems. The commander of SS 6 found it hard to fill his unit's equipment lists because "the nature of my squadron was kept so secret that the relevant supply departments knew nothing about us". Unable to get personal weapons for his pilots through the proper channels, he made an unauthorized flight to Tokyo and "by all but threatening an officer at the Navy Ministry" obtained 50 revolvers and a supply of ammunition. On the trip back, he encountered Vice-Admiral Sentaro Omori, overall commander of torpedo boat training, who had a fearsome reputation as a disciplinarian. Questioned, the officer confessed his breach of regulations—"and Admiral Omori wept! 'Do they really have to make a commander who may go to his death at any moment worry about this sort of thing?' he said". But the sentiments expressed by Vice-Admiral Komatsu, commander of Sasebo Naval Base, were more conventional: he ended his rousing address to an outward-bound

EMB squadron with "a thunderous shout of 'Go, then, into battle!'" —
being careful *not* to use the Japanese form of speech that implies
"go — and return again".

Deployment of the EMBs

The deployment of shinyo and maru-ni units in the Philippines before
and during the American landings at Leyte that began in October 1944
was as follows:

> Shinyo Squadrons 7, 8, 9, 10, 11, 12 and 13, with a total strength of
> 300 Type 1 boats, at Corregidor;
> Advanced Combat Units (Army) Nos 11 and 12, with a total
> strength of 200 maru-ni, around Lingayen Gulf, west-central
> Luzon;
> Advanced Combat Units Nos 7, 9 and 17, with a total strength of
> 300 maru-ni, around Lamon Bay, southeast Luzon;
> Advanced Combat Units Nos 14, 15 and 16, with a total strength of
> 300 maru-ni, around Batangas Bay, southern Luzon.

Thus, a total of 300 shinyo guarded the island fortress of Corregidor at
the entrance to Manila Bay, while 800 maru-ni were deployed to cover
the most likely invasion beaches. In addition, two torpedo boat squadrons, equally ready for conventional or, if necessary, suicidal operations, were available:

> Torpedo Boat Squadron No 25, with 10 boats, based on Cebu
> Island, west of Leyte;
> Torpedo Boat Squadron No 31, with 10 boats, based at Manila.

The hurried deployment of the early EMB units had caused
problems. On 1 October 1944, SS 6, which had been transported to
Manila aboard two oil tankers, was ordered to be ready for action
within two weeks. Its pilots had received no practical training: "our
boats were still crated up, as they had been received from our workshops. It was highly unlikely that we could get full power from them
without a proper working-up period; and loading the explosive warheads by hand-winch would take about 10 days". In response to his
protests, SS 6's commander was assigned 100 more support personnel,
a miscellaneous collection of survivors from sunken ships: "all in
short-sleeved shirts and shorts, with white kerchiefs round their heads
and not a weapon between the lot of them. They were like primary
schoolchildren filing out on to the playground for sports day!"

Although SS 6 had reached Manila intact, considerable losses were
suffered by other EMB units en route to the Philippines, whence a total
of more than 1,000 shinyo and maru-ni was dispatched in September-
October 1944. Some transports were sunk; accidents were caused by
the instability of the boats' explosive charges and the unreliability of
their engines; and men succumbed to tropical diseases. The greatest
danger came from air attacks: to escape these, while awaiting the
expected Allied invasion, SS 6 was posted from its base at Zamboanga,
western Mindanao, to Sandakan in North Borneo. The Allied landing
at Leyte on 17 October 1944 trapped SS 6 at Sandakan for the rest of
the war. Establishing a base on a small, swampy island in Sandakan
Bay, the Squadron trained for the attacks it would never have the
chance to make; and by August 1945 more than two-thirds of its

personnel had died from tropical diseases aggravated by rough living and semi-starvation.

The Army's maru-ni units experienced similar vicissitudes. Captain Takahashi's Advanced Combat Unit No 12 (ACU 12; the Army units were sometimes called "Sea Raiding Battalions"), formed at Etajima on 1 October 1944 with a strength of 100 boats, took ship for the Philippines only two days later. By 15 November, after suffering the loss of several boats in a typhoon, it had established a base just north of San Fernando, on Lingayen Gulf, central Luzon. Thus, such training as was possible had to be carried out in the combat zone where, while exercising on 15 December, the unit lost several boats to air attack.

On 26 December, Takahashi was ordered by Major-General Nishiyama's 3rd Division HQ to move ACU 12's base from San Fernando to Sual in the southwest of Lingayen Gulf. Because only one small transport vessel was available, many of the maru-ni had to make the voyage of some 20nm (23 miles, 37km) under their own power, and two boats and their crews were lost on the way. The movement was not completed until 4 January 1945, only two days before the US Navy's Task Group 77.2 entered Lingayen Gulf to begin a pre-invasion bombardment. Although both kamikaze and conventional aircraft struck hard at Vice-Admiral J.B. Oldendorf's battleships, cruisers and destroyers, Japanese forces ashore suffered severely. Nine of ACU 12's pilots were killed by naval gunfire on 7 January and as many more on the morning of 9 January, when US landings began. On that day, 3rd Division HQ ordered ACU 12 to attack Allied invasion shipping.

Disaster at Corregidor

The Imperial Japanese Navy had hoped to have the honour of launching the first EMB attack, but this was prevented by an accident of a kind all too common. On 23 December 1944, Japanese commanders at Corregidor were warned that major Allied warships were moving north in coastal waters from Mindoro. Shinyo Squadrons Nos 7-13, based at Corregidor under the overall command of LtCdr Oyamada, were ordered to readiness. In the hurried preparation, the engine of one boat of Lt Ken Nakajima's SS 9 caught fire. Since the Squadron's boats were packed tightly together in the cave chosen as base, the fire quickly spread, detonating the boats' warheads in a chain of explosions that wiped out all the shinyo and most of their pilots. No sortie could be made.

The frequent engine fires and failures of the shinyo (the maru-ni seem to have suffered less from such accidents) had more than one cause. Japan had failed to develop an efficient small-boat engine, and the automobile engines which powered the shinyo were not purpose-designed and had often had hard usage before conversion. And although petrol engines are better suited to small, fast craft than are diesels—giving a better power-to-weight ratio and being capable of running at full power for longer periods—they are also more prone to take fire and require much more careful maintenance. Since time and facilities for training shinyo personnel were so limited, skilled maintenance was not always available.

As at Corregidor, EMB units facing the constant threat of air attack often established their bases in natural caves or pens blasted from rock or coral. When engines were run up in such cramped, semi-enclosed quarters, the air became so thick with petrol vapour that any chance spark might trigger off a holocaust. A former shinyo squadron commander states:

> "Most personnel had no combat experience at all before they were called upon to sortie, and it is not surprising that young, inexperienced seamen should have neglected some vital precaution when preparing their boats in such circumstances. The Imperial Navy, it must be admitted, provided very little training in fire precautions, and fire-fighting equipment for shinyo squadrons was practically non-existent."

Although Japanese officers consulted by the author had no criticisms of the explosives supplied for their boats, most Allied authorities agree that Japanese explosives were not of a high degree of stability, especially when exposed to excessive heat or humidity.

Date: **10 January 1945**
Place: **Lingayen Gulf, Luzon, Philippines**
Attack by: **Maru-ni EMBs, Imperial Japanese Army**
Target: **Allied invasion shipping**

During daylight on 9 January, some 70,000 US troops, meeting little initial opposition, established a beachhead at Lingayen. The invasion transports and their escorts, commanded by Vice-Admiral Theodore S. Wilkinson, lay close inshore, ready to recommence landing men and materiel next morning and meanwhile on the alert for kamikaze air attack. But the major threat was to come from the sea: Captain Takahashi of the Imperial Japanese Army was ready to launch the first and most successful of the mass suicidal surface attacks.

Takahashi had at readiness about 40 maru-ni of ACU 12, most of them belonging to Lt Womura's 3rd Company, reinforced by some 50 boats of ACU 11. Since the Army's maru-ni units were generally much larger than the Navy's shinyo squadrons — with as many as 200 pilots and 600 support personnel to a unit of about 100 boats — it was not uncommon for a single maru-ni to go into action with a crew of up to four men, rather than the "official" one or two. Personal honour led supernumary pilots, and even support personnel, to demand their chance of a glorious death in battle. This was the case at Lingayen, where US combat reports spoke of EMB's crews attacking with small arms and grenades as well as depthcharges. The same reports suggest that a number of small MTBs may have taken part in the attack — but the majority of the boats committed were maru-ni, carrying either one 441lb (200kg) or two 265lb (120kg) depthcharges and with up to four crewmen armed with light machine guns, rifles and pistols, hand grenades and Molotov cocktails.

A Japanese officer denies US reports that the maru-ni incorporated a device that allowed the rudder to be locked in position, so that the crew could take to the water after setting the boat on a collision course:

> "Imperial General HQ and the Army and Navy staffs wished for escape provisions of this kind to be made on the maru-ni and

shinyo—but in most cases *the pilots themselves refused, saying that this was not necessary.* I believe that this stemmed from their personal sense of honour.'

The maru-ni sortied from Sual, some 5nm (6 miles, 9km) northwest of the Lingayen beaches, before 0300 on 10 January. They approached the Allied anchorage with engines throttled down, hoping to evade the screen of escorts and strike at the soft-skinned transports. The first alarm appears to have been given by the radar watch aboard the destroyer USS *Philip* (Cdr J.B. Rutter), when three "blips" too small to be aircraft registered at 0320. The night was too dark for unassisted lookouts, but in the glare of starshell a number of small boats were spotted. The maru-ni pilots speeded up to attack.

At 0353 the battleship USS *Colorado* picked up a TBS appeal from the 1,625-ton (1651 tonne) tank landing ship *LST-925:* ". . . damaged by enemy torpedo boats . . . taking on water . . . send rescue boats". At least three maru-ni had dropped depthcharges alongside *LST-925*, holing her beneath the waterline and knocking out her starboard engine. These three boats had *not* rammed their target but had executed a drill-book attack: coming in at about 20kt (23mph, 37kmh) from astern—one boat to port, one to starboard, and one some 50-

The deployment of "special attack" weapons, including **kamikaze** aircraft, in the Philippines.

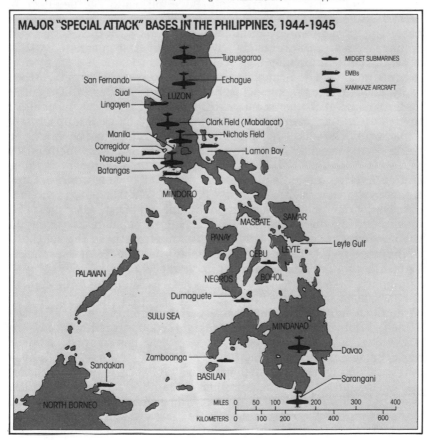

100yds (46-90m) to the rear backing up; dropping depthcharges on a four-second fuze as close as possible to the ship's most vulnerable areas—amidships, below the stacks or at the stern to damage propellers and rudders; and then veering sharply away.

Most of the maru-ni, however, made straightforward ramming attacks to ensure that their depthcharges exploded directly beneath their targets. Such an attack was made on *LST-1028:* explosions stove in her bottom and sent water pouring into her engine compartments. Near the two stricken LSTs, the 6,200-ton (6300 tonne) transport *War Hawk* was rammed by a single maru-ni. Signalling that his ship had been "torpedoed", her skipper gave the order to abandon ship; but *War Hawk*, with a 12ft (3.6m) gash in her side and 73 casualties, survived.

Soon after 0400, when a general warning of attack by "torpedo boats" was given throughout the Allied fleet, USS *Philip* narrowly escaped damage when a maru-ni racing in on a collision course exploded only 25yds (23m) away when raked by 20mm fire. The Allied ships were hampered in their evasive manoeuvring by the crowded anchorage (two transports and an LST were damaged in collisions) and their fire against the diminutive attackers was limited by the danger of hitting their own ships. The US destroyers *Robinson* and *Leutze,* engaging a group of maru-ni between 0415 and 0445, were rarely able to move at more than 5kt (5.75mph, 9.25kmh), and the small craft pressed so close that only light automatic weapons could be brought to bear. The attack was beaten off, but *Robinson* sustained superficial damage from a maru-ni exploded by gunfire at close quarters. By that time, the general warning had been extended to include midget submarines and "suicide swimmers", as well as torpedo boats and EMBs.

By about 0500, the surviving maru-ni had withdrawn. They had suffered heavily: about 45 boats were lost and ACU 12 was incapable of further operations. Relying on explosions reported by shore observers, Japanese official sources claimed that 20-30 US ships had been sunk or seriously damaged. In fact, apart from the ships already mentioned, *LCI(M)-974* and *LCI(G)-365*—246-ton (250 tonne) infantry landing craft converted for duties as mortar and gun/rocket armed escorts respectively—had been sunk; *LST-610* and *LST-925* had been seriously damaged; and seven transports had suffered lesser damage. The results were serious enough for the US Navy immediately to expedite the northward deployment of PT-boat squadrons from the southern Philippines and significantly to increase the number of escorts assigned to guard attack transports' anchorages.

Suicidal Conduct by Survivors

From the conduct of Japanese survivors found in the water after the attack stemmed the legend of the "suicide swimmers of Lingayen"—of naked Japanese swimmers with explosive charges strapped to their backs being mopped up by boatloads of US sailors armed with knives and small arms. (It is true that the IJN trained teams of suicidal swimmers and frogmen, as described briefly in Chapter 6, but these were not committed at Lingayen.) The legend originated in the intransigence of the maru-ni survivors. For example, the destroyer-transport USS *Belknap* lowered a boat to rescue two Japanese afloat on a piece of wreckage—and had to machine-gun both when they attempted to fling grenades at their would-be rescuers. Eleven more survivors were killed under similar circumstances that same morning by *Belknap* alone, and many more by other ships.

Resistance to rescue by Japanese who preferred suicide to capture was nothing new. Of many incidents, one of the most striking occurred off New Ireland in the Bismarck Archipelago on 22 February 1944, when the IJN's 750-ton (762 tonne) salvage and repair vessel *Nagaura*, mounting two 25mm guns, attempted to engage the five US destroyers of Captain Arleigh A. ("Thirtyone-knot") Burke's Desron 23, and was blown apart by 5in (127mm) fire. Of some 150 survivors, about half allowed themselves to be rescued (and within one day were volunteering to act as ammunition carriers during the bombardment of a Japanese-held island!). Of the remainder, some cut their throats while others, unarmed, deliberately drowned themselves, sometimes diving many times before the determination to die triumphed over the instincts of self-preservation.

Similar suicidal determination was displayed by survivors of an action on 26 March 1945, when four British destroyers led by HMS *Saumarez*, assisted by B-24 bombers, sank two Japanese transports and their escorts, the 440-ton (447 tonne) submarine-chasers *Ch 34* and *Ch 63*. Only 53 survivors from the four ships were picked up, of whom one subsequently hanged himself aboard HMS *Volage;* the rest simply swam away to drown. One man swam to HMS *Saumarez* carrying a 25mm shell and, hanging on to the rescue net, hammered on the destroyer's side in a desperate attempt to detonate it until he was clubbed into the sea.

Recruiting in the Homeland
While the first hastily-recruited and partly-trained EMB units were preparing for action in the Philippines, an official programme of recruitment and training had begun in Japan. The formation of kamikaze aircraft units was officially announced on 27 October 1944 and, at the beginning of November, Captain Tameichi Hara was ordered to find volunteers for suicidal surface weapons among his 400-strong intake of students at Kawatana Torpedo School. The order was conveyed by Captain Toshio Miyazaki, who brought with him three shinyo and a number of frogman suits (the latter to equip the *fukuryu*, "crawling dragon", demolition swimmers described in Chapter 6).

According to Hara, both he and Miyazaki had serious doubts about the efficacy, and morality, of suicide weapons, but comforted themselves with the rationalization that, because of the way in which the war had developed, the men they were training were doomed to die in any case. Calling together Hara's students, they explained the nature of the new weapons and called for volunteers. Each man was allowed to give his decision secretly to Hara, who guaranteed that no pressure would be exerted. Of 400 men, 200 elected to remain in conventional torpedo boat training; 150 volunteered for EMB duties; and 50 were prepared to become demolition frogmen.

Some historians have suggested that Japanese "special attack" personnel were not volunteers in the true sense—that they were brainwashed, indoctrinated with the rhetoric of patriotic self-sacrifice, whipped up into hysteria by senior officers, and made to feel that they would be branded as cowards if they did not volunteer. That such men as Captain Hara (who had made his reputation as one of the IJN's most successful destroyer skippers) and the naval airman Saburo Sakai (whose status as an "ace" gave him a prestige that far outweighed his junior rank) seem to have made little secret of their opposition to suicide tactics; that 50 per cent of Hara's students saw no dishonour in opting for non-suicidal duties; and that their decisions were unquestioningly accepted: all these facts are strong evidence to the contrary. (This is discussed further in Chapter 4.)

Rewards and Promotions

Allegations that kamikaze airmen were granted extreme licence to persuade them to volunteer are dealt with in Chapter 4. Two former shinyo squadron commanders were asked if any special privileges were granted to EMB volunteers:

"We did get some extra rations, small luxuries such as *sake* and sweetmeats. Regarding pay, there was a regulation providing for higher allowances for special attack personnel, but these were only paid after a man had left for the front — where money was of little use to him!"

"There was an extra ration allowance, to keep up the men's stamina for hard training for night operations; but there were no special recreation facilities."

A popular feature of EMB service, although it can hardly have influenced men faced with a choice between life and death, was the uniform worn by pilots. Japanese military uniforms were, to western eyes, functional to the point of sloppiness. EMB pilots, however, were issued with flying suits which, according to a veteran, "were very popular because they were both smart and comfortable, allowing great freedom of movement. In addition, each pilot was issued with a revolver — and this, too, was very popular". (Many writers on military psychology have noted the "status symbol" aspect of the hand gun.)

It is often assumed that all special attack personnel went into action wearing *hachimaki* emblazoned with patriotic slogans. The EMB pilots did not, as a former commander explains:

"I don't know of any EMB units that wore *hachimaki;* in my unit, and those of my friends, we certainly didn't intend to wear them — mainly because, in a night attack, for which we were trained, a white head-band isn't a good idea!"

Officer-man relationships within special attack units were, according to veterans, generally more relaxed than in conventional formations: brutal discipline was out of place in a unit where all were sworn to die together. It should be noted, however, that all Japanese officers were officially encouraged to form close personal relationships with their men. An officer was expected to share his men's meals, visit their homes, take a close interest in their families — and even lend them money on occasion. He was also expected to reward minor acts of merit out of his own pocket: Captain Hara records that he presented his own watch to an exceptionally efficient seaman. On the other hand, officers and NCOs, down to senior enlisted men, were allowed to reinforce discipline with kicks, blows and even severe beatings.

It might be claimed that promotion was a bait for special attack volunteers; but this was a reward received only after death in action. In the same way, medals—which *were* awarded for gallantry, the claims of some western writers notwithstanding—were usually given post-humously. Men killed in suicide operations received a posthumous promotion of two ranks, compared to the one-rank promotion given to all Japanese servicemen killed in battle. (This was of practical value to their families, who received increased pensions—as well as greater honour.) Shinto doctrine held that seniority at Yasukuni Shrine, where those killed in battle were re-united as *kami* ("demi-gods"), depended on order of arrival rather than rank at the time of death; thus, it was a favourite joke among enlisted men that their officers, if not among the first to fall, would find themselves on fatigue duties in the hereafter. The most common good-luck wish among Japanese servicemen was "See you at Yasukuni!"

PT-boats versus EMBs

Four days after the maru-ni attack at Lingayen, US PT-boat squadrons arrived in Luzon waters. With air support, they would henceforth be the major enemies of the EMBs. With the LCI ("Elsie Item") gunboats and rocket- and mortar-armed landing craft, the PT-boats—usually without their torpedoes, but bristling with as many 40mm, 37mm and 20mm guns, heavy machine guns and rocket launchers as could be "found" and fitted on improvised mounts—constituted the "Cactus Navy", charged with the interdiction of Japanese inter-island traffic and the destruction of the EMBs in their concealed bases. The US Navy's success in seeking out and destroying the suicide craft before they could be committed to action was facilitated by the breaking of Japanese codes—the "Ultra"/"Magic" intelligence operation—and also by the capture at Gehh islet, during the Kwajalein operations of early 1944, of a large number of secret charts of Japanese-held anchorages throughout the Pacific.

From early 1945 onward, it is difficult to speak with any certainty of the deployment of individual EMB units. Harried from sea and air, unit and sub-unit commanders were forced to attack when and where opportunity decreed and, apart from the two mass attacks described below, were largely confined to "run-and-hit" sorties by small groups or individual boats. In spite of their theoretical range, the difficulties of maintenance, the unreliability of engines and the vulnerability of small boats to weather conditions made it hard for EMBs to attack enemy vessels other than those close inshore. Their best hope was to lie hidden near the shore line, on launching dollys that could be run down rails to the water's edge, carefully camouflaged, in areas where Allied landings were expected. If the EMBs had been the "high-speed craft" envisaged by their originators, they might have been more successful; but most were considerably slower than the Allied escort warships deployed to counter their attacks.

In May 1945, the US Navy issued a "Confidential" bulletin (CinCPac-CinCPOA Bulletin 126-45) on Japanese suicide weapons, giving the following advice on counter-measures to EMB attacks:

"Small boat attacks can be expected wherever there is enemy-held territory nearby which can shelter and hide the craft . . . Many attacks have occurred at night, especially between the hours of 2400 and 0400. Experience has demonstrated the wisdom of having visual lookouts, searchlights, and machine gun batteries fully manned during these hours . . . Limitations of train and depression of armament on most vessels have made it necessary to have patrols equipped with small arms for firing on approaching small craft . . . In preparing such defenses, however, it has been necessary to caution personnel against illuminating and shooting into friendly ships' boats.

"Battle experience has shown that suicide boats rarely are detected by radar, as a result of their low freeboard and small size. [And, it might have been added, because most were constructed of wood.] There have been instances of a few being picked up by sound gear. The combination of a small blip on the radar and high speed screws on the sound gear may, together, foretell the approach of this craft."

However, the best counter-measure proved to be aggressive daylight patrolling by PT-boats and aircraft, to destroy the EMBs in their bases. Typical actions took place near Lingayen on 29-31 January 1945.

On 29 January, 10 maru-ni on a beach near San Fernando were destroyed by the gunfire of *PT-523* and *PT-524*, covered by aircraft of 85th Fighter Command. Farther south on the same day, a maru-ni base on Batangas Bay, southern Luzon—reported to US forces by Filipino guerrillas—was raided by four PT-boats from Caminawit Point, northern Mindoro, where 25 PT-boats were based under the command of LtCdr N. Burt Davis. Supported by two P-38 Lightning fighters ("fork-tailed devils" to the Japanese) and two B-25 Mitchell bombers, which silenced shore batteries, the PT-boats strafed the shore for more than one hour, destroying several maru-ni.

Next day, LtCdr Davis took two PT-boats, covered by two aircraft, into Batangas Bay, and led ashore a party to capture an intact EMB, which they attempted to tow back to Caminawit Point. But Davis's force, without air cover on the homeward run, was attacked by trigger-happy US aircraft which sank the maru-ni. The EMB base at San Fernando was hit again on 31 January, when two PT-boats supported by P-38 fighter-bombers claimed to have destroyed five suicide boats and many other small craft.

Date: **31 January-1 February 1945**
Place: **Nasugbu, southern Luzon, Philippines**
Attack by: **Shinyo EMBs, Imperial Japanese Navy**
Target: **US landing craft and escorts**

On 31 January 1945, two regimental combat teams of the US 11th Airborne Division were landed against little opposition at Nasugbu, just south of Manila Bay. Because of the landing area's steep gradient, several tank and infantry landing craft were forced to wait off the beaches until they could unload on the high tide at 2400. Japanese EMBs were known to be in the area, and appropriate precautions were taken to guard the transports. Three destroyers and the amphibious force flagship USS *Spencer* (Rear-Admiral William M. Fechteler) were on general patrol. Ranged in a 5-mile (8km) arc around the beachhead were the DE *Richard W. Suesens* and the submarine-chaser *PC-623* to the north; the DE *Tinsman*; and the DE *Lough* and sub-chaser *PC-1129* to the south. Within this screen, close to the transports, were the destroyers *Flusser* and *Claxton*.

Although the sea was calm, a full moon rising in a cloudless sky soon after 2100 made EMB operations more hazardous. Nevertheless, a shinyo squadron that had recently established a base on Balayan Bay, some 25nm (29 miles, 46km) northwest of Nasugbu, was ordered to sortie.

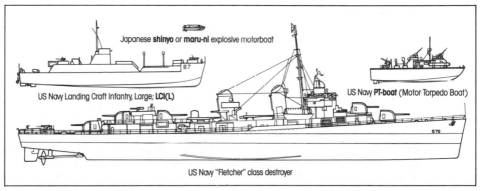

Shinyo and opposing warships, all drawn to the same scale. Minimum close-range armament: PT-boat, 2 x 20mm; LCI(L), 5 x 20mm; "Fletcher" class destroyer, 6-10 x 20mm and 40mm.

At around 2235, *PC-1129* registered the intruders and radioed a warning of "skunks in the area". LtCdr Blaney C. Turner of *Lough* immediately ordered his crew to general quarters and headed for the action, soon sighting 20 or more boats in line ahead formation. *Lough* manouevred for a position from which she could enfilade them, but before she could fire the shinyo had overwhelmed *PC-1129*, swarming in from all angles as the 280-ton (284 tonne) escort blazed away with her single 3in (76mm) gun and 40mm AA. Two shinyo were blown apart, but a third rammed *PC-1129* amidships, tearing a 6ft (2m) gash at the waterline. The subchaser capsized and sank.

Meanwhile, *Lough* had scattered the remaining shinyo with enfilading 40mm fire. Abandoning their attempt to reach the transports, the shinyo broke into small groups and attempted to engage *Lough*, *Tinsman* and *Claxton*. The latter, illuminating with starshell, found herself the target of a new menace: a torpedo was fired by a unseen opponent which *Lough's* battle report designated a midget submarine. (It is more likely that one or more of the Japanese MTBs of Torpedo Boat Squadron 31, based at Manila, had ventured out to support the shinyo.) But the torpedo was evaded and the shinyo, having taken heavy losses—*Lough* alone claimed six destroyed— withdrew. The Japanese claimed to have sunk or damaged eight ships: in fact, *PC-1129* was the only loss, and all but one of her 80-strong crew survived. Two EMBs, stragglers from the night attack, were sunk next morning by patrolling aircraft.

Next night, US warships were naturally on full alert at Nasugbu. Admiral Fechteler had requested support from LtCdr Davis's Caminawit-based PT-boats, and Davis had sent *PT-77* and *PT-79* to patrol off Talin Point, 6nm (7 miles, 11km) south of Nasugbu. The PT-boats were instructed not to go north of the Point, into waters where Fechteler's ships were patrolling with orders to shoot on sight. Although the PT-boats obeyed, they were sighted and pursued by *Lough* and the destroyer *Conyngham* and, apparently failing to make speedy and adequate recognition signals, were taken under 5in (127mm) and 40mm fire at c.1,200yds (1100m) range. Knowing the attackers were US ships, Lt John H. Stillman headed *PT-77* towards the destroyers, making the light signal "PT . . . PT . . . PT . . .". This only convinced the destroyer skippers that the small craft were Japanese: for to advance under fire while making improvised "friendly" signals seemed an obvious ruse for a suicide attacker. Both PT-boats were sunk by the destroyers' gunfire—the last PT-boats lost in action in the Pacific. It was, says the US Navy's historian, a victory for the suicide boats, which had so unsettled the US seamen.

The US Navy was able to declare the Lingayen area "clear" by 11 February, by which time the strength of the EMB units had been seriously depleted both by losses and by the re-deployment of many support personnel as infantry. From late January onward, the EMBs had suffered considerably at the hands of Luzon-based Douglas SBD Dauntless divebombers of the US Marine Corps (the "Diving Devil-dogs"). Especially heavy losses were sustained during the massive naval bombardment of Corregidor begun on 10 February: a few shinyo made a desperate sortie against the bombardment force on the night of 10-11 February, but with no result other than the loss of more boats. By mid-February, fewer than 60 of the Corregidor-based shinyo commanded by LtCdr Oyamada remained operational. However, in seeking the capture of the island fortress, the US invaders gave the EMBs the chance to make their last mass attack.

Date: **15-16 February 1945**
Place: **Mariveles, Corregidor Channel, Luzon**
Attack by: **Shinyo EMBs, Imperial Japanese Navy**
Target: **US landing ships**

On 15 February, Rear-Admiral A.W. Struble's Amphibious Group 9 put ashore some 4,300 US troops at Mariveles on the north shore of the Corregidor Channel. As at Nasugbu, a steeply-sloping beach and heavy surf delayed the operation, and at nightfall five LSTs were still waiting to unload on the next high tide. Rear-Admiral R.S. ("Count") Berkey was understandably unwilling to hazard his cruisers and destroyers in the restricted waters of Mariveles harbour in darkness. The warships withdrew, leaving five LCS(L)s—246-ton (250 tonne) converted landing craft, each mounting at least six 40mm guns, 10 rocket launchers and many smaller automatic weapons—to guard the tank landing ships.

Oyamada ordered that all shinyo still operational at Corregidor should be committed to an attack on these tempting targets little more than 5nm (5.75 miles, 9km) away. After nightfall, about 50 shinyo were wheeled from their revetments on dollys to the water's edge. The five LCS(L)s, ranged across the mouth of Mariveles anchorage, made radar and visual contact with the attackers at around 0315; by that time, the shinyo were so close that, although they failed to pierce the defensive screen, they were able to swamp the armoured support craft with mass attacks. *LCS(L)-27* was the first US ship to open fire; her gunners claimed to have blown apart five shinyo before a sixth detonated so close aboard that she was severely damaged and was run ashore by her skipper. *LCS(L)-7, LCS(L)-26* and *LCS(L)-49* were all sunk by massive explosions — but so many shinyo were lost in the fierce mêlée that they could not press home their attack to the transports.

Japanese artillery observers at Mariveles signalled to Corregidor: "Shinyo have sunk one cruiser, one destroyer and two transports". There were no Japanese survivors to set the record straight, for not one shinyo returned from the sortie. The destroyers *Conyngham*, *Nicholas* and *Young* accounted for several stragglers in the light of morning. The surviving personnel of the Corregidor EMB squadrons fought to the death as ground troops following the US airborne and amphibious invasion of 16 February 1945.

EMBs at Iwo Jima and Okinawa

Neither shinyo nor maru-ni played a significant part in the defence of Iwo Jima. Shinyo Squadrons 3 and 4 were transported from Hahajima to Iwo Jima — some 175nm (200 miles, 325km) to the south — shortly before the US landings. On 16-19 February, however, the big guns of Rear-Admiral Bertram S. Rodgers's Task Force 54, with air cover from the 10 escort carriers of Rear-Admiral C.T. Durgin's Task Group 52.2 and support from USAF bombers, subjected Iwo Jima to a massive pre-invasion bombardment. LtGen Tadamichi Kuribayashi's 23,000-strong garrison was able to weather the storm without great loss, in a labyrinth of caves and bunkers, but there were few suitable beach areas on the small, volcanic island for the concealment or protection of EMBs, and most were destroyed.

At the end of March 1945, LtGen Mitsuri Ushijima's 32nd Army stood ready to fight to the death in the central Ryukyus — on Okinawa and its offshore islands. Of Ushijima's garrison of some 100,000 men, about 9,000 were naval personnel under Rear-Admiral Minoru Ota. The naval special attack forces comprised a midget submarine unit, Dragon Squadron No 2, with seven boats, based on Unten on the east side of the Motobu Peninsula, northwest Okinawa; and Shinyo Squadrons Nos 22 and 42.

Both EMB squadrons suffered considerable pre-invasion losses. SS 22, formed late in December 1944, reached Okinawa on 15 January, and thus had time to prepare a satisfactory base for its 45 boats near Chinen, southeast Okinawa. But on 14 March, while the squadron was engaged in early-morning training offshore, a surprise raid by B-24 bombers killed 15 pilots and sank several boats. SS 42 left Japan much later and the squadron's transports sustained heavy air attacks; by the time SS 42 reached its base at Yonabaru, in the south of Nakagusuku Wan (Buckner Bay), southeast Okinawa, on 1 March, it had only 17 operational boats remaining.

The Imperial Army's maru-ni were much stronger, with eight units — Advanced Combat Units Nos 1, 2, 3, 4, 26, 27, 28 and 29; with a total establishment of 720 boats — deployed in the Okinawa area. Some 300 of these boats were based on the Kerama Retto, the chain of small islands about 15 miles (24km) west of Okinawa. Of the remainder, most were based on the Motobu Peninsula or in and around the estuary of the Bisha Gawa at Hagushi, west-central Okinawa, which was thought, rightly, to be a likely area for landings.

Clearing the Kerama Retto

Vice-Admiral Richmond K. Turner, commanding the Joint Expeditionary Force in "Operation Iceberg", was well aware of the importance of the Kerama Retto to the Okinawan operations and was determined to secure them in advance of D-Day (1 April) as a supply and repair base. The Japanese garrison was weak — no more than 1,000 men — and, by unhappy chance, the US 77th Infantry Division's landing on 26 March came at a time when the overall maru-ni commander, Captain Omachi, and many of his pilots were away on a training exercise in Okinawa itself. Thus, no general order was given for maru-ni to strike at the invasion force off Kerama Retto: about 10 boats are believed to have sortied, but without result.

At a cost of only 31 dead and 81 wounded, US forces had by 31 March secured a vital base and, an important contribution to the safety of the Allied invasion fleet, had destroyed or captured most of the Kerama Retto-based maru-ni. Some 250 EMBs were found in concealed anchorages or improvised shelters, many on launching dollys. Some had been carefully booby-trapped; others had been wrecked by their crews. A US Army report stated that the boats were powered by "6-cylinder Chevrolet automobile engines" and that each carried two 264lb (120kg) depthcharges on a stern rack — "the fragility of the boats made survival highly unlikely". A later US Navy report stated that the boats captured in the Keramo Retto were one-man craft, some capable of no more than 6.5kt (7.5mph, 12kmh), carrying either time-fuzed or impact-fuzed charges. Charts and operational instructions captured with the boats not only gave detailed information on the deployment of EMBs at Okinawa but also enabled the US Navy to draw up a manual of suicide boat tactics, based on captured Imperial Japanese Army instructions.

A few maru-ni survived in the Kerama Retto to strike back. On the night of 28 March, one of a group of boats hidden on Hokaji Shima made a well-judged attack on the netlayer USS *Terebinth* as she lay at anchor. The maru-ni made its approach from dead ahead, so that the "horns" of the netlaying gear on the US vessel's bows prevented her guns from being brought to bear, and itself opened fire with a light machine gun as it rushed in. Then, with every prospect of success, the maru-ni turned sharply to starboard, dropped a single depthcharge some 50ft (15m) from *Terebinth,* doing no damage, and raced away into the darkness. The pilot may have lost his nerve; or he may have been over-cautious in the hope of preserving his boat to make further attacks. On the same night, three maru-ni attempting to make the passage between Tokashiki Shima and Okinawa were intercepted and

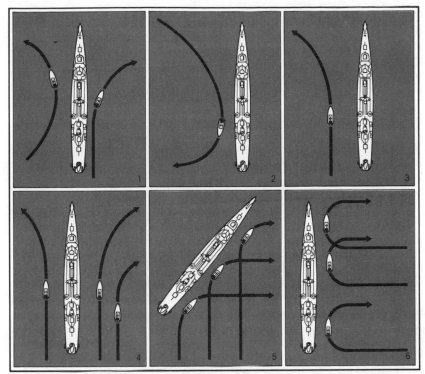

Attack plans for **Maru-ni** EMBS, from an IJA manual of early 1945. Boat(s) approach at c.20kt; at the moment of turning away, a stern-mounted 441lb (200kg) depthcharge (or two smaller charges) on a 4-second fuze is dropped a few feet from a vulnerable point on the target ship. According to Japanese veterans, most **Maru-ni** pilots chose to make ramming attacks to ensure a certain hit, and stayed in their boats, like the IJN's **Shinyo** pilots, to perish in the moment of success.

sunk by LCI gunboats; and three more which attempted a dawn attack on *LSM(R)-189* were destroyed by the rocket-gunboat's fire.

The last attacks by Kerama Retto-based EMBs appear to have been made on 29 March, in daylight, when the destroyer-transport USS *Bunch*, with escorting destroyers, took Underwater Demolition Teams into the Bisha Gawa estuary to destroy the maze of landing obstacles the Japanese had erected there. Two maru-ni racing in from seaward, probably from Keise Retto, were destroyed by gunfire; so was a third which emerged at high speed from the estuary itself.

Attacks by Okinawa-based EMBs

The part played by Japanese EMBs in the long and bitter struggle for Okinawa—described more fully in Chapter 4—was a minor one. Nevertheless, the suicidal surface craft scored some successes, and most certainly contributed to the adverse effect on Allied morale exerted by the long-sustained and suicidal resistance of Okinawa's defenders from 1 April 1945 onward.

During the immediate pre-invasion air bombardment of Okinawa on 25-31 March, EMB bases had a target priority second only to airfields. The Bisha Gawa area, where many EMBs were based, was subjected to heavy napalm strikes on 28 March; the midget submarines and shinyo at Unten received special attention on 29 March. On the latter day, SS 42 suffered heavily: 15 boats sortied after dark, found no targets and, returning to base after dawn, were caught by US aircraft and sunk. A group of boats from SS 22 was also sighted by aircraft and tracked back to its base at Chinen, which was thereafter subjected to heavy bombing. By 31 March, the two squadrons had fewer than 20 operational boats between them.

The maru-ni at Bisha Gawa also took severe losses from air attack. Enough survived, however, to make a mass attack on the night of 31 March, as the Allied invasion armada moved towards the Hagushi beaches. Some 50 maru-ni sortied, but, betrayed by the roar of their engines and by the phosphoresence of their wakes on the moonlit water, they came under fire while still far from the soft-skinned transports. But at least one maru-ni penetrated the wall of fire to ram the 520-ton (528 tonne) *LSM-12*. Temporarily kept afloat despite a gaping hole amidships, the landing ship at last foundered on 4 April.

As US troops poured ashore on the western beaches on 1 April, the shinyo squadrons on the east coast launched their last attacks. Lt Imoto, commander of SS 42, played his *shakuhachi* (a bamboo flute) as he led out his two remaining boats. Neither boat was seen again, although a Japanese observation post ashore reported "a pillar of fire in Nakagusuku Wan".

The end of SS 22 was not long delayed. By 3 April, the US ground advance threatened the Chinen base from landward and Admiral Ota's HQ ordered all remaining shinyo to sortie. SS 22 had 14 boats left; but because so many launching dollys had been destroyed in air raids, only four could be got into the water, on the night of 3-4 April. Each manned by two men (for supernumary pilots had insisted on the honour of taking part), the four shinyo, led by Lt Toyohiro, headed south. Not far from Chinen they sighted two LCI gunboats, and split into two pairs, one to each enemy vessel. Although the LCI(G)s were capable of only about 14kt (16mph, 26kmh), the poorly-engined shinyo were probably even slower, especially with double crews; and one pair of EMBs missed their target, passing astern. But the boat crewed by POs Ichikawa and Suzuki was successful: their shinyo rammed and sank *LCI(G)-82*, killing 8 and wounding 11 of her crew of 65.

Successful Strikes by Maru-ni

Although LCI gunboats claimed to have destroyed 71 suicide boats during the first week of April, and although US ground forces were overrunning their bases, the Imperial Army's maru-ni still retained some offensive capability. ACU 26 had established a well-concealed base at Naha on the southeast coast, just north of the Oroku Peninsula and only some 10nm (11.5 miles, 18.5km) south of the Hagushi beaches. From this base, a group of maru-ni launched an attack on US transports and escort off the "Brown" landing beaches at c.0300 on 9 April. Approaching in darkness, the maru-ni split into two groups to assault transports and escorts simultaneously.

At 0400, as the 2,050-ton (2083 tonne) destroyer USS *Charles J. Badger* (Cdr J.H. Cotten) was lying to after completing a shore bombardment task, she was the victim of a "text-book" attack by a maru-ni. Charging out of the darkness, the EMB unloaded a single time-fuzed depthcharge and wheeled away before *Badger* could open fire. The explosion tore a gash in the destroyer's starboard side and sent sea water pouring into the after engine-room. Although there were no casualties, the destroyer was only with difficulty kept afloat. Towed to Kerama Retto, she took no further part in the war.

Concentrated fire from the destroyer USS *Purdy* deterred another maru-ni, which dropped a depthcharge too far away to do any damage. The 6,318-ton (6419 tonne) attack cargo ship USS *Starr* had a closer escape: a maru-ni on a collision course struck a medium landing ship, *LSM-89*, moored alongside, inflicting only superficial damage. The destroyer USS *Porterfield* was also damaged—by gunfire from other US ships as they lashed at the diminutive attackers. Even after the maru-ni had all been sunk or driven off, further fire was necessary to dispose of swimming survivors armed with hand grenades.

For the rest of April, maru-ni activity was limited to lone sorties. An EMB damaged the motor minesweeper *YMS-331* on 15 April; and a greater blow was struck by a single maru-ni in Nakagusuku Wan on 27 April, when the 2,050-ton (2083 tonne) destroyer USS *Hutchins* was "lifted several feet" by the impact of a suicide boat. With 18 men wounded and her port engine and propeller shaft wrecked, *Hutchins* remained out of commission until the war's end. Two days later, the rocket-gunboat *LCS(L)-37* was rammed; only four of her 70-strong crew were wounded, but the fire support craft was a write-off.

The last significant operation by suicide boats at Okinawa took place on 3-4 May, when almost all the remaining EMBs were deployed in the amphibious phase of a Japanese counter-offensive. Some served as communication boats and transports; others made suicidal attacks timed to coincide with kamikaze air strikes and banzai attacks by ground troops. (Naval shinyo squadrons ordered to Okinawa from Formosa, Ishigaki-shima and Amami-O-shima to support these attacks failed to arrive because their transports were bombed en route.) Some 15 maru-ni were expended in attacks that resulted in serious damage to the 4,380-ton (4450 tonne) cargo ship USS *Carina*.

Admiral Ota's Suicide

By mid-May, the EMBs at Okinawa had spent their strength. The surviving members of the EMB units fought on as infantry, holding out on the Oroku Peninsula, around Naha, until mid-June, and putting up a savage resistance to the advancing US 6th Marine Division.

On 6 June, Rear-Admiral Ota sent a signal to Tokyo praising the gallantry of the naval troops and expressing "deepest apologies to the Emperor for my failure to defend the Empire more efficiently". His last message to General Ushijima, on 10 June, announced that "the Naval Base Force is now dying with glory". When US Marines entered Ota's HQ on 15 June, they found the Admiral and five of his staff, their bodies reverently composed, lying with their throats cut. Some 200 more naval personnel had committed ritual suicide elsewhere in the Admiral's headquarters.

Thereafter, the EMBs would be deployed for the final defence of Japan. This is described in Chapter 6, as is the tragic action at Hong

Kong following Japan's surrender, and the reactions to the surrender of EMB units outside the home islands.

SUICIDE BATTLESHIP: THE YAMATO SORTIE

Between 6 April and 22 June 1945 (as described in Chapter 4) the Allied forces at Okinawa sustained ten *kikusui* ("floating crysanthemum") mass attacks by kamikaze aircraft. The aerial onslaught was supported by other suicidal actions: by EMBs; by midget submarines and kaiten manned-torpedoes; by banzai attacks by ground troops; and—during the kikusui attack of 6-8 April—by a unique special attack force consisting of the Imperial Japanese Navy's last task force, headed by the super-battleship *Yamato*.

This sacrificial sortie, openly acknowledged as a "death ride" with little practical value, was largely provoked by inter-service bitterness. At Imperial General HQ, the Army's commanders stressed the heroic deeds of the defenders of Saipan and Iwo Jima, which, they promised, would be surpassed at Okinawa. Admiral Soemu Toyoda, C-in-C of Combined Fleet, was taunted by references to the "Hashirajima Force", the fleet seemingly content to lie at its main base south of Hiroshima until it was sunk piecemeal by air attack. The giant *Yamato* was derided by Army officers at Imperial General HQ as a "floating hotel for idle and inept admirals".

Under such psychological pressure, Toyoda drafted the order for what he described to his staff as "the most tragic and heroic attack of the war": "Operation Ten-Ichi", the surface force's part in "Ten-Go", first of the kikusui attacks. Sailing with only enough fuel oil for a one-way voyage, *Yamato* was to smash through the screen of US warships around Okinawa, delivering the *coup de grâce* to enemy ships previously crippled by kamikaze air strikes; run aground on the Hagushi beaches; and thereafter constitute a mighty fortress, turning her great guns against both sea and land forces. With all ammunition expended, her surviving crewmen were to rig demolition charges, abandon ship, and fight to the death alongside Ushijima's soldiers.

The Mighty Sisters: Yamato and Musashi

Until the commissioning of the nuclear-powered aircraft carrier USS *Enterprise* (CVN-65) of 89,600 tons full load in November 1961, the IJN's Yamato-class battleships were the largest warships ever constructed. Commissioned on 16 December 1941, *Yamato* displaced 69,100 tons in trial condition and 72,809 tons full load. The building of the battleship and her sister-ship *Musashi* in 1936-41 was carried out in the strictest secrecy. Two further ships of the class were planned: *Shinano* (whose fate is described in Chapter 4), completed as an aircraft carrier, and a fourth giant, scrapped at Kure in December 1941 when about 30 per cent complete.

Yamato was also the most heavily-armoured and -armed warship to be built. Her 16.1in (409mm) side armour extended from her 7.8in (198mm) armoured deck to her bottom plates, sloping outward a little to form a near-impregnable bulkhead with an outer torpedo-bulge. Her side armour plates were designed to withstand 18in (457mm) gunfire, as were the 22in (599mm) front plates of the main armament barbettes. The armoured deck was supposedly proof against anything up to a 2,200lb (1000kg) AP bomb dropped from 10,000ft (3050m). The total weight of the battleship's armour was c.23,500 tons—some 34 per cent of her total tonnage. Each of her three 18.1in (460mm) triple turrets weighed 2,774 tons, and each gun could throw a 3,240lb (1470kg) shell some 45,200yds (41,330m); that is, more than 25.5 miles (41km). Her secondary and AA armament (in 1945) comprised 6 x 6.1in (155mm); 24 x 5in (127mm); and 150 x 25mm. She had a maximum speed of 27.5 knots (31.6 mph, 50.9 kmh) and carried a crew around 2,900 strong. (The data given apply equally to *Musashi*.)

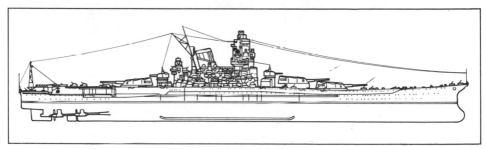

HIJMS **Yamato** (72,809 tons, 73 974 tonnes, full load) was the biggest, most powerful battleship ever built. Note her clipper bow; streamlined and heavily-armoured foremast; and raked stack.

For all this, *Yamato's* war record was not distinguished. As Admiral Yamamoto's flagship, kept well to the rear, she accomplished nothing at the vital Battle of Midway; did little around Guadalcanal; and spent much of 1943 lying idle at Truk, where a single torpedo from the submarine USS *Skate* put her out of action until mid-April 1944. During the greatest of all sea battles, Leyte Gulf, in October 1944, *Yamato* and *Musashi* formed part of Vice-Admiral Takeo Kurita's Centre Force; *Yamato* serving as flagship after the sinking of the cruiser *Atago*. And at Leyte, *Musashi* was sunk—in circumstances that give her end a definite sacrificial aspect.

A Japanese account states that when she sailed from Brunei with Kurita's force on 22 October 1944, *Musashi* had been newly-painted light grey, in contrast to the drab, near-black paintwork of the other ships. This had been done with the deliberate intention of making her a "decoy": Kurita expected little air support (and got none) and *Musashi* was intended to save her consorts by serving as the focus of attention for enemy aircraft. Certainly, when successive waves of US carrier aircraft attacked Kurita's ships in Tablas Strait, *Musashi* was their prime target, taking between 11 and 20 torpedo hits and at least 17 direct bomb hits before sinking, at 1650 on 24 October. More than 1,000 of her crew were lost with her, including Captain Kenchiki Kato, whose last order was for his officers to tie him to the binnacle so that he might not involuntarily survive the loss of his ship.

Apart from two bomb hits on *Yamato.* doing little damage, and a crippling torpedo strike on the cruiser *Myoko*, Kurita's force suffered no other losses in the seven-hour series of air attacks. Next morning, he was able to pass through the San Bernardino Strait and surprise Rear-Admiral Clifton A.F. Sprague's Task Group 77.4.3—six escort carriers, protected by three destroyers and four DEs. These escorts, in a desperate attempt to give Sprague time to launch his aircraft, charged Kurita's battle-line of four battleships, six cruisers and 13 destroyers. According to the US Navy's historian, the skipper of USS *Samuel B. Roberts* (DE 413) informed his crew that they were entering "a fight against overwhelming odds from which survival could not be expected, during which time we would do what damage we could"—as clear an expression of "special attack" doctrine as could be made.

The US warships closed to within 10,000yds (9140m) before launching torpedoes, throwing Kurita's ships into confusion. The part played by USS *Johnston* (DD 557), commanded by Cdr Ernest E. Evans (a Cherokee Indian), may be singled out. At 0727, a torpedo from *Johnston* struck the heavy cruiser *Kumano*, blowing off her bow. Three minutes later, *Johnston* took three 14in (356mm) hits, followed by three 6in (152mm), wounding Cdr Evans, killing or injuring many of his crew, and doing extensive damage. Evans was bringing his ship out of the action, with all torpedoes expended, when he encountered the destroyers *Hoel* and *Heermann* and the *Samuel B. Roberts* heading in for a second attack. He immediately took station with the attackers "to provide fire support".

Over a period of two hours, *Johnston* was hit again and again. Soon all her remaining guns were being served manually, and in this state she was seen to engage the 27,000-ton battleship *Kongo*. At 0940, with all power gone, all communications out, and only one 5in (127mm) gun firing spasmodically, *Johnston* was surrounded and sunk by Japanese destroyers. Survivors, of whom Cdr Evans was not one, reported that Japanese officers were seen to stand at the salute as *Johnston* went down. Only one of Sprague's escort carriers was sunk by Kurita's force.

Orders for a One-Way Sortie

On 5 April 1945, the "Ten-Ichi" order was conveyed by Vice-Admiral Ryunosuke Kusaka, Toyoda's chief-of-staff, to Vice-Admiral Seiichi Ito, aboard his flagship *Yamato* at Tokuyama. Ito showed no emotion as he read what he knew to be the death-warrant for himself, for many men of the Second Fleet—and for *Yamato*. The most powerful battle-ship built had now been declared as expendable as a wooden shinyo.

The first of the commanders of the suicide task force to learn of the plan was Rear-Admiral Keizo Komura, commander of Destroyer Squadron 2, who flew his flag in the light cruiser *Yahagi*. Returning from his briefing aboard *Yamato*, he called together on *Yahagi* the other commanders of the force: Rear-Admiral Kosaku Ariga, captain of *Yamato*; the eight destroyer skippers concerned; and Captain Tameichi Hara, the former reluctant recruiter of special attack personnel, now captain of *Yahagi*. He confronted them with Toyoda's order which, according to a Japanese historian, read:

> "The Second Fleet is to charge into the enemy anchorage of Kadena, Okinawa Island, at daybreak on 8 April. Fuel for only a one-way passage will be supplied. This is a special attack operation."

The reaction of the assembled officers was intensely critical. Admiral Komura, in tears, denounced the mission as useless—and thus dishonourable. Captain Kiichi Shintani, commanding Destroyer Division 17, called it "a ridiculous operation", and was strongly supported by the destroyer skippers. He suggested that the men whose lives were to be thrown away would be more valuably employed as last-ditch defenders of the home islands. Captain Hara, saying that the plan was as unrealistic as "throwing an egg at a rock", proposed that instead he should take the newly-refitted *Yahagi*—with her efficient radar, homing torpedoes and proximity-fuzed AA guns—on a high-speed raiding mission. Commander Yoshiro Sugihara of the destroyer *Asashimo*, suspecting like his colleagues that the sortie would receive no air cover, declared that they would all be sunk before reaching Okinawa. Captain Hisao Kotaki, commanding Destroyer Division 21, spoke scathingly of the naval high command issuing such orders "from its air-raid shelter".

Komura relayed this angry and unprecedented criticism to Kusaka and Ito aboard *Yamato*. Kusaka defended the order by promising that *Yamato* and her escorts would not be sacrificed in vain, even if they did not reach Okinawa. The real purpose of the sortie, he argued, was to lure enemy air cover away from the island, so that the kamikaze air squadrons based on southern Kyushu might fling themselves un-opposed on the Allied invasion fleet. Playing on Komura's pride, Kusaka referred to *Yamato's* undistinguished record and declared that "the whole nation will hate the Navy if the war should end with *Yamato* still intact". But it was Vice-Admiral Ito, who would have to lead the sortie, who at last broke his silence with an unanswerable argument. "I think," he said, "that we are being given an appropriate chance to die." He added the Bushido proverb: "A samurai so lives that he is always prepared to die."

Komura returned to *Yahagi* and told the commanders that he had unconditionally accepted the order for the death ride. There was no more to be said: "We must now make the best of the situation", remarked Hara. And in spite of the initial reaction, morale throughout the "Surface Special Attack Force" was high: cadets and unfit personnel, who were to be left behind, wept as they pleaded to be allowed to remain aboard; many ratings began to sharpen their bayonets in anticipation of hand-to-hand combat on Okinawa. That evening, Admiral Komura presided at a party held by the force's officers aboard *Yahagi*, where vast quantities of *sake* were consumed and patriotic and sentimental songs sung:

"Flowers of the same cherry-tree,
You and I bloom in the courtyard of the same house,
Opening our petals on the same day.
So shall the day we fall be the same:
We shall scatter our sweet blossom bravely for our country."

Date: **6-7 April 1945**
Place: **East China Sea**
Attack by: **Yamato Task Force, IJN**
Target: **Allied sea and land forces, Okinawa**

Sailing time for the *Yamato* force was at 1520 on 6 April. From the early hours of that day, the force was kept under observation by high-flying

B-29s. At the appointed time, *Yahagi* led the way from the Tokuyama anchorage, followed by the destroyers *Isokaze* (Cdr Saneo Maeda), *Hamakaze* (Cdr Isami Mukoi) and *Yukikaze* (Cdr Masamichi Terauchi); then *Yamato,* flanked by the destroyers *Fuyutsuki* (Cdr Hidechika Sakuma) and *Suzutsuki* (Cdr Shigetaka Amano); and finally the destroyers *Asashimo* (Cdr Yoshiro Sugihara), *Kasumi* (Cdr Hiroo Yamana) and *Hatsushimo* (Cdr Masazo Sato) in column astern.

Initial air cover consisted only of two reconnaissance seaplanes, which almost immediately reported the presence of enemy submarines in Bungo Suido, the channel leading from the southwest Inland Sea to the Philippine Sea. Emerging from Bungo Suido at c1950, the force's own search equipment also detected submarines and the ships began to zig-zag at around 22 knots. In spite of this precaution, the US submarines *Threadfin* and *Hackleback,* with orders to observe rather than attack, were able to keep fairly close track of the Japanese warships throughout the night.

At 0600 on 7 April, a dismal sunrise on a day of low cloud and frequent rain squalls, the *Yamato* force was steaming westnorthwest, with *Yahagi* and the destroyers in circular formation around the battleship for all-round AA defence. A few Japanese fighters took off from southern Kyushu early in the day in a vain attempt to deter enemy reconnaissance aircraft, but no other effort was made to provide air cover. Vice-Admiral Marc A. Mitscher had deployed no less than four US carrier task groups to the northeast of Okinawa, and a minimum of eight carriers was available at any one time for operations against the IJN sortie. US reconnaissance planes from Kerama Retto and search aircraft from the carrier groups sought to pinpoint the Japanese position, while strike planes were held at readiness on the carriers' decks.

At 0823 a Hellcat from USS *Essex* (CV 9) reported the *Yamato* force's position as 31°22′ N, 129°14′ E, to the southwest of Koshiki Retto. Mitscher warned Vice-Admiral Morton L. Deyo's heavy units at Okinawa to be on the alert for a breakthrough by *Yamato;* Deyo planned to interpose six battleships, seven cruisers and 21 destroyers between the Japanese ships and the Okinawa invasion force. But Deyo's big guns would not be needed.

Throughout the morning, two Martin PBM Mariners from Kerama Retto kept track of the Japanese warships, in spite of *Yamato's* sporadic efforts to drive them away by firing Type 3 *sanshiki-dan* AA shells (producing a shot-gun scatter of 20mm incendiaries, theoretically effective over several thousand square yards) from her 18.1in (460mm) guns. At 1000 hours, as the *Yamato* force swung south towards Okinawa, the launching of some 280 aircraft was begun from the carriers of USN Task Groups 58.1 and 58.3.

The *Yamato* force's first warning of the approaching air attack was given by a shore station at 1200. At 1210 and 1221, the destroyer *Asashimo,* which had dropped well behind with engine trouble, reported that she was under air attack. At 1232, some 200 aircraft were sighted about 12nm from *Yamato.* The battleship opened sanshiki-dan fire but, because of her inefficient radar and the prevailing low cloud and rain, made poor practice. Many of the US pilots were, in fact, guided to their target by the massive air bursts. At 1235, as the Japanese force raced south at close on 30kt in AA formation, with an interval of about 5,500yds (5030m) between each ship, the first wave of US aircraft began what the Japanese were to call the Battle of Bonomisaki (an island some 80nm to the north).

Meeting no air opposition, Corsairs and Hellcats—each carrying three 500lb (227kg) bombs—and Helldivers, with one 1,000lb (454kg) semi-AP or GP bomb and two 250lb (113kg) bombs, swarmed over the Japanese ships in an attempt to knock out their AA mountings, while torpedo-carrying Avengers stood by. *Yamato's* big guns were now silent: they could not be worked without endangering the men at the many AA mountings on the main deck. Still, the force put up an impressive barrage of multi-coloured AA fire. while zig-zagging violently at flank speed.

At 1241, two bombs from aircraft of USS *Bennington* (CV 20) struck just aft of *Yamato's* main mast, and at 1243 a *Bennington* Avenger scored the first torpedo hit, tearing a great gash in the battleship's port bow. *Yahagi's* engine room was wrecked by a torpedo hit amidships at 1246, leaving the light cruiser dead in the water. *Hamakaze*, struck by one bomb and one torpedo from aircraft of USS *San Jacinto* (CVL 30), quickly sank by the bows. When the first wave of aircraft withdrew just before 1300, they left *Yahagi* a battered wreck after 12 direct bomb hits and six torpedo strikes, with *Isokaze* standing in to pick up survivors. The second attacking wave plastered this destroyer with bombs and she reeled away from *Yahagi*. (With more than 100 of her crew dead, *Isokaze* had to be sunk after the action by *Yukikaze*, while *Fuyutsuki* performed the same office for the shattered *Kasumi*. *Susutsuki*, her bows mangled by a bomb, was later able to creep back to Japan stern first.) *Asashimo*, still far from the main force, was sunk at around 1250.

But *Yamato*, still escorted by *Fuyutsuki* and *Yukikaze*, was the prime target. Two torpedoes struck on the port beam, knocking out all communications. At around 1335, three more torpedoes struck along the port side, increasing the battleship's flooding to such an extent that a list of some 30 degrees could not be corrected by counter-flooding starboard compartments—although Admiral Ariga's order for this to be done resulted in the deaths of many men scalded or drowned at their posts below decks.

The End of a Giant

From about 1400 onward, aircraft from USS *Intrepid* (CV 11) and *Yorktown* (CV 10) closed in for the kill. *Yamato* now lay over some 35 degrees to port, creeping in a circle with her rudder jammed and only one pair of propellers turning, with only a few AA guns still firing. Six of *Yorktown's* Avengers came in on the starboard side, where the battleship's list had exposed her underside beneath the armoured belt. Five torpedoes struck home, the last at about 1420. Aboard the dying giant, Admiral Ito had ordered the crew to save themselves at about 1405, himself retiring to his cabin to await death alone. Admiral Ariga ordered the Emperor's portrait (which occupied a hallowed place in all Japanese warships) to be put in the care of a strong swimmer; then he had himself roped to the compass mounting: "My last request — and it is an order!"

Only about 300 of *Yamato's* crew were clear of the battleship when the end came. The remaining shells in her magazines tore loose as she listed farther to port, setting off a chain of internal explosions, and at 1423 the world's biggest battleship rolled briefly on to an even keel and then, with a massive eruption of orange-brown flame and smoke, slid quickly beneath the waters of the East China Sea. She had taken between 11 and 15 torpedo hits and at least seven direct hits from bombs. In the water, *Yahagi's* survivors, bombed and machine-gunned by US aircraft, interrupted their singing of the "Warrior's Song" (". . . even though I fight at sea and become a water-logged corpse, I will die for my Emperor and never once look homeward") to give a last banzai for the great battleship. Then they began to sing the Japanese national anthem, *Kimigayo.*

The death ride had resulted in the loss of a battleship, a light cruiser, four destroyers (with another crippled) and some 3,700 men. The USN's loss was 10 aircraft and 12 aircrew (a PBM Mariner landed among Japanese survivors immediately after the action to pick up downed US airmen). The sortie had ostensibly been launched to draw away air cover from Okinawa to allow for devastating kamikaze strikes: in fact, the main effort of the first kikusui offensive was made on 6 April; and on 7 April, the day of *Yamato's* sinking, kamikaze attacks at Okinawa resulted in heavy damage to the battleship USS *Maryland* and destroyer *Bennett* (neither repaired before the war's end) and lesser damage to the fleet carrier *Hancock,* a destroyer, a destroyer-escort and a minesweeper.

GERMAN EXPLOSIVE MOTORBOATS

The inspiration for the EMBs used by German forces during World War II came directly from the Italian Navy's MTM boats, described earlier in this chapter. After Italy's surrender in September 1943, some members of the 10th Light Flotilla — notably Cdr J. Valerio Borghese and Lt Eugenio Wolk — remained loyal to the Axis cause. The services of these veterans were at first denied to the German Navy by *SS-Sturmbannführer* Otto Skorzeny, who quickly pre-empted them to instruct his own commando force, recruited largely from within the SS. It was at first intended that SS personnel and naval volunteers for "special weapons" should train together. However, a number of the SS men were from punishment units: they had been persuaded to "volunteer" for hazardous duties with the promise that their crimes would be forgotten — if they survived. Most naval officers made no secret of their reluctance to work with such individuals.

Thus, the first German EMB operations were carried out by Skorzeny's commandos, who trained at Langenargen near Friedrichshafen, on the north shore of Lake Constance. Their sorties against Allied shipping in the Tyrrhenian Sea, off the Anzio-Nettuno beachheads, went almost un-noticed. Their boats, patterned on the Italian MTMs but somewhat more lightly constructed, appear to have been entirely unsuited to operations in the open sea. Their major effort was made on the night of 20-21 April 1944, in conjunction with an attack by *Neger* ("Nigger") manned-torpedoes (see Chapter 5). The small craft were located in the darkness by the radars of USN submarine-chasers—280-ton escorts mounting one 3in (76mm) and one 40mm gun—and were repulsed with heavy losses.

K-Force: the German Naval Commandos

While Skorzeny's men carried out their abortive operations in Italian waters, the *Kriegsmarine* (German Navy) had been forming its own "special attack" units. The moving spirit was Vice-Admiral Hellmuth Heye, who throughout 1943 had badgered the naval high command to take action in this field. The loss of the battlecruiser *Scharnhorst* in December 1943 finally persuaded Grand Admiral Dönitz to give Heye his chance: he was ordered to organize and take command of the *Kleinkampfmittel Verband* ("Small Battle Force", usually called the *KdK* or K-Force).

Because the SS had temporarily monopolized the EMB project, the K-Force's early efforts were mainly concerned with the development of midget submarines (see Chapter 2) and manned-torpedoes (see Chapter 5) and the training of frogmen. But by the late spring of 1944, EMB formations—called *Kleinboote Verbände* ("Small Boat Units")—had been established on the Baltic coast, at Timmendorfer Strand, Lübeck Bay.

Initial training was carried out in some 30 MTM-derived boats designed for the *Brandenburgerdivision* (the "special force" from which Skorzeny drew many of his commandos). The unseaworthy nature of these craft was soon apparent, and their first operational deployment was a total failure. Thirty boats were rushed to Le Havre, whence they were to strike at Allied invasion shipping in the Seine Bay. Since the EMBs were not capable of making the voyage of some 20-25nm to the beachheads under their own power, they were to be towed as far as the Orne estuary, on the eastern flank of the invasion area, by motor minesweepers.

On the evening of 29 June 1944, as the EMB pilots were making final tests on the firing mechanisms of their boats' warheads, one EMB blew up, sinking a minesweeper. The remainder left as planned, each minesweeper towing 3-5 EMBs, but in a choppy sea all but six of the boats sank or slipped their tows and made for the shore. Reaching the Orne estuary, the survivors attempted to sortie but were driven ashore by foul weather.

Germany's EMB: the Linse

As a result of this failure, the German EMB was hurriedly re-designed, emerging as an adequately seaworthy craft, if somewhat complex in operational theory. Like all EMBs, it was an extremely hazardous weapon—but most German writers deny that it was a suicide boat. However, evidence to the contrary is to be deduced from the scale of operational losses incurred; from the fact that, like the Italians before them, German EMB pilots sometimes made no attempt to escape from boats set on collision courses; and, most importantly, from the fact that the German pilots themselves referred to their duties as *Opferkampfer* ("sacrifice missions").

The EMB used by the Kriegsmarine in the English Channel and the Mediterranean was code-named *Linse* ("Lentil"). In dimensions and performance it closely resembled the Italian MTM and, like the Italian boat, it was of wooden construction. The Linse was, however, longer and less beamy than the MTM—18.9ft (5.75m) long overall and 5.7ft (1.75m) in the beam—and displaced about 1.3 tons. It was propelled by twin screws powered by two 95hp V-8 automobile engines (Ford units were found in captured examples) giving a maximum speed of 30-35kt (34-40mph, 55-65kmh). It had an action radius of about 60nm (69 miles, 111 km) at high speed and an endurance of 4.5 hours at 15kt

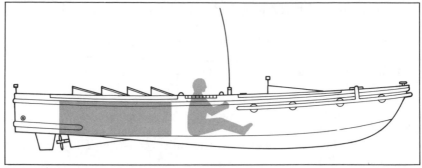

German **Linse** EMB; note "bumper" at bow; guidance lights fore and aft, and radio aerial.

(17mph, 28kmh). An explosive charge of 660-880lb (300-400kg) was mounted towards the stern, the pilot's cockpit being amidships.

In theory, Linsen operations were more complex than those of Italian or Japanese EMBs. Each section of three Linsen comprised two one-man explosive-carrying boats and one two-man control boat. The boats were intended to attack under cover of darkness, their major targets being transports at anchor. They approached the target area at slow speed (the Linse's engines were supposedly silent at a speed below 8kt), with the control boat a little to the rear of the pair of EMBs. When within a few hundred yards of the target, the Linsen increased to full speed. Some 100yds (90m) from the target, the pilots of the explosive-carrying Linsen tripped switches that turned over their craft to radio guidance by the control boat. Then the pilots ditched, to be kept afloat by their lifejackets until picked up by the control boat.

The radio operator in the control boat was equipped with an ultra-shortwave transmitter based on the remote guidance system developed in c1943 for the BIV *Funklepanzer* demolition tank. It was his task to steer an un-piloted Linse into its target by keeping in line recognition lights (green in the bows; red in the stern) switched on by the EMB's pilot before ditching, when his boat was on a collision course. These lights were shielded so that they could be seen only from astern. The radio operator's simple control box was capable of altering the Linse's course to port or starboard; stopping, starting, slowing or accelerating its engine; or detonating its explosive charge as close as possible to the target if the EMB itself appeared likely to miss.

When the Linse struck its target a metal "bumper" framework around the bows was compressed, triggering a small charge that blew off the boat's bow and also primed the fuze of the main, stern-mounted charge. The latter was set to explode on a delay of some seven seconds, by which time the Linse should have sunk below its target.

This was the prescribed operational method for which Linsen units were trained in the Trave Estuary on Lübeck Bay. However, there appear to have been alternative procedures. Skorzeny wrote that Linsen could, if necessary, be remote-controlled by the pilots of *Neger* manned-torpedoes—and a British naval historian records that Linsen pilots captured off Normandy claimed that their boats were meant not to attack, but for the rescue of *Neger* operators. German writers also refer to Linsen being on occasion controlled by whistle signals from a back-up boat—and of Linsen operating in the same way as Italian MTMs or Japanese shinyo, with the individual pilot being responsible for a simple ramming attack. Experiments were also made in fitting Linsen with smoke projectors to emit a defensive screen, but there are no records of this equipment being used in action and the EMBs were, in any case, almost invariably committed at night.

Experimental EMBs: "Tornado" and "Sledge"

Although in theory fairly effective against ships at anchor off invasion beaches, the task for which it was primarily intended, the Linse was not suitable for attacks on defended anchorages. To escape the probability of destruction by shore batteries or warships' defensive fire, greater speed was a prime necessity. One answer was the *Tornado,* a boat built around two floats from the Junkers Ju 52 seaplane and powered by the Argus 109-014 pulse-jet engine developed for the Fieseler Fi 103 (V-1) flying bomb. This was to operate in much the same way as the Linse, delivering a bow-mounted 1,550lb (700kg) explosive charge at a much higher speed. On trials, however, the Tornado prototype rarely made more than 35kt (40mph, 65kmh) and capsized in all but fair weather. This, with the probable non-availability of the Argus power units, caused the project to be abandoned.

As well as experimenting with a number of torpedo-armed hydrofoils, the K-Force was also concerned in the development of what was—in view of its projected mission—a truly suicidal weapon. This (possibly to be identified with the experimental boat code-named *Schlitten,* "Sledge") was a one-man catamaran powered by a 600hp engine giving a maximum 65kt (75mph, 120kmh). A 2,650lb (1200kg) explosive charge was to be packed between its hulls.

German design for a high-speed EMB, **Tornado**: an Argus pulse-jet unit mounted on seaplane floats.

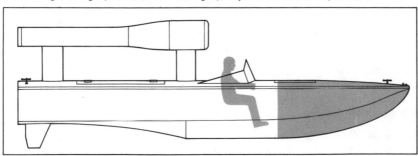

The catamaran was to be carried to its operational area and launched from a Gotha Go 242C-1 glider (a variant with a planing hull, flotation bags and stabilizing floats). Late in 1944, several of these gliders were assigned to *Oberleutnant* Kempke's *6 Staffel* of *Kampfgeschwader 200*. This unit was equipped with Heinkel He 111Z aircraft ("Z" for *Zwilling*, "Twin"), the five-engined, long-range aircraft formed by linking together two He 111 airframes and fitting a fifth engine into the central wing section. Each of these aircraft could tow three Go 242s; and it was planned that the gliders, each carrying a catamaran, should be delivered to the British fleet anchorage at Scapa Flow, in the Orkneys. Launched from the floating gliders, the catamarans' pilots would set their craft on collision courses, ditching at the last moment to be rescued by submarines or seaplanes. It may well be supposed that the possibility of such a rescue was even more unlikely than that of the pilots' survival! Shortage of aviation fuel was the official reason for the abandonment of this suicidal scheme.

Allied Countermeasures: the 'Trout Line"

The massive air and surface superiority of the Allies prevented the Kriegsmarine's major surviving units—destroyers and the larger U-boats—from effective action against the invasion armada off the Normandy beachheads from 6 June 1944 onward. Nevertheless, the invasion was threatened by the activities of minor craft, notably R-boats (MGBs), E-boats (MTBs)—and the K-Force's manned torpedoes, midget submarines and EMBs.

Night bombing of the bases of these small craft—Le Havre, Dieppe and Boulogne—by RAF Lancasters, and daylight patrols by fighter-bombers, notably the Beaufighters of Coastal Command, inflicted heavy losses on the Kriegsmarine's light forces. For surface defence, the Allies formed, in July, the Support Squadron Eastern Flank (SSEF), commanded by Cdr K.A. Sellar, RN.

The SSEF consisted of some 80 support craft: LCGs (Landing Craft, Gun) mounting two 4.7in (119mm) guns and up to 15 x 20mm; LCFs (Landing Craft, Flak) mounting four 4in (102mm) AA guns and up to 8 x 20mm; LCT(R)s (Landing Craft, Tank, Rocket) armed with around 1,000 5in (127mm) salvo-fired rockets; LCSs (Landing Craft, Support) mounting 4in (102mm) smoke mortars, 20mm AA and heavy and light machine guns; and MLs (Motor Launches), 20-knot craft of some 70 tons, usually mounting one 40mm and two 20mm guns.

At night, the SSEF formed two patrol lines to protect the invasion shipping: the armoured landing craft in fixed stations on the outer line, called the "Trout Line", and the MLs patrolling on an inner line. Outside the Trout Line, British, American and Canadian MGBs and MTBs prowled nightly.

Date: **2-3 August 1944**
Place: **Off Courseulles-sur-Mer, English Channel**
Attack by: **Linsen EMBs, Kriegsmarine**
Target: **Allied invasion shipping**

The first successful sortie by Linsen was made on the night of 2-3 August, when the K-Force's head of operations, *Kapitän-sur-See*

Böhme, ordered *Kapitänleutnant* Bastian's Small Battle Unit Flotilla 211 to strike at Allied shipping off Courseulles-sur-Mer (the area where British and Canadian troops had landed on "Sword" and "Juno" beaches on 6 June). Sixteen Linsen and eight control boats, half the Flotilla's strength, sailed from Houlgate—a small port about 15 miles (24km) northeast of Caen and some 15nm from the invasion area—after nightfall on 2 August.

Hugging the coast except when forced out to skirt minefields, the EMBs approached the "Trout Line" at some time after 0100 on 3 August. Authoritative British accounts say that the first indication of an attack—which had been anticipated two nights' earlier, at full moon—came when *Marder* manned torpedoes (see Chapter 5) launched torpedoes at escorts to the north of the Trout Line at 0200-0300. The German historian of the *Kdk* claims that manned-torpedoes did not take part in this or in any other Linsen operation; he ascribes Allied reports of their presence to the Linsen's ruse of dropping plexiglass buoys, each with the outline of a human head painted upon it and thus counterfeiting the observation dome of a *Neger* or *Marder,* to drift into the Allied defence line with the prevailing tidal stream. Allied claims that up to 50 *Marder* were deployed are, however, more convincing than German denials.

In fact, the greater part of the damage to Allied shipping on the night of 2-3 August appears to have been inflicted by torpedoes from *Marder.* The main assault by Linsen of Flotilla 211 (now joined by an unspecified number of EMBs from other units; the British official history states that 32 Linsen in all were committed) was not made until c.0400 according to Allied reports. By that time, the destroyer HMS *Quorn* and the minesweeping trawler HMS *Gairsay* had been sunk and the Liberty ship *Samlong* (later declared a constructive total loss) and a large freighter badly damaged. (Some sources state that *Quorn* was sunk by an EMB; but the destruction of a 1,000-ton destroyer, with the loss of 130 men, seems far more likely to have been the result, as the British official history states, of torpedo hits. *Gairsay* is a more likely victim of the Linsen.)

Between 0400 and 0615, Linsen made determined efforts to break the Trout Line. The first attacking swarm was sighted towards the northern end of the Line, in the glare of star-shell, by the trawler HMS *Gateshead* and *ML 185: Gateshead's* 12-pounder gunners and the sailors manning the 20mm and 40mm automatics of the motor launch claimed to have detonated four EMBs almost immediately. At least 14 more Linsen were destroyed in similar skirmishes. Their one indisputable success was the destruction of the 570-ton *LCG(L)(4)-764* (landing craft, gunboat, Mark 4), which was rammed almost simultaneously by two EMBs after her defensive fire had sunk their control boat. Whether the EMBs' pilots ditched before impact or died with their boats is uncertain.

The surviving boats withdrew at first light under cover of smoke floats. It had been intended that E-boats (German MTBs) from Le Havre, armed with *Dackel* ("Dachshund") pattern-running torpedoes, should sortie to cover the retreat of the K-men. But an RAF bombing raid on Le Havre had prevented embarkation of the new torpedoes and the E-boats that did venture out were badly mauled by British MTBs. In the night's work, the Linsen had taken at least 50 per cent losses in boats—and a German account gives Flotilla 211's personnel loss as one officer and eight men (ie, about 25 per cent of those committed). Losses on such a scale—which were, as will be seen, to be maintained throughout Linsen operations—certainly allow the craft to be classed as extra-hazardous, if not truly suicidal.

The deployment of EMBs had not come as a great surprise to the senior Allied commanders, who were well informed of German intentions through "Ultra" and other intelligence. They were, however, anxious to obtain an intact Linse (which the Allies then called "Weasel"). Two attempts were made to secure a specimen on 3 August. Lt J.P. Fullarton, RNVR, commanding *ML 131*, boarded an abandoned boat in spite of the ominous ticking of its self-destruction charge; he took it in tow, but within ten minutes it detonated. This was witnessed by Lt S.N. Orum, RNVR, in *ML 146*, who, in the process of trying to tow another EMB, which foundered, was able to examine the craft closely and make a useful report.

Transports Tasks for Linsen

The sinking of a small escort vessel on 3 August was to be the Linsen's major achievement in their designed role. They did, however, prove useful as silent and unobtrusive shallow-draft transports for the demolition frogmen (non-suicidal; unlike the Japanese *fukuryu* described in Chapter 6) who also formed a part of the *Kdk*. In this role, Linsen carried assault teams in coastal, estuarine and riverine missions: against the Orne River locks (as early as July 1944); against British artillery positions around the Seine Bay; against Antwerp harbour; and, towing torpedo-mines, against the Moerdijk Bridge over the Hollandschdiep, which was badly damaged on 15 November 1944.

Missions in the designed role continued unsuccessful. On the clear, calm night of 8-9 August 1944, some 28 Linsen approached the Trout Line. Allied reports indicate a certain lack of determination among the German pilots: illuminated by star-shell, they were hunted down by the Allied escorts and destroyed by close-range fire. Among combat reports, *LCF 1* recorded the destruction of four, possibly five, EMBs by her 4-inch and 20mm fire over a period of 60 minutes; *MTB 714* claimed four victims, all engaged at ranges below 200yds (183m), in the same period—adding that "No survivors were picked up". Indeed, only six prisoners were taken from an estimated 20 Linsen (16 explosive and 4 control boats) destroyed.

A Heavy Loss Rate

Following the fall of Le Havre to the Allies, the *KdK* moved north to operate against Allied shipping in the Scheldt estuary. The overall German plan for denying the Allies the benefit of the port of Antwerp, vital for supply traffic, called for attacks by conventional and midget submarines on shipping off the British southeast coasts; E-boat hit-and-run raids on convoys at sea; minefields laid by aircraft or light vessels off the Belgian coast; and, within the Scheldt, strikes by EMBs and human torpedoes. Both sides perceived the minefields to be the vital element in this plan—and this perception resulted in the Linsen taking heavy losses through over-tasking.

Thus, on the night of 5-6 October, in spite of adverse weather conditions, 50 or more Linsen sortied from their base near Vlissingen on Walcheren Island for a mass attack on Allied coastal minesweepers. Foul weather, rather than defensive fire, resulted in the loss of 36 Linsen (by both Allied and German estimates) with no damage to their target. The EMBs had to contend not only with wintry weather and with aggressive inshore patrolling by the escorts of the Allied "Force T", but also with Bomber Command's hammer-blows at their bases. In open water, they were subject to the attentions of Allied fighter-bombers. By late December 1944, the Allies claimed that 115 Linsen had been destroyed (including accidental losses) without damage to Allied ships. A British official history states that only *an order from Admiral Dönitz for the continuance of suicide operations (Opfer-kampfer)* prevented the Linsen and other "special" weapons from being withdrawn.

The Linsen's final actions in the Channel/North Sea areas were fought in April 1945. On the night of 7-8 April, six E-boats of the 9th Flotilla set out from Ijmuiden to ferry Linsen and their crews to ambush points inside the Scheldt. Foul weather killed the mission— and within a week the E-boat force in the narrow seas was no longer operational, with bases bombed and fuel exhausted. Linsen retained some offensive capability: sorties were made in the Scheldt on 11-12 April, when the frigate HMS *Ekins* destroyed two EMBs; and, finally, on 20-21 April, when a group of 12 Linsen heading for Dunkirk was intercepted and broken up, losing four boats, by the frigate HMS *Retalick*.

In January-May 1945, according to British official figures, 54 Linsen were lost in a total of 171 sorties (ie, a loss rate for boats of c.32 per cent; although no figures for personnel losses are available). During that period, no Allied ship was sunk or damaged by a Linse.

EMBs in the Mediterranean Theatre

In August-September 1944, a *KdK* base was established at Pola (now Pula, Yugoslavia) on the Adriatic. Its equipment included both German and Italian midget submarines and EMBs, crewed by Germans and by Italians loyal to the Axis. At about the same time, K-units became operational in the Ligurian Sea, working out of San Remo and La Spezia against the shipping of the Allied "Dragoon"/ "Anvil" landings in the south of France.

In the Adriatic, an unsuccessful sortie was made against an Allied coastal bombardment force on the night of 30 September 1944: five EMBs and two control boats were destroyed. The nearest the EMBs came to making a score was on 12 February 1945, when the cruiser HMS *Delhi*, at anchor in Split harbour, was near-missed by a boat reported to be of Italian type. In the same month, heavy air raids on Pola forced the withdrawal of the *KdK* craft to Brijoni Island, northwest of Pola, where they ceased operations as a result of losses incurred in an air raid on 24 April.

Although more active than their colleagues farther east, the

Ligurian EMBs operating out of La Spezia were from the first kept in subjection by Allied escorts; the US Navy's PT-boats proving particularly effective. Even so, the EMB pilots did not lack spirit—as their attacks on destroyers showed. USS *Gleaves* (DD 423), patrolling near San Remo, was the target of a group of Linsen shortly before dawn on 2 October 1944. Undeterred by the 1,630-ton bulk of the modern destroyer, with its 5-inch main armament, the small boats headed in on collision courses: only the sighting by *Gleaves*'lookout of a phosphorescent wake saved the destroyer from a hit to port. To starboard, a 300lb (136kg) depth charge from the destroyer's K-gun (D/c projector Mk 6 Mod 1) deflected the course of another attacker, which was quickly detonated by .50 cal fire. Two of the surviving boats took station astride *Gleaves*'wake, apparently intending a stern chase. As they drew nearer to the speeding destroyer (the antagonists' designed speeds were approximately equal at c.35kt), depth charges from stern rack and K-gun tore them apart. When full daylight came, *Gleaves* retrieved two uninjured German pilots and one intact Linse. A similar attack was made on the French destroyer *Le Fortuné* off San Remo on the early morning of 10 January 1945: she beat off her assailants and emerged unscathed.

BRITAIN'S EMB: THE BOOM PATROL BOAT

Among the many small craft developed or adapted during World War II for British Commandos and "special forces", one at least must be described here. If it had been committed to action as planned, the Vosper Boom Patrol Boat would have been as extra-hazardous, if not properly suicidal, as the Italian EMB which inspired it.

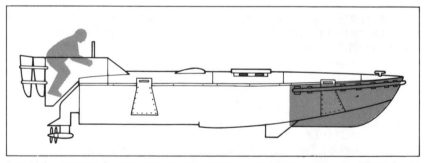

British EMB, the Vosper Boom Patrol Boat, closely resembled the Italian **MTM** It was to be para-dropped, the pilot at that time being strapped into a padded cockpit amidships.

The suicidal attack on Valletta, Malta, made by Italian MTM explosive boats in July 1941 has already been described (pages 80-83). After close study of an intact MTM captured there, the British firm of Vosper was asked to construct a similar boat—with the added capability of being air-dropped, with its pilot, into a target area. This requirement was probably originated by LtCol H.G. "Blondie" Hasler, RM, commander of the raiding force with the innocent cover-name of Royal Marine Boom Patrol Detachment (RMBPD) and best known as the planner and leader of the "Cockleshell" canoeists' assault on shipping at Bordeaux in December 1942.

The Vosper-built EMB, cover-named the Boom Patrol Boat (BPB), closely resembled its Italian model. It weighed c.1.5 tons and was 18ft (5.5m) in length and 5ft (1.52m) in beam. Its internal combustion engine, an American-built, 12-cylinder, 140hp Gray Fireball, gave a maximum speed of above 30kt (34.5mph, 55.5kmh), with an action radius of some 60nm (69 miles, 111km) at cruising speed. Its bow-mounted charge of c.500lb (226kg) of TNT was somewhat smaller than that of the Italian boat, but its fuzing system — impact, hydrostatic or time-fuze — was electrical rather than mechanical, thus allowing the pilot to select a system at any time during an attack. Operational procedure was the same as that of the MTM: in the target area, the pilot would select his victim, aim his boat, bring it to maximum speed, and then ditch with his back-rest/life-raft (called a "flutterboard").

Air-dropped EMBs: the Bergen Plan

In the case of the BPB, however, air-delivery created an added hazard for the pilot. Furthermore, it was accepted that even if he survived the drop and the attack, he would almost certainly be taken prisoner — and there were many cases, including that of the "Cockleshell" raiders, in which captured British commandos had been executed out of hand by the Germans. In air-dropping experiments, more than one BPB prototype with a dummy pilot was smashed to pieces on impact with the sea. Three extra-large parachutes (of 96ft/29.3m flat diameter) were found necessary for safe delivery of the boat; while for the preservation of the pilot a padded cockpit with safety harness had to be added amidships. On landing, the pilot must trigger the quick-release gear that jettisoned the parachutes, unstrap from the midships position, and scramble into the control cockpit aft.

The first manned drop was made on 10 June 1944, when Lt D. Cox, RMBPD, climbed through a hatch leading from the fuselage of an Avro Lancaster bomber to its bomb-bay, where his BPB was suspended in a cradle; strapped himself into the forward cockpit, with a personal parachute which he *might* have the chance to use if the main 'chutes failed; and was launched by the Lancaster's bomb-aimer from an altitude of c.5,000ft (1550m). Cox's successful descent lasted for some five minutes: if he had been dropped by a low-flying bomber over an AA-defended harbour — even at night, as was planned — his chances of survival must have been small.

Late in 1944, six Lancasters of 617 Squadron (the famous "Dambusters"; but at that time sometimes known within the RAF as the "Suicide Squadron" because of the scale of losses incurred in their low-level operations) were fitted out to carry BPBs. Under cover of a conventional bombing raid, it was planned to para-drop the explosive boats into the harbour at Bergen, Norway, to strike at the U-boat pens and depot ships there. (The same target was chosen for the Welman midget submarine; see Chapter 2.) First postponed, when two of the modified Lancasters were lost on conventional operations on 12 January 1945, the mission was abandoned when reconnaissance revealed that the German defences had become so strong as to render a BPB sortie both ineffective and truly suicidal.

"Nothing you can lose by dying is half so precious as the readiness to die, which is man's charter of nobility"

George Santayana

Chapter Four
Divine Wind

A "Confidential" CinCPac-CinCPOA Bulletin on suicide attacks, circulated among Allied forces in the Pacific in May 1945, warned at the outset: "Generalities about Kamikaze attacks must be treated with caution". I would repeat that warning to the reader of my necessarily brief account of the aerial suicide units of World War II.

In this book I have tried to give a full description of suicide weapons, such as explosive motorboats, which receive little or no mention in other sources. And within this chapter, devoted to aerial weapons, I have chosen to give considerable space to the *Ohka* piloted bomb, the *STo* aircraft-carrying submarines, and the Luftwaffe's "special attack" weapons, at the expense of the suicide pilots popularly known as the *kamikaze*. In their case, I concentrate upon the evolution of the kamikaze squadrons, on the major manifestation of the kamikaze effort in the first *Kikusui* mass attack at Okinawa, and on operational techniques and Allied countermeasures. (The deployment of aerial ramming squadrons in defence of the Japanese home islands is described in Chapter 6.) The reader seeking an overall account of the kamikaze is directed to the *Bibliography;* no completely satisfactory work is known to me, but the books by Inoguchi and Nakajima; Karig; Larteguy; Morison; Morris; Nagatsuka; Okumiya and Horikoshi; Roscoe; Sakai; and Wood; are all to be recommended.

A Note on Nomenclature

Japan's suicide squadrons have become universally known as the *kamikaze* ("divine wind"; originally the typhoon that destroyed a Mongol invasion fleet in the 13th century). This term has rarely been used in Japan: it is a rendering, with pejorative overtones of foolish or reckless behaviour, of the Sino-Japanese characters with the same meaning but with the more dignified transliteration of *shimpu* (cf, *hara-kiri* and *seppuku*). The first "official" suicide units of the Imperial Japanese Navy were known as the *Shimpu Tokubetsu Kogekitai* ("Divine Wind Special Attack Force"). This was frequently abbreviated to *Tokko-Tai* ("Special [Attack] Force"); *tokko* or *toku* ("special") being a euphemism for suicide operations. Other such euphemisms were *tai-atari* ("body-crashing") and *jibaku* ("self-destructing"). The Imperial Japanese Army's suicide units were often called the *Shimbu Tokubetsu Kogekitai: shimbu* may be translated as "brandishing the sword" or "the gathering of heroic warriors".

It has been suggested, convincingly in my opinion, that the term *kamikaze* may have been popularized by *Nisei* (Americans of Japanese descent, serving in noncombatant roles in the Pacific theatre; in Europe, a *Nisei* battalion was the most-decorated US infantry unit), who used the term for the special attack squadrons in much the same spirit as that with which they belittled the threat of the *ohka* ("cherry blossom") piloted bomb by referring to it as the *baka* ("foolish" or "crazy") bomb. This said, I use the term *kamikaze* in this chapter for the sake of brevity and convenience.

Evolution of the Suicide Squadrons

The name most closely associated with the organization of the kamikaze squadrons is that of Vice-Admiral Takijiro Onishi. However,

Onishi's creation of an "official" suicide unit in October 1944 was anticipated in actions by junior officers of both the IJN and IJA. Nor were Japanese aerial suicide tactics unforeseen by the Allies. As early as October 1940, Capt (later Rear-Admiral) Ellis M. Zacharias, head of the Far Eastern Section of the US Office of Naval Intelligence, reported an alleged Japanese plan for a surprise air raid on a major base of the US Pacific Fleet, during which at least four bomb-laden aircraft would attempt to dive down the stacks of US battleships at anchor. Admiral James O. Richardson took this report seriously enough to alert the San Diego base, but his successor, Admiral Husband E. Kimmel, gave it less credence when Zacharias repeated the warning in March 1941. When the Japanese "sneak attack" was made on Pearl Harbor, no such dives were reported.

Who was the "first kamikaze"? Since the Japanese suicide pilots have been condemned by certain western writers as "inhuman fanatics" and "barbarians", it is worth remembering a wartime myth. It was widely believed in the United States that Capt Colin P. Kelly, Jr, USAAF, had been awarded a posthumous Medal of Honor for deliberately crash-diving his B-17D into the Japanese battleship *Haruna* during the Japanese landings at Aparri, northern Luzon, on 10 December 1941. In fact, this gallant officer's aircraft was badly damaged by a Zero fighter piloted by PO Saburo Sakai, while returning from an attack on Japanese transports. Kelly sacrificed his life by staying at the controls of his blazing Fortress to hold it steady while his crew parachuted to safety; he was awarded a posthumous Distinguished Service Cross. A number of similar "kamikaze" claims were made for American pilots by an overheated propaganda machine.

There were instances throughout the war, in all theatres, of pilots in damaged aircraft, possibly knowing themselves to be mortally wounded, whose last actions were to set a ramming course — but such instances, however heroic, cannot be described as kamikaze attacks: the essence of "special attack" is that the mission should be *planned* from the outset to be suicidal.

An attack on the carrier USS *Enterprise* on 1 February 1942 is sometimes cited as the first kamikaze strike. Seven Mitsubishi G4M "Betty" bombers approached Admiral Halsey's carrier task group off Wotje in the Marshalls: six were quickly shot down by AA fire and fighter cover but the survivor attempted to crash on *Enterprise*'s flight deck, striking its edge and falling into the sea. Halsey himself commented that the Betty "was undoubtedly on fire when she hit us ... I doubt if this Japanese even knew he was a kamikaze". Similarly, although a popular reference work cites an attack on US transports off Guadalcanal on 8 August 1942, in which USS *George F. Elliot* (AP 13) was lost after being struck by an Aichi D3A "Val" divebomber, as the "first premeditated suicide attack", it seems certain that this crash-dive was made by an aircraft already in flames with a dying pilot at the controls. The carrier *Hornet* (CV 8) and destroyer *Smith* were similarly struck by doomed aircraft during the Battle of Santa Cruz, 26 October 1942.

So far as "official" kamikaze operations are concerned, it is probable that the adoption of *overtly* suicidal weapons and tactics of all kinds was first discussed at high level in Japan in 1943, but that no decision was taken until July-August 1944, when the plans for *Sho-Go* ("Operation Victory") were drawn up by Imperial General HQ. *Sho-Ichi-Go* ("Operation Victory, Plan One") called for the concentration of all available resources for a "decisive battle" in the Philippines, and it may be that suicide operations figured from the planning stage, especially if we accept an assertion that Emperor Hirohito's agreement "in principle" to such operations was obtained during a conversation with his brother, Prince Takamatsu, a naval officer, in June 1944. If this scenario is correct, then the "independent" actions of Major Takata, Captain Miura and Admiral Arima, described below, may have been officially sanctioned in order to further the acceptance of self-sacrificial missions—even to provoke demands for their adoption—among all ranks of the Japanese fighting forces. This is not a view to find favour in Japan or among the more emotional admirers of the kamikaze; but I cannot see that the fact that their patriotism may have been manipulated in this way by the high command in any degree detracts from their heroism.

Date: **27 May 1944**
Place: **Biak Island, Geelvink Bay, NW New Guinea**
Attack by: **5th Army Air Squadron, IJA**
Target: **US invasion shipping**

In my opinion, the first true kamikaze sortie was flown by pilots of the Imperial Japanese Army on 27 May 1944, against the newly-established US beachhead on the south coast of Biak Island, New Guinea. Major Katashige Takata, commanding the New Guinea-based 5th Army Air Squadron, called upon his pilots for volunteers for a *tai-atari* attack on the US invasion transports. His unit flew twin-engined Kawasaki Ki-45-KAI Toryu ("Dragon Killer, Modified") heavy fighters, cover-named "Nick" by the Allies, already specially modified to carry two 551lb (250kg) bombs for anti-shipping "skip-bombing".

At 1700 hours on 27 May, Takata led in a strike by two Nicks, escorted by five Nakajima Ki-43 "Oscar" fighters, against the US ships. The aircraft came in low from landward over Biak, swooping over the clifftops into a curtain of fire from US Army M55s (.50in multiple MG mounts) on the beach and from escort warships. One Nick crashed almost at once, narrowly missing the tank landing ships inshore. The surviving bomber, although hard hit and on fire, was skilfully piloted towards the largest warship in sight, the destroyer USS *Sampson,* flagship of Rear-Admiral W.M. Fechteler's VII Amphibious Force. Almost grazing the destroyer's stern, the Nick struck the water with its left wingtip and cartwheeled with a massive explosion into the submarine chaser *SC-699.* Although the 95-ton (96.5 tonne) wooden-hulled craft was temporarily engulfed in a mast-high sheet of flame and many of her 28-strong crew were blown overboard, she was not sunk and had only two killed.

Captain Jyo's Initiative
Barely three weeks after the attack at Biak, which the IJA was quick to publicize with the announcement of posthumous honours for

Takata and his men, the IJN suffered a crushing defeat in the Battle of the Philippine Sea, 19-20 June. In what the US Navy christened the "Great Marianas Turkey Shoot", the IJN lost three aircraft carriers and between 300 and 400 aircraft. Even more serious than the materiel loss was the loss of trained aircrews.

Among the Japanese warships damaged in the battle was the light carrier (former midget-submarine carrier, see Chapter 2) *Chiyoda*, commanded by Capt Eiichiro Jyo (sometimes given as Iyo or Jo). Even before the June débâcle, Jyo had been aware of a growing mood of depression and fatalism among the fleet's carrier pilots; a mood which, coupled with the fact that replacement aircrew with only a bare minimum of training were being drafted to the carriers, manifested itself in an increasing number of fatal accidents during routine training at sea. Pilots were beginning to voice their belief that if orthodox tactics continued to prevail, they were doomed to die uselessly. And although death in combat was honourable, death that wrought no good for the Emperor or the homeland was felt to be both pointless and shameful.

After sounding out the mood of his pilots, Jyo (a man of some influence, having been a naval attaché in Washington and an aide-de-camp at the Imperial court) addressed a memorandum to his immediate superiors, Rear-Admiral Soemu Obayashi and Vice-Admiral Jisaburo Ozawa. His message was forthright: conventional attack methods were no longer enough; crash-diving "special attack" units must be formed immediately; he himself volunteered as their commander. Jyo's plea met with a favourable response from Obayashi and Ozawa, but was initially opposed by Admiral Soemu Toyoda, CinC Combined Fleet. Since Toyoda, as Chief of Naval General Staff from May 1945, was to be one of the diehards implacably opposed to surrender, it is probable that his apparent lack of enthusiasm was simply a reflection of the policy that the initial impetus for the kamikaze effort should not appear to come from the high command.

Captain Miura's Exhortation

Meanwhile, another relatively junior naval officer was seeking to initiate "special attack" operations. The fighter "ace" Saburo Sakai has recorded that Captain Kanzo Miura, commanding Sakai's Air Wing at Iwo Jima, *ordered* 17 of his pilots to make a suicidal attack on the US invasion fleet on 4 July 1944. Flanked by samurai banners and patriotic slogans, Miura made an emotional speech to his men, exhorting them to crash-dive US carriers. Sakai, while accepting that a crash-dive was the proper action to be taken by the pilot of an aircraft crippled beyond hope of return, found Miura's histrionics distasteful, "a sign of weakness ... resorting to what amounted almost to witchcraft"; he recorded, however, that most of his comrades were imbued with fresh spirit by this fighting talk.

Before take-off, the chosen pilots ceremonially discarded the parachutes that had been compulsory wear for Japanese fliers only since 1942. (They were disliked both because they were bulky, hampering the pilot in his cockpit, and because, if used over enemy territory, they might lead to the final dishonour of capture.) The mission proved ineffective: the formation of Zeros was broken up by US interceptors far short of its objective. Faced with overwhelming odds and with no chance of success, Sakai led a handful of survivors back to base. To return in such circumstances was not regarded as being dishonourable: the kamikaze were warned against throwing away their lives to no purpose.

Admiral Arima's Example

The final push towards the acceptance of suicide tactics on a large scale was provided by Rear-Admiral Masafumi Arima, commander of the Manila-based 26th Air Flotilla. On 15 October 1944, aircraft of his command were preparing to strike at a US carrier task force off Luzon. As the second attack wave—13 Mitsubishi G4M2 "Betty" bombers, with an escort of 16 Zeros and 70 Army fighters—prepared to take off from Nichols Field, Arima declared that he would lead the attack in person. Like most of the kamikaze who were to follow his lead, Arima was no fire-breathing fanatic: fifty years old, he was a taciturn, dignified and scholarly man, known for a frugal lifestyle in adherence to the Zen discipline of the true samurai. He had stripped from his flying suit all badges of rank: this was interpreted as symbolic of his determination to die in battle.

In spite of the protests of his staff, Arima took off at the controls of a Zero. The Japanese claim, accepted by some western writers, is that the Admiral himself succeeded in crash-diving the heavy carrier USS *Franklin*. In fact, the only damage to *Franklin* during the strike by Arima's aircraft was caused by a Betty shot down by AA fire: the bomber struck the sea some 30yds (25m) from the carrier and a part of its wing ricocheted on to the flight deck. Twenty aircraft of the attack wave failed to return, Arima's among them; he had, said a Japanese communiqué, "lit the fuze for the ardent wishes of his men".

Whether or not it was sanctioned,or even suggested, by the high command, Arima's sacrifice had prepared the way for Onishi who, two days later, took command of the 1st Air Fleet in the Philippines. He had no more than 200 effective aircraft (fewer than 100, according to some sources) with which to provide air cover for Vice-Admiral Takeo Kurita's main battle fleet in the "decisive battle" in the Philippines.

Father of the Kamikaze: Takijiro Onishi

Vice-Admiral Takijiro Onishi had been one of the pioneers in establishing the IJN's paratroop forces and had built a fine reputation as a combat leader in China. In 1941, after initially opposing Admiral Yamamoto's Pearl Harbor plan, he had become one of its driving forces. He was a man of fierce enthusiasms and somewhat mystical temperament: he had strongly advocated the employment of a phrenologist and graphologist to assist in pilot selection and had even briefly espoused a scheme put forward by a self-styled sage who claimed to be able to transform water to petrol. Such eccentricities, allied to an abrupt and arrogant manner, had alienated many of his contemporaries, and before taking command of the IJN's land-based air forces in the Philippines he had held an unspectacular, although important, supply post at Naval General HQ. It may be that his faults, as much as his virtues, recommended him for his position as what was called the "father of the kamikaze".

Within two days of taking up his new appointment, after consultation with his predecessor, Vice-Admiral Kimpei Teraoka, Onishi set about the formation of a "special attack" corps. On the evening of 19 October 1944, at Mabalacat, Luzon, he called together senior staff officers and the commanders of the 201st Air Group and delivered a brief and unemotional lecture on Japan's grave situation and of their responsibilities in *Sho-Ichi-Go*. He concluded that, in order to give the IJN's surface forces a chance to counter the US invasion, the US carriers must be "neutralized" for at least one week. With the limited resources available, there was only one way this could be done: ". . . suicide attack units composed of Zero fighters armed with 250kg bombs, with each plane to crash-dive into an enemy carrier".

Mitsubishi A6M7 Model 63 **Reisen** (Zero; "Zeke") with a 1,102lb (500kg) bomb on a purpose-designed mounting. The first "official" **kamikaze** missions in October 1944 were flown by A6M5 Model 52 Zeros, each with a 551lb (250kg) bomb on its belly-mounted drop-tank fitting.

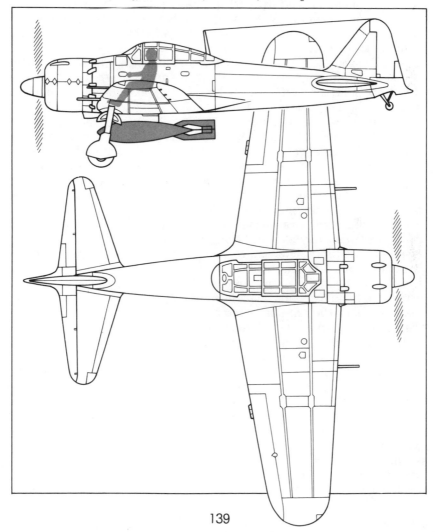

He ended with a question which, in the circumstances, could only be rhetorical: "What do you think?". The assembled officers could have only one answer. Mindful of the *Imperial Rescript* demanding that duty be done at any cost; reared in the tradition of the samurai "always prepared to die"; and confronting a senior officer who surely spoke with the authority of the high command in so grave a matter, they could not but agree to Onishi's "suggestion". Nevertheless, Cdr Asaichi Tamai of 201st Air Group called for an opinion on the effectiveness of a bomb-carrying crash-diving Zero—it would be far more effective than conventional bombing, he was told—and held a brief consultation on his unit's morale with Lt Masanobu Ibusuki, before assuring Onishi that he would form a "special attack" unit at Mabalacat. Onishi's expression was, according to Cdr Rikihei Inoguchi, present at the conference, one of "relief . . . with a shadow of sorrow".

The High Command and the Kamikaze

It has been claimed by Japanese writers that Onishi envisaged only a temporary kamikaze effort, perhaps limited to those pilots asked to volunteer at Mabalacat for a single specific task in the Philippines. I cannot agree. The kamikaze of Mabalacat, and the hundreds who were to follow them, may have believed—indeed, it was necessary that they should believe—that their sacrifice would alter the course of the war. But in acting through Onishi to initiate a kamikaze *strategy*, I believe that Imperial General HQ was looking farther ahead, even beyond the war's end in case of Japan's defeat.

The suicide strategy (embracing all the Japanese "special attack" weapons described in this book) was, in my opinion, seen by the high command not as a way of "winning" the war—but of ending it in an "honourable" way. The suicide strategy had three major aims. In order of priority: to give such awe-inspiring proof of Japan's inflexible will to fight to the last that the enemy would consider a negotiated peace, rather than demanding unconditional surrender; to delay enemy conquest of islands as air bases and stepping-stones to invasion until full preparations for defence of the home islands could be made; and to inspire the entire population to take part in the final defence in the spirit expressed in the slogan: "One hundred million will die for Emperor and Nation!". I am supported by former members of "special attack" units in believing that the most important—but not unexpected—result of the kamikaze strategy was not apparent until *after* Japan's defeat, when the self-sacrifice of the kamikaze enabled Japan to bear the dishonour of surrender and thus made possible the post-war miracle of reconstruction.

There were, of course, also immediate practical reasons for the formation of the kamikaze squadrons. Shortage of aircraft was not one of them: although Onishi was initially starved of aircraft in the Philippines—thus temporarily justifying his creation of the kamikaze—some 2,000 replacements would be received by the end of the campaign. And although Japan's first-line aircraft were, by 1944, significantly inferior to those of the Allies, there was little shortfall in quantity. Japan produced 16,693 aircraft in 1943 and 28,180 in 1944, the highest total of any war year; production in the first seven months of 1945 totalled 11,066. The crucial shortage was that of aircrew, caused both by combat losses and by a lack of training facilities largely due to the fuel crisis.

In normal times, home production of oil amounted to below 10 per cent of Japan's annual requirement. By 1944, some two-thirds of the tanker fleet bringing oil to Japan from the South Pacific fields captured in 1941-42 had been destroyed by the Allies: 40 per cent of the oil produced in southern fields reached Japan in 1942; only 13.5 per cent in 1944 — and none in 1945. In 1944, Japan's total consumption of oil was 19.4 million US barrels, but total production, both imported and home, amounted to only 7.81 million US barrels, and the reserves built up in the pre-war and early war years were rapidly dwindling.

Thus, there was insufficient fuel even for Japan's front-line aviation, and precious little for the training of replacement aircrew. The period of instruction for trainee pilots had to be cut from 100 hours in 1943 to 40 hours in 1944. Operational training was also slashed and, with the inception of the kamikaze, navigation was often omitted altogether: one experienced pilot could lead a whole group of half-trained kamikaze to their target area. Although brief, training was extra-hazardous: what fuel was issued was diluted with an increasing proportion of alcohol, beginning at 50 per cent in 1944, giving it an extremely low flashpoint which made it near-impossible to restart the engine after a stall. Accidents were increasingly frequent.

Kamikaze in the Philippines: the First Sorties
Within one day of Onishi's visit, 24 volunteer pilots at Mabalacat had formed four "special attack" units equipped with the Mitsubishi A6M5 Zero carrying a 551lb (250kg) bomb (or sometimes two smaller bombs) in place of the belly-mounted drop tank. The five pilots of the *Yamato* unit left immediately for Cebu, some 400 miles (640km) to the south, where they formed the nucleus of another kamikaze group with the 601st Air Group. The pilots left at Mabalacat were eager to sortie, but bad weather, the difficulty of locating targets and strikes by US carrier planes all contributed to delay.

Meanwhile, news of the newly-formed kamikaze force was spreading to other units and receiving an enthusiastic reception. It may have inspired an attack on the Allied bombardment force off Leyte on 21 October when, at c.0600, a small group of Japanese aircraft flew out of the dawn haze from landward to strike at the US and Australian cruisers and destroyers of Rear-Admiral R.S. Berkey's Task Unit 77.3. An Aichi D3A2 "Val" divebomber, possibly damaged by AA fire from HMAS *Shropshire*, dived through a wall of shells from HMAS *Australia*'s multi-barrelled pom-poms and, moments after releasing an anti-personnel bomb, smashed into the cruiser's bridge, killing her captain and 29 others and wounding 64 crewmen. *Australia*, "the first Allied ship to be hit by a suicide aircraft" according to the RAN's official historian, was out of action for one month. Later the same day, the first kamikaze sortie was flown from Cebu by a group headed by Lt Yoshiyasu Kuno. Two bomb-carrying Zeros and one escort fighter took off at 1625: one kamikaze and the escort returned, but Kuno, who had vowed to find a target or perish when his fuel ran out, did not. No result is recorded for the sortie. On 24 October, the fleet tug USS *Sonoma* was sunk in San Pedro Bay, Leyte, by a crash-diving aircraft which also badly damaged the "Liberty" ship *Augustus Thomas;* but this, like the strike on *Australia,* appears to have been an impromptu attack by an already-damaged aircraft.

Date: **25 October 1944**
Place: **Leyte Gulf, off Samar Island, Philippines**
Attack by: **Kamikaze Zeros from Cebu and Mabalacat**
Target: **US carrier task units**

Early on 25 October 1944, the second day of the great naval battle of Leyte Gulf, the kamikaze units struck their first major blows. At the very moment when the US escort carriers and destroyers of Rear-Admiral C.A.F. Sprague's Task Unit 77.4.3 ("Taffy 3") were making their desperate fight against Admiral Kurita's Centre Force (described on pages 117-118), at c.0725, the five kamikaze Zeros and four escort fighters of Lt Yukio Seki's *Shikishima* unit took off from Mabalacat. They received a final farewell from Onishi himself. Seki, in a parting gesture of the kind that was to be widely recorded as illustrative of the kamikaze's burning patriotism, thrust into the hands of a staff officer the sum of 2,000 yen with a request that it should be sent to the homeland to help build new aircraft. But although Seki's flight was to be the most widely publicized, it was not the first of the day.

At 0740, just as the four escort carriers of Rear-Admiral T.L. Sprague's TU.77.4.1 ("Taffy 1") had launched a strike wave to the aid of "Taffy 3", some 30 miles (50km) to the north, six Zeros of an unidentified kamikaze unit (almost certainly from the 601st Air Group at Cebu) broke cloud cover almost immediately overhead. With machine guns blazing, a bomb-laden Zero dived vertically into USS *Santee*, smashing through the flight deck forward, where the explosion of its bomb blew a hole 450sq ft (42sq m) in extent, and penetrating to the hangar deck. Sixteen US sailors were killed and 47 wounded. Seconds later, another Zero, driven away from *Suwanee* by AA fire, dived on *Sangamon*. A direct hit from *Suwanee*'s 5in (127mm) AA splashed it some 500yds (460m) short, while *Petrof Bay*'s AA claimed another Zero. At 0800 *Suwanee*'s gunners engaged a Zero dodging through the clouds at c.8,000ft (2440m). Trailing smoke, the kamikaze rolled into a dive and struck the carrier's flight deck before exploding, killing 71 men and injuring 82. Almost simultaneously, *Santee* was struck by a torpedo from the submarine *I-56* (LtCdr Masahiko Morinaga). It is probable that Morinaga had no advance intelligence that enabled him to coordinate his attack with that of the kamikaze: such coordination, which might have been extremely effective, was to be very rare. It was a tribute to the tough construction of the "Sangamon"-class escort carriers (converted fleet oilers of 11,400 tons, 11,582 tonnes) that by c.1000 both *Santee* and *Suwanee* had put out their fires, patched up their decks and were operating their aircraft.

At 1050, Seki's group from Mabalacat struck "Taffy 3", already mauled and with the escort carrier *Gambier Bay* sunk in the battle with Kurita's heavy units. The Zeros were sighted coming in fast and low (to escape radar detection) out of a haze. Once in sight of their objective, the Japanese aircraft climbed steeply to c.6,000ft (1830m) and then hurtled into their dives with machine guns hammering. One Zero struck the edge of *Kitkun Bay*'s deck to port and rebounded into the sea, where its bomb detonated and caused damage below the waterline. *Fanshaw Bay*'s gunners claimed two kills and *White Plains* knocked down another Zero which splashed close aboard, wounding 11 of her crew. Another aircraft, damaged by *White Plains*'s AA, reeled away over *St Lô* and smashed down on the centre line of the 7,800-ton (7925 tonne) escort carrier's flight deck aft. The kamikaze's bomb load went through to the hangar deck, near the ready supply of aviation fuel. Minor explosions below decks culminated in a massive detonation at 1058: *St Lô* erupted amidships, spewing up a 750ft (230m) geyser of flame and debris, and, after burning for some 30 minutes, sank with the loss of about 100 men.

Three of the four escort fighters of Seki's flight returned to Mabalacat to report the sinking of an aircraft carrier and, oddly, a light cruiser. But "Taffy 3's" ordeal was not over. At c.1110, a force of about 15 aircraft—Yokosuka D4Y2 "Judy" divebombers with Zero escorts— attacked the hard-hit carriers while rescue work was still in progress. "Taffy 3's" own surviving Wildcats beat off the raiders, but not until three more crash-dives had been made by flaming aircraft, slightly damaging *Kalinin Bay* and *Kitkun Bay.* These Japanese bombers had flown either from Mindanao or Davao: it is apparent that even on the first day of fullscale kamikaze operations, the "special attack" spirit had spread to units throughout the Philippines.

Volunteers for Death

From the first, there was no lack of volunteers for kamikaze missions. And there can be little doubt that the suicide pilots who flew the earlier missions in the Philippines were volunteers in the truest sense, motivated by sincere patriotism and a sense of honour. It is difficult to judge whether personal or national honour was the greater spur. "I do this not solely for the Emperor, but for my beloved wife", Lt Seki (unusual in that he was a married man; the selection procedures described on pages 177-178 applied also to the kamikaze pilots) is reported to have declared before take-off. Collections of the last letters of "special attack" personnel (work by Larteguy, *Bibliography*) display a wide variety of motives, not excluding the Christian religion; but many of these scripts show, in their stilted wording, signs of having been too consciously written for posterity.

It is all too easy, in reaction to contemporary Allied descriptions of the suicide pilots as blood-crazed, nationalistic fanatics, to sentimen- talize the kamikaze as starry-eyed patriots, the flower of their generation, going joyfully and unthinkingly to their spectacular ends in the light of the setting sun. This is to create a stereotype as unreal, and ultimately as insulting, as the goggle-eyed, buck-toothed "Jap" of the comic books. It is no more true than are the tales, mainly in US wartime accounts, of kamikaze pilots chained in their cockpits, wearing funeral shrouds (although some may have flown in the regalia of various nationalistic societies), drugged, drunk, or numbed by pre-mission sex orgies.

143

The truth is that the kamikaze were, like Rudyard Kipling's "Tommy" of the Boer War, "single men in barracks, most remarkable like you". And, as Kipling remarked, "single men in barracks don't grow into plaster saints". The kamikaze drank when they could, whored when they could, often complained and sometimes despaired, at times became arrogant when the propaganda machine acclaimed their glory,and at times wished themselves anything but what they were. And when they were told to go out and die, they obeyed. In this, they did no more and no less than was done by many Allied and Axis winners of awards for gallantry—and unknown thousands whose deeds went unobserved. Anyone who doubts this should study the loss-rate of the RAF's Bomber Command or the US 8th Air Force over Germany in 1943-1944.

Japanese and Allied Opinions of the Kamikaze

Perhaps the best single summing-up of the overall motive of the kamikaze was given by LtGen Torashiro Kawabe, when interrogated after the war by the US Strategic Bombing Survey (USSBS). Kawabe went on record as stating:

"We believed that our spiritual convictions and moral strength could balance your material and scientific advantages. We did not consider our attacks to be 'suicide'. The pilot did not start out on his mission with the intention of committing suicide [ie, of immolating himself in a spirit of despair]. He looked upon himself as a human bomb which would destroy a certain part of the enemy fleet . . . [and] died happy in the conviction that his death was a step towards the final victory."

On the Allied side, a USSBS report described the kamikaze as:

"Macabre, effective, *supremely practical under the circumstances*, [my italics], supported and stimulated by a powerful propaganda campaign."

Mention of propaganda raises an important point. Although there is no reason to doubt that all the kamikaze were volunteers, it must be admitted that the Japanese pilot who declined to volunteer when given the opportunity to do so would himself have displayed moral courage of a high order. When radio propaganda and movies presented the image of the "wild eagles" to Japan in terms of the heroic past; when the Ministry of Information, in November 1944, exhorted the population to "Stand firm . . . or how can you justify yourselves before the departed spirits of the Kamikaze Special Attack Force?"; and when it was widely reported that Emperor Hirohito had said, on being told of Lt Seki's success, "They certainly did a good job" (but prefacing it with the question, "Was it necessary to go to this extreme?"), and had ordered the typical "last meal" of a kamikaze— rice and beans, fish and *sake*—served in the Imperial Palace on New Year's Day; it was almost impossible for a young pilot to resist the pressure to volunteer.

However, although raised to fever pitch by propaganda, the enthusiasm of the vast majority of the kamikaze was genuine. A pilot who volunteered for "special attack" might have to wait weeks or months before making his sortie; and the fact that so few appear to

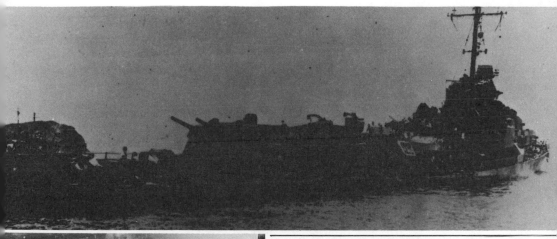

Above: On Radar Picket Station No 10 off Okinawa, the light minelayer USS **Aaron Ward** took six **kamikaze** hits in one hour during the fifth **kikusui** mass suicide attack on 3 May 1945. Fortyfive men were killed; the ship was scrapped.

Left: During the second **kikusui** attack, on 11 April 1945, a **kamikaze** heads in at wave-top height against the battleship USS **Missouri**. In the moment before impact (**Below**), it seems that the **kamikaze** will strike a twin 5in (127mm) AA mount – but the aircraft struck the starboard quarter and "damage was confined to scorched paint", says the US Navy's historian.

Right: The destroyer USS **Laffey** (DD 724) was subjected to 22 **kamikaze** attacks in 80 minutes on 16 April 1945. Her AA gunners shot down nine of the attackers, but six **kamikaze** and four bombs struck, knocking out all armament but four 20mm guns, killing 31 men and wounding 72.

Below: Fire on the flight deck of the veteran heavy carrier USS **Saratoga** after **kamikaze** hits off Iwo Jima, 21 February 1945. "Sara" took five hits inside three minutes and a sixth one hour later, with 123 killed and 192 wounded. She was retired from combat duty for the rest of the war.

Top: A flaming Zero dives on HMS **Indomitable** as the British carrier force operates off Sakishima Gunto, May 1945. (**Above**) **Indomitable** is near-missed. The British carriers, with armoured flight decks, were better able to withstand **kamikaze** hits than their USN equivalents.

Below: In an attempted crash-dive, a Kawasaki Ki-61 "Tony" of the IJAAF passes within 25ft (8m) of the flight deck of the escort carrier USS **Sangamon** off Kerama Retto, 4 May 1945.

Right: A giant **STo**-type submarine of the IJN, with a USN crew after the war's end. The long hangar amidships housed three seaplane-bombers, catapult-launched from the ramp forward.

Far right: The aircraft-carrying submarines **I-14, I-401** and **I-400,** seen after surrender, were to have launched a **kamikaze** strike on the US fleet anchorage at Ulithi in August 1945.

Below: Damage to the heavy carrier USS **Randolph** after the single hit achieved by 24 Yokosuka P1Y1 "Frances" bombers that flew a long-range **kamikaze** mission to Ulithi on 11 March 1945.

Above: Japanese naval pilots relax near a Mitsubishi G4M2 "Betty" bomber with an MXY7 **Ohka** piloted-bomb semi-recessed beneath it.

Right: The cockpit of an **Ohka**. Note the armoured bucket-seat, control column, simple instruments, fuze arming handle (above left), sighting ring immediately forward of the windshield, and, forward again, the suspension lug by which the **Ohka** was slung beneath a "Betty" bomber.

Far right: Formal photograph of pilots of the **Jinrai Butai** ("Divine Thunderbolt Corps"), the unit formed to operate the **Ohka**.

Below: The Model 11 **Ohka**, seen here, was the only model to be used operationally. The Allied estimate of 298 so-called **Baka** ("Idiot") bombs expended is almost certainly too high.

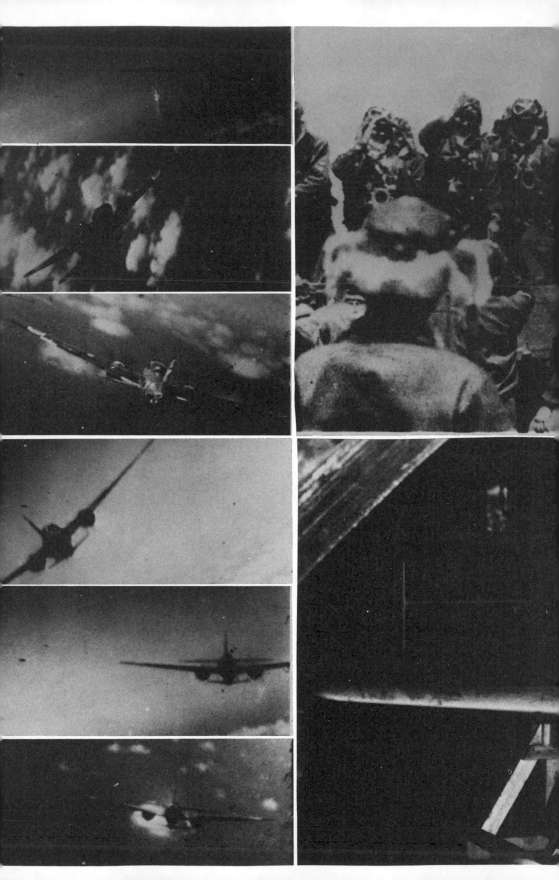

Far left: Gun-camera shots show the manoeuvres of "Betty" bombers, slow and ungainly with **Ohka** slung beneath them, as they vainly attempt to evade Hellcats from USS **Hornet**, 21 March 1945.

Left: Immediately before the disastrous combat début of the **Ohka** on 21 March 1945, LtCdr Goro Nonaka's bomber pilots of the 721st **Kokutai** prepare to go to their aircraft at Kanoya Naval Air Base. All 18 **Ohka**-carrying "Betty" bombers were intercepted and shot down by US carrier planes before launching their piloted-bombs.

Above: An RAF officer examines a Model 11 **Ohka** found at Seletar air base, Singapore.

Below: Many **Ohka** deployed for the defence of the Japanese home islands against invasion were stored in shelters near potential landing beaches.

Above: Focke-Wulf Fw 190 (top) and Junkers Ju 88 in **Mistel** (``Mistletoe'') combination. The pilot of the upper aircraft guided the combination towards the target, releasing the pilot-less, explosive-packed lower unit at the last moment. There were plans to air-launch the Messerschmitt Me 328B or Heinkel He 162 by this method.

Right: An Allied technician sits in a **Reichenberg III**, the powered training model, with ballasted dummy warhead, of the manned version of the Fieseler Fi 103 ``V-1'' or ``doodlebug''.

Below: **Reichenberg** piloted-bomb in operational paintwork. Note position of Argus pulse-jet unit atop the fuselage: a pilot attempting to bale out after putting the aircraft into a dive would almost certainly be dashed against it.

Below right: This Heinkel He 162A-2 **Volksjäger** (``People's Fighter''; unofficially the **Salamander**) was captured in an unpainted condition and with a shattered cockpit canopy, May 1945.

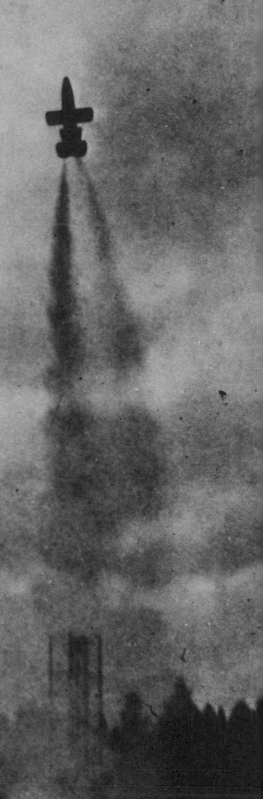

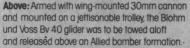

Above: Armed with wing-mounted 30mm cannon and mounted on a jettisonable trolley, the Blohm und Voss Bv 40 glider was to be towed aloft and released above an Allied bomber formation.

Above: The Bachem Ba 349A **Natter** (`Adder') rocket-propelled interceptor has its nose-cone removed to show a battery of 24x73mm **Föhn** spin-stabilized rockets. Note ring sight forward.

Right: Boosted by jettisonable, tail-mounted, solid-fuel rockets, giving an initial climb rate of c.36,500ft (11,125m) per minute, the liquid-fuelled **Natter** blasts off from its ramp.

have given way under the strain of awaiting certain death proves that their dedication was not based merely on passing emotional fervour. There were certainly few material rewards: the minor privileges granted to "special attack" personnel, and the ceremonies that attended their departure on their missions, are adequately described in the section later in this chapter dealing with the *Ohka*, and in other chapters, and need not be repeated here.

Material and Moral Effects

The USSBS was to characterize the kamikaze as "effective [and] supremely practical under the circumstances". The truth of this is illustrated in the accompanying Table showing the results of kamikaze operations, as opposed to conventional air attacks, in the Philippines from 25 October 1944 to 31 January 1945. Compiled from the US Navy's "Chronology" and "Official History" and from various Japanese sources, these figures cannot claim complete accuracy, since sources are frequently at variance, but I believe that they are a true reflection of the relative efficiency of kamikaze and conventional methods. A Japanese source (Inoguchi and Nakajima) shows a total of 378 kamikaze aircraft and 102 kamikaze escorts expended in the Philippines (together with 43 kamikaze and 102 escorts that returned from sorties). These figures refer only to IJN aircraft; it is not possible to ascertain figures for IJA aircraft or, of course, for aircraft making impromptu suicide attacks.

Something that the Table cannot show is the effect of the kamikaze on Allied morale. "The American soldier [and sailor] has a very active imagination . . . and is inclined to endow the death-dealing weapons of

ALLIED SHIPS SUNK/DAMAGED BY AIR ATTACK IN THE PHILIPPINES, 25 OCTOBER 1944-31 JANUARY 1945				
Type	SUNK BY KAMIKAZE	SUNK BY CONVENTIONAL AIR ATTACK	DAMAGED BY KAMIKAZE	DAMAGED BY CONVENTIONAL AIR ATTACK
Battleship (BB)	–	–	5	1
Aircraft carrier (CV)	–	–	8	–
Aircraft carrier, small (CVL)	–	–	3	–
Aircraft carrier, escort (CVE)	2	–	13	–
Heavy cruiser (CA)	–	–	7	–
Light cruiser (CL)	–	–	7	–
Destroyer (DD)	3	–	27	6
Destroyer escort (DE)	–	–	5	–
Submarine (SS)	–	1	1	–
High speed minesweeper (DMS)	1	2	1	–
Attack transport (APA)	1	–	5	–
High speed transport (APD)	3	–	2	1
Minor warships/auxiliaries	8	1	16	11
"Liberty" ships	3	8	10	6
"Victory" ships	1	–	–	–
Total	22	12	110	25

Note: In the case of figures for ships damaged; several ships were struck more than once and these figures refer to the number of hits made.

the enemy with extraordinary qualities . . .", noted General George C. Marshall in a report to the US Secretary of War in 1945, "[and] if given slight encouragement the reaction can be fatal to the success of our forces". From the inception of the kamikaze, strict censorship had ensured that the Allied public at home knew nothing of the suicide attacks (the news embargo was not lifted until 13 April 1945), and the official figures of losses incurred were deliberately understated; but there was obviously no way in which such a spectacular threat could be hidden from Allied servicemen in the Pacific theatre.

In 1944-45, there was a significant increase in psycho-neurotic illness among Allied personnel in this theatre. In the case of the US Navy, which bore the main weight of the kamikaze onslaught, mental disease case incidence increased from 9.5 per thousand of total strength in 1941 to 14.2 per thousand in 1944. Fleet Admiral King, in his report to the US Secretary of the Navy, attributed this increase to "the increase in tempo of modern war with its *grueling, unfamiliar horrors*" (my italics; the phrase surely refers to the suicide attacks).

During the Okinawa campaign, when the kamikaze fury reached its climax, the US Navy's commanders were forced to discontinue the practice — made possible partly by the breaking of Japanese codes — of warning their crews when mass suicide attacks were imminent. "The strain of waiting", wrote the American war correspondent Hanson Baldwin, "the anticipated terror, made vivid from past experience, sends some men into hysteria, insanity, breakdown". The US Army's "Official History" notes that at Okinawa "nonbattle casualties were numerous, a large percentage being neuro-psychiatric or 'combat fatigue' cases . . . The rate of psychiatric cases was probably higher on Okinawa than in any previous operation in the Pacific".

Attack Methods of the Kamikaze

In considering the tactics of kamikaze aircraft attack, it must be remembered that many suicide attacks were impromptu crash-dives on targets of opportunity and that kamikaze units were often the creation of local commanders, operating in whatever way best suited their individual circumstances. The aerial Special Attack Corps, embracing both IJN and IJA units, cannot be regarded as a single command — in the sense, say, of RAF Bomber Command — guided by overall operational directives.

The earlier kamikaze missions were flown by groups no more than five to seven strong; typically by three or four suicide aircraft with two or three escorts. The major function of the escorts was not so much to protect the kamikaze, by engaging interceptors or drawing AA fire, as to guide them to the target area and observe and report the results of their attacks. Later, particularly at Okinawa, kamikaze attacked in much larger groups, sometimes without escorts, being led to the target by the most experienced pilot in the group, and sometimes accompanied by one or two fast recce-bombers — such as the IJN's Yokosuka P1Y "Frances" and the IJA's Kawasaki Ki-48 "Lily" or Mitsubishi Ki-46 "Dinah" — which kept well clear of the action. There were, of course, instances of escort aircraft, despite their lack of explosive loads, making impromptu crash-dives.

The Allied navies had excellent search radar, capable of picking up intruders at any altitude at a range of up to about 150 miles (240km), and, to deal with close-in attackers, radar control for their heavier AA weapons (see below, and Table on page 164). But there were, inevitably, gaps in radar coverage which the Japanese sought to exploit. "Window", strips of metal foil cut to lengths corresponding to radar frequencies, proved only marginally useful; a more effective method of radar evasion, favoured in the Philippines by geographical factors, was to approach ships from landward, since shore "echoes" often cluttered ships' radar. To avoid visual sighting, the kamikaze were instructed to make maximum use of cloud cover and to attack out of the sun whenever possible.

Diversionary raids by conventional aircraft, or simultaneous kamikaze strikes in different locations, were made to draw off or confuse the guardian interceptors of the Allied carrier forces' Combat Air Patrols (CAPs). Monitoring Allied R/T channels, the Japanese observed that

Yokosuka D4Y4 **Suisei** (Comet; Allied name ``Judy'') Special Attack Bomber Model 43; a single-seat version of the standard carrier-based divebomber-fighter, specially designed for **kamikaze** attacks. It carries a semi-recessed 1,764lb (800kg) bomb. Three RATOG (**R**ocket **A**ssisted **T**ake **O**ff **G**ear) auxiliary rockets might be fitted to the fuselage to boost its diving speed.

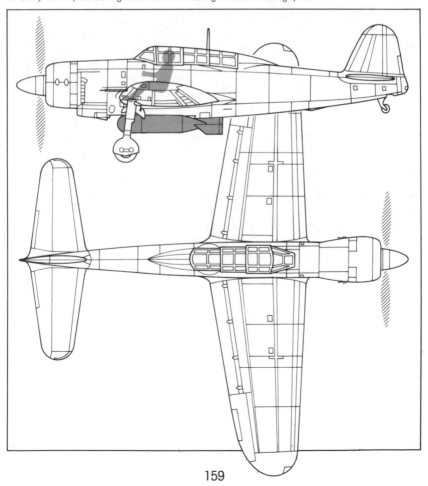

poor radio discipline by excited pilots often clogged the limited number of channels available to the ships' Fighter Direction Officers (FDOs). Diversionary raids ensured the maximum traffic on these vital communication links, allowing the kamikaze to evade interception. Single kamikaze often attempted to approach Allied ships by tagging on to formations of aircraft returning to their carriers, while larger groups might copy their formations and flight procedures.

Target Selection and Bomb-Loads

The kamikaze were recommended to achieve visual sighting of their targets from an altitude of above 20,000ft (6100m). While more than 5 miles (8km) from the target, a kamikaze group should disperse so that its aircraft would make their attacking runs from as many different directions, levels and angles as possible—again, to present maximum difficulty to the FDOs and to AA gunners. Targets were specified in order of precedence as aircraft carriers, battleships, cruisers and transports; in fact, kamikaze showed a tendency to concentrate on the largest ship in any formation, or on the first ship to be damaged. The kamikaze pilot was instructed to aim for the central flight deck, abreast the island, of a carrier, or the base of the bridge on other ships.

At the commencement of his final run-in, the kamikaze pilot must arm his bomb by pulling a toggle in the cockpit which freed the fuze arming vane on the missile. Judging from US reports of bombs which failed to detonate, this procedure was not infrequently overlooked by pilots facing their last few moments of life. The bomb-loads of kamikaze aircraft varied from the 1,764lb (800kg) of the IJA's "Lily", through the 551lb (250kg) of the Zero (or 1,102lb, 500kg, in the A6M7), to the 110lb (50kg) of the Kyushu K9W1/Ki-86 "Cypress" biplane trainer. Occasionally, depending on the aircraft or on ordnance availability, torpedoes or even heavy artillery shells were used instead of bombs. In the IJA's purpose-adapted Kawasaki Ki-48-II KAI ("Lily") and Mitsubishi Ki-67-I KAI ("Peggy"), internal charges of explosives (up to 6,393lb, 2900kg, in a "Peggy") were carried, to be impact-detonated by a long rod mounted in the aircraft's nose; I can find no certain instance of their combat deployment.

The accompanying Table lists purpose-adapted kamikaze aircraft (purpose-designed kamikaze are covered in the section of this chapter dealing with the *Ohka* piloted-bomb, and in Chapter 6). Most of the IJN and IJA's standard aircraft were used at some time or another in kamikaze attacks, but it is worth noting that although it is generally

Mitsubishi Ki-67-I KAI ("Peggy") purpose-modified for **kamikaze** attack, with faired-over turrets, a three-man crew, and nose-mounted rod to detonate internal explosive charge of 6,393lb (2900kg).

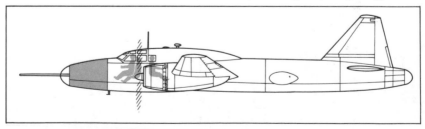

accepted that the Zero was the most common kamikaze, a US Navy publication of May 1945 estimated that the Aichi D3A "Val" divebomber was most frequently encountered in the suicide role.

In the earlier attacks, the kamikaze usually crashed with their bombs still attached to the aircraft. Later, as more efficient bomb-release gear replaced improvised racks, it became more usual, when the aircraft type permitted, to release bombs just before impact. There are Allied reports of pilots who attempted to parachute from their planes in a terminal dive, after releasing bombs, but none appears to have survived in this way.

JAPANESE "SPECIAL ATTACK" AIRCRAFT (PURPOSE-MODIFIED)

Aircraft:	MITSUBISHI A6M REISEN (ZERO FIGHTER) ("ZEKE")*	KYUSHU K11W1 SHIRAGIKU (WHITE CRYSANTHEMUM)	KAWASAKI Ki-48-II (TYPE 99 SPECIAL PLANE) ("LILY")	NAKAJIMA Ki-49-II DONRYU (STORM DRAGON) ("HELEN")	MITSUBISHI Ki-67-I-KAI HIRYU (FLYING DRAGON MODIFIED) ("PEGGY")
Type:	Single-engined carrier-based fighter	Single-engined trainer	Twin-engined light bomber	Twin-engined heavy bomber	Twin-engined heavy bomber
Span:	36.09ft (11m)	49.15ft (14.98m)	57.25ft (17.45m)	67.01ft (20.42m)	73.82ft (22.5m)
Length:	29.92ft (9.12m)	33.59ft (10.24m)	41.83ft (12.75m)	54.14ft (16.5m)	61.35ft (18.7m)
Height:	11.51ft (3.51m)	12.89ft (3.93m)	12.47ft (3.8m)	13.94ft (4.25m)	25.26ft (7.7m)
Loaded weight (normal):	6,025lb (2733kg)	5,820lb (2640kg)	14,330lb (6500kg)	23,545lb (10 680kg)	30,347lb (13 765kg)
Engine(s):	(A6M5) 1 x Nakajima NK1F Sakae 21 radial, take-off rating 1,130hp (A6M7) 1 x Nakajima Sakae 31 air-cooled radial, take-off rating 1,130hp	1 x Hitachi GK2B Amakaze 21 air-cooled radial, take-off rating 515hp	2 x Nakajima Ha-115 (Army Type 1) air-cooled radials, take-off rating 1,130hp	2 x Nakajima Ha-109 (Army Type 2) air-cooled radials, take-off rating 1,500hp	2 x Mitsubishi (Army Type 4) air-cooled radials, take-off rating 1,900hp
Maximum speed:	351mph (565kmh) @ 19,685ft (6000m)	143mph (230kmh) @ 5,580ft (1700m)	314mph (505kmh) @ 18,375ft (5600m)	306mph (492kmh) @ 16,405ft (5000m)	334mph (537kmh) @ 19,980ft (6090m)
Service ceiling:	38,520ft (11 740m)	18,440ft (5620m)	33,135ft (10 100m)	30,510ft (9300m)	31,070ft (9470m)
Normal range:	c.1,160 miles (1866km)	1,093 miles (1759km)	1,274 miles (2050km)	1,243 miles (2000km)	1,740 miles (2800km)
Armament:	(A6M5) 2 x 7.7mm Type 97 MG; 2 x 20mm Type 99 cannon (A6M7) 3 x 13.2mm Type 3 MG; 2 x 20mm Type 99 cannon	(as kamikaze) Nil	(non-kamikaze) 3 x 7.7mm Type 89 MGs	(as kamikaze) Nil	(as kamikaze) Nil
Bomb load for kamikaze missions:	(A6M5) 1 x 551lb (250kg) bomb on drop-tank fitting (A6M7) 1 x 1,102lb (500kg) bomb on bomb-rack	1 x 551lb (250kg) bomb under fuselage	1,764lb (800kg) of bombs/explosives carried internally and impact-detonated by nose-mounted rod	3,527lb (1600kg) of bombs carried internally	2 x 1,764lb (800kg) bombs or 1 x 6,393lb (2900kg) explosive charge carried internally and impact-detonated by nose-mounted rod
Crew:	1	Normal: 5; Kamikaze: 1	Normal: 4; Kamikaze: 1	Normal: 8; Kamikaze: 2 or 3	Normal: 6-8; Kamikaze: 3
Number built:	11,291 (A6M, all types)	798	1,408 (Ki-48-II, all types)	669	698 (Ki-67, all types)

*Unless otherwise indicated, all data refer to A6M5 Model 52, which flew the first "official" kamikaze missions. The A6M7 Model 63, designed with a bomb-rack, is sometimes said to have been specifically intended for "special attack" operations.

Note; Many other aircraft types of the Imperial Japanese Navy and Army flew "special attack" missions with no modification other than an improvised bomb-rack or -shackle where necessary.

High-Level and Low-Level Attacks

At first sight, the high-level attack method recommended to the kamikaze appears to be the simplest and potentially most destructive approach. It consisted of an approach to the target at c.20,000ft (6100m) and a dive at a shallow angle from the point of visual sighting, up to 10 miles (16km) away, to a position above the target, culminating in a crash-dive from c.5-6,000ft (1500-1850m) at a near-vertical angle. At this angle, radar-guided heavy AA was "blind" and the ship had little time for evasive action, while a high terminal velocity maximized damage. However, many kamikaze pilots lacked sufficient skill to hold an aircraft on course in a full-power dive, while making adjustments for wind and target movement. Experienced pilots, in aircraft not designed as divebombers, sometimes lowered their landing-gear to act as dive-brakes. (The "Val" had fixed landing-gear: Zeros diving in this way may have been misidentified, thus leading to the conflict of views mentioned above.)

At Iwo Jima and Okinawa, low-level attacks were much more common. An IJA manual for kamikaze, issued in February 1945, included diagrams and tables showing the altitudes, diving angles and speeds recommended for attacks by ten different aircraft types, ranging from the fast, twin-engined "Dinah" to the Tachikawa Ki-9 "Spruce" biplane trainer. The approach to the target was still to be

Recommended methods of **kamikaze** attack, adapted from an instruction manual issued by the Imperial Japanese Army in February 1945. Note that the two upper diagrams show the approaches recommended to pilots attacking warships other than aircraft carriers.

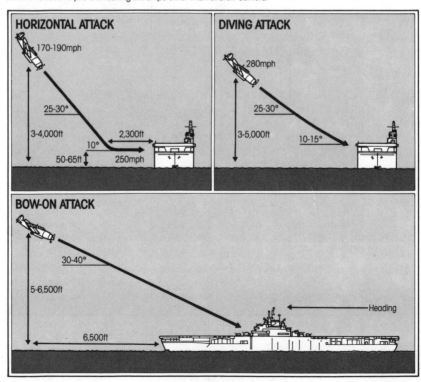

made at high altitude, but within c.5 miles (8km) of the objective the kamikaze were to descend to c.150-350ft (45-110m) for a high-speed run-in, zooming to c.1,500ft (450m) immediately before the terminal dive. Alternatively, the aircraft might hold a level course for a horizontal collision. The simplest of all methods recommended was a shallow dive from c.5,000ft (1500m).

Allied Countermeasures to Kamikaze Attack

"The best defence against the suicide bomber", stated the US Navy in May 1945, "is a well trained and coordinated CIC [Combat Information Centre; a director post in each ship, with one ship in the group, usually the flagship, providing the CIS, the central coordination of all combat information] and fighter plane team". The measures taken by the Japanese to confuse FDOs and CICs are described above. They proved effective in the Philippines where, according to USN estimates, only 17 per cent of all kamikaze encountered were knocked down by CAPs, as compared to 50 per cent falling to AA fire. Even after the measures (described below) taken to improve CAP cover in December 1944 onward, AA remained the major killer of those kamikaze which succeeded in making contact with their targets.

The only sure way to stop a kamikaze, remarked a USN bulletin, was "total disintegration"—and the weapon for this was the 5in (127mm) Dual-Purpose (DP) gun of the US Navy and its Allied equivalents. From January 1943 onward, these heavy AA weapons could fire shells equipped with the British-invented, US-developed proximity (or "influence") fuze, with an inbuilt radio transmitter-receiver which "bounced" its signals off a solid object—eg, an aircraft—and detonated the shell when the intervals between "bounces" were at their shortest. So effective was the proximity fuze in 1943-44 that the US Navy's official historian states that it was the major factor in forcing the Japanese to adopt kamikaze tactics. Even without proximity fuzes, the 5in AA, with radar and computer guidance that trained, elevated, set time fuzes and fired the guns, was the most effective weapon against kamikaze, supplemented at closer range by a wall of fire put up by 40mm and 20mm mounts (see Table on next page).

Guided missiles were considered for anti-kamikaze use, notably the British "Stooge" missile, under development by Fairey Aviation from early 1944. This radio-guided missile, 7.54ft (2.3m) long and weighing 738lb (335kg) with a 220lb (100kg) warhead, resembled a small pilotless aircraft. Blasted off from a 10ft (3m) ramp, small enough to be fitted aboard a warship, it could reach a climbing speed of up to 500mph (804kmh) and had a range of c.8 miles (13km). Successfully flown from February 1945 onward, it never reached operational status. It was also suggested that German scientists captured at Peenemünde in May 1945 should be assigned to a crash programme to bring the more powerful *Wasserfall* ("Waterfall") liquid-fuelled, radio-guided AA missile into anti-kamikaze service. With a range of c.22 miles (35km), a proximity-fuzed 320lb (145kg) warhead, and a maximum speed exceeding Mach 1, *Wasserfall* had been flown, with varying success, from February 1944 onward.

ANTI-AIRCRAFT GUNS OF THE U.S. NAVY IN 1945			
Type:	5in (127mm) Dual Purpose (DP)	40mm AA	20mm AA
Projectile weight:	54lb (24.5kg)	2lb (0.9kg)	0.5lb(0.23kg)
Muzzle velocity:	2,600f/s (792m/s)	2,800f/s (853m/s)	2,725f/s (831m/s)
Horizontal range:	18,000yd (16 460m)	11,000yd (10 060m)	5,000yd (4570m)
Vertical range/ceiling:	12,500yd (11 430m)	5,000yd (4570m)	c.2,000yd (1830m)
Rate of fire Maximum: Sustained:	22rpm 15rpm	160rpm c.120rpm	450rpm c.300rpm
Typical mountings "Iowa" BB "Essex" CV "Independence" CVL "Casablanca" CVE "New Orleans" CA "Cleveland" CL "Fletcher" DD "John C. Butler" DE (Royal Navy) "King George V" BB "Illustrious" CV "S"/"T" DD	 20 (10 x 2) 12 (4 x 2; 4 x 1) None (in 1945) 1 (1 x 1) 8 (8 x 1) 12 (6 x 2) 5 (5 x 1) 2 (2 x 1) 16 (5.25in DP) (8 x 2) 16 (4.5in DP) (8 x 2) 4 (4.7in DP) (4 x 1)	 60-80 (15-20 x 4) 44 (11 x 4) 38 (4 x 4; 11 x 2) 16 (8 x 2) 16 (4 x 4) 28 (4 x 4; 6 x 2) 6-10 (3-5 x 2) 4-10 (2 x 2 or 1 x 4; 3 x 2) 8 (2 x 4) (and 16-40 2pdr AA) c.5-10 (x 1) (and 48 2pdr AA) 2 (1 x 2)	 49-60 (49-60 x 1) 44 (44 x 1) 40 (40 x 1) 24 (24 x 1) 19 (19 x 1) 21 (21 x 1) 7-11 (7-11 x 1) 10-16 (10 x 1 or 3 x 2; 10 x 1) 16-40 (x 1 and x 2) 40 (18 x 2; 4 x 1) 8-12 (4 x 2 or 6 x 2)

Note: Mountings of AA armament sometimes varied between ships of the same class; an attempt has been made to show guns actually carried, regardless of the authorised provision.

Evasive Tactics: Kamikaze versus Destroyer

Even with the weight of AA fire at the disposal of the Allied ships, it was difficult to stop a kamikaze aircraft on its run-in. Japanese training manuals stressed the importance of evasive tactics up to the last moment; and although many pilots lacked the skill to do more than head straight into defensive AA fire, others proved harder to hit.

On 25 March 1945, just before the Okinawa invasion (when US reports noted that a higher proportion of obviously skilled pilots were making kamikaze attacks), the "Fletcher" class destroyer USS *Kimberly* was the subject of an attack by two "Vals". When 5in fire was opened at 7,500yds (6860m), both briefly turned away out of range. Then a single Val began its run-in. The destroyer manoeuvred to keep the maximum number of guns bearing, but fire control, in the words of *Kimberly*'s combat report, was "further complicated by the pilot's radical maneuvers, including zooming, climbing, slipping, skidding, accelerating, decelerating and even slow rolling". At 4,000yds (3660m), 40mm fire was opened, but although the Val "seemed to be completely surrounded with 5in bursts and 40mm tracers", the Japanese pilot banked sharply and then bored in from c.1,500yds (1370m) at an altitude of c.150ft (45m) towards the destroyer's stern, "performing continuous right and left skids". *Kimberly* was turning on full right rudder, but "the target skidded to always remain inside the ship's wake". Inside 1,200yds (1100m), when 20mm fire was opened and the aircraft began trailing smoke, "only the after guns would bear and each 5in salvo blasted the 20mm crews off their feet". Scarfed with flame and raked by automatic fire by gunners lying back almost prone to bring their weapons to bear, the Val swept in over the destroyer's stern, aiming for the bridge, and crashed aft the rear stack between two 5in mounts, its bomb exploding almost instantaneously.

(Note that all the action described in this paragraph took place inside one minute; on average, ships' AA had no more than 20 seconds in which to destroy a kamikaze once it came within range.)

The "Big Blue Blanket"

On 24-26 November 1944, the US Pacific Fleet's high command met in conference at Pearl Harbor to discuss the kamikaze menace. As a result, significant changes were made in the US Navy's dispositions of aircraft and ships.

First came a change in the aircraft complements of the carriers of Task Force 38 (TF 38; the US Fast Carrier Force). From December onward, an "Essex"-class CV, previously with an establishment of c.38-45 fighters, 36 divebombers and 18 torpedo-planes, carried some 73 fighters (or more; *Wasp* had more than 100 in January 1945) and only 15 divebombers and 15 torpedo-planes. Some compensation for the loss of strike power was achieved by progressive modification of the fighters—F6F Hellcats and, from late December, F4U Corsairs—to carry up to 2,000lb, 900kg, bombloads. At about the same time, as kamikaze attacks by night intruders (which sometimes tried to "ride down" the streams of tracer emitted by their targets) increased, USS *Enterprise* (CV 6) began operating as a night carrier, with 27 radar-carrying TBM-3D Avengers to locate targets and guide 18 radar-equipped F6F-5N/P Hellcats to interceptions. The light carrier USS *Independence* had been operating 9 Avengers and 16 Hellcats in a similar role since August 1944, and soon some other carriers would have a proportion of night-fighters and guides.

With increased fighter complements, the carriers could strengthen CAPs and also pursue a policy of pre-emptive strikes against the kamikaze. In support of the Mindoro landing operations, on 14-16 December, a daytime force of some 500 Hellcats, supported by around 40 night-fighters, swarmed over the Japanese airfields on Luzon. The fighter umbrella, called the "Big Blue Blanket" from the dark-blue livery of the US fighters, destroyed more than 170 Japanese aircraft, many on the ground or soon after take-off, at a cost of only 27 US planes. Damage by kamikaze to the invasion fleet was light.

Defensive Formation and Radar Pickets

By December 1944 also, TF 38 had been regrouped into three Task Groups, rather than four, for better close-in AA defence. A typical Fast Carrier Task Group now comprised 2-3 heavy carriers (CV), 2 light carriers (CVL), 2-3 battleships, 3-5 heavy and light cruisers (CA and CL, and including an AA-cruiser, CLAA; USS *San Diego* and *San Juan* had added AA armament for this role), and 18-20 destroyers. In the standard AA defence formation, one heavy carrier steamed at the centre of a circle of 2,000yds (1830m) radius formed by the remaining carriers, with the battleships, cruisers and destroyers in an outer cirlce of c.4,000yds (3660m) radius. Normally, course and speed were set by the central carrier, the ships manoeuvring independently only to avoid such immediate threats as torpedoes. Under kamikaze attack, more flexibility was necessary, although fighting instructions continued to stress that concentration of AA fire and continual fighter cover were more important than manoeuvre as anti-kamikaze measures.

But Vice-Admiral J.S. McCain, commanding TF 38 in December 1944, was determined that the kamikaze must be stopped before reaching the task groups. With Rear-Admiral W.D. Baker and Captain J.S. Thach (after whom the "Thach Weave", a scissoring manoeuvre for mutual support by a pair of aircraft, was named), McCain evolved a system for which many destroyermen — and many kamikaze — were to curse him, but which undoubtedly saved many Allied carriers from destruction or damage.

Destroyers fitted with best available radar and homing equipment were disposed on picket lines up to 60 miles (95km) from the carrier groups, not only to give early warning of the kamikaze's approach but also to direct interceptions. The picket ships had their own guardian fighters: "Jack Patrols", that made low-level sweeps outside the screen; and CAPs controlled by designated "Tom Cat" destroyers. All US carrier aircraft returning from strikes were instructed to circle the "Tom Cats" so that they could be "de-loused" of kamikaze attempting to tag along. Kamikaze might be identified visually or through IFF (Identification, Friend or Foe), an electronic device in Allied aircraft that automatically responded (when switched on; there were numerous instances of pilots who neglected this precaution and were shot down by friendly forces) to a radar pulse from a ship or shore station.

But all countermeasures could not prevent some kamikaze from reaching the carrier groups. During the Lingayen landings of January 1945 (before the introduction of radar pickets), some 80 kamikaze sorties by IJN aircraft resulted in the sinking of the escort carrier USS *Ommaney Bay,* serious damage to two escort carriers and lesser damage to two more. Two large transports and a minesweeper were also sunk and some 20 other warships suffered varying degrees of damage. During the Iwo Jima campaign of February-March 1945 (when fighter sweeps over the kamikaze's airfields in Kyushu were launched from fast carrier groups, and strikes by B-29s were stepped-up), only one escort carrier was lost to suicide attack, USS *Bismarck Sea* on 21 February. On the same day, the fleet carrier *Saratoga* took five hits from a wave of six kamikaze Zeros inside three minutes and then, one hour later, one more hit from a group of five, killing 123 of her crew and wounding 192. The veteran carrier went stateside for repair, doing no further combat duty.

Date: **11 March 1945**
Place: **Ulithi atoll, Western Carolines**
Attack by: **Yokosuka P1Y1 "Frances" kamikaze bombers**
Target: **US Navy Task Force 58 at anchor**

The US Navy's fleet anchorage at Ulithi atoll in the Western Carolines had, as described in Chapter 5, first been the target of "special attack" by *kaiten* human torpedoes, in late 1944. In March 1945, when Task Force 58 (ie, the Fast Carrier Task Force when commanded by Vice-Admiral Marc A. Mitscher) lay there preparing for pre-Okinawa strikes at the Japanese home islands, it was the objective of a kamikaze raid which, because it was better-planned than most, is worth describing in some detail.

For "Operation *Tan*", the IJN formed at Kanoya, southern Kyushu, the *Azusa* Special Attack Unit, to which were allocated 24 of the newly-operational Yokosuka P1Y1 *Ginga* (Milky Way; "Frances") twin-engined medium bombers. These fine aircraft had a maximum speed of 340mph (547kmh) and, with a normal range of 1,192 miles (1918km) and a maximum 3,338 miles (5317km), the c.1,400-mile (2253km) flight to Ulithi, each carrying a single 1,764lb (800kg) bomb, was within their range. (According to some sources, the Franceses staged at Minami Jima, some 800 miles, 1290km, north of Ulithi.) For once, pre-strike reconnaissance was not neglected: on 9 March a Nakajima C6N *Saiun* (Painted Cloud; "Myrt") flew from Truk over Ulithi and reported no fewer than 15 carriers at anchor. Although initial garbling of the message from Truk to Kanoya resulted in the operation being aborted on 10 March, the 24 Franceses, preceded by a patrol of four "Betty" bombers and guided by four flying-boats, took off at c.0900 on 11 March.

It must be assumed that the recently-delivered Franceses had not been fully proved, for 13 of them developed engine trouble and dropped out en route. Bad weather delayed the formation, and after the guiding aircraft were forced to leave the strike group at c.1830 the force had difficulty in locating its target. A Japanese account states that all 11 Franceses remaining eventually made crash-dives at Ulithi, but since US reports speak of only two attackers it may well be that more bombers were forced to ditch before the atoll was sighted at c.1930, after dark.

Principal **kamikaze** airfields and bases of midget submarines and explosive motorboats in the Ryukyu Islands prior to "Operation Iceberg", the Allied invasion of Okinawa on 1 April 1945.

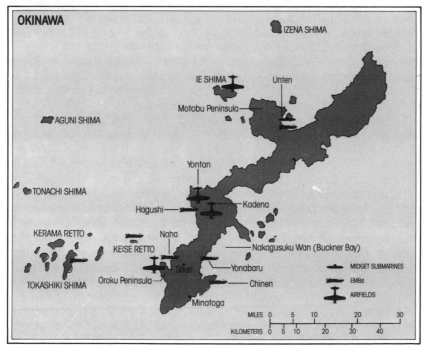

Supposedly secure behind a radar screen and defensive air patrols, workshops ashore at Ulithi were brightly lit, and although blackout was observed aboard the carriers, transports alongside loading stores were also lit up. Aboard the heavy carrier *Randolph*, many men were at a cinema show on the hangar deck when a single Frances smashed into the deck aft. Twentythree men died and sufficient damage was done to keep *Randolph* out of action for a fortnight. A second Frances crash-dived harmlessly into a coral reef and any other bombers that had succeeded in reaching the atoll must have plunged into the sea, aiming blindly at shadows, as an immediate and total blackout shrouded the fleet.

Even without *Randolph*, TF 58 struck heavily at the kamikaze's bases on Kyushu on 19-22 March, claiming the destruction of 528 Japanese aircraft. Kamikaze counterattacks (including the first use of the *ohka* piloted-bomb, described later in this chapter) failed to inflict significant damage on the carriers—although the destroyer *Halsey Powell* was crippled by a kamikaze that narrowly missed *Hancock* (CV 19)—but the heavy carrier *Franklin* was put out of the war, with a toll of 724 dead and 265 wounded, by a conventional bombing attack (*not* by kamikaze, as some sources state).

Date: **6 April-22 June 1945**
Place: **Okinawa, Ryukyu Islands**
Attack by: **"Kikusui" kamikaze aircraft of the IJN and IJA**
Target: **Allied warships and invasion transports**

Both the Allies and the Japanese knew well that Okinawa in the Ryukyus, only about 330 miles (530km) south of Kyushu, was the major "stepping-stone" for the invasion of the home islands. Yet by dusk on 1 April 1945, the first day of "Operation Iceberg", more than 50,000 US troops had crossed the invasion beaches virtually unopposed. LtGen Mitsuru Ushijima had concentrated his forces around strong-points in the interior. But in spite of their soft landing, the Allies rightly expected a struggle no less bitter and bloody than those at Guadalcanal, Saipan and Iwo Jima—and they were determined that Ushijima should receive no help from seaward.

The huge invasion fleet was shielded from attack, whether from kamikaze or conventional aircraft or from surface or submersible craft, and the way for potential blockade runners from Japan blocked, by a complex and efficient defensive screen. Under Vice-Admiral Richmond K. Turner's direction, transports lay close to the beaches at all times, instead of retiring seaward at nightfall, and were always ready to raise a smokescreen at short notice. Between the transports and the beaches, patrolling LCIs (landing craft, infantry) kept watch and "fly-catcher" flotillas of LCI(G)s (landing craft, gunboat) and smaller craft, mounting every available automatic weapon, each group with an attendant destroyer or light cruiser, stood constant guard.

On the outer fringes of the transports' area, destroyers formed an anti-submarine screen, while more destroyers and destroyer-escorts held an anti-submarine cordon extending in a wide sweep from the Motobu peninsula in northwest Okinawa to Ara Saki on the south, taking in the Kerama Retto group (where a major US supply and repair base was built). A group of at least five destroyers and DEs steamed nightly across the routes which blockade runners might use. Finally, up to 100 miles (160km) from the beaches, destroyers and DMSs ("Bristol" class destroyers re-rated as high-speed minesweepers, with torpedo tubes and the aft 5in turret removed), supported by LCI(G)s with 40mm AA in every available mount, manned the radar picket stations as the first line of defence against the kamikaze. Between 8 and 12 of the 16 designated stations were manned at all times, the ships patrolling on a 5,000yd (4570m) circle with a CAP permanently overhead.

British Carriers in Action
In the immediate pre-invasion period, the important task of interdicting Japanese air strength in the southern Ryukyus went to Task Force 57, the Royal Navy force of 4 heavy carriers, 2 battleships, 5 cruisers and 11 destroyers, commanded by Vice-Admiral B. Rawlings, RN. A British heavy carrier operated on average only c.54 aircraft (typically some 38 fighters — Supermarine Seafires, Fairey Fireflies, Hellcats and Corsairs — and 16 Avengers) compared to the 80-plus of their USN equivalents. However, the 3in (76mm) armoured flight decks that contributed to this lesser capability proved invaluable against the kamikaze.

Early on 1 April, off Sakishima Gunto, three of a group of seven Zeros broke through TF 57's CAP. Two were shot down by a single Seafire, but the third achieved an optimum kamikaze hit — on HMS *Indefatigable*'s flight deck at the base of the island. Fourteen men were killed and 16 wounded, but within a few hours *Indefatigable* was again operating her aircraft: the same hit on a USN heavy carrier, it was estimated, would have necessitated lengthy repairs at a well-equipped base.

Kamikaze at Okinawa: the Statistics
On the Japanese side, the threat to the home islands posed at Okinawa partly succeeded, as nothing else ever did, in forcing the IJN, with its surface forces now practically non-existent, and IJA to abandon their bitter rivalry. Now they would cooperate in planning and launching air attacks in which their kamikaze and conventional aircraft operations would be coordinated.

No two sources agree on the total number of aircraft committed at Okinawa: the figures given by the USSBS and accepted by British official histories — a total of c.1,900 kamikaze sorties and c.5,000 conventional sorties — seem to me the most acceptable. The US Navy's historian puts the number of kamikaze sorties at above 3,000, out of a total of some 6,300 sorties. Takushiro Hattori's "General History of the Pacific Battle" (quoted by Nagatsuka) gives a total of 2,571 kamikaze sorties at Okinawa in the period 3 March-16 August: 1,637 by IJN aircraft, 934 by the IJA. Overall, it seems safe to say that the total number of "official" kamikaze sorties at Okinawa from 1 April onward was around 2,000, of which at least 60 per cent were made by IJN aircraft, as compared to 5,000-plus sorties by conventional aircraft. Estimates of the number of Japanese aircraft lost at

Okinawa, in reliable sources, range from 4,100 to 7,830; Allied aircraft losses in the same period (26 March-22 June) are officially stated as 763, including 98 British aircraft.

The accompanying Table, compiled from a variety of sources, illustrates the comparative effectiveness of kamikaze and conventional aircraft at Okinawa. It agrees fairly closely with the British official histories, which give overall figures of 24-26 ships sunk and 176-202 damaged. The US Navy historian's figures are higher — 34 ships sunk and 368 damaged, with more than 4,900 US sailors killed and 4,800 wounded. What is beyond argument is that the kamikaze once again proved far more effective than conventional air attack.

Mass Attacks by Kamikaze

Between 6 April and 22 June, the main kamikaze thrust against Allied shipping at Okinawa was made in 10 mass attacks by aircraft of both the IJN and IJA. These were called by the Japanese the *Kikusui* ("Floating Crysanthemum") attacks, a name common in "special attack" operations; its derivation is described in Chapter 5.

The first and largest of the kikusui offensives was made on 6-7 April, when a total of 355 kamikaze (230 IJN; 125 IJA) and 341 conventional aircraft was committed. In spite of an interdiction strike

---

ALLIED SHIPS SUNK/DAMAGED BY AIR ATTACK IN THE OKINAWA AREA, 20 MARCH-13 AUGUST 1945

Type	SUNK BY KAMIKAZE	SUNK BY CONVENTIONAL AIR ATTACK	DAMAGED BY KAMIKAZE	DAMAGED BY CONVENTIONAL AIR ATTACK
Battleship (BB)	–	–	10	–
Aircraft carrier (CV)	–	–	12	1
Aircraft carrier, small (CVL)	–	–	1	–
Aircraft carrier, escort (CVE)	–	–	3	–
Heavy cruiser (CA)	–	–	2	–
Light cruiser (CL)	–	–	2	–
Destroyer (DD)	9	1	63	13
Destroyer escort (DE)	–	–	19	4
Submarine (SS)	–	–	–	1
Light minelayer (DM)	–.	–	12	1
High speed minesweeper (DMS)	1	–	17	2
Minelayer (CM)	–	–	1	–
Minesweeper (AM)	1	–	9	4
Submarine chaser (PC)	1	–	1	–
Attack transport (APA)	–	–	9	1
High speed transport (APD)	3	2	14	3
Other auxiliaries/ landing ships	2	3	23	11
"Liberty" ships	–	–	19	4
"Victory" ships	3	–	–	–
Total	20	6	217	45

Note: In the case of figures for ships damaged; several ships were struck more than once and these figures refer to the number of hits made.

It should also be noted that a number of the ships shown as damaged only were, in fact, subsequently scrapped, or were not repaired until after the war.

at dawn on the Kyushu airfields by Allied carrier planes, some 400 Japanese aircraft sortied against Okinawa on 6 April, making their heaviest strikes in the afternoon (as the *Yamato* task force began its suicide run to Okinawa; see Chapter 3). Although early warning was given by radar pickets and US pilots claimed to have destroyed more than 300 Japanese aircraft (reporting that many of the kamikaze pilots appeared to lack basic skills), some 40 kamikaze hits or near-misses were recorded. A major blow to US ground forces was the sinking by kamikaze of the 7,600-ton (7722 tonne) transports *Hobbs Victory* and *Logan Victory*, carrying most of 10th Army's mortar ammunition: the offensive against Ushijima's southern stronghold was temporarily stalled. In addition, two destroyers, a DMS and an LST were sunk; three destroyers and a DE were damaged so badly that they were subsequently scrapped; and a destroyer, a DMS and a minesweeper received damage that put them out of the war for good.

In this first kikusui attack, there became apparent a pattern that would be repeated throughout. On Picket Stations No 1 and 2, some 50 miles (80km) north of Okinawa, the destroyers *Bush* and *Colhoun* (DD 801) had escaped damage from conventional bombers earlier in the day. But at about 1500, kamikaze struck en masse: more than 40 aircraft began to circle above *Bush* at between 500 and 20,000ft (150-6100m), peeling off in ones, twos or threes for attacking runs. The ship's AA knocked down two Vals and drove off others, but at 1503 a lone Nakajima B6N2 "Jill" torpedo-bomber made a 7,000yd (6400m) run at sea-level through the destroyer's full broadside fire to smash down between the ship's stacks. The detonation of its 1,764lb (800kg) bomb in the forward engine room knocked out all power: with fire breaking out and her 5in AA jammed in train, *Bush* lay dead and listing almost helpless in the water.

Although *Bush* appeared to be in a sinking condition, kamikaze continued to concentrate on her (a frequent tactical fault already noted). *Colhoun* closed in with her 12-strong CAP, but the fighters were low on fuel and reinforcements dispatched from the carrier group met strong Japanese formations and failed to arrive. Now facing some 15 attackers, Cdr R. Westholm of *Bush* ordered 150 of his men to abandon ship while the remainder manned the 40mm mounts. *Colhoun* had meanwhile splashed three Zeros within a few minutes; then a Zero struck her main deck, starting fires and cutting speed by more than half. At 1717, with kamikaze still arriving, two Vals and a Zero made simultaneous dives on *Colhoun*. The destroyer's 5in claimed one Val; *Bush* and the supporting *LCS-84* got another; the Zero struck *Colhoun* forward, knocking out all power.

At 1725, seven kamikaze headed in on *Colhoun* from varying angles, while more dived on *Bush*. *Colhoun* took another hit, holing her below the waterline; *Bush* was almost cut in half by a Zero that crashed amidships. At 1745, yet another Zero hit the shattered *Bush*, setting her afire end to end, and at 1830, after *Colhoun* had taken yet another Zero hit, *Bush* broke apart and sank. Of her 307-strong crew, 94 were dead and 33 wounded. *Colhoun*, with 35 dead and 21 wounded, was ablaze and slowly sinking; late that night, she was abandoned and sunk by gunfire from the destroyer *Cassin Young*.

Self-Defeating Tactics

Again and again during the kikusui offensives, kamikaze were to waste their strength against the radar pickets, often making repeated attacks on ships that were already obviously doomed. It is said that one picket destroyer's crew erected on the stern of their ship an enormous pointing arrow, with the legend: "TO JAP SUICIDERS— CARRIERS ARE *THAT* WAY"! Of 33 destroyers deployed on picket duty during the Okinawa campaign, six were sunk and 18 damaged (13 seriously), and of the AA-armed landing vessels supporting them, four were sunk and eight damaged. It was estimated that more than 300 kamikaze attacks (ie, perhaps 15 per cent of *all* kamikaze sorties at Okinawa) were made during April on Picket Station No 1 alone. The accompanying Diagram details the most spectacular of these attacks, on USS *Laffey* (DD 724) on 16 April.

But in subjecting the radar pickets to this ordeal the kamikaze were defeating their own ends: the carriers and, even more important at Okinawa, the invasion transports were their essential targets if they were to affect the course of the campaign. This they failed to do.

Date: **July-August 1945**
Place: **Ulithi atoll, Western Carolines**
Attack by: **Submarine-launched Aichi M6A1 Special Attack bombers**
Target: **US fleet anchorage**

Kamikaze sorties from the home islands following the loss of Okinawa are described in Chapter 6; but one unusual, although abortive, plan for the offensive rather than the defensive deployment of kamikaze aircraft may be described here.

Early in 1943, the IJN began construction of the first of its *Sen-Toku* (*STo;* "Submarine, Special") boats, the largest submarines of World War II. Each of these 400ft (122m) long monsters had a normal displacement of 5,223 tons (5306 tonnes) surfaced and 6,560 tons (6665 tonnes) submerged. With a horizontal rather than the conventional vertical figure-eight hull form, the STo boats were 39.3ft (12m) in beam and incorporated a 102ft (31m) long hangar amidships, to house three seaplane-bombers for catapult-launching from an 86ft (26.2m) ramp forward. Only three of the projected 18 STo boats— *I-400*, *I-401* and *I-402*—were completed; but to supplement them in the submersible aircraft-carrier role, the large *Kai-Ko* ("Modified A-Class") boats *I-13* and *I-14* (3,603/4,762 tons, 3660/4838 tonnes; 372.75ft, 113.7m, long overall) were modified during building to carry and launch two seaplane-bombers.

Aichi Kokuki K.K. designed and built a special aircraft for these submarines: the Aichi M6A1 *Seiran* ("Mountain Haze"), with detachable floats and folding wings and tail surfaces for storage in the submarines' hangars, whence, it was estimated four skilled men could prepare the Seiran for launching inside seven minutes. Although the original role of the submarines was said to be long-range reconnaissance for the surface fleet (the STo boats had a 37,500-mile, 60,340km, action radius at 14kt), with possible air strikes on targets of opportunity, it is likely that "special attack" operations figured in planning from an early stage. By December 1944, when *I-400* and *I-13* were completed, it

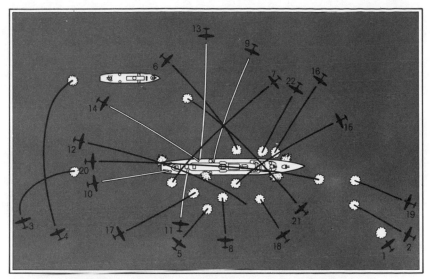

The destroyer USS **Laffey** (DD 724) is attacked by 22 **kamikaze** aircraft out of a 50-strong swarm in a period of 80 minutes, on Radar Picket Station No 1 at Okinawa during the third **Kikusui** mass suicide offensive, 16 April 1945. **Laffey** (6 x 5in DP; 12 x 40mm; 11 x 20mm) receives support from **LCS-51** (6 x 40mm), stationed some 500-900yds (460-820m) to port. Events in sequence:

(1) 0827. The **kamikaze** begin their attack while **Laffey** awaits the arrival of a new CAP. A "Val" is shot down by the destroyer's 5in fire at 9,000yds (8230m) range.
(2) 0830. "Val" shot down by **Laffey**'s AA at 3,000yds (2740m).
(3) 0830. Another "Val" shot down by **Laffey**'s AA at 3,000yds (2740m).
(4) 0830. "Val" shot down by **LCS-51**.
(5) 0835. "Judy" shot down by **Laffey**'s 40mm and 20mm fire at 3,000yds (2740m).
(6) 0835. "Judy" shot down by **Laffey**'s AA close to port; explosion damages fire-control radar.
(7) 0839. "Val" glances off stern hatch on **Laffey** and splashes a few feet away.
(8) 0843. Aircraft shot down by **Laffey**'s 40mm and 20mm fire. Cdr Frederick J. Becton is manoeuvring his ship brilliantly: he will succeed in taking most damage astern and preserving full engine power throughout.
(9) 0845. KAMIKAZE HIT. "Judy" strikes 20mm/40mm mounts aft, starting fires with burning fuel.
(10) 0847. KAMIKAZE HIT. "Val" strikes aft.
(11) 0847. KAMIKAZE HIT. Aircraft strikes No 3 5in mount.
(12) 0848. BOMB HIT. "Val" drops bomb which strikes aft, crosses ship, and escapes.
(13) 0849. KAMIKAZE HIT. Aircraft strikes after deck house.
(14) 0850. KAMIKAZE HIT. After deck house struck a second time; fire and flooding aft; all remaining guns now firing under local control.
(15) 0850 **Laffey**'s new CAP has now arrived. With a Corsair on its tail, an "Oscar" strikes
    –0945. the destroyer's mast before splashing to starboard. The Corsair, having followed the **kamikaze** through **Laffey**'s AA barrage, is also shot down; its pilot bales out.
(16)   BOMB HIT. A "Judy" is shot down by CAP close to the port bow, after its bomb damages No 2 5in mount. Cdr Becton declares his intention "never to abandon ship as long as a gun will fire".
(17)   "Judy" shot down by 20mm and 40mm AA at 800yds (730m).
(18)   "Oscar" shot down by 5in AA at 500yds (460m).
(19)   "Val" shot down by No 2 5in AA at 600yds (550m).
(20)   KAMIKAZE HIT/BOMB HIT. A "Val" flies the length of the ship, dropping a bomb which strikes aft, glances off the starboard yardarm, and is shot down by CAP.
(21)   BOMB HIT. "Val" crosses **Laffey**, dropping bomb which strikes 20mm mount forward, and is shot down by CAP.
(22) 0947. "Judy" is shot down by combined CAP and ship's AA fire. **Laffey** now has only four 20mm guns still firing.

The attack ends at c.0950. **Laffey** has 31 men dead and 72 wounded; her rudder is jammed and she is burning and flooded aft. She is taken in tow to Hagushi, Okinawa, for temporary repair, and within a week is able to proceed to Guam under her own power.

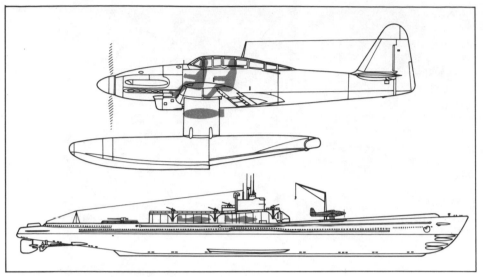

The Aichi M6A1 **Seiran** ("Mountain Haze") seaplane-bomber was specially designed to be carried by and launched from the giant **STo**-type submarines of the IJN for **kamikaze** missions.

was thought that they might be used to launch strikes (obviously kamikaze raids, for moral rather than material effect) against New York and/or Washington, D.C.

(The Japanese only twice succeeded in bombing the American mainland. On 28-29 August and 9-10 September 1942, the submarine *I-25* launched a Yokosuka E14Y1 "Glen" seaplane which dropped a total of four 167lb (76kg) incendiaries in coastal Oregon, vainly hoping to set forest fires. In November 1944-March 1945, the IJA's "Special Balloon Regiment" launched from east Honshu some 9,300 *Fu-Go*—layered-paper balloons, hydrogen-filled and about 35ft (10.7m) in diameter—to drift some 6,000 miles (9650km) in the prevailing winds across the Pacific and fall in the USA. Fu-Go, each carrying two small incendiaries and a 35lb (15.9kg) anti-personnel bomb, were found from Alaska to Mexico—but the only casualties were one woman and five children who unwisely approached a specimen at Lakeview, Oregon, in May 1945. All attempts to produce a bomber capable of a return trip to the US mainland came to nothing.)

In May 1945, *I-400, I-401, I-13* and *I-14,* under the overall command of Capt Tatsunoke Ariizumi, formed Submarine Squadron 1 (SubRon 1). By this time, mainly at Ariizumi's urging, US mainland targets had been abandoned in favour of a more practical attack on the Gatun Locks of the Panama Canal. Air raids on the Aichi workshops, fuel shortages that hindered pilot training in the specially-formed 901st Air Group, and air-dropped mines that interfered with submarine exercises in the Inland Sea, delayed the programme; but by mid-June the Seiran pilots had joined SubRon 1 for pre-mission training against full-sized mock-ups of the Gatun Locks in Toyama Bay, Honshu.

The four boats of SubRon 1 were to sail to Oahu on the route taken by the Pearl Harbor attack force in December 1941. Then they would head south for the Colombian coast; then move stealthily northward in coastal waters to launch all 10 of their bombers, each with one 1,764lb (800kg) bomb or torpedo, when within the Seirans' range (739 miles, 1190km) of the Panama Canal. The Seiran pilots would jettison the floats of their aircraft to increase speed in the terminal dive.

But before training was completed, the target was changed again. Now naval high command decided on a coordinated attack on the US fleet anchorage at Ulithi atoll by the aircraft of SubRon 1 and by *kaiten*-carrying submarines (see Chapter 5). Only *I-400* and *I-401* would launch Seiran; *I-13* and *I-14* were to carry crated Nakajima C6N1 "Myrt" long-range reconnaissance planes to Truk, where they would be assembled to scout over Ulithi in preparation for an attack that was planned to take place on 25 August.

I-13 (Cdr Ohashi) and *I-14* (Cdr Shimizu) sailed for Truk on 15 July. Next day, some 630 miles (1000km) east of Honshu, *I-13* was located by aircraft of a hunter-killer group headed by USS *Anzio* (CVE 57). Damaged by aircraft rockets, the submarine was finished off by "Hedgehog" rounds from the DE *Lawrence C. Taylor*. *I-400* (Cdr Utsunosuke Kusaka) and *I-401* (Cdr Shinsei Nambu) sailed later, separately, for a rendezvous off Ponape Island in the eastern Carolines, where they were to meet on 16 August and await orders to launch their aircraft. The end of the war on that day found them still waiting; their orders were to return to Japan and surrender. At the end of the month, when the ineffectual monsters entered Yokosuka naval base, Capt Ariizumi made honourable atonement for the failure of his "special attack" force by shooting himself.

JAPANESE PILOTED BOMBS
The Origin of the "Ohka"
The only purpose-designed suicide aircraft to reach full operational status in World War II was the Imperial Japanese Navy's Yokosuka MXY7 *Ohka* ("Cherry Blossom"), which the Allies called the *Baka* ("Idiot") bomb. The weapon, a piloted missile, was also known in Japan as the *Jinrai* ("Divine Thunderbolt").

Credit for the origin of the ohka is generally given to a junior officer, Ens Mitsuo Ohta, a transport pilot with the 405th Kokutai of the JNAF. However, it is fairly certain that discussion of a piloted bomb antedated Ohta's advocacy of a rocket-propelled, manned missile early in 1944. As in the case of other suicide weapons, the high command at first put up token resistance; but when preliminary designs drawn up by Ohta with the help of the Aeronautical Research Institute, University of Tokyo, were submitted to the Dai-Ichi Kaigun Koku Gijitsusho (First Naval Air Technical Arsenal) at Yokosuka, the decision to proceed with the weapon was quickly made. It is important to note that the ohka was approved — and the recruitment of personnel begun — in August 1944, some two months *before* Admiral Onishi's formation of the first "official" kamikaze squadrons.

A team headed by LtCdr Tadanao Miki worked intensively to produce 10 operational ohka by late September 1944, along with a number of unpowered models for flight trials. These trials, with both powered and unpowered models launched from beneath "Betty" bombers, began in October: the first powered flight was made at

175

Kashima, near Sasebo, by Lt Kazutoshi Nagano, who declared that the ohka handled "better than a Zero". His enthusiasm was not shared by other test pilots; one of whom described the aircraft as "a flying coffin". The IJN had, however, gone ahead with full production even before studying the results of the trials. Thus, the programme was not set back by the deaths in November of two test pilots: Lt Tsutomo Kariya, killed when his ohka stalled immediately after release from its parent aircraft; and CPO Kita, killed in a crash-landing.

The Ohka Model 11

The Ohka Model 11, of which 155 were built at Yokosuka and 600 by the Dai-Ichi Kaigun Kokusho (First Naval Air Arsenal) at Kasumigaura, between September 1944 and March 1945, was the only mark carried into action. The small mid-wing monoplane, with an alloy (duralumin) fuselage and wooden wings and stabilizers, was powered by three solid-propellant rockets mounted in the fuselage aft the cockpit. (See Table and Diagram for full technical details.)

The cockpit was surprisingly well-finished for a one-trip aircraft, as Allied observers noted when undamaged ohka were captured on Okinawa and elsewhere. The pilot's bucket-seat was protected by

(**Top**) **Ohka** Model 22, longer but lighter than the Model 11, for launching from a ``Frances'' bomber.
(**Centre**) **Ohka** Model 43 K-1 KAI, a powered trainer in which a second cockpit replaced the warhead.
(**Bottom**) **Ohka** Model 11: side and front elevations of the piloted bomb used operationally.

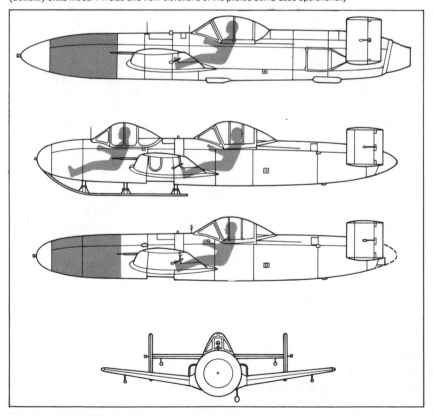

"OHKA" PILOTED BOMB: PRODUCTION MODELS				
Type:	MODEL 11	MODEL 22	K-1	MODEL 43 K-1 KAI WAKAZAKURA ("YOUNG CHERRY")
Span:	16.8ft (5.12m)	13.5ft (4.12m)	16.8ft (5.12m)	16.8ft (5.12m)
Length:	19.9ft (6.06m)	22.6ft (6.88m)	19.9ft (6.06m)	19.9ft (6.06m)
Height:	3.8ft (1.16m)	3.77ft (1.15m)	3.8ft (1.16m)	3.8ft (1.16m)
Wing area:	64.6sq ft (6sq m)	43sq ft (4sq m)	64.6sq ft (6sq m)	64.6sq ft (6sq m)
Maximum loaded weight:	4,718lb (2140kg)	3,197lb (1450kg)	4,718lb (2140kg)	4,718lb (2140kg)
Power:	3 x Type 4 Mk I Model 20 solid-propellant rockets with total thrust of 1,764lb (800kg)	1 x Tsu-11 turbojet with total thrust of 441lb (200kg)	None (replaced by water ballast)	Powered glider with one tail-mounted Type 4 Mk I Model 20 solid-propellant rocket with total thrust of 573lb (260kg)
Maximum speed Level:	403mph (649kmh) @ 11,500ft (3505m)	276mph (444kmh) @ 13,125ft (4000m)	n.a.	n.a.
Dive:	580mph (933kmh)	not known	n.a.	n.a.
Range:	c.20nm (23 miles, 37km)	c.70nm (80 miles, 130km)	n.a.	n.a.
Warhead:	2,646lb (1200kg) Tri-nitroaminol	1,323lb (600kg)	None (replaced by water ballast)	None (replaced by second cockpit)
Carried/Launched:	Mitsubishi G4M2e ("Betty") bomber	Yokosuka P1Y3 Model 33 Ginga ("Frances") bomber	Towed by trainer	Towed by trainer
Crew:	1	1	1	2
Number built:	755	50	45	2

0.3-0.6-inch (7.62-15.24mm) armour plate and had a rubber-padded head rest. The controls were kept simple, since the pilots would be given little flight training: besides a control column, instrumentation comprised rocket ignition switches, compass, altimeter, turn-and-bank and airspeed indicators, and an arming handle for the fuzes at the base of the warhead (an impact fuze was also mounted at the nose). The pilot had a quick-release cockpit catch: this was purely a token gesture, for his chance of baling out during his terminal dive was nonexistent. A simple sighting ring was mounted on the fuselage immediately forward of the windshield. Forward of the sight was the suspension lug, by which the ohka was slung beneath its carrier.

The Model 11 was designed to be carried beneath and launched from a Mitsubishi G4M2e Model 24J twin-engined bomber. In this variant of the G4M2 "Betty", the bomb-bay doors were removed to allow carriage of the ohka in a semi-recessed position beneath the bomber's belly, shackled to the mother plane by its suspension lug. The Betty's unprotected fuel tanks—armour having been sacrificed to range in its design—had already earned it the nickname of the "one-shot lighter" from US airmen: as an ohka carrier, increased weight and degradation of handling characteristics made it even more vulnerable.

The Divine Thunderbolt Corps

Personnel for ohka operations were recruited from among naval air units, where posters urging men to volunteer for "special attack" duties appeared in August 1944. Although the suicidal nature of the work was not concealed, volunteers were numerous: even when married men, elder and only sons and others with heavy family responsibilities were weeded out, some 600 men were quickly chosen.

On 1 October 1944, antedating the formation of the first kamikaze squadrons by some three weeks, the 721st Kokutai (Naval Air Corps)—nicknamed the *Jinrai Butai*, "Divine Thunderbolt Corps"—was formed at Hyakurigahara Naval Air Force Base in central Honshu. The commander was Cdr Motoharu Okamura, a veteran airman who, as commander of the 341st Air Group in the Tokyo area in June 1944, had been a major advocate of the formation of kamikaze squadrons, promising Vice-Admiral Shigeru Fukudome that he would "turn the tide of war" with 300 suicide aircraft. Fukudome had reported that conversation to Vice-Admiral Seiichi Ito of the Naval General Staff—and Okamura's enthusiasm was now rewarded. In charge of operations under Okamura were LtCdr Goro Nonaka and LtCdr Kunihiro Iwaki. In November the Jinrai Butai moved to Konoike NAFB northeast of Tokyo, where its organization was finalized. From late November, it consisted of four "Cherry Blossom Squadrons", each at first with some 10 ohka and 40 kamikaze Zeros. At first, the Zeros of 721st NAC were A6M5s, each carrying a 551lb (250kg) bomb; but from May 1945 the Corps was equipped with the new A6M7 Model 63, purpose-adapted for suicide attack and carrying a 1,102lb (500kg) bomb. These were nicknamed *Kembu* ("strengthening the warrior spirit") bombers. The Corps' bomber wing comprised the 708th and 711th Squadrons, each with 18 Mitsubishi G4M2e bombers as ohka carriers. Its escort wing comprised the 306th and 308th Squadrons, each with 36 Zero fighters.

Before being expended in suicide attacks, the Zero fighters attached to each Cherry Blossom Squadron were used to train ohka pilots. The first volunteers had been selected largely from pilots who had already received conventional training. Because of the shortage of time and fuel, their ohka training consisted largely of familiarization with the weapon on the ground; training in attack methods while flying a Zero with the engine switched off; and, for some, a single powered flight in an air-launched ohka fitted with landing skids and with water ballast replacing the warhead. Later in the programme, the Ohka K-1, an unpowered craft in which water ballast replaced both warhead and rocket motors, was introduced to allow less-experienced volunteers to receive limited flight training. Fortyfive K-1s were built at Yokosuka. The Ohka Model 43 K-1 KAI *Wakazakura* ("Young Cherry") was a more practical trainer, for it was a two-seater (a second cockpit replacing the warhead) and was powered by a single tail-mounted rocket unit; but only two of these were completed.

Combat Deployment Frustrated

The speed with which the first ohka volunteers were trained may be judged from the initial plans for the weapon's combat deployment.

On 28 November 1944, the newly-commissioned aircraft carrier *Shinano* sailed from Tokyo Bay for the Matsuyama fleet training area, near Kure. Begun as the third of the Yamato-class super-battleships, *Shinano* was converted to a carrier while building. On her launch, 8 October 1944, she displaced 70,755 tons (71,890 tonnes) fully loaded; with an overall length of 872.75ft (266m) and an 840ft (256m) armoured flight deck, she was the largest and best-protected carrier of World War II. She was intended as a "supply carrier" and carried only 47 aircraft for her own operational use: the greater part of her immense bulk was crammed with complete aircraft, spares and ordnance—including 50 Ohka Model 11s, the first operational batch, with which it was planned to establish bases in the Philippines. It was thought possible that *Shinano* herself might become such a base—a mobile airstrip from which ohka-carrying bombers would be launched.

Shinano sailed with a young, inexperienced crew; with dockyard hands still aboard, working on her multiple watertight compartments; and without proper pumping gear. At 0310 on 29 November, still in Japanese coastal waters, she was struck by at least four torpedoes from the submarine USS *Archerfish* (Cdr Joseph F. Enright), which had tracked its huge quarry on the surface throughout the night. Although *Shinano* was badly holed, Captain Toshiro Abe held his original course at 18-20 knots for some hours: the flooding below grew worse; the civilian workers and many crewmen panicked; and by the time Abe realized the true extent of the damage, his ship was past saving. At 1055, some 120nm (138 miles, 222km) SSE of Cape Shiono, Honshu, the giant carrier rolled over to starboard and went down by the stern, taking with her Captain Abe, some 500 of his 1,400-strong crew—and the first 50 operational ohka. Her period of commission had lasted for no more than 17 hours.

The only ohka eventually deployed outside Japan were a number of Model 11s sent to Okinawa, where intact specimens were captured after the invasion of 1 April 1945, and to some other bases, notably Singapore. However, so far as can be ascertained, no ohka missions were flown from bases outside the home islands.

Boosting Morale
Training at Konoike was carried on at a hectic pace, encouraged by morale-boosting visits from the IJN's high command. Fleet Admiral Soemu Toyoda, Chief of Naval General Staff, and Fleet Admiral Osami Nagano arrived on 1 December, followed by Navy Minister Admiral Mitsumasa Yonai on 3 December. Admiral Toyoda exhorted the ohka pilots to combat the enemy's material superiority with their spiritual force, and presented each man with a white hachimaki, bearing the Jinrai Butai ideographs, and a short sword engraved with the recipient's name. Early in January, when preparations were made to move to an operational base at Kanoya in southern Kyushu, the Corps' pilots travelled to Tokyo to pray for success at Yasukuni Shrine, at Meiji Shrine, and outside the Imperial Palace. Informed of the impending move, Emperor Hirohito sent an aide-de-camp to Konoike with his personal good wishes.

The 1st Cherry Blossom Unit of the 721st Kokutai, commanded by Lt Kentaro Mitsuhashi following the death of Lt Kariya in flight testing, arrived at Kanoya Naval Air Base in March, ready for the ohka's first combat mission. All that was needed was a worthwhile target. On 21 March, one appeared: the ten heavy and six light aircraft carriers of US Task Force 58 which, on 18-20 March, had launched heavy strikes against airfields in Kyushu and the remnants of the

Combined Fleet in the Inland Sea, as a preliminary to the invasion of Okinawa. Determined Japanese counter-strikes by both kamikaze and conventional bombers had resulted in damage to several carriers, and early on 21 March a Japanese reconnaissance flight reported three US carriers, apparently damaged and without protective air cover, some 320nm (368 miles, 592km) southeast of Kyushu. Vice-Admiral Matome Ugaki, commanding Fifth Naval Air Fleet, ordered Okamura to commit the Jinrai Butai to action immediately.

Date: **21 March 1945**
Place: **Philippine Sea**
Attack by: **Ohka piloted bombs**
Target: **USN Task Group 58.1**

Okamura's first preoccupation was to secure an adequate fighter escort for his vulnerable Betty bombers which, according to a Japanese source, were limited to a maximum cruising speed of little more than 130mph (240kmh) when burdened with the 4,718lb (2140kg) ohka. When he found that the escort force, 201st Air Group, could provide only 55 Zeros, he sought to cancel the mission, but agreed to go ahead on Admiral Ugaki's urging. Unwilling to stay behind while his men faced heavy odds, Okamura now declared that he himself would lead the attack. Again he was frustrated: LtCdr Goro Nonaka, chief flight officer, claimed this as his right and flatly refused to stand down in Okamura's favour.

Eighteen Betty bombers were prepared for takeoff; 16 of them with ohka beneath their bellies. (According to Japanese eyewitnesses, the ohka of this first mission were painted bright blue, with the unit's cherry blossom emblem in red on the side of the fuselage. The colour scheme reported from later missions was for the bomb's upper surface to be painted pale green; its underside grey; and the unit marking and cherry blossom symbol—and sometimes the imperial crysanthemum emblem, on the nose—in red. Training ohka were normally bright orange.) Two Bettys, one the aircraft of LtCdr Nonaka, flew without ohka. The ohka pilot appointed to launch first and lead his comrades to their targets was Lt Kentaro Mihashi. Each pilot wore the hachimaki presented by Admiral Toyoda; Admiral Ugaki was present on the airstrip to pour the *sake* in which the pilots drank a toast to success. After checking the controls of their weapons, the ohka pilots took their places beside the pilots of the parent aircraft, leaning from the windows to salute Ugaki as they taxied to takeoff at 1130 hours.

As LtCdr Nonaka entered his aircraft, he remarked "This is my Minatogawa"—a reference to Masashige Kusunoki's heroic fight, with 700 men against many thousands, at the Minato River in 1336. The odds would be even greater than Nonaka expected, for of the 55 Zeros detailed to escort the ohka force, only 30 were able to sortie: 8 failed to get off the ground and 17 turned back with engine trouble. Even so, Admiral Ugaki decided not to call back the ohka force. The 18 Bettys with their depleted escort pressed on towards their target, which was in fact, Rear-Admiral J.J. Clark's Task Group 58.1,with the fleet carriers *Hornet, Bennington* and *Wasp* (the latter badly damaged by a kamikaze hit on 19 March, but still operational) and the light carrier

Belleau Wood escorted by the battleships *Massachusetts* and *Indiana* and a strong force of cruisers and destroyers.

Ohka Operational Procedure

Although it was not followed in the mission of 21 March, the standard operational procedure for the ohka may properly be described here.

Until reaching the target area, the ohka pilot remained in the parent aircraft. Some 50 miles (80km) from the target, having said a formal farewell to the bomber's crew, he crawled through the bomb-bay and into the cockpit of his weapon, which was secured from the outside by a crewman. He remained in contact with the bomber pilot through a speaking tube or telephone link until the moment of launching. Then, advised by the bomber's pilot, the ohka pilot pulled the lever releasing the shackle from the suspension lug, aiming to launch from the mother plane at an altitude of 20-27,000ft (6100-8230m) when about 20nm (23 miles, 37km) from the target. The ohka's flight began as a shallow, unpowered glide, reaching a speed of 230-280mph (370-450kmh). When less than one minute away from the target, the pilot triggered the electrical ignition of his rocket motor: its 1,764lb (800kg) thrust, with a duration of 8-10 seconds, gave a maximum speed of 403mph (649kmh) at 11,500ft (3505m). In its final dive on the target, at an angle of c.50°, the ohka reached a terminal velocity of some 580mph (933kmh). If he could, the pilot levelled out

Standard attack procedure for an **Ohka** Model 11 launched from a "Betty" bomber. **Ohka** were to prove most effective when launched from no more than 10 miles (16km) range at c.20,000ft (6100m)

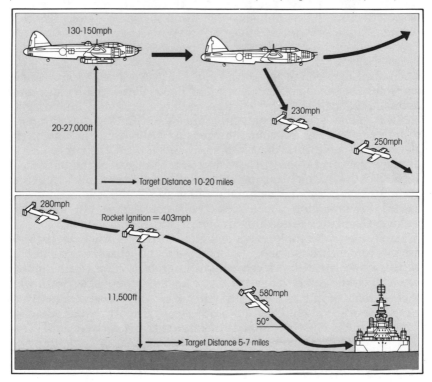

from his dive at the last moment, to strike his target at the waterline.

Such a weapon as the ohka, with its 2,646lb (1200kg) warhead of tri-nitroaminol, was a potential killer of major warships. Once approaching its terminal velocity, it was too fast for interception by any aircraft then available, and virtually unstoppable by AA fire. Its fallibility, as its first mission so graphically demonstrated, lay in its method of delivery to the target area.

Interception and Destruction

The bombers of 721st Kokutai and their escorts were picked up by radar while still some 70nm (80 miles, 130km) northwest of the USN Task Group, and additional fighters immediately launched from the US carriers to supplement the normal CAPs. Of some 150 US interceptors airborne, the first to find the ohka force—some 60nm (69 miles, 111km) from the US carriers—were 24 Grumman F6F Hellcats from *Hornet* (VF-17 and VBF-17) and *Belleau Wood* (VF-30).

The ohka pilots never had the chance to enter their weapons, which were jettisoned as soon as the Bettys came under attack. Even this could not save the clumsy bombers: in a 20-minute melee all 18 were chopped down by *Hornet*'s Hellcats, Lt Henry E. Mitchell, Jr, of VBF-17 claiming five kills. Meanwhile, *Belleau Wood*'s fighters, assisted by F4U Corsairs, engaged the escorting Zeros. It is difficult to escape the conclusion that the Zero pilots were either inexperienced or had little stomach for their mission: for the loss of only one Hellcat, some 15-20 Japanese fighters were destroyed. Japanese sources state that only "one or two" Zeros returned to Kanoya to tell of the total destruction of the first ohka mission—and the same sources say that Admiral Ugaki was seen to weep on receiving the news.

Ohka at Okinawa

The Allied invasion of Okinawa began on 1 April 1945—and on the same day the second ohka mission was flown. Three Bettys and three kamikaze Zeros took off from Kanoya late in the day, intending to strike at the invasion shipping after dusk and thus lessen the chances of interception. Approaching the landing fleet from the north, the Bettys were able to avoid air patrols and launch their missiles. A diving ohka struck one of the twin 16-inch turrets of the battleship USS *West Virginia*, causing considerable damage and inflicting several casualties. The remaining ohka and kamikaze aircraft succeeded in damaging the attack transport *Alpine* (16 killed, 27 wounded) and the cargo ships *Achernar* and *Tyrrell*.

In all, about 300 ohka were available during April-June 1945 for attacks on Allied shipping at Okinawa. Of these, according to Japanese records, only 74 were committed to action, of which number some 56 either succeeded in making attacks or were shot down with their parent aircraft. It was difficult for the Japanese accurately to gauge the effect of ohka sorties, since escort aircraft that approached Allied shipping closely enough to observe the attacks were unlikely to return. The Allies nicknamed the weapon the *Baka* ("idiot" or "foolish") bomb. This was not altogether appropriate: because the ohka was virtually unstoppable, *when* it could be successfuly launched, it exerted an adverse effect on Allied morale out of all proportion to its operational success.

Date: **12 April 1945**
Place: **East China Sea, off Okinawa**
Attack by: **Ohka piloted bombs**
Target: **US radar picket destroyers**

Apart from stepping up attacks on the Kyushu airfields from which they flew against Okinawa, the Allies' only sure defence against the ohka was to intercept the parent aircraft before the piloted bombs were launched. A vital role was played here by radar picket destroyers (see page 166). On 12 April, in the course of the second kikusui mass attack, this cordon of ships became a target for ohka strikes.

Eight ohka-carrying Bettys took off from Kanoya, escorted by both kamikaze and conventional Zeros. On the way to the target area, the force split up, to approach from widely separated directions and thus lessen the chance of a single interception prejudicing the entire mission. At least four Bettys reached the Allied defence perimeter, where the radar pickets were on station. A much quoted example of the ohka pilots' sang-froid was the behaviour on this mission of Lt Saburo Doi, whose parent plane was the only one of the mission to return to Kanoya. Doi's last action before boarding his Betty was to enquire into the provision of new bedding for the Jinrai Butai's spartan living quarters. Once aboard the aircraft, he lay down on an improvised cot and, asking to be woken 30 minutes before ETA in the target area, fell asleep. Duly awoken, he remarked how quickly the time had passed, shook hands all round, entered his ohka, and was launched from the Betty at what was thought to be the ideal range (11 miles, 18km) and altitude (19,700ft, 6000m).

Lt Doi was credited by the Japanese with a direct hit on a battleship—but although USS *Tennessee* and *Idaho* were both damaged by suicide attack on this day, USN records attribute the hits to kamikaze aircraft. No doubt exists, however, concerning the fate of the 2,200-ton Sumner-class destroyer *Mannert L. Abele* (LtCdr A.E. Parker). Manning Radar Picket 14, some 70nm (80 miles, 130km) northwest of Okinawa, along with two rocket-armed landing ships, *Abele* was subjected to a determined kamikaze attack at c.1440 hours. Three Zeros dived on the destroyer from different angles: one hit home, smashing into the starboard side and penetrating the after engine room before its bomb detonated, fracturing the shafts, breaking the destroyer's back and leaving her dead in the water.

One minute later, the big destroyer was a sitting target for a diving ohka: again she was struck to starboard, and again the attacker penetrated the ship before exploding. *Abele* broke in half, sinking within three minutes, with 79 men killed and 35 wounded. More would have died if *LSM(R)-189* and *-190* had not been on hand to pick up survivors, while engaging and shooting down two Zeros that were bombing and machine-gunning men in the water. During the rescue work, a Zero crashed *LSM(R)-189*, wounding four of her crew.

Also hastening to the relief of *Abele*'s survivors was the destroyer minesweeper USS *Jeffers* from Radar Picket 12. At 1435 engaged an approaching Betty bomber which released an ohka at close range. The DMS's fire was believed to have damaged the piloted bomb, which dived into the sea some 50yds (46m) from the ship—but even at that distance the ohka's detonation caused sufficient damage to send *Jeffers* for repair to the base at Kerama Retto.

Meanwhile, on Radar Picket 1, the destroyer USS *Cassin Young* had been badly damaged by a kamikaze aircraft. The destroyers *Stanly* and *Lang* were ordered to her relief, coming under kamikaze attack on the way. Within 20 minutes, as the destroyers manoeuvred beneath a CAP controlled by *Stanly*'s fighter-director, more kamikaze closed in, ohka-carrying Betty bombers among them. Diving through the screen of US aircraft, and then levelling out and seemingly unaffected by numerous hits from the destroyer's 20mm and 40mm AA guns, an ohka struck *Stanly* on the starboard bow just above the waterline. The body of the ohka tore clear through the ship and its warhead emerged through the port side before exploding. *Stanly* was still able to fight, and a few minutes later her gunners engaged a second ohka. Its pilot showed great skill and determination, passing so low over the destroyer as to tear the ensign from its gaff and then attempting to bank for a second run. Concentrated 40mm fire tore a wing from the attacker, sending it into the sea some 2,000yds (1830m) away. Only three men aboard *Stanly* were wounded by the impact of the first ohka—which left the remains of the ohka pilot thinly plastered over a bulkhead within the destroyer.

On 14, 16 and 28 April, ohka missions were sent from Kanoya against ships at Okinawa. Seven ohka sorties were flown on 14 April without recorded success—although no Bettys returned.

On 16 April, as part of the third kikusui attack, six ohka-carrying Bettys sortied against the Royal Navy's Task Force 57: Rear-Admiral Philip Vian's four fleet carriers—HMS *Formidable, Indefatigable, Indomitable* and *Victorious*—were striking at Japanese airfields in the southern Ryukyus. Fighter-director teams on the carriers picked up the fast-moving ohka on radar, but no attempt at interception was necessary: the piloted bombs had been launched too far from their targets and splashed harmlessly into the sea. It is probable that the same fate befell the four ohka sorties made from Kanoya on 28 April.

The Ohka's Limited Range

From the foregoing instances, it may be inferred that the *effective* range of the ohka was far less than the 50 miles (80km) attributed to them in some non-Japanese sources—and less even than the Japanese figure of 20-plus miles (32+ km). They proved effective only when launched at close range—some 10 miles (16km) or less—at times when Allied CAPs were fully occupied in beating off kamikaze and conventional aircraft. The chronic shortage of aviation fuel and pilots for escort aircraft meant that, when committed independently of mass kamikaze attacks, the ohka were usually shot down with their parent aft or wasted by launching at extreme ranges.

ever, on 4 May during the fifth kikusui offensive, the ohka were ectively. Seven ohka-carrying Bettys took off from Kanoya for where heavy air attacks had been made on Allied shipping from dawn onwards. Shortly before 0900, a single Betty was sighted about 5nm (5.75 miles, 9.25km) from Radar Picket 14. CAP aircraft were directed to the bomber, which succeeded in launching its ohka before it was knocked down. A smoke haze from the transports off the Hagushi beaches limited surface visibility to less than 2,000yds (1830m), and the ohka's track was lost until it burst from the murk only 1,000yds (915m) from the picket ships. Undeterred by 40mm fire, the ohka steered into the light minelayer USS *Shea*, its tremendous velocity taking it through the starboard bridge structure to detonate on the port side. With her upper works a mangled wreck, 27 men dead and 91 wounded, *Shea* was able to reach the Hagushi anchorage, but took no further part in the war. Later that morning, a little farther north, the minesweeper USS *Gayety* had two men wounded when she was near-missed by an ohka. A single Betty bomber returned to Kanoya from this mission.

Date: **11 May 1945**
Place: **Okinawa**
Attack by: **Ohka bombs and kamikaze aircraft**
Target: **US radar picket ships**

The ohka's last successful mission — proving again the potential of the weapon when used as one element of mass kamikaze attack — was flown on 11 May, when four Bettys (one of which returned after launching its ohka) sortied during the second and final day of the sixth kikusui offensive.

On Radar Picket 15, the destroyers *Evans* (Cdr R.J. Archer) and *Hugh W. Hadley* (Cdr B.J. Mullaney), the latter acting as fighter-control ship, along with three landing ships, fought one of the fiercest anti-kamikaze actions of the battle of Okinawa. Between 0750 and 0930, it was estimated that some 50 enemy aircraft were destroyed by the 12 Corsairs of the picket station's CAP, while at least 50 more evaded the air cover and struck at the ships. While manoeuvring at high speed, *Evans* and *Hadley* were subjected to repeated attacks by groups of four to six kamikaze coming in from different angles. At 0920, *Hadley*'s gunners were engaged with ten aircraft simultaneously: four to starboard, four to port, two astern. All ten were destroyed, but the destroyer sustained a bomb hit and a kamikaze crash aft, followed by a hit from an ohka released by a low-flying Betty at very close range. Holed and flooding, with 28 men dead and 67 wounded, Cdr Mullaney gave the order to abandon ship; but a skeleton crew remained aboard and brought under control the fires that threatened *Hadley*'s magazines. With *Evans*, which had taken four kamikaze hits, *Hadley* was towed to Kerama Retto and later scrapped. The two destroyers' gunners were credited with the destruction of 46 enemy aircraft in less than two hours.

On 24 May, as the seventh kikusui offensive raged at Okinawa, the carrier pilots of US Task Force 58 struck at the kamikaze's airfields on Kyushu. The Jinrai Butai's base at Kanoya was a prime target: US pilots claimed the destruction of 70 Betty bombers awaiting takeoff with ohka beneath their bellies. Such a total seems unlikely — and the raid did not prevent a sortie the next day by 11 ohka-carrying Bettys, when Admiral Toyoda was present to bid the suicide pilots farewell as they took off for Okinawa at 0500 hours.

Approaching the target area, a heavy and prolonged squall cut down visibility so far—it was reported as nil to below 4,000ft (1220m)—that a number of the Bettys jettisoned their ohka and returned to base; only to be forced to land at a nearby Army base when Kanoya was found to be again under attack. One Betty, however, pressed on. Disregarding standing orders that forbade ohka to launch below 15,000ft (4570m), the Betty came down almost to sea-level for a run in on Radar Picket 5—but was shot down by the combined fire of the destroyers *Braine* and *Anthony* before the ohka could launch.

The Last Ohka Mission

On 22 June, the second and last day of the tenth and final kikusui offensive, the last ohka mission of the war was flown by six Bettys of the 10th Cherry Blossom Unit. The chief ohka pilot was Lt Toshihide Fujisaki; but neither he nor his comrades found a target. Two of the Bettys returned safely to base.

The total losses of the Jinrai Butai, almost all incurred during the kikusui attacks at Okinawa, are given in Japanese sources as 467 men; of whom some 55-60 were ohka pilots and 229 the pilots and crews of parent aircraft. An Allied estimate of 298 ohka expended is almost certainly an overstatement: if it is accepted as in any way accurate, it must be concluded that far more ohka were shot down with their parent aircraft or jettisoned than ever achieved operational launching. The ohka sank one destroyer (*Mannert L. Abele*) and shared in damaging another (*Hugh W. Hadley*) so badly that she was scrapped; a light minelayer was so badly damaged as to take no further part in the war, and damage of varying degree was inflicted on a battleship, a destroyer, a destroyer-minesweeper, a minesweeper, an attack transport and a cargo ship. The deaths of some 150 American sailors and the wounding of about 250 may be attributed to ohka attacks.

Ohka in the Final Defence

Following the mission of 22 June, the remaining ohka were redeployed in the home islands to meet the expected Allied invasion. It was planned to establish a chain of small bases along the coasts from which ohka, carried by bombers or launched from catapults, could sortie against invasion shipping. Launching catapults for the Ohka Model 43B (described below) were to be mounted in natural or specially-excavated caves facing potential landing beaches; and a pilot-training centre for this weapon was established at a requisitioned Buddhist monastery on a mountain near Kyoto, Honshu.

Of the Cherry Blossom Units already operational, some remained at Kanoya, but most were moved to Komatsu Air Base in central Honshu, while the kamikaze aircraft units allied to them went to Matsuyama Air Base on Shikoku. The main training echelon—Squadron I, commanded by Lt Akira Hirano—continued its work at Konoike, where Hirano strove to bring a new, 300-strong operational unit—722nd Naval Air Corps (called *Tatsumaki Butai*, "Tornado Corps")—to operational readiness.

On 15 August, Emperor Hirohito's broadcast of the decision to surrender put an end to all these activities. Like many other officers of the "special attack" forces, the Jinrai Butai's commanding officer, Cdr Motoharu Okamura, decided that honour demanded expiation of his "failure": he committed seppuku in the traditional manner.

Non-Operational Ohka Models

At the war's end, several Ohka models were under construction or in development, although none achieved operational status. The only one built in any quantity—apart from the unpowered K-1 training glider; 45 completed—was the Model 22, 50 examples completed.

Since the Betty bomber had proved so vulnerable as a carrier, the Ohka Model 22 was designed to be carried and launched by a variant of the much faster and more manoeuvrable Yokosuka P1Y "Frances". The P1Y3 Model 33, with an enlarged fuselage and increased wingspan to operate the Ohka Model 22 and the projected Model 21 (with the rocket engine of the Model 11 and the smaller dimensions of the Model 22), was planned to have a maximum speed of 340mph (547kmh) and a range of more than 4,000 miles (6440km). The aircraft never left the drawing board.

Even had the P1Y3 become available, it is doubtful whether the Ohka Model 22 would have been successful. Its designers aimed at improved range and, of necessity, smaller dimensions—achieving both, but at heavy cost. By using a Campini-type, 551lb (200kg)

"OHKA" PILOTED BOMB: EXPERIMENTAL MODELS

Type:	MODEL 21	MODEL 33	MODEL 43A	MODEL 43B	MODEL 53
Span:	13.5ft (4.12m)	not known (planned as enlarged version of Model 22)	29.53ft (9m)	29.53ft (9m)	not known (also an enlarged version of Model 22)
Length:	22.6ft (6.88m)	not known	26.8ft (8.16m)	26.8ft (8.16m)	not known
Height:	3.77ft (1.15m)	not known	3.77ft (1.15m)	3.77ft (1.15m)	not known
Wing area:	43sq ft (4sq m)	not known	139.9sq ft (13sq m)	139.9sq ft (13sq m)	not known
Maximum loaded weight:	3,197lb (1450kg)	not known	5,005lb (2270kg)	5,005lb (2270kg)	not known
Power:	3 x Type 4 Mk I Model 20 solid-propellant rockets with total thrust of 1,764lb (800kg)	1 x Ne-20 axial-flow turbojet with total thrust of 1,047lb (475kg)	1 x Ne-20 axial-flow turbojet with total thrust of 1,047lb (475kg)	1 x Ne-20 axial-flow turbojet with total thrust of 1,047lb (475kg)	1 x Ne-20 axial-flow turbojet with total thrust of 1,047lb (475kg)
Maximum speed Level:	not known	not known	345mph (555kmh) @13,125ft(4000m)	345mph (555kmh) @13,125ft(4000m)	not known
Dive:	not known	not known	not known	not known	not known
Range:	not known	not known	c.150nm (173 miles, 278km)	c.150nm (173 miles, 278km)	not known
Warhead:	not known	1,764-1,984lb (800-900kg)	1,764-1,984lb (800-900kg)	1,764-1,984lb (800-900kg)	1,764-1,984lb (800-900kg)
Carried/Launched:	Yokosuka P1Y3 Model 33 Ginga ("Frances") bomber	Nakajima G8N2 Renzan ("Rita") heavy bomber **or** own take-off	Folding-wing model to be catapult-launched from submarine	Catapult-launched from land	Towed by aircraft and released in target area
Crew:	1	1	1	1	1
Number built:	Nil	Nil	Nil	Nil	Nil

JAPANESE & GERMAN FLYING BOMBS						
Type:	KAWANISHI BAIKA ("PLUM BLOSSOM")	FZG 76 ("V-1")	REICHENBERG I	REICHENBERG II	REICHENBERG III	REICHENBERG IV
Span:	21.7ft (6.6m)	17.4ft (5.3m)	17.4ft (5.3m)	17.4ft (5.3m)	17.4ft (5.3m)	18.75ft (5.7m)
Length:	22.9ft (7m)	25.3ft (7.7m)	27.9ft (8.5m)	27.9ft (8.5m)	27.9ft (8.5m)	26.25ft (8m)
Loaded weight:	3,155lb (1430kg)	4,807lb (2180kg)	n.a.	n.a.	n.a.	4,960lb (2250kg)
Power:	1 x Maru Ka-10 pulse-jet with total thrust of 794lb (360kg)	1 x Argus As 109-014 pulse-jet with total thrust of 770lb (350kg)	Unpowered glider	Unpowered glider	1 x Argus As 109-014 pulse-jet with total thrust of 770lb (350kg)	1 x Argus As 109-014 pulse-jet with total thrust of 770lb (350kg)
Maximum speed:	460mph (740kmh)	400mph (644kmh)	n.a.	n.a.	400mph (644kmh)	c.497mph (800kmh) @ 8,000ft (2440m)
Range:	Not known	163-250 miles (260-400km)	n.a.	n.a.	n.a.	c.205 miles (330km) from air-launch at 8,200ft (2500m)
Warhead:	551lb (250kg)	1,000-1,870lb (450-850kg)	None (replaced by ballast)	None (replaced by second cockpit)	None (replaced by ballast)	1,870lb (850kg) Amatol
Carried/ Launched	Take-off under own power (with jettisonable undercarriage)	Ground-launched from ramp **or** air-launched from Heinkel He 111H bomber	Towed by trainer	Towed by trainer	Air-launched from Heinkel He 111H bomber	Air-launched from Heinkel He 111H bomber
Crew:	1	Unpiloted	1	2	1	1
Number built:	Nil	c.29,000	Not known	Not known	Not known	c 175

thrust, Tsu-11 jet engine, with a 100hp *Hatsukaze* ("Fresh Wind") piston engine as a compressor, the Model 22 achieved a range of c.80 miles (130km), nearly four times that of the Model 11. But its maximum speed was only about 276mph (444kmh), which would have made it extremely vulnerable to both interception and AA fire *after* launching. Its warhead was only half the size of that of the Model 11.

A one-third reduction in wing area meant that the handling characteristics of the Model 22 were far worse than those of the Model 11, itself a tricky aircraft. It was impossible to land the Model 22, which had a stalling speed of 207mph (333kmh); for testing flights, its pilot was equipped with a special parachute and instructed to bale out at 3,000ft (914m). On 26 June, Lt Kazutoshi Nagano, chief ohka test pilot, was killed when a Model 22 launched from a P1Y1 at 12,000ft (3660m) went out of control immediately: Nagano escaped from the rolling, diving ohka but received mortal injuries when his parachute failed to open fully. But although flight testing was never satisfactorily completed, the Model 22 was put into production: the Dai-Ichi Kaigun Kokusho planned to build the weapon in underground workshops, dispersed to escape the effects of US bombing.

The Ohka Model 21, combining the rocket motor of the Model 11 with the airframe of the Model 22, was never built; and nor were the projected Models 33, 43A and 43B, which were to be powered by the Ne-20 axial-flow turbojet, a 1,047lb (475kg) thrust engine.

The Model 33, about the same size as the Model 11, was intended to be launched from the Nakajima G8N1 *Renzan* ("Mountain Range"), but only four of these four-engined heavy bombers, called "Rita" by the Allies, were completed.

The much larger Model 43A (with folding wings) was intended to be catapult-launched from a fleet submarine; the Model 43B was to be catapult-launched from shore installations. Yet another method of delivery was envisaged for the projected Model 53, which was to be towed aloft by a bomber and released on sighting a target.

The Kawanishi Baika

Japan's other piloted-bomb project, the Kawanishi *Baika* ("Plum Blossom"), was based on the German *Reichenberg-IV*, the piloted

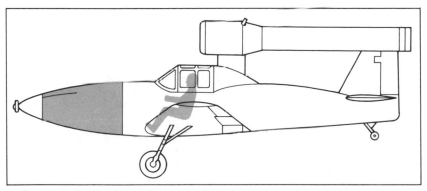

The Kawanishi **Baika** ("Plum Blossom") piloted bomb, based on the German **Reichenberg** manned "V-1".

version of the V-1 flying bomb (described below). After detailed study of plans and an example of the Argus As 109-014 pulse-jet engine, brought from Germany by submarine in late 1944, Professors Ichiro Tani and Taichiro Ogawa of the Aeronautical Institute, Tokyo Imperial University, worked with the Kawanishi Kokuki K.K. to produce a design for a piloted bomb.

As designed, the Baika was a low-winged monoplane with a pulse-jet engine mounted above the fuselage aft the cockpit. The Maru Ka-10 pulse-jet unit, giving a maximum 794lb (360kg) thrust, allowed the aircraft to take off under its own power with the use of a jettisonable wheeled dolly. With a maximum speed of c.460mph (740kmh), and a 551lb (250kg) warhead in its nose, the Baika might have proved a most effective suicide weapon had it progressed beyond the design stage.

GERMAN "SPECIAL ATTACK" AIRCRAFT
The Piloted Bombs

German experiments with piloted bombs began late in 1943, inspired largely by increasing fears of an Allied invasion of continental Europe. In the face of the Luftwaffe's increasingly apparent inadequacy, it was felt that guided bombs — manned and un-manned — offered the best method of attacking small, heavily-defended targets, such as ground strong-points and major warships. A number of remote-controlled missiles, such as the fairly successful "Fritz X" air-to-ground guided bomb, were in production or under development by 1943—but these have no place in this narrative.

Prime movers in the *piloted*-bomb programme were SS-Sturmbann-führer Otto Skorzeny, the Reich's principal commando leader, and Flugkapitän Hanna Reitsch, the famous woman test pilot. However, even before Skorzeny's involvement with the project early in 1944, the Deutsche Forschungsinstitut für Segelflug (DFS; German Flight Research Institute) had begun consideration of precision attacks made by piloted, explosive-laden aircraft. Initial suggestions for the use in this role of a piloted Fieseler Fi 103—the "flying bomb" designated *Vergeltungswaffen Eins*, or V-1—were laid aside in favour of the projected Messerschmitt Me 328.

An Expendable Aircraft: Me 328A/B

The Me 328A was designed in 1941-42 as an expendable, air-launched interceptor, powered by two Argus As 014 pulse-jets. It would be pole-towed to its operational area by a He 177 or Me 264 bomber and released to engage enemy aircraft; the pilot either baling out or crash-landing on completion of his mission. By late 1943, this concept had been abandoned in favour of the Me 328B, a single-sortie bomber powered by two or four pulse-jet units, towed aloft or carried in the *Mistel* ("Mistletoe") pick-a-back configuration by a bomber, and released at c.10,000ft (3050m) to make a high-speed, low-level run on a ground target or warship. Once he had aimed his aircraft at the target, the pilot had the chance to escape by triggering explosive bolts that jettisoned all the fuselage aft of his seat.

Gliding trials revealed that the Me 328 had extremely unpleasant handling characteristics; and powered trials, early in 1944, showed graver faults. The acoustic effects of the pulse-jet units caused vibration that had literally shattering consequences for both air-frame and pilot, and this drawback, although partly rectified by mounting the pulse-jets farther aft, so that they exhausted beyond the tailplane, was never wholly conquered. Thus, it was decided that the Me 328 would operate as an unpowered glider bomb.

The Leonidas Staffel

The Me 328 was to be operated in this role by 5.II/KG 200 (ie, the Fifth *Staffel*, or Squadron, of the Second *Gruppe*, or Wing, of

Powered version of the Messerschmitt Me 328B, with pulse-jets set well back under the wings.

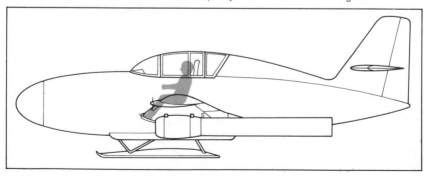

Kampfgeschwader 200). This squadron of an elite bomber group, commanded by Hauptmann Heinrich Lange and sometimes called *Kommando Lange,* had been specially formed to test and operate "experimental" weapons. The probable nature of such weapons was suggested by the unit's nickname, "Leonidas Staffel"—a reference to the Spartan king who, with his 300-strong royal guard, fought to the death against the Persian hordes in the pass of Thermopylae.

Bombers were to carry the Me 328 aloft in the Mistel configuration, releasing it near the target area. Once released, the missile's pilot would glide at an angle of 5:1, reaching a speed of c.155mph (250kmh), and would make his attack at an angle of 12:1, at an estimated 440mph (708kmh). At this speed, he was expected to aim his aircraft, with its 1,100-2,200lb (500-1000kg) bomb-load, at the target before baling out. Although a factory order was placed for this suicidal glider-bomb, the project had been abandoned by around May 1944.

It was now planned to use Focke-Wulf Fw 190 fighters in a similar role, as manned, powered bombs, each carrying an impact-fuzed, 2,205lb (1000kg) SB/SC 1000 bomb. Again, the pilot had a theoretical chance of survival by baling out during the terminal dive. The pilots of the Leonidas Staffel subjected heavily-laden Fw 190s to the most extreme diving tests; but although these showed that a pilot prepared to sacrifice his own life would have a good chance of hitting a precision target, it was decided that an Fw 190 slowed by a heavy bomb-load would have little chance of reaching its target area against fighter opposition. This project, too, was abandoned; but it is worth noting that, early in 1945, the Fw 190-G1s of *Nachtschlachtgruppe 20,* commanded by Major Kurt Dahlmann, were specially converted to carry the 3,968lb (1800kg) SC 1800 bomb, with which they made semi-suicidal attacks on such vital ground targets as the Remagen Bridge (which was attacked on 7 March 1945).

The Manned V-1

It was at this juncture that Skorzeny and the intrepid Hanna Reitsch (who had not long recovered from multiple skull fractures incurred while testing the Me 163 rocket fighter) pressed for reconsideration of a piloted Fi 103. According to Skorzeny's own account, Adolf Hitler was at the time (late 1944) dubious of the moral effect of suicide weapons; but, by misrepresenting the Führer's views to Erhard Milch at the Air Ministry and to Reichsminister Albert Speer, Skorzeny pushed forward the project. Once the DFS was authorized to proceed with designs, work went ahead at great speed: within two weeks, four *Reichenberg* models, manned versions of the Fi 103—the unpowered R-I and R-II; the R-III powered trainer; and the operational R-IV (see Table on page 188 for full technical details)—had been produced and facilities established for bulk production.

The operational model, Reichenberg-IV, differed surprisingly little from the unpiloted Fi 103 weapon. Modifications consisted of the addition of ailerons to the trailing edges of the wings; the fitting of a truncated nose-cone covered by a plywood fairing in place of the unmanned missile's faired warhead; and the provision of a cockpit. Space was made for the latter by removing the compressed air bottle

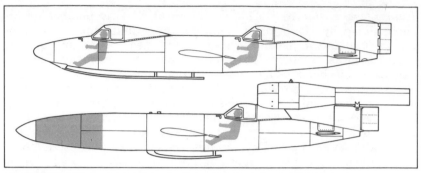

(**Top**) **Reichenberg II**, an unpowered trainer in which a second cockpit occupied the warhead space.
(**Bottom**) **Reichenberg IV**, a piloted version, never operational, of the Fieseler Fi 103 flying-bomb.

needed in the V-1 to power the control system and resiting the second bottle, for fuel tank pressurization, in the aft compartment that formerly housed the auto-pilot. The R-IV's pilot sat beneath a single-piece cockpit hood with an armour-glass windscreen, on which were engraved guide lines for diving angles. He had a plywood bucket seat with a padded headrest. On his eye-level instrument panel were, from left to right, a switch to arm the warhead; clock; airspeed indicator; altimeter; and turn-and-bank indicator. Running from the panel to the cockpit floor, forward of the control column, was a bracket mounting a gyrocompass.

Like the air-launched V-1, the R-IV was to be carried to its launching point beneath the starboard wing, inboard of the engine, of a Heinkel He 111H bomber. (Experiments were made with rocket-assisted takeoffs from a launching dolly, and it was reported—although later historians deny this—that Hanna Reitsch was badly injured in such a trial.) The R-IV was to launch at c.8,000-9,000ft (2440-2740m), its pilot remaining in contact with the parent aircraft through a telephone link until the moment of separation. With a maximum speed in level flight of c.400mph (644kmh), the R-IV had a powered endurance of 30-plus minutes, giving a range of c.205 miles (330km) from a launch made at the optimum altitude.

Having sighted his target, the pilot was to arm his warhead, begin his terminal dive—reaching a speed of c.490-530mph (790-850kmh)—and, at the last moment, trip a canopy-jettison lever positioned to his left and bale out. In fact, his chance of survival was infinitesimal: the canopy had to move through an angle of 45° to starboard before it would detach itself—and at terminal velocity, air pressure was not likely to permit this. Even if the pilot succeeded in leaving the cockpit, the rush of air would probably hurl him on to the pulse-jet unit.

The Weapon Tested—and Abandoned

Flight testing in air-launched, unpowered R-Is, begun at Lärz in North Germany in September 1944, quickly revealed the weapon's faults. The first launch ended in a crash after the pilot accidentally jettisoned the cockpit canopy; the second flight also ended in a wreck. It seemed that Milch might put an end to the project; but this was averted largely by Hanna Reitsch, who—without authorization, according to

Skorzeny—made a successful flight and skid-landing. Soon after-wards she survived without injury a spectacular crash when the sand ballast that replaced the warhead in the powered training model broke loose in flight. A second experienced test pilot, Heinz Kensche, now joined Reitsch, and some 20 successful flights were made.

Although the weapon's suicidal nature must have been obvious, there was no lack of volunteers for Reichenberg operations. Some 30 men from Skorzeny's own commando force—dedicated members of the SS, who had already received some pilot training—were joined by about 60 selected Luftwaffe personnel for training in the two-seat R-II. Pilots of the Leonidas Staffel were to carry the self-styled *Selbstopfermänner* ("suicide personnel") into action. By October 1944, about 175 R-IVs were ready for use. Had they been available earlier, for deployment against the Normandy invasion fleet in June 1944, they would almost certainly have been used—and, judging from the evidence of Japanese operations, might have proved effective against Channel shipping.

There had, however, always been considerable opposition to the Reichenberg project among the German high command. Skorzeny later claimed that the Air Ministry killed the scheme by refusing to allocate sufficient fuel for training with the powered R-III; whereupon he himself lost interest and took back the majority of the Reichenberg trainees into his commando units. Be that as it may, the Reichenberg plan was shelved following the appointment to command of KG 200 of O erstleutnant Werner Baumbach, in October 1944. Baumbach, influential through his association with Major Hajo Herrmann in the establishment of the *Wilde Sau* ("Wild Boar") night-fighter project in July 1943, let the Reichenberg programme lapse in favour of experi-ments with the various Mistel combinations using unmanned aircraft.

When the Allies launched "Operation Paperclip", specifically aimed at securing the secrets of Germany's "special" weapons, in 1945, one investigating team discovered near Dahlenburg, in the Hamburg area, a cache of V-1s which included most of the R-IVs.

Experimental "Special Attack" Aircraft
Germany's increasingly severe losses of aircraft and veteran pilots and the Allies' implementation of an "area bombing" policy led in 1943-45 to the initiation of several projects for "special attack" aircraft. Not to strike at surface targets—but to attempt to stem the tide of heavy bombers of the US 8th Air Force that flooded daily over the cities of the Reich. The main effort was the organization of close-attack squadrons (described below), whose pilots resorted to ramming if all else failed; but several designs for cheap and easily-produced interceptors, capable of being flown by inexperienced pilots, had suicidal aspects that make them worthy of note.

One of the earlier attempts at an interceptor of this kind, initiated in mid-1943 and akin to the Me 328 project described above, resulted in the Blohm und Voss Bv 40, a wood-and-metal glider of 25.9ft (7.9m) span, armed with two 30mm cannon. One or two of these craft would be towed aloft by a Messerschmitt Bf 109G fighter and released some 800-2,500ft (240-760m) above the approaching bomber formation. The

Bv 40 would make its firing pass in a shallow dive at c.290 mph (470 kmh); its pilot, lying prone behind a 122mm armour-glass windshield, might hope to be saved from the massive firepower of a B-17 formation by the narrow frontage presented by his engine-less craft; by his high closing speed; and by a heavily-armoured cockpit. If he retained sufficient altitude after firing, he might make a second attack with the *Gerät-Schlinger*, a small bomb trailed on a cable beneath the glider. Although the latter option was later discarded, development of this semi-suicidal aircraft continued until late 1944, when it was abandoned in favour of expendable rocket- and jet-propelled interceptors.

The "Natter" Rocket-Plane

Apart from the Messerschmitt Me 163 *Komet* ("Comet"), which is dealt with in its Japanese incarnation as the Mitsubishi J8M *Shusui* in Chapter 6, the most notable of the rocket-interceptors was the Bachem Ba 349 *Natter* ("Adder"). This aircraft was proposed as early as 1939 but was rejected until, in mid-1944, its designer Dipl Ing Erich Bachem secured the interest of Reichsführer SS Heinrich Himmler. With such support, intensive development began in August 1944.

The Natter emerged as a 20ft (6.1m) long, stub-winged (11.8ft, 3.6m, span) monoplane built largely of laminated wood in a process

Bachem Ba 349A **Natter** ("Adder") expendable interceptor, powered by liquid-fuel rocket motor.
Note the tail-mounted, jettisonable, solid-fuel rocket motors fitted to boost take-off from a ramp.

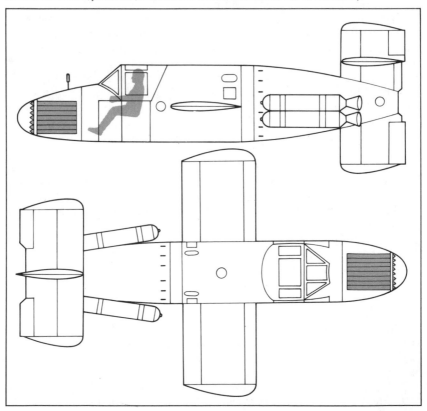

consuming no more than 1,000 man-hours of mostly unskilled labour. It was powered by a Walter rocket motor fuelled by the highly volatile mixture of *T-Stoff* (hydrogen peroxide/water) and *C-Stoff* (hydrazine hydrate/methanol); take-off, from a near-vertical 80ft (24.4m) ramp, was boosted by two or four jettisonable solid-fuel rocket motors. Once in flight, the final model of the Natter had a maximum endurance of 4.36 minutes at 9,840ft (3000m) and a maximum speed of 497mph (800kmh) at sea level or 620mph (1000kmh) at 16,400ft (5000m), giving it a range of 24-36 miles (39-58km), depending on altitude.

The Natter was to be launched into the path of the bomber stream. Since the g-forces at launch might cause the pilot to black out, an auto-pilot would guide the interceptor to a pre-determined altitude some 1,800-3,500yds (1650-3200m) from the approaching bombers. The pilot would then take control, jettison the cone that covered a nose-mounted battery of 24 x 73mm spin-stabilized *Föhn* ("Spring Storm") rockets (or 33 x 55mm R4M rockets), and, using a simple ring-sight, fire his missile salvo at close range while in a shallow dive. It was originally planned that he should then pull out of the dive and set the Natter on a ramming course before ejecting; although this requirement was dropped, it may be thought that the operation remained near-suicidal. After firing, the pilot unstrapped his harness and released catches that freed the entire section of the Natter forward of his seat: the aircraft broke apart, the pilot descending on one parachute and the rear section, with the re-usable Walter motor, on another. It was believed that only basic training on the ground would be needed to produce Natter pilots: with this in mind, the SS made an intial order for 150 aircraft, while 50 were ordered for the Luftwaffe.

Unmanned test launchings of Natters from November 1944 onward were only moderately successful; but on 28 February 1945 the first manned flight was scheduled. A few seconds after leaving its ramp, the Natter's cockpit cover broke away, probably knocking unconscious the pilot, Oberleutnant Lothar Siebert. The aircraft climbed inverted to c.4,900ft (1500m) and then dived into the ground, killing Siebert. Even so, volunteers to pilot the Natter were not wanting, and seven successful manned flights were subsequently made. Of 36 completed Ba 349A Natters (with an endurance of only 2.23 minutes at a maximum speed of c.560mph, 900kmh), 10 were operationally deployed near Stuttgart in April 1945, but the rapid advance of Allied armour towards the launching area necessitated their destruction unlaunched. Japan, equally in need of cheap and simple interceptors for "special attack" on B-29s, purchased the plans of the Natter, but failed to complete any examples before August 1945.

Heinkel He 162: the "People's Fighter"
Although the jet-propelled Heinkel He 162 (unofficially named the "Salamander") was not in essence a suicide plane, the plans for its operations, reflected in its designation of *Volksjäger* ("People's Fighter"), gave it a suicidal aspect. The cannon- or MG-armed interceptor, propelled by a 1,760lb (800kg) turbojet unit mounted atop the fuselage aft the cockpit, had a maximum speed of 522mph (835kmh) at 19,690ft (6000m). The result of an incredibly rapid

195

development programme—specifications were issued on 8 September 1944; the prototype flew on 6 December 1944—the wood-and-metal-bonded Volksjäger was intended to be in production at a rate of 1,000 a month by April 1945, rising thereafter to 4,000 a month. Swarms of these fighters were to take on the fighter escorts of the Allied bomber formations, while jet-propelled Me 262s struck at the bombers.

Although a test flight on 10 December 1944 ended in the death of the pilot when defective bonding resulted in the disintegration of a wing—and although subsequent tests showed that even experienced pilots found the aircraft difficult to handle—it was planned that thousands of teenagers of the *Hitlerjugend* would receive primary training on gliders before converting directly to the Volksjäger, gaining their jet-training on operational flights! That a modicum of sanity still existed in command circles is demonstrated by the fact that although more than 120 He 162s reached operational status with the Luftwaffe in January-May 1945, they were kept out of combat.

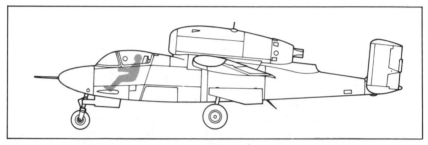

Heinkel He 162A-2 **Volksjäger** ("People's Fighter"; called the "Salamander"); a mass-produced jet-propelled interceptor intended to be flown by half-trained teenagers of the **Hitlerjugend**.

Germany's Aerial Ramming Squadrons

In the latter half of 1941, as German forces thrust inexorably into the Soviet Union, the hard-pressed Red Air Force had increasingly resorted to suicidal tactics. Ramming attacks (which pilots often survived, according to Soviet accounts) on German bombers were not uncommon. Pilots of the *Komsomoltsi* (Young Communist) units are reported to have formed semi-kamikaze squadrons, pledged to bring down the enemy either by ramming or by *Taran* attack, in which a Polikarpov I-16 fighter with a steel-plated propeller attempted to close in astern of a bomber and "buzz-saw" its tail surfaces. By late 1943, the Luftwaffe in its turn was forced to consider similar desperate measures against Allied bombers.

A plan for the formation of interceptor squadrons dedicated to close attack and pledged to ram as a last resort was mooted by a junior officer (a veteran glider pilot) in September 1943, when it was also suggested that explosive-packed Junkers Ju 88s might be aimed at bomber formations by pilots who would attempt to parachute at the last moment. Such schemes were viewed unfavourably by General der Jäger Adolf Galland, head of Germany's fighter arm, who rightly believed that the Luftwaffe should seek efficient methods of dealing with Allied escort fighters before tackling the heavy bombers; but later in the year, Major Hans von Kornatski's advocacy of *Sturm-*

staffeln (Assault Squadrons) equipped with heavily-armoured interceptors—called *Rammjägers* ("Battering Rams")—was successful.

The first Sturmstaffeln were formed in March-April 1944 and were equipped with Focke-Wulf Fw 190A-6 fighters, with increased armour and mounting 4 x 20mm cannon. Later, the Sturmstaffeln received a few Fw 190A-8/R7s, which had armoured wing leading edges to facilitate ramming—but initially, close-in "storm" attacks proved so effective that ramming was usually unnecessary. On 2 November 1944, when almost 1,000 heavy bombers of the US 8th AF, escorted by more than 600 P-51 Mustangs and P-38 Lightnings, appeared in two groups over the Reich, nearly 500 Luftwaffe interceptors rose to meet them, including 61 Fw 190s of two Sturmstaffeln. The Rammjägers claimed 30 out of a total of some 80 bombers destroyed (US figures admit only 40 heavies lost, but credit no fewer than 24 of these to close-attack groups), one by ramming attack by Leutnant Werner Gerth, who died when his parachute failed to open after a deliberate collision with a B-17. Thirty of the 61 Rammjägers were lost.

At first, Sturmstaffeln pilots were volunteers, but soon men were being pressed into service by offers that serious disciplinary charges pending against them would be dropped if they undertook to destroy at least one enemy bomber on each mission, by ramming if necessary—failure to do so involving a capital charge of cowardice! And by the spring of 1945, with both pilots and aircraft in increasingly short supply, the Sturmstaffeln relied more and more on all-out ramming attacks. "The *Rammjägers* are now to make suicide attacks", wrote Propaganda Minister Joseph Goebbels in his diary on 31 March 1945, ". . . 90 per cent casualties are expected . . . [but] extraordinary success is anticipated". He noted also that "50 to 90 per cent are volunteers"; perhaps the lower figure was nearer to the truth.

The climax came on 7 April when, with Nazi marching songs blasting from their radios, 120 Fw 190s and Bf 109Gs of Oberst Hajo Herrmann's *Rammkommando Elbe* took off agianst a force of more than 1,000 heavy bombers and 800 escorts over North Germany. With support from Me 262s, the Rammjägers dived from c.35,000ft (10,670m) on to the bomber stream. In what the USAAF's historians characterize a "suicidal, frenzied effort", lasting some 45 minutes, at least eight B-17s and B-24 Liberators were brought down by ramming attacks. The cost was immense: only 15 of the Rammjägers returned to their bases at Stendal and Gardelegen; 28 pilots had made successful parachute jumps; 77 were dead or missing.

"Our suicide fighters have not produced the hoped-for success", wrote Goebbels next day, ". . . [but] this is only an initial trial which is to be repeated . . . hopefully with better results". In this hope, as in so many more, he was to be disappointed.

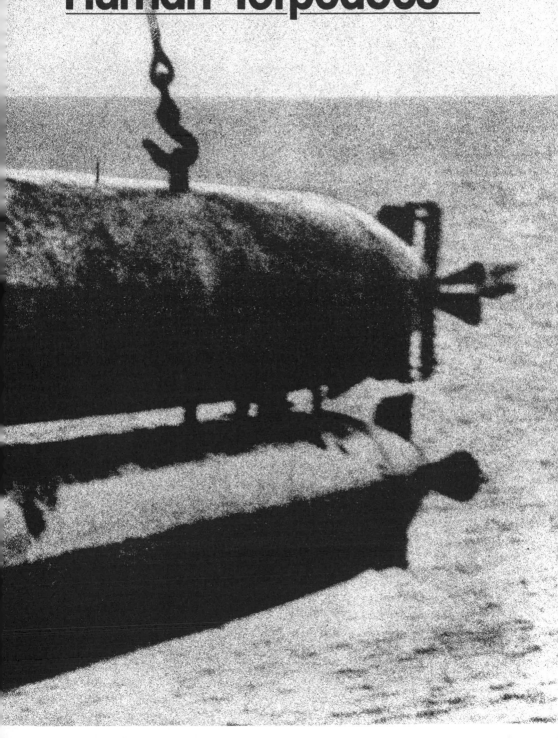

Chapter Five:

Human Torpedoes

Although a number of craft fall within the category of "human torpedoes", only one, the Japanese *Kaiten*, was a purpose-built suicide weapon; and it is with the operations of the kaiten that this chapter is chiefly concerned. The German *Neger, Marder* and *Hai* might be classified either as midget submarines or as manned-torpedoes. I have chosen to put them into the latter category and, since their loss rate was so great as to justify their being designated semi-suicidal craft at least, I describe their development and operations in some detail.

I term the kaiten a "human torpedo", applying that phrase to a suicide weapon. Therefore, the Italian *Maiale* and the British *Chariot* are better described as "manned-torpedoes", for although they were extremely hazardous weapons (and the *Maiale* was at least once used suicidally, see pages 81-82) they cannot properly be called suicide craft. But because they were designed to fulfil the same purpose as the kaiten — and because the reader will find them referred to in many other sources as "human torpedoes" — an account of their development and deployment is necessary. All the more so because, although not suicide craft, they proved in combat to be among the most effective and economical (in terms of both cost and personnel) "special attack" weapons of World War II.

World War I: the "Mignatta"

As in the case of the midget submarine and the explosive motorboat, the Italian Navy pioneered the use of the manned-torpedo in 20th-century warfare. During World War I, as in World War II, the light forces of the Italian Navy distinguished themselves by daring raids made by small torpedo boats and other "special attack" craft. The attack on the Austrian fleet's Adriatic base at Pola by the *Grillo*, in May 1918, is mentioned in Chapter 3; it was probably that gallant failure that inspired the first of the manned-torpedoes, the *Mignatta* ("Leech") of Engineer-Major (naval rank) Raffaele Rossetti and Surgeon-Lt Raffaele Paolucci.

At first working independently, both Paolucci and Rossetti had realised that earlier attacks had resulted in the defences of such major bases as Pola being greatly strengthened, and both sought to develop weapons as small and unobtrusive as possible. Paolucci designed a time-fuzed explosive canister supported by flotation tanks, planning to swim by night from a motor launch into Pola harbour, towing his mine, which he would affix to a warship. Rossetti, meanwhile, worked on a vehicle to carry such a charge. Taking the empty shell of a German 20in (510mm) torpedo, he filled its interior with a compressed-air tank to power a 40hp single-shaft motor. On this basic vehicle, some 27ft (8.2m) long and displacing c.1.5 tons (1.52 tonnes), two men in protective rubber suits could sit astride, "steering" with their arms and legs like men on a toboggan, and proceed in an awash position at a speed of c.2kt (2.3mph, 3.7kmh) to a maximum range of c.8nm (9 miles, 15km), given a calm sea.

The two inventors joined forces to perfect the craft's detachable warhead, which consisted of two bow-mounted metal canisters, each containing 375lb (170kg) of explosive. A clockwork time-fuze allowed for a delay in detonation of up to five hours. Built into the surface of each canister were magnetic clamps (the "leeches" that gave the craft its name; cf, the "limpets" of World War II) by which they could be affixed to the hull of an enemy ship.

Date: **31 October-1 November 1918**
Place: **Pola harbour, Adriatic**
Attack by: **Italian "Mignatta" manned-torpedo**
Target: **Austrian battleships at anchor**

On 31 October 1918, after some four months' intensive training, Rossetti and Paolucci embarked with their craft on the torpedo boat *65 PN* (Cdr Costanzo Ciano). At 2000 that evening the Leech was lowered into the sea off Pola and towed by an electric-powered (ie, silent-running) launch to within 500yds (457m) of the harbour mole. Straddling their craft, with Rossetti at the stern controlling the motor, the Italians headed in. Having negotiated the first net-and-boom defence successfully, they were almost run down by a submarine underway on the surface: fearing discovery, as he later reported, Paolucci prepared "to fire the mines and destroy the machine [and himself and Rossetti], so as to fulfil my debt of honour." Such a suicidal action proved unnecessary and the Leech crept onward, often with both men swimming and manhandling their balky craft over booms against a strong current, until the anchored line of Austrian dreadnoughts was reached. It was now 0430; well over half the Leech's compressed-air reservoir was exhausted and both men realised that there was no chance of returning, as planned, to make rendezvous with the launch outside the harbour.

At c.0500 Rossetti detached one of the charges and swam with it beneath the Austrian battleship *Viribus Unitis* (20,000 tons, 20 320 tonnes). A long and noisy struggle to fix the mine to the warship's hull ensued and would, in normal circumstances, surely have led to the swimmer's detection. Unknown to the Italians, the Austrian Empire had collapsed and the fleet had been handed over that day to Yugoslavia, with concomitant confusion and indiscipline. Not until after reveille sounded aboard the battleship were Rossetti and Paolucci discovered alongside and hauled aboard as prisoners. By this time, one mine on a one-hour fuze was safely in place—and Paolucci's last action before capture was to set the fuze ticking on the remaining charge, still in place on the Leech, and send the lethal craft drifting away on the current.

Once apprised of the Yugoslavian take-over, the Italians warned that the battleship was in immediate danger and urged its evacuation. Their revelation seemed likely to result in a lynching; they, and many crewmen, were still aboard at 0645, when the charge detonated. With her bottom ripped open, the battleship began to settle, took on a heavy list, and capsized. Her Yugoslavian commander, Capt V. Voukovitch, went down with his ship, but few other lives were lost. As well as sinking *Viribus Unitis*, the abandoned Leech had drifted beneath the armed merchant cruiser *Wien* (7,400 tons, 7518 tonnes)—not to be confused with the Austrian battleship of the same name, sunk in December 1917—severely damaging her with its detonation.

Preparing for World War II

It has already been noted that the development of the Italian Navy's "special attack" weapons was stimulated in 1935 by the international tension consequent upon Mussolini's Abyssinian adventure. In September of that year, two young naval engineers, SubLt Teseo Tesei and SubLt Elios Toschi, submitted a plan for a manned-torpedo based on the Leech but with significant improvements—notably the capability of travelling fully submerged over short distances. The design was quickly approved by Admiral Domenico Cavagnari and two prototypes were built at the San Bartolomeo Torpedo Workshops, La Spezia. In January 1936, crewed by its inventors, the weapon ran successful secret trials, and later in the year the training of manned-torpedo personnel was begun under Cdr Catalano Gonzaga di Cirella, commanding 1st Submarine Flotilla.

The pace of development slackened as the Abyssinian crisis passed, but picked up again with increasing threats of war in 1939. The programme was now under the direction of Cdr Paolo Aloisi of the 1st Light Flotilla; Tesei and Toschi, now promoted and relieved of all other duties, made further design improvements to their manned-torpedo. Early in 1940, three manned-torpedoes were launched from the submarine *Ametista* (Cdr J. Valerio Borghese) in the Gulf of Spezia: in a mock-attack by night, one succeeded in penetrating the harbour of La Spezia and fixing a dummy charge to the hull of a target ship. According to Borghese's account, a short-wave radio link to guide the torpedoes back to the mother boat was tested then but was not proceeded with—largely because the torpedoes' operators felt that any provision made for their return might affect their determination to succeed at all costs. (This was an argument used by Japanese servicemen who opposed the fitting of ejector-seats in explosive motorboats and escape hatches in kaiten; weapons which they, if not the high command, acknowledged to be suicidal.) Further, Borghese quotes Tesei (whose suicidal end at Malta in July 1941 is described on pages 81-82) as declaring that "what really counts is that there are men ready to die . . . [to] inspire and fortify future generations . . ."

The "Maiale" Manned-Torpedo

As a result of the successful exercise, the construction of a first batch of 12 manned-torpedoes at San Bartolomeo was ordered. Officially, the weapon was designated the *SLC (Siluro a lenta corsa*, "Slow-running Torpedo"); to the men who manned it, it was almost always known, probably because of its frequent perversity in handling, by the cover-name of *Maiale* ("Pig").

The Pig was 22ft (6.7m) long overall and 1.8ft (533mm) in diameter, displacing 1.5 tons (1.52 tonnes). It was powered by a 1.1hp (later uprated to 1.6hp) electric motor, giving near-silent running at a maximum 4.5kt (5.2mph, 8.3kmh) to a range of 4nm (4.6 miles, 7.4km) or at 2.3kt (2.6mph, 4.25kmh) to a range of c.15nm (17 miles, 28km). Its crew were clad in protective rubber suits and equipped with self-contained breathing-apparatus fed by a six-hour supply of bottled oxygen, and the Pig was capable of full submergence, to a safe depth of c.100ft (30m), over a fairly short distance. The bow-mounted

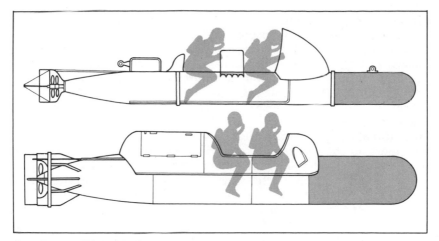

Upper: The Italian **SLC** (**Maiale**, "Pig") manned-torpedo. Note suspension-ring forward, used to sling warhead beneath target ship's hull by means of a cable passed through magnetic clamps.
Lower: In the **SSB**, the final model of the **Maiale**, the operators were partly enclosed.

detachable warhead was at first of 485lb (220kg) explosive weight, later rising to 550lb (250kg) and at last to 660lb (300kg). A time-fuze allowed up to five hours' delay in detonation.

The Pig's operators sat astride their craft with their feet held in place by metal stirrups. The officer-pilot, forward, was protected by a chest-high curved metal screen on which was mounted a luminous magnetic compass, a depth-gauge, a spirit-level, and instruments for monitoring the electric motor. He controlled the rudders with a steering-column of aircraft type; trim-levers admitted water to or "blew" the tanks. Separated from the pilot by the protuberance of the crash immersion tank, the co-pilot (usually a petty-officer/diver) sat with his back against a metal storage locker containing spare breathing gear and tools.

In the last few of the 80-plus Pigs built in 1940-43, the operators were provided with greater security by the provision of an overall metal casing, which gave the craft an appearance something like that of a dual-cockpit aircraft fuselage. These later examples, called the *SSB* (*Siluro San Bartolomeo*, "San Bartolomeo Torpedo"), are believed to have been of improved performance; their operational deployment was, however, forestalled by Italy's collapse.

Transport to the Attack Zone

The first operation planned for the Pigs was an attack on British warships at Alexandria, Egypt, scheduled for the night of 25-26 August 1940. The submarine *Iride* (Lt Francesco Brunetti) was to carry four Pigs clamped to her casing, releasing them some 4nm (4.6 miles, 7.4km) from the harbour. With the unprotected Pigs aboard, the submarine could not dive deeper than the Pigs' maximum tolerance of c.100ft (30m), which would certainly have put her at risk from aircraft patrolling the clear coastal waters. In the event, *Iride* was caught on the surface while training for the mission in the Gulf of Bomba, off Libya, and sunk by torpedo-planes from HMS *Eagle*. Among the survivors were Tesei and Toschi, who had both volunteered for the first combat mission of their weapon.

Meanwhile, thought had been given to the safety of the mother boats on Pig missions. Beginning in August-September 1940, five fleet submarines were fitted with watertight steel cylinders to house Pigs in transit. The "Perla" class boat *Ambra* and the "Adua" class *Gondar* and *Scirè*, with the forward 3.9in (99mm) gun removed, mounted one cylinder forward and two aft; the "Flutto" class *Grongo* and *Murena*, completed in 1943, were both designed to mount four cylinders on the side casing, one pair just fore and aft the conning tower on either side. The Pigs could be taken from their cylinders by crewmen in "frogman" outfits (I employ the term for convenience; it was not in use in 1940-41) and mounted by their operators while the mother boat lay submerged.

One of the mother boats was soon lost. Late in September 1940, *Gondar* and *Scirè* (the former commanded by Lt Brunetti, who had survived *Iride's* sinking) sailed to launch simultaneous Pig strikes against Alexandria and Gibraltar respectively. The missions were aborted when intelligence reported the absence of major warships at both anchorages, but on the homeward run *Gondar* was intercepted by the destroyers HMS *Diamond* and HMAS *Stuart*, supported by Short Sunderland flying-boats. Badly damaged by depthcharges after a 12-hour hunt, *Gondar* surfaced and was scuttled by her crew. Among those taken prisoner were Capt Toschi, co-inventor of the Pig, and Cdr Mario Giorgini, commanding 1st Light Flotilla. (Giorgini's place was taken by Cdr Vittorio Moccagatta, under whom the "special weapons" section took the name by which it is best known: *Decima Flottiglia MAS*, 10th Light Flotilla.)

The nearest approach to operational success during the first year of manned-torpedo operations was made by Pigs launched from *Scirè* (Cdr Borghese) in Algeciras Bay, Gibraltar, on the night of 29-30 October 1940. One of the three Pigs launched sank within 30 minutes. A second, piloted by the now Major Tesei, with Sgt-Diver Alcide Pedretti, reached the mouth of the inner harbour before failure of both men's breathing-apparatus, and of the reserve set, caused Tesei to abort the mission. Scuttling their craft (the eventual fate of which is described on page 220) Tesei and Pedretti swam to the Spanish shore where, like the crew of the other sunken Pig, they were able to contact Italian agents and return safely to Italy.

The third Pig, crewed by Lt Gino Birindelli and PO-Diver Damos Paccagnini, although handling sluggishly because of a faulty trimming tank, penetrated the military harbour while running just awash, surfaced fully to clear the boom defences, and at last crept along the harbour bottom at c.50ft (15m) towards the battleship HMS *Barham*. Within about 75yds (70m) of this rich prize, the Pig's motor failed: Birindelli, single-handed because Paccagnini's breathing-gear had failed, attempted to drag the warhead along the harbour bottom towards the battleship. After some 30 minutes, increasing symptoms of carbon-dioxide poisoning forced him to abandon the Herculean task. Setting the time-fuze (the charge later exploded harmlessly), Birindelli swam ashore and, like Paccagnini, was taken prisoner.

Above: Based on the shell of a German 20in (510mm) torpedo, the **Mignatta** ("Leech") manned-torpedo was developed by the Italian naval officers Rossetti and Paolucci in World War I.

Left: An Italian **Maiale** ("Pig") manned-torpedo of World War II. The warhead separates from the main body at the ring immediately forward of the metal screen protecting the pilot.

Below: Watertight metal cylinders like this one, mounted forward on the Italian submarine **Scirè**, housed either a **Maiale** manned-torpedo or an **MTR** (a smaller **MTM**) explosive motorboat.

Above: The **SSB** (**Siluro San Bartolomeo**; "San Bartolomeo Torpedo"), the final model of the **Maiale**, was given a streamlined metal casing which improved performance. None was operational.

Right: Prince Junio Valerio Borghese, wartime commander of the Italian Navy's 10th Light Flotilla, sits in an **SSB** manned-torpedo at the Imperial War Museum, London, April 1953.

Far right: Wearing a rubberized twill "Sladen suit" and self-contained breathing-gear, a British "Charioteer" bestrides a manned-torpedo from which the warhead has been removed.

Below: Like the Italian **Maiale** on which it was based, the British **Chariot** approached its target while awash, under cover of darkness, and submerged only for the final run-in.

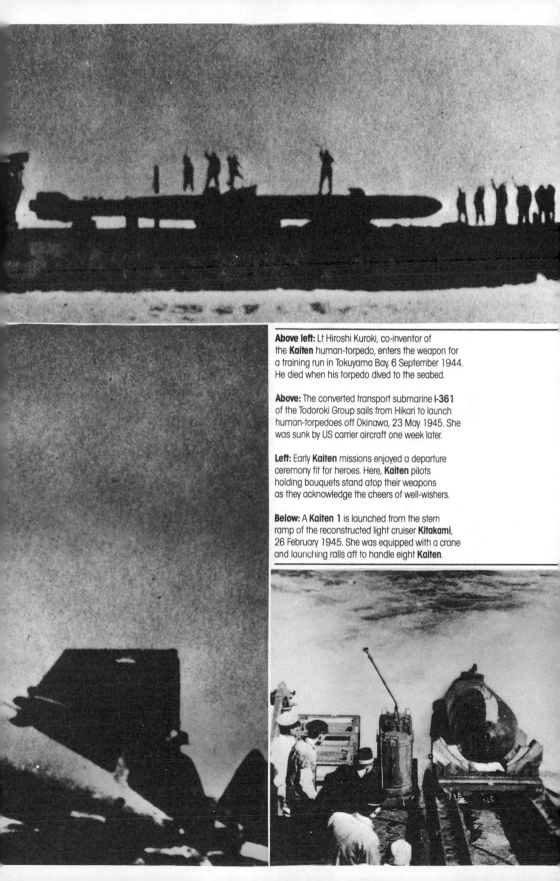

Above left: Lt Hiroshi Kuroki, co-inventor of the **Kaiten** human-torpedo, enters the weapon for a training run in Tokuyama Bay, 6 September 1944. He died when his torpedo dived to the seabed.

Above: The converted transport submarine **I-361** of the Todoroki Group sails from Hikari to launch human-torpedoes off Okinawa, 23 May 1945. She was sunk by US carrier aircraft one week later.

Left: Early **Kaiten** missions enjoyed a departure ceremony fit for heroes. Here, **Kaiten** pilots holding bouquets stand atop their weapons as they acknowledge the cheers of well-wishers.

Below: A **Kaiten 1** is launched from the stern ramp of the reconstructed light cruiser **Kitakami**, 26 February 1945. She was equipped with a crane and launching rails aft to handle eight **Kaiten**.

Above: The 1,500-ton fast transport/landing ship **T 1**, May 1944. The 21 ships of this class had stern ramps with rollers or rails for launching landing craft, midget submarines or **Kaiten.**

Far left: A column of smoke and flame rises over the US fleet anchorage at Ulithi atoll, western Carolines, after the fully-loaded, 11,300-ton fleet oiler USS **Mississinewa** is struck by a **Kaiten** human-torpedo, 20 November 1944.

Bottom left: This **Kaiten**, launched off Ulithi on 20 November 1944, ran on to a reef. Its warhead detonated, but the salvaged wreck provided information on the new suicide weapon.

Centre left: These 3,418lb (1550kg) warheads for **Kaiten** human-torpedoes were found by US occupation forces at Maizuru Naval Base, southern Honshu, after Japan's surrender.

Left: LtCdr Mochitsura Hashimoto, IJN, arrives in Washington after the war to give evidence at the court martial of the captain of USS **Indianapolis**, sunk by Hashimoto's **Kaiten**-carrying submarine **I-58** on 29 July 1945.

Below: Some **Kaiten** deployed in defence of Japan were to be shore-launched from rail trolleys.

Above: A **Neger** ("Nigger") manned-torpedo of the German Navy's "K-Force" is lowered to the water for a trial run early in 1944.

Right: German naval technicians inspect a **Neger**. Note the improvisational appearance of the control rudders at the stern of the upper body, and the narrow clearance between the two bodies.

Below right: **Negers** were first used off the Anzio-Nettuno beachhead, Italy, on the night of 20-21 April 1944. This specimen was found drifting by the Allies next morning: the dome was smashed to bring out the pilot, who had died from carbon-dioxide poisoning.

Below centre: Returning from a **Neger** sortie off Normandy, 8 July 1944, Cpl-Clerk Walter Gerhold is congratulated on sinking a light cruiser.

Below: The original **Neger**, designed by Richard Mohr in 1943-44, from which the operational models and, later, the similar but fully-submersible **Marder** ("Marten"), were developed.

Above: More than 24,000 of the 30,000-strong Japanese garrison died in defence of Saipan; some 3,000 in a **Banzai** charge on the night of 6-7 July 1944. This was its aftermath.

Above right: Realizing that Saipan must fall, many Japanese servicemen and civilians committed suicide. The man in the background, wearing a naval mechanic's badge, has apparently pulled the trigger of his rifle with his toe.

Below: Aftermath of the night raid on the US airfield at Yontan, Okinawa, by men of the IJA's **Giretsu** ("Heroic") Airborne Unit, 24 May 1945. About 10 of the 13 volunteer suicide commandos aboard (**Bottom**) the single Mitsubishi Ki-21-IIb "Sally" heavy bomber that succeeded in crash-landing at Yontan, did considerable damage with grenades and demolition charges.

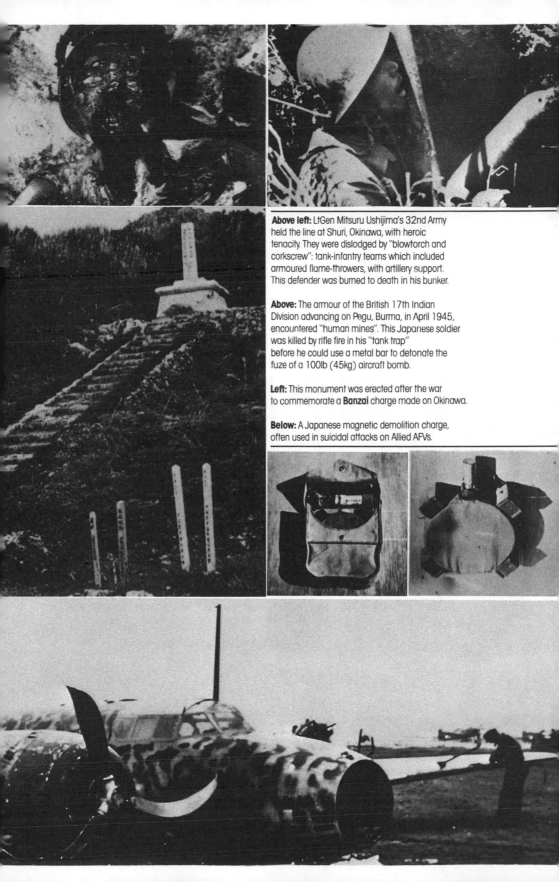

Above left: LtGen Mitsuru Ushijima's 32nd Army held the line at Shuri, Okinawa, with heroic tenacity. They were dislodged by "blowtorch and corkscrew": tank-infantry teams which included armoured flame-throwers, with artillery support. This defender was burned to death in his bunker.

Above: The armour of the British 17th Indian Division advancing on Pegu, Burma, in April 1945, encountered "human mines". This Japanese soldier was killed by rifle fire in his "tank trap" before he could use a metal bar to detonate the fuze of a 100lb (45kg) aircraft bomb.

Left: This monument was erected after the war to commemorate a **Banzai** charge made on Okinawa.

Below: A Japanese magnetic demolition charge, often used in suicidal attacks on Allied AFVs.

Above: A Japanese soldier commits suicide to avoid capture: a sequence of photographs shot in Papua-New Guinea. (**Top left**) A Japanese who has attempted to swim away begins to wade ashore, watched by an Australian soldier, who realizes (**Top right**) that he holds a grenade and (**Bottom left**) comes on guard. But the Japanese holds the grenade to his head and pulls out the pin.

Left: "One hundred million will die for the Emperor"! Japanese militia drill with bamboo spears for the defence of the home islands.

Below: Damage at Cowra PoW camp, New South Wales, after Japanese prisoners attempted a break-out on 5 August 1944. Of the 234 who died in the incident, many committed suicide in desperation.

Scirè returned to Gibraltar on the night of 26-27 May 1941, launching three Pigs. One sank; the others reached merchant shipping anchored in deep water outside the military harbour but failed to carry through their attacks because of mechanical failures. Within a few weeks, Tesei was to meet his suicidal end on a Pig at Malta and, with Toschi a PoW, neither of the Pig's inventors would take part in its long-delayed operational success. Indeed, I would suggest that the suicidal determination displayed by Tesei at Malta was largely provoked by the Pigs' poor operational record to date.

Date: **19-20 September 1941**
Place: **Algeciras Bay, Gibraltar**
Attack by: **Italian "Maiali" manned-torpedoes**
Target: **Allied shipping at anchor**

That record was now to improve dramatically. On the night of 19 September 1941, Borghese took *Scirè* yet again into Algeciras Bay, releasing three Pigs at its northern end for the run-down of some 3nm (3.5 miles, 5.5km) with the current to the military harbour on the southeast of the Bay. The Pigs left *Scirè* at 0100 on 20 September. Italian intelligence reported the presence of a battleship, an aircraft carrier and two cruisers in the military harbour and these were, of course, the assigned targets. But the British were by now well-apprised of the Italian threat: the Algeciras roadstead and the entrance to the military harbour were intensively patrolled by launches which dropped depthcharges at regular intervals.

As it approached the entrance to the military anchorage, well protected by booms and netting, the Pig crewed by Lt Decio Catalano with PO-Diver Giuseppe Giannoni was tracked by a launch. Alternately surfacing and submerging while dodging between merchantmen anchored in the roadstead, Catalano at last evaded the hunter — but by 0350 he had been driven far from the harbour entrance. With dawn approaching, he decided on a merchantman as his target, and he and Giannoni had already fixed their warhead to a sizeable ship when they discovered that she was a captured vessel of Italian registration. Quixotically, they unshipped their charge and transferred it to the nearby armed motorship *Durham* (10,900 tons, 11 075 tonnes), fixing magnetic clamps to the target's bilge keel and slinging the warhead beneath it by means of a rope passed through the suspension-ring on its upper side, with the fuze on a four-hour delay. At c.0600, after setting the self-destruction charge that was now part of the Pig's design, Catalano and Giannoni scuttled their craft and swam to safety on the Spanish shore, whence they were able to observe the detonation of their warhead at 0916. Badly damaged, *Durham* was beached by harbour tugs.

Allied patrols had also driven the Pig of Lt Amadeo Vesco and PO-Diver Antonio Zozzoli away from the entrance to the military harbour — and they, too, had chosen a target in the roadstead. At c.0800, as Vesco and Zozzoli watched from a Spanish coastguard station, the warhead they had fixed in place broke in half the small tanker *Fiona Shell* (2,444 tons, 2483 tonnes).

It was left to Lt Licio Visintini and PO-Diver Giovanni Magro to

217

show that the Pig was truly capable of the task for which it was intended—the penetration of a heavily-defended anchorage and the destruction of shipping therein. After dodging patrolling launches, Visintini submerged to c.35ft (11m) to thread his Pig between the steel cables supporting netting across the mouth of the military harbour. Inside, he surfaced near a British cruiser. Deciding that he had insufficient time—it was now 0405—to penetrate the harbour more deeply in search of HMS *Ark Royal,* his assigned target, Visintini decided against the cruiser in favour of a large tanker riding low in the water nearby, hoping to start an oil fire that would engulf the harbour. Submerged to 23ft (7m) below the tanker, and more than once shocked by depthcharge detonations that flung them against its hull, Visintini and Magro fixed their charge by 0440, remounted their Pig, and again evaded the patrols to make a clean getaway. By 0630 they were in the hands of Italian agents in Spain, disappointed only in that when a violent explosion broke the back of the Royal Fleet Auxiliary oiler *Denbydale* (8,145 tons, 8275 tonnes) at 0843, the holocaust they had hoped for did not follow.

The genesis and development of the Pig, its early failures and its first successful mission have been described in sufficient detail to enable the reader to compare the Italian manned-torpedo with the Japanese and German weapons, suicidal and semi-suicidal, of the same "family" which are treated of later in this chapter. But since the Pig cannot be described as a suicide weapon, my account of its further operations, and of the British *Chariot* derived from it, must be brief.

Triumph at Alexandria

Had the Italian naval general staff proved more resolute, and their German opposite numbers more supportive of an ally, the Pigs' greatest success might significantly have affected the course of the war. On the night of 18-19 December 1941, three Pigs launched from *Scirè* penetrated Alexandria harbour, slipping awash through the gate in the net-and-boom barrier in the wake of British destroyers. Although special precautionary measures had been ordered only two days before by Admiral A. B. Cunningham, CinC Mediterranean, the Pigs avoided patrolling launches and negotiated their targets' anti-torpedo netting while surfaced.

Lt Luigi Durand de La Penne and PO-Diver Emilio Bianchi were assigned the battleship HMS *Valiant* (30,600 tons, 31 090 tonnes). Although Bianchi's breathing-gear failed, forcing him to the surface, and the Pig was immobilized by a fouled propeller, de La Penne succeeded in manhandling his craft along the bottom for the last few yards and setting the fuze on its warhead. The two Italians then surfaced alongside the battleship and were captured. Refusing to respond to questioning, they were imprisoned in *Valiant's* hold, very near the site of the charge, and were still aboard when detonation occurred at 0620. A few minutes earlier, the charge placed beneath *Valiant's* sister-ship HMS *Queen Elizabeth* by Engineer-Capt Antonio Marceglia and PO-Diver Spartaco Schergat had detonated: Admiral Cunningham himself, then standing right aft on the battleship's deck, reported being "tossed about five feet into the air" by the whiplash of the massive warship. Marceglia and Schergat were captured ashore three days later.

The third Pig, crewed by Gunner-Capt Vincenzo Martellotta and PO-Diver Mario Marino, had been assigned a laden tanker as target and, in addition to the Pig's warhead, the men were equipped with six small calcium-carbide incendiary charges. Setting their main charge beneath the tanker *Sagona* (7,554 tons, 7675 tonnes), the Italians fuzed their incendiaries to detonate later than the warhead and released them to float nearby, hoping that an oil fire would be started. Although this stratagem failed, *Sagona* and the destroyer HMS *Jervis*, moored alongside, were both severely damaged. Martellotta and Marino were captured ashore.

Admiral Cunningham ordered the Italian prisoners to be held incommunicado for six months but this and other disinformation measures almost certainly failed to prevent the Axis commanders from learning the full extent of the damage. *Valiant*, with a 1,800 sq ft (167 sq m) rent in her lower bulge forward and much internal damage, was out of action until July 1942. *Queen Elizabeth* was worse hit: with her double bottom stove in over an area of 5,400 sq ft (502 sq m) and serious damage to her machinery, she settled on the harbour bottom. An attempt to finish her off by Pigs launched from *Ambra* on 14 May 1942 failed; she was patched up and dispatched to the United States for permanent repairs, which were not completed until June 1943.

Cunningham praised "the cold-blooded bravery and enterprise of these Italians" and rated the damage to the battleships "a disaster". Ordering the construction of far heavier barriers at the harbour entrance, he commented that after the attack "everyone has had the jitters, seeing objects swimming about at night . . . That must stop". One immediate counter-measure was to order warships at anchor to keep their engines running slow astern: the wash thus created beneath the hull would, it was thought, "flush out" enemy swimmers or at least hinder their nocturnal activities.

For the expenditure of three Pigs and six men captured, the 10th Light Flotilla had reversed the balance of naval power in the Mediterranean, but the Italian high command (subsequently blaming the Germans for failing to provide an adequate fuel supply for increased naval operations) did not take full advantage of this sudden superiority in capital ships.

Pigs and "Gamma Groups"

In mid-1942, Borghese became commander of the 10th Light Flotilla, handing over *Scirè* to Cdr Bruno Zelik (who was lost with all his crew on 10 August 1942 when the submarine was sunk by the AS-trawler HMS *Islay* while attempting to launch Pigs off Haifa harbour, Palestine). Under Borghese's driving leadership, "special attack" operations flourished.

In late 1941, Borghese had been instrumental in forming the "Gamma Groups" to operate in conjunction with the Pigs. Originally intended as "underwater infantry" who would walk the seabed in much the same way as the Japanese *Fukuryu* (see Chapter 6), the Gamma men soon evolved into assault swimmers. These "frogmen", clad in protective rubber suits with swim-fins on their feet, had self-contained breathing-gear which gave them an underwater endurance of c.30-40 minutes. Each man carried on a waist-belt four or five "bugs", 4.4-6.6lb (2-3kg) time-fuzed explosive charges, with suction cups by which they were affixed to enemy hulls. The "bugs" were later replaced by magnetic "limpets" of 9.9lb (4.5kg), which incorporated both time- and distance-fuzes; when it was learned that the British had formed an anti-limpeteer team of frogmen at Gibraltar under Lt. L.K.P. "Buster" Crabb, RN, a booby-trap device was added to the Italian swimmers' charges. A fully-equipped Gamma man was expected to operate to a range of up to c.4nm (4.6 miles, 7.4km) at an average speed of 0.8kt (0.9mph, 1.5kmh), leaving a mother boat along with the Pigs, making his approach to the target on the surface, and diving only for the final run-in.

The major successes of the combined Pig-Gamma teams were scored against Allied shipping at Gibraltar, where an Italian base was established in Algeciras Bay itself. The Italian freighter *Olterra* had been sabotaged at the beginning of the war and lay half-sunken in Spanish territorial waters. On the pretext of being repaired and handed over to Spain, she was raised and towed into Algeciras harbour, across the Bay from the Allied military anchorage. With what must have been the connivance of the Spanish authorities (although Borghese was to deny this), her hold became the base for Pigs and Gamma men, who slipped out through an underwater door for a series of raids on the Algeciras roadstead. Between September 1942 and August 1943, manned-torpedoes and swimmers from *Olterra* sank or badly damaged 11 Allied merchant ships totalling some 54,200 tons (55 070 tonnes). In addition, on 12 December 1942, three Pigs and ten Gamma swimmers were launched from the submarine *Ambra* (Cdr Mario Arillo) as she lay submerged in the Algiers roadstead, sinking or damaging four merchantmen totalling c.22,300 tons (22 660 tonnes). At the time of Italy's collapse, preparations were being made aboard *Olterra* to launch the newly-received *SSB*-type Pig against Gibraltar.

"CHARIOT": THE BRITISH MANNED-TORPEDO

The Pig scuttled by Tesei and Pedretti in Algeciras Bay on 30 October 1940 (see page 204) had been washed ashore in Spain, where British intelligence was able to discover full details of the weapon; and other Pigs were soon recovered intact at Gibraltar and Alexandria. By mid-1942, the Royal Navy had made a prototype copy called the *Chariot*, and training under Cdr W. R. Fell, RN, and Cdr Geoffrey Sladen, RN, was underway in the far north of Scotland, from the depot ship HMS *Titania*.

The British Chariot differed very little from the Italian Pig. It was slightly longer overall—25ft (7.62m) with its warhead, as compared to 22ft (6.7m)—but of the same diameter (21in, 533mm) and displacement (1.5 tons, 1.52 tonnes). The added length was due to a somewhat larger warhead, a maximum of 700lb (318kg) of explosive on the Chariot Mark I. Its electric motor was superior to the Italian unit, giving a maximum speed of above 4kt (4.6mph, 7.4kmh) and a range of up to 18nm (21 miles, 33km) at 3kt (3.5mph, 5.5kmh). Although its safe

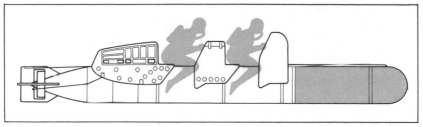

The British "Chariot" manned-torpedo closely resembled the Italian **SLC**, on which it was based, but had a superior performance and carried a larger warhead of up to 700lb (318kg).

diving depth was rated at only 35ft (10.7m), this limit was frequently exceeded during both training and operations.

The rubberized twill "frogman" suits worn by Charioteers, designed by Cdr Sladen and incorporating the self-contained breathing-gear of the Davis Submarine Escape Apparatus, were more durable but also more bulky than those used by the Italians. This was partly due to a need to provide added protection for men who were expected to operate the Chariots in cold northern waters: the Italians had not thought it possible for manned-torpedoes to operate at water temperatures of below c.50°F (10°C).

"Operation Title": Chariots against "Tirpitz"

Indeed, northern waters were the destination of the first Charioteers deployed. Late in October 1942, the Norwegian fishing boat *Arthur* sailed from the Shetlands; ostensibly an innocent coaster carrying a cargo of peat to Trondheim, Norway. But her skipper, Leif Larsen, and his crew were members of the Norwegian Resistance; concealed on deck were two Chariots; and in a secret compartment in the hold were six British Charioteers, two attack crews and two "dressers".

The target was *Tirpitz*, then based at Trondheim. On a small, uninhabited island off the Norwegian coast, the Chariots would be unloaded and slung beneath *Arthur's* hull by wire traces fixed through eye-bolts in her keel. With false papers, *Arthur* would bluff her way into the heavily-guarded Trondheimsfjord, where the Chariots would be slipped at night for a run against *Tirpitz*. After laying their charges, the Charioteers would scuttle their craft, swim ashore, and be helped home via Sweden by the Norwegian Resistance.

All went to plan until, in the final run up Trondheimsfjord, a heavy swell battered the Chariots on their slings against *Arthur's* keel. Both broke free and sank when the fishing boat was no more than 8nm (9 miles, 15km) short of the battleship. *Arthur* herself was in a poor state; she was scuttled and her crew and the Charioteers began the perilous journey home. An added hazard of "special attack" operations in European waters was now made manifest: the Charioteer AB R. Evans, RN, was wounded and captured in a skirmish near the Swedish frontier. Nursed back to health by the Germans, he was interrogated and then—on the insistence of Gen Wilhelm Keitel, Chief of the High Command of the Armed Forces, in pursuance of Hitler's notorious "anti-commando" order of 18 October 1942—tried on a charge of espionage, condemned, and executed by firing-squad.

Successful Chariot Operations

In December 1942, a Chariot base was established at Malta under Cdr Sladen. Three submarines of the 10th Flotilla—HMS *Trooper, Thunderbolt* and *P.311* (ex-*Tutankhamen*)—were fitted with containers much like those used by the Italians and were thus able to carry two or three Chariots apiece.

All three submarines sailed from Malta on 28-29 December to launch Chariots off Palermo, Sicily, where the new Italian light cruiser *Ulpio Traiano* (3,747 tons, 3807 tonnes) was approaching completion after her launch in November. En route, *P.311* was lost with all hands, almost certainly sunk by a mine. Off Palermo on the night of 2-3 January 1943, *Thunderbolt* launched two Chariots and *Trooper* three; the manned-torpedoes were launched while the mother boats lay surfaced, although later it proved possible to launch while submerged at a depth of c.50ft (15m).

Fighting a heavy sea whipped up by a Force 4 gale (which forced one of *Trooper's* Chariots to abort its mission when a crewman was incapacitated by seasickness), a Chariot from *Thunderbolt* crewed by Lt R.T.G. Greenland, RNVR, and Ldg-Sig A. Ferrier negotiated a spiked buoy-and-net barrier and anti-torpedo netting and ran on the surface towards the Italian cruiser. At c.0400, Greenland put his warhead in place on a two-hour fuze—and then continued to move on the surface around the harbour while he and Ferrier affixed 5lb (2.3kg) "limpets" to four small craft. Their task completed, the Charioteers attempted to make rendezvous with *Thunderbolt,* but complete failure of the Chariot's compass caused them to scuttle their craft and swim ashore. Both were captured—having witnessed the explosion that sank *Ulpio Traiano,* which was never repaired.

Of the ten Charioteers taking part in this successful operation, six were taken prisoner, two were lost, and two returned. Of the remaining Chariots, two were prevented from completing their missions by mechanical failure or crew sickness; of their four operators, two were drowned and two rescued by a patrolling British submarine. However, a Chariot from *Trooper* crewed by SubLt R.G. Dove, RNVR, and Ldg-Seaman J. Freel penetrated the anchorage and placed a charge beneath the transport *Viminale* (8,700 tons, 8839 tonnes), which was badly damaged by the subsequent explosion.

Italo-British Chariot Teams

Late in 1943 the British Chariot teams were reinforced by those members of the Italian 10th Light Flotilla, led by Cdr Ernesto Forza, who had chosen not to follow Borghese in continued adherence to the Axis cause. A number of operations by Italo-British manned-torpedo teams and "frogmen" were carried out against units of the Italian fleet that had fallen into German hands.

On the night of 21-22 June 1944, Pigs and Chariots launched from the Italian destroyer *Grecale* and the British *MTB 74* penetrated La Spezia to sink the heavy cruiser *Bolzano* (11,065 tons, 11 242 tonnes); a few night later, in a similar attack, the heavy cruiser *Gorizia* was badly damaged. In the last manned-torpedo operation in European waters, on the night of 19-20 April 1945, the uncompleted aircraft carrier *Aquila* (27,000 tons, 27 432 tonnes), which the Germans planned to use as a blockship at Genoa, was sunk in her dock by Italo-British manned-torpedoes and swimmers.

Mark II Chariots in the Far East

The comparative fragility of the Chariot had necessitated the fitting of transport containers to its mother boats, had prevented submerged launching below c.50ft (15m), and had caused the abandonment of plans for deploying Chariots by towing them behind fast coastal motorboats or carrying them in and launching them from Sunderland flying-boats. The Chariot Mark II (or "Terry Chariot", after Cdr S. Terry, RN, a leading figure in British manned-torpedo design) was a more sturdy vehicle.

As in the Italian *SSB*, the two Charioteers (sitting back to back in the Mark II) were partly enclosed by a metal shell. Better hydrodynamic qualities and an up-rated motor increased both speed and range, to a maximum of c.30nm (34.5 miles, 55.5km) at 4.5kt (5.2mph, 8.3kmh), and allowed the fitting of a warhead of up to 1,100lb (500kg) of Torpex. No special container was needed to transport the Mark II, which was able to withstand pressure to a depth of 300ft (91m).

The first Charioteers trained on the Mark II were sent to establish a base at Trincomalee, Ceylon (Sri Lanka), for operations against Japanese shipping. On 22 October 1944, the submarine HMS *Trenchant* sailed with two Chariots aboard for an attack on the harbour at Phuket town, Phuket Island, Andaman Sea, where the Japanese were refitting several captured merchant ships. Launched some 5nm (6 miles, 9km) offshore on the night of 27-28 October, both Chariots penetrated the harbour and placed their charges, sinking the ex-Italian freighter *Sumatra* (4,859 tons, 4937 tonnes) and badly damaging the *Volpi* (5,292 tons, 5377 tonnes). Both returned safely to rendezvous with *Trenchant*, where they were scuttled and their crews taken aboard the submarine.

However, it was known that the Japanese intended to treat captured "special attack" personnel with exceptional severity. (In 1945, the survivors of a Commando raid on shipping at Singapore, in which electrically-powered submersible canoes called 'Sleeping Beauties" were used, were tried by a military court and, having been praised in the most extravagant terms by the prosecuting officer for valour which should be "taken as a model by the Japanese", were condemned and executed.) The Charioteers at Phuket had been provided with elaborate escape kits—including poison capsules—but the British high command hesitated to commit men to missions that often necessitated the surrender of the participants after their task was completed. Thus, it was decided that Chariot operations against the Japanese were too hazardous to be continued.

JAPANESE HUMAN TORPEDOES

Enough has been said of the Pig and the Chariot to make it clear that they were hazardous but not suicidal weapons. The *Kaiten*, the weapon with which the Imperial Japanese Navy hoped to "make a tremendous change" in the Pacific War, was a manned-torpedo (better

223

described as a "human torpedo") which gave its operator no chance of survival, in spite of an "official" gesture to that end.

The "Long Lance" Torpedo

The IJN's interest in large-diameter torpedoes dated from the decade following the Russo-Japanese War, when an experimental 24in (610mm) harbour-defence weapon was ordered from Whitehead of Fiume. Japanese experiments with enriched-air propulsion units began in c.1926 and were stimulated by intelligence reports of British experiments with hydrogen-peroxide and oxygen systems. In fact, the Royal Navy's effort ceased after 1928, because of the instability and high corrosion factor of the liquid oxygen used in the excessively-bulky Mark VII torpedo.

A team of Japanese designers at Kure, led by Vice-Admiral Toshihide Asaguma and Rear-Admiral Kaneji Kishimoto, persevered, and by 1933 had brought to fleet-testing stage the 24in (610mm) *Shiki Sanso Gyorai Type 93*—the "Long Lance". It was a formidable weapon, outweighing and outranging the torpedoes of other major navies. Unlike compressed-air torpedoes, it was wakeless.

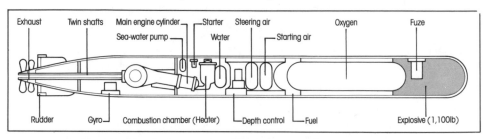

The Imperial Japanese Navy's massive **Type 93** "Long Lance" oxygen torpedo, developed in extreme secrecy from c.1926 onward, provided the basis of the **Kaiten** human torpedo. The "Long Lance" was carried by cruisers and destroyers; the similar but smaller **Type 95** by submarines.

The massive power of the Long Lance—and the liability of its ultra-sensitive fuze to malfunction—was first apparent to the Allies at the Battle of the Java Sea, on 27 February 1942, when Rear-Admiral Doorman's ABDA (American-British-Dutch-Australian) force was engaged at long range by Rear-Admiral Takagi's cruisers and

TORPEDOES OF JAPANESE AND U.S. SURFACE SHIPS, c.1941		
Type:	Type 93 "Long Lance" (Japan)	Mk 15 (USA)
Length:	29.5ft (8.99m)	23ft (7m)
Diameter:	24in (610mm)	21in (533mm)
Weight:	6,107lb (2766kg)	3,289lb (1490kg)
Machinery:	Type 93 petrol/liquid oxygen engine	Turbine
Max speed:	49kt (56mph, 91kmh)	48kt (55mph, 89kmh)
Range:	43,744yd (40000m) @ 36kt (41mph, 67kmh) 34,995yd (32000m) @ 40kt (46mph, 74kmh) 24,059yd (22000m) @ 48kt (55mph, 89kmh)	15,190yd (13890m) @ 27kt (31mph, 50kmh) 10,130yd (9260m) @ 33kt (38mph, 61kmh) 6,100yd (5580m) @ 45kt (52mph, 83kmh)
Warhead:	1,100lb (498kg)	660lb (299kg)
Note: Japan developed the "Type 95" oxygen torpedo for use by submarines. This was a 21in (533mm) diameter torpedo, with a range of 40,478yd (37000m) @ 36kt (41mph, 67kmh) or 21,880yd (20000m) @ 50kt (57mph, 92kmh).		

destroyers. The Japanese warships released some 43 Long Lance torpedoes from a range of more than 16,000yds (15 000m): some 20 blew up while running and no hits were made. But one of a subsequent spread—again released at such a range that the Allied vessels, with no Japanese warships in sight, believed themselves to be under submarine attack—struck the Dutch destroyer *Kortenaer*, literally tearing her in half. In the night action which followed, the Dutch cruisers *De Ruyter* and *Java* fell to the Long Lance.

Genesis of the Kaiten

But in spite of its range and power, the Long Lance was by 1942 obsolescent as a major weapon for surface ships. In a conventional gunnery engagement, opening at c.20 miles (32km) and with the range closing thereafter, it was a battle-winning weapon: in the Pacific War, where major naval battles were fought by aircraft at ranges of 200 miles (320km) or more, its advantages were lost.

By 1944, Allied carrier task forces had established air supremacy and Japan was beginning to strangle in the noose of blockade. The operational capability of the Japanese surface ships armed with the

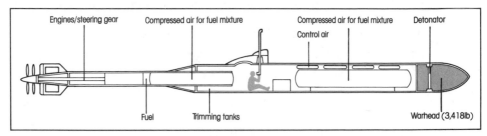

The **Kaiten 1** human torpedo, the only model of this suicide weapon to be used operationally, was basically a "Long Lance" torpedo lengthened to incorporate a pilot's compartment and a small conning tower amidships. It carried an impact-detonated warhead of 3,418lb (1550kg).

Long Lance was drastically curtailed by mounting losses and fuel shortages. When more than 400 aircraft were lost, with their irreplaceable crews, and the Japanese carrier force shattered in the Battle of the Philippine Sea, 19-20 June 1944, the naval high command was ready to give serious consideration to a plan to use the Long Lance as a suicide weapon.

Development of such a weapon had begun in 1942, when two junior naval officers, SubLt Hiroshi Kuroki and Ens Sekio Nishina, enlisted the aid of Hiroshi Suzukawa, a designer at Kure Naval Arsenal, in an effort to produce a midget submersible which, unlike the "Type A" midget submarine, could be launched from a *submerged* fleet submarine. From the first, their designs were based on a Long Lance torpedo lengthened to include a pilot's compartment amidships. Even with the weight increase this entailed, and with a warhead heavy enough to break the back of a battleship, it was estimated that a Type 93 torpedo engine would provide the necessary speed and range.

The design for the manned-torpedo that was to be called the *Kaiten* (variously translated as "turn towards heaven" or "make a tremendous change") was completed early in 1943. Nishina and Kuroki eagerly approached the Naval General Staff—who flatly refused even to examine the plans. The young officers stressed the potential of the weapon: the Type A midgets used in the surprise raids of 1941-42, they argued, had to be launched from surfaced submarines or mother ships; in either case, the parent craft was extremely vulnerable. The kaiten, launched from a submerged submarine, could be released far closer to the target, at less risk, with a much better chance of success. But the high command refused to consider an openly suicidal weapon.

This attitude changed in late 1943-early 1944. Japanese historians are inclined to cite Nishina and Kuroki's submission of a petition written in their own blood, as a sign of deepest sincerity, as a reason for the Naval General Staff's change of mind. It is more likely that the high command was swayed by Japan's mounting losses of conventional warships, submarines and aircraft.

The Naval General Staff agreed to accept the kaiten on one condition: it might be a suicide weapon—and everyone concerned must have been well aware that it was—but it must not *appear* to be one! Nishina and Kuroki met this requirement by incorporating into their design an escape hatch below the pilot's seat. In theory, the pilot could now set his torpedo on a collision course and, when about 50yds (46m) from the target, press a switch that would eject him into the water. The fact that he would have no hope of surviving the

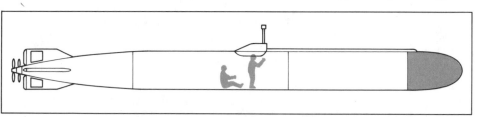

The experimental **Kaiten II** had a crew of two and a maximum range of more than 50 miles at 20kt.

KAITEN HUMAN TORPEDOES				
Type:	KAITEN I	KAITEN II	KAITEN III	KAITEN IV
Length:	48.39ft (14.75m)	54ft (16.47m)	55ft (16.77m)	54ft (16.47m)
Diameter:	3.28ft (1m)	4.6ft (1.4m)	5.5ft (1.67m)	4.5ft (1.37m)
Submerged Displacement:	8.3 tons (8.43 tonnes)	18.37 tons (18.66 tonnes)	18.3 tons (18.59 tonnes)	18.17 tons (18.46 tonnes)
Machinery:	Type 93 petrol & liquid oxygen engine of 550hp =30kt (34.5mph, 55.5kmh) or 40kt (46mph/74kmh) for a short distance	Type 6 hydrogen-peroxide/ hydrazine (Perhydrol) engine of 1,500hp=40kt (46mph, 74kmh)	Type 6 (improved) engine of 1,800hp=30/40kt (34.5mph, 55.5kmh/ 46mph, 74kmh)	Type 6 petrol & liquid oxygen engine of 1,800hp =40kt (46mph, 74kmh)
Range:	85,300yd (78000m) @ 12kt (14mph, 22kmh) 47,025yd (43000m) @ 20kt (23mph, 37kmh) 25,153yd (23000m) @ 30kt (34.5mph, 55.5kmh)	90,770yd (83000m) @ 20kt (23mph, 37kmh) 54,680yd (50000m) @ 30kt (34.5mph, 55.5kmh) 27,340yd (25000m) @ 40kt (46mph, 74kmh)	67,800yd (62000m) @ 20kt (23mph, 37kmh) 43,700yd (39960m) @ 27kt (31mph, 50kmh) 41,500yd (37950m) @ 30kt (34.5mph, 55.5kmh)	67,800yd (62000m) @ 20kt (23mph, 37kmh) 41,560yd (38000m) @ 30kt (34.5mph, 55.5kmh) 29,530yd (27000m) @ 40kt (46mph, 74kmh)
Warhead:	3,418lb (1550kg)	3,418lb (1550kg) uprated to 3,968lb (1800kg)	3,307lb (1500kg)	3,968lb (1800kg)
Crew:	1	2	2	2
No completed:	c.300	fewer than 10	prototype only	fewer than 100

subsequent detonation of the kaiten's 3,418lb (1550kg) warhead was officially ignored. In fact, although the escape hatch was never used for its designed purpose, it was to become an important feature of the weapon, as will be seen.

The Kaiten I was accepted by the Naval General Staff in February 1944, under conditions of strictest secrecy and with a variety of cover names, including *maru-roku kanamono* ("zero-six metal fittings") and *kyukoku heiki* ("national salvation weapon"). A construction programme was initiated at Kure Navy Yard, later extended to Yokosuka and Hikari, and the first training centre, "Base P", was established at Otsujima in Tokuyama Bay.

Data for the Long Lance torpedo and the four types of kaiten developed from it are given in the accompanying tables. It should be noted that the one-man Kaiten I was the only model to be carried into

JAPANESE SUBMARINES CONVERTED TO CARRY KAITEN HUMAN TORPEDOES						
Type:	Number	Surfaced displacement	Length overall	Action radius in NM (surfaced/submerged)	Complement	No of Kaiten carried
FLEET TYPES:						
J3	I-8	2,231 tons (2267 tonnes)	358.5ft (109.3m)	14,000nm @ 16kt 60nm @ 3kt	100	4
B1	I-36	2,198 tons (2233 tonnes)	356.5ft (108.7m)	16,000nm @ 16kt 96nm @ 3kt	94	4 (later 6)
B1	I-37	as I-36	as I-36	as I-36	as I-36	4
B2	I-44	2,320 tons (2357 tonnes)	356.5ft (108.7m)	16,000nm @ 16kt 96nm @ 3kt	94	4 (possibly 6)
C2	I-47	2,184 tons (2219 tonnes)	358.5ft (109.3m)	14,000nm @ 16kt 60nm @ 3kt	95	4 (later 6)
C2	I-48	as I-47	as I-47	as I-47	as I-47	4
C3	I-53	2,095 tons (2129 tonnes)	356.5ft (108.7m)	21,000nm @ 16kt 105nm @ 3kt	94	4 (later 6)
B3	I-56	2,140 tons (2174 tonnes)	356.5ft (108.7m)	21,000nm @ 16kt 105nm @ 3kt	94	4 (later 6)
B3	I-58	as I-56	as I-56	as I-56	as I-56	4 (later 6)
KD3B	I-156	1,635 tons (1661 tonnes)	330ft (100m)	10,000nm @ 10kt 90nm @ 3kt	89	2
KD3B	I-157	as I-156	as I-156	as I-156	as I-156	2
KD3A	I-158	as I-156	as I-156	as I-156	as I-156	2
KD3B	I-159	as I-156	as I-156	as I-156	as I-156	2
KD4	I-162	as I-156	320.5ft (97.7m)	10,800nm @ 10kt 60nm @ 3kt	60	2
KD5	I-165	1,575 tons (1600 tonnes)	as I-162	as I-162	89	2
TRANSPORT TYPES:						
D1	I-361	1,440 tons (1463 tonnes)	241ft (73.5m)	15,000nm @ 10kt 120nm @ 3kt	60	5
D1	I-363	as I-361	as I-361	as I-361	as I-361	5
D1	I-366	as I-361	as I-361	as I-361	as I-361	5
D1	I-367	as I-361	as I-361	as I-361	as I-361	5
D1	I-368	as I-361	as I-361	as I-361	as I-361	5
D1	I-369	as I-361	as I-361	as I-361	as I-361	5
D1	I-370	as I-361	as I-361	as I-361	as I-361	5
D1	I-372	as I-361	as I-361	as I-361	as I-361	5

action. The two-man Kaiten II, with an experimental hydrogen peroxide/hydrazine engine, was produced only in very small numbers, and the Kaiten III, with an improved peroxide-hydrazine unit, did not progress beyond a prototype. Up to 100 Kaiten IVs, propelled by a Type 6 petrol and liquid oxygen engine based on that of the Long Lance, were built, but these two-man craft were deployed only in the home islands, for use against the expected invasion fleet.

Parent craft for kaiten

Between autumn 1944 and late spring 1945, 15 fleet submarines and 8 transport submarines were stripped of their main gun armament—and in some cases had aircraft hangars and catapults removed—and were fitted with chocks to carry between two and six kaiten. In addition, a number of surface ships were refitted to carry and launch kaiten but, because of the severe limitations on the activities of Japanese surface ships in the last months of the war, were never operational in this role. (See Table below for surface ships thus equipped.)

The most interesting conversion was that of the veteran light cruiser *Kitakami*. Torpedoed and severely damaged by HM submarine *Templar* on 25 February 1944, *Kitakami* was reconstructed at Sasebo

JAPANESE SURFACE SHIPS EQUIPPED TO CARRY KAITEN HUMAN TORPEDOES							
Type:	Name/No	Completed	Standard Displacement	Length overall	Machinery	Armament	No of Kaiten
"KUMA" CLASS LIGHT CRUISER	KITAKAMI	April 1921 (final rebuild December 1944)	5,100 (5192 tonnes)	535ft (163m)	2-shaft Gihon GTU = 23kt	4 x 5in DP 67 x 25mm AA 18 DC	8 (4 each side of upper deck)
"MINEKAZE" CLASS DESTROYER	NAMIKAZE	November 1922 (final rebuild late 1944)	1,215 tons (1234 tonnes)	336.5ft (102.5m)	2-shaft Parsons GTU 3 Kampon boilers=28kt	1 x 4.7in DP 20 x 25mm AA 8 x 13mm MG – DC	2 (in tandem on centre line of quarterdeck)
"MINEKAZE" CLASS DESTROYER	SHIOKAZE	July 1921 (final rebuild February 1945)	as NAMIKAZE	as NAMIKAZE	as NAMIKAZE	1 x 4.7 DP 19 x 25mm AA 8 x 13mm MG – DC	4 (2 on each side of upper deck)
"MATSU" CLASS DESTROYERS	TAKE KAEDE* KASHI* KIRI* MAKI* SUGI*	June 1944 (conversion early 1945; ships marked* =conversion probably not completed)	1,262 tons (1282 tonnes)	328ft (100m)	2-shaft GTU 2 Kampon boilers=27.8kt	3 x 5in DP 24-29 x 25mm AA 4 x 24in (610mm) TT 36 DC	1 (at stern)
"TYPE 1" LANDING SHIPS	T.1 to T.21	May 1944 to July 1945	1,500 tons (1524 tonnes)	315ft (96m)	1-screw GT 2 boilers =22kt	2 x 5in HA 15-33 x 25mm AA 5 x 13mm MG 42 DC	6 (on wooden launching cradles; or 2 koryu midget submarines)
"TYPE A" LIGHT ESCORTS (STEEL HULLS)	20 ordered	2 partly completed	278 tons (282.5 tonnes)	167.3ft (51m)	2-shaft diesel =15kt	1 x 40mm AA 6 x 25mm AA 4 DC	2 (on cradles on rails, on quarterdeck)
"TYPE B" LIGHT ESCORTS (WOODEN HULLS)	60 ordered	19 partly completed	290 tons (295 tonnes)	132ft (40.2m)	2-shaft diesel =12.5kt	1 x 40mm AA 6 x 25mm AA 8 DC	1 (on quarterdeck)

later that year. The six quadruple Long Lance torpedo tubes were removed from her deck and her anti-aircraft armament re-sited to make room for eight kaiten on launching rails aft. A 20-ton crane was mounted on her mainmast and her stern rebuilt to form an overhanging ramp. Thus equipped, it was estimated she could launch all her kaiten within eight minutes. The two turbines in her aft engine-room were removed — reducing her maximum speed from 36 to 23 knots — and the space used for the storage of kaiten parts and maintenance equipment.

As well as conversions, new warships were purpose-designed to handle kaiten. The 21 "Type 1" fast transports/landing ships completed in 1944-45 were built with rails and stern ramps to carry and launch landing craft, amphibious tanks, two midget submarines, or six kaiten. The steel-hulled "Type A" and wooden-hulled "Type B" light escorts planned for mass-production in 1945 were designed to carry two (Type A) or one (Type B) kaiten, but only two of these vessels were completed by the war's end.

Selection of kaiten pilots
Potential pilots for kaiten operations were mainly drawn from among trainee naval aviators; for whom, late in 1944, there were likely to be

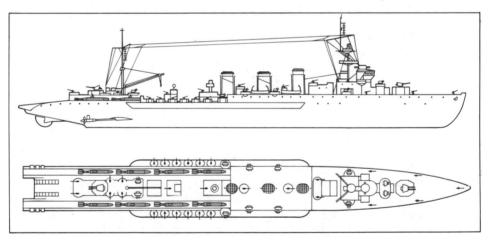

Above: The "Kuma" class light cruiser **Kitakami**, as converted in 1944-45 to carry and launch up to eight **Kaiten**. Note overhanging stern ramp, crane mounted on mainmast and launching rails aft.

Below: "Type A" light escort, with ramp and rails to carry and launch two **Kaiten**. Of a projected class of 20 of these steel-hulled, 278-ton (282.5 tonne) ships, only two approached completion.

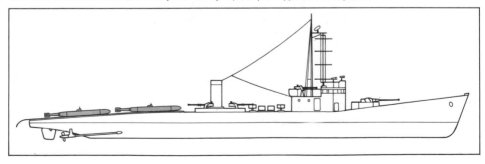

few available aircraft and fewer still instructors and fuel allocations. Like all other "special attack" personnel, the kaiten pilots were volunteers — and of all the volunteers for suicidal operations, they needed to be the most highly dedicated and intensively trained.

In August 1944, students at the naval air bases at Tsuchiura and Nara were assembled by their commandants and given a truthful summary of the war situation. Only desperate measures, they were told, could change the course of events in Japan's favour. Those who wished could now volunteer for training with a new weapon capable of inflicting enormous damage on the enemy — a suicide weapon.

At Tsuchiura, in a secret vote, more than 1,000 of the 2,000 students volunteered. Obviously, there were no facilities to train so many with the kaiten, so a rigorous selection procedure reduced the number to about 100. Only the best physical specimens were accepted; all married men and those with family responsibilities were rejected. There were also psychological criteria: men who were to undergo long and hazardous training with a complex weapon, knowing that death was the reward for proficiency, needed to be emotionally stable. Ill-balanced fanatics and hotheads might crack up in training or, worse, when committed to action. Nevertheless, many of the men rejected for kaiten training would later be accepted as kamikaze aircraft pilots.

The volunteers were cheered by their comrades as they left for an unknown destination — "Base P". After receiving an official welcome from the commandant, they were allowed to make a brief inspection of a kaiten. Then, having seen the weapon in which they would attack the enemy and die, they were given a final chance to withdraw: any man who wished to return to conventional pilot training could do so, with no questions asked and no imputation of dishonour. Very few took advantage of this offer.

Training for kaiten operations

Western historians have stated that Japanese volunteers for suicide operations were given only the most rudimentary training: the implication being that they were sent out to die as quickly as possible, before their febrile enthusiasm could wane. This may be partly true in the case of the kamikaze aircraft pilots in the last months of the war, when planes, fuel and qualified instructors were all in miserably short supply. It is certainly untrue of the kaiten pilots, who spent many weeks training on land before even entering a kaiten in the water.

The kaiten required as much skill to pilot as a fighter aircraft; but there were other reasons for the length of the training period. The weapon was at first in short supply: in September 1944, "Base P" possessed only six kaiten, enough to run a training programme for only about 30 of the 200 volunteers there. The situation improved later that year: by November, a second training centre at Hikari, on the coast just south of Tokuyama, had more than 70 kaiten. But there was always a critical shortage of technicians to maintain and service the torpedoes at the training bases.

"Wet" training, obviously the most important part of the course, was limited by Japan's fuel shortage. The 16.4ft (15m) launches specially constructed to transport two kaiten, lashed alongside, and to act as target boats and recovery vehicles were powered by 80hp petrol engines; and although many of these *sagyo-tei* (working boats) were ordered, only 20 were built and obsolescent torpedo-boats and escorts, burning even more fuel, had to be pressed into service. Thus, kaiten trainees were lectured on the need to attain proficiency with the minimum of "wet" training and were perpetually reminded that "a drop of petrol is as precious as a drop of blood".

However hard a student worked during shore training, his first session at the controls of a kaiten in the water was nerve-wracking. Having squeezed into the tiny cockpit, he was faced by the single eyepiece and training handles of the periscope, raised and lowered by a hand-crank to his right. Above this crank was the valve that regulated the flow of oxygen to the engine, and also to the pilot's right was the rudder control lever. Overhead and behind the pilot lay the lever that started the engine. The valve for admitting sea-water to the trimming tanks, to compensate for the fuel used, was situated on the pilot's left, and above it was the control lever for the diving planes. On the dimly-lit instrument panel were a gyro-compass, clock, depth-indicator, fuel gauge and oxygen pressure gauge.

During training, the pilot had yet another vitally important control to manipulate. If, as quite often happened, his craft dived too deep and became stuck on the muddy bottom of Tokuyama Bay, he could free the kaiten by using a blow valve that forced compressed air into the water-filled practice warhead, thus giving the kaiten buoyancy. Because of its position, it was all too easy to open the fuel valve instead of the blow valve, thus forcing the kaiten deeper into the mud. The kaiten might then be recovered after a diver was sent down to fix raising lines, but this was often too late to save the pilot. After much experiment, an air purifier that would enable an undamaged kaiten to remain submerged for up to 20 hours was developed. It is a striking comment on the dedication of the kaiten pilots that the fate they most feared, according to one veteran, was that of the man who *survived* the loss of a kaiten in training—dismissal from the special attack forces!

Ironically, of the 15 men to die in kaiten training accidents, the first was the weapon's co-inventor, Lt Hiroshi Kuroki, whose kaiten became stuck on the sea-bed on 6 September 1944. With him died Lt Takashi Higuchi: as was not uncommon, two men had crammed into the kaiten for the training run. Like other kaiten pilots, Kuroki had taken great pains to leave his kit and personal effects in good order against just such an eventuality: his will, found on his body, was read to his comrades as an inspirational document.

A Training Run

The trainee entered his kaiten as it lay on a launching trolley on the dockside, secured the entrance hatch, and checked out his instruments and controls. The kaiten was lifted into the water by a crane and lashed alongside a launch for transport to the training area. A simple code of knocks on the kaiten's casing allowed instructors to check that the pilot was ready to be launched. Reaching up and back, the pilot pulled the starting lever and moved away from the training launch.

After thoroughly testing the diving controls with a series of descents to 75ft (23m), the pilot had to tackle a navigational problem, with the aid of a stop-watch and gyro-compass, while keeping the kaiten at an average depth of 15ft (4.6m). This was the optimum depth for an attacking run, and to break the surface was to fail the test. If the kaiten went seriously off-course and appeared to be heading for trouble, the training boat fired a burst from its machine gun to warn the pilot. Once the pilot was fully confident of his controls, he progressed to making dummy attacks on the training boat and on larger ships assigned for the purpose. Moving away from the training boat, the kaiten pilot was required to make a run-in on a moored target ship up to six miles (9.6km) distant, completing the attack by taking his torpedo beneath the target ship's bow. This too was a hazardous procedure: several trainees died after colliding with the hulls of target ships and displacing the kaiten's upper hatch. Ashore, after a training session, the pilot shared his experience with other trainees in an exhaustive debriefing.

As well as training with the kaiten ashore and afloat, students underwent hard physical training, in a programme that included sumo wrestling, judo, kendo fencing, athletics, rowing, rugby football and baseball. Living conditions were good: at a time of general shortage, kaiten trainees received extra rations and ample supplies of cigarettes and sweetmeats. At "Base P", one trainee recorded, they even had the luxury of western-style beds. As in most elite units, the tough discipline of the Japanese services was not so much in evidence: instructors rarely beat or hectored their men. On the debit side, the training bases were strictly isolated. There was no access to women (the tales told by some western writers of the "orgies" permitted to special attack personnel have little basis in fact) and leave was only given immediately before a combat mission. Kaiten men were not supposed to reveal to their families and friends that they were to undertake suicide missions, but this prohibition does not seem to have been strictly observed.

Into Action

By the autumn of 1944, the kaiten construction and training programme was far enough advanced for the Naval General Staff to decide to commit the weapon to action. There was then, and would remain, a basic division on the question of operational doctrine. One faction held that the kaiten should be launched against ships at sea; another that it would be better deployed against anchorages. Because of the traditional insistence on attacking capital ships at all costs, the policy of attacking anchorages at first prevailed. Such locations, it was argued, could be subjected to air reconnaissance in advance, and aircraft carriers or battleships pinpointed as targets. The fact that the kaiten would probably have had far greater success if used, from the first, against convoys and task forces at sea—although transports and escorts would then have been more likely victims than major warships—and the fact that this must have been obvious to naval planners, suggests that the moral value of the kaiten was valued above the material, even before it was sent into action.

The target selected for the first kaiten attack was Ulithi atoll in the Western Carolines, which had been abandoned by the Japanese in August 1944 and promptly occupied by US forces in an unopposed landing on 23 September. The natural deep-water anchorage of Ulithi lagoon soon became the centre of USN operations in the western Pacific. For maximum effect on US morale, the Japanese planned to make a simultaneous attack on the Kossol Passage anchorage, off Palau Island.

Three fleet submarines were assigned to carry four kaiten each to the attack: *I-47* (commanded by the "ace" submariner LtCdr Zenji Orita) and *I-36* to sortie to Ulithi; *I-37* to Kossol Passage. Lt Sekio Nishina, the surviving co-inventor of the weapon, would be one of the kaiten pilots aboard *I-47*, along with Lt Hitoshi Fukuda and Ensigns Akiro Sato and Kozo Watanabe. In *I-36* were Lt Kentaro Yoshimoto and Ensigns Kazuhisa Toyozumi, Taichi Imanishi and Yoshihiko Kudo; in *I-37*, Lieutenants Yoshinori Kamibeppu and Katsumi Murakami and Ensigns Shuichi Utsunomiya and Kazuhiko Kondo. Besides winning undying glory as demi-gods at Yasukuni Shrine, each pilot could look forward to a posthumous promotion of one or two ranks when the completion of his mission was reported.

The Kikusui Group

As their unit's emblem, the men of the first kaiten mission were given the most honoured of Japan's warrior symbols: the *kikusui* ("floating crysanthemum") crest of Masashige Kusunoki (1294-1336). At the Battle of Minatogawa, according to tradition, Kusunoki, champion of Emperor Godaigo, with 700 men withstood for seven hours the onslaught of 35,000 warriors of the Ashikaga faction. Having sustained 11 great wounds, he committed seppuku along with his brother Masasue. (The latter's dying words—"I wish only that I could be reborn seven times to fight the enemies of my Emperor"—were adopted by Japanese servicemen during World War II as the slogan: "Seven lives for the Emperor!"). Along with the flag of the rising sun, the ideographs for *kiku* and *sui* were painted on the conning towers of the kaiten mission's submarines.

The ceremonies that marked the departure of the Kikusui Group must be described in some detail, for they set a pattern for the rites that accompanied succeeding kaiten missions. On the afternoon of 7 November 1944 (only two weeks after the first successful kamikaze aircraft attack; a fact which must have added to the determination of the kaiten pilots), the men of the Kikusui Group paraded in new uniforms, with the green crysanthemum badge of the Special Attack Forces on the left sleeve, for an address by Vice-Admiral Shigeyoshi Miwa, commanding Sixth Fleet (the IJN's submarine force). Standing on the quayside beneath the battle flag of the Imperial Japanese Navy, Miwa frequently gestured towards the submarines moored nearby with the kaiten on their decks, as he delivered a patriotic homily. He concluded by presenting each of the kaiten pilots with a *wakizashi*, the short sword traditionally carried by a samurai and used in the act of seppuku, and a *hachimaki*, the strip of cloth that a samurai bound round his forehead before going into battle, to keep his long hair from

233

obstructing his vision. The hachimaki bore patriotic slogans.

That evening, before attending a farewell party given by the officers of the training base, the kaiten pilots packed their personal belongings for shipment to their next-of-kin. These effects were accompanied by their wills and by their last letters—some couched in conventionally patriotic terms; some genuinely thoughtful and moving—and by hair-clippings and fingernail parings to be offered at the family altar before cremation and burial in the homeland. The farewell party itself began decorously with a further speech from Admiral Miwa, answered by Lt Kamibeppu on behalf of his fellow pilots. A solemn moment was Miwa's toast to the mission's success, drunk in *sake* announced as the gift of the Emperor himself. There followed a banquet which included such scarce luxuries as canned fruit, as well as fish, rice, dried seaweed and *kachi kuri* ("victory chestnuts"), the latter a delicacy traditionally served to express wishes for success. The meal was followed by more *sake* and, as most Japanese do not have strong heads for liquor, emotional scenes ensued: martial songs were sung and the warriors embraced and wept freely.

At 0800 next morning the kaiten pilots, with swords at their right sides, wakizashi in their left hands and hachimaki bound round their heads, marched through the ranks of their comrades to the quayside, stopping on the way to pray at a Shinto shrine specially dedicated to their activities. Lt Nishina bore an honourable burden: the square, white box containing the ashes of Hiroshi Kuroki, which he would carry with him in his kaiten when he made his attack. Before embarking, the pilots drank a solemn farewell toast in water, symbol of purity, the *mizu-sakasuki*, while a military band played the national anthem, *Kimigayo*. Finally, a group photograph was taken of the kaiten pilots, their senior training officers, the submarine skippers and Admiral Miwa.

At 0900 the submarines sailed slowly from the bay, escorted by an honour guard of training boats and other small craft. The kaiten pilots stood in the open hatches of their torpedoes, brandishing their swords, while the onlookers cheered and chanted their names repeatedly. They had 12 days to live: the attacks were scheduled for dawn on 20 November 1944.

The Voyage Out

While carrying kaiten, a submarine was forbidden to make attacks with conventional torpedoes. Much of the voyage to the target areas, through enemy-dominated waters, was spent submerged. The kaiten pilots supervised the routine maintenance of their weapons by petty officers or leading seaman technicians assigned from the training base for this duty. They practised judging attack angles with the aid of a mock-up periscope and a model warship on the wardroom table, and relaxed by playing chess, *go* and cards. As incipient demi-gods, they were regarded with some awe by the submarine's crew, and their offers to help in the boat's daily routine were usually politely refused.

Whenever the parent submarine's situation allowed, the kaiten pilots practised manning their weapons—and now the kaiten's "token" escape hatch was put to practical use. By rigging a flexible tube with a diameter of c.24in (610mm) between a hatch in the submarine's casing and the escape hatch on the underside of the kaiten, the pilot was enabled to enter his weapon while the submarine lay submerged. A crewman followed the pilot through the access tube to secure the escape hatch after he had entered the torpedo; the submarine's hatch was then secured and the access tube flooded, but a telephone cable running through the tube allowed voice contact between the pilot and the submarine's skipper up to the moment of launching, when both cable and tube tore free from the kaiten. Only two of the four kaiten on each submarine of the Kikusui Group had the access tube facility, but on later missions all kaiten were thus equipped.

By 19 November, both elements of the Kikusui Group had reached their target areas. Here, *I-37's* part in the mission came to a premature end. Shortly before 0900 on 19 November, *I-37* surfaced briefly at the western entrance to Kossol Passage, where she was sighted by the net-layer USS *Winterberry*. The DEs *Conklin* and *McCoy Reynolds* were quickly on the scene. *I-37* dived deep, but after a sonar hunt lasting several hours the submarine was located, subjected to eight depthcharge attacks, and sunk with all hands without having had the chance to launch her kaiten.

Date: **20 November 1944**
Place: **Ulithi, Western Carolines**
Attack by: **Kaiten human torpedoes**
Target: **US warships at anchor**

I-36 and *I-47* reached their launching area off Ulithi without incident. A few days before the attack, a high-altitude reconnaissance aircraft from Truk reported that Ulithi lagoon was crammed with shipping, including aircraft carriers and battleships. The intelligence, relayed to the submarines from Japan, was good: present at the time of the attack were the four fleet carriers, three battleships, cruisers and destroyers of Rear-Admiral Frederick Sherman's Task Group 38.3; the heavy cruisers and destroyers of Task Group 57.9; a number of major and minor units under repair; and the many fleet auxiliaries of Commodore W.R. Carter's Service Squadron 10—perhaps some 200 ships in all.

LtCdr Orita surfaced some 50 miles (80km) west of Ulithi, late on 18 November, to allow for a final check on *I-47's* kaiten. By noon on 19 November he had made a submerged approach to the southern of the two main entrances of the 20-mile (32km) long lagoon. LtCdr Iwao Teramoto brought *I-36* to a similar position not far from the eastern entrance channel. The kaiten pilots made their farewells, thanking the submarine crews for bringing them safely to the target area, tied on their hachimaki, and said a brief prayer for success at the boats' shrines. Following Shinto practice, Nishina affixed a written prayer to the shrine in *I-47:* "My offering . . . one large aircraft carrier". It remained there throughout *I-47's* operational life as an inspiration to Nishina's successors. (Handed over by Orita to LtCdr Shokichi Suzuki in May 1945, *I-47* survived the war and was surrendered.)

Around midnight, both boats surfaced to allow the pilots whose weapons had no access tubes to enter their kaiten. Two of the four cables holding the kaiten on their chocks were now released. The pilots of the remaining kaiten entered their torpedoes while the parent craft lay submerged, at around 0300 hours. Nishina took with him into the cramped cockpit the ashes of Kuroki, stowing them beneath his seat along with the emergency rations of rice, dried fish and a small flask of whiskey—the food, it may be supposed, being more for the pilot's psychological support than his sustenance.

At 0400 hours, while lying submerged within one mile of the lagoon's entrances and able to see through their periscopes the working lights of the USN repair crews, Orita and Teramoto prepared to launch their kaiten. Sealed in their torpedoes, the pilots checked their instruments and plotted their attack courses with the aid of the information passed through the telephone link from the submarine's skipper at his periscope. Final ranges and bearings were given: the pilots confirmed their readiness. From within the submarine, holding steady some 35 feet (11m) below the surface, the third securing cable was released. The kaiten pilots started their engines. The fourth cable was released and the kaiten began to move away. As Lt Fukuda, last to launch, broke from *I-47*, his final words came clearly over the telephone link a moment before its parting: *"Tenno heika banzai!"* ("May the Emperor reign for ten thousand years").

All four kaiten were successfully launched from *I-47:* Nishina at 0415; Sato at 0420; Watanabe at 0425; Fukuda at 0430. Each was to pursue a different attacking course, in order to strike targets in widely separated locations within the lagoon at approximately 0500 hours. Orita took *I-47* out to sea, intending to surface at 0500 and watch for explosions through binoculars. Aboard *I-36*, things did not go so smoothly: the engines of the first two kaiten were started and the weapons were found to be immovably wedged on their chocks. A third kaiten failed to start: sea water had leaked into its mechanism. Only one torpedo, that piloted by Ensign Imanishi, got away—at 0454. Immensely distressed at their failure, Yoshimoto and Toyozumi re-entered the submarine through their access tubes, blown free of flooding, and Kudo was retrieved when the submarine surfaced briefly before moving out to sea.

In the five kaiten running into Ulithi lagoon at 20-30 knots (23-34.5mph/37-55.5kmh), the pilots juggled with their controls in order to stay at the optimum depth of 15ft (4.6m), operating diving planes and rudder controls, manipulating the valve that admitted sea water to compensate for the fuel used, checking gyro-compass and stop-watch to hold the predetermined attack course. To avoid detection, and probable destruction from enemy guns, the periscope should not be raised until an estimated 15 seconds before impact. At that time, the kaiten should be making its final run in to the target at its maximum speed of 40 knots (46mph/74kmh), and only slight rudder corrections should be necessary to ensure a direct hit amidships. This was the theory: in practice, it was unlikely that the directions given by the parent submarine's skipper—viewing the target area at a distance, through a periscope, often in poor light—would be sufficiently accurate to enable the kaiten pilot to steer to a predetermined target without visual reference. As US combat reports reveal, the kaiten pilot, having reached the vicinity of enemy ships, was often forced to reveal his presence by raising his periscope to seek a target before beginning his final run in at maximum speed.

The submarine commanders observing Ulithi from seaward recorded explosions within the lagoon at 0507, 0511, 0545, 0552 and 0605. Aboard *I-47*, LtCdr Orita ordered one minute of silent prayer for the dead heroes before setting course for home, easily avoiding a single US destroyer encountered heading toward Ulithi after the attack. The disappointed kaiten pilots on *I-36* pressed LtCdr Teramoto to resurface at a safe distance and attempt to repair their torpedoes for a follow-up strike; but a wide-ranging depthcharge hunt by US warships racing from the atoll immediately after the explosions forced *I-36* to remain submerged for the rest of the day. Teramoto was unable to surface until 2340 on 20 November and, after recharging his batteries, began the homeward run on the surface at flank speed.

Apart from the disappointed pilots, the crews of both submarines were jubilant; and their joy was shared in Japan where, after a debriefing at Kure on 2 December, Sixth Fleet officially announced that the kaiten of the Kikusui Group had sunk three aircraft carriers and two battleships.

The American View
The reality was somewhat different. The first encounter between US warships and the kaiten occurred at about 0530 hours, just outside the lagoon's southern entrance, where the destroyers *Cummings* and *Case,* putting to sea with TG 57.9, spotted a periscope approaching the heavy cruiser *Pensacola.* Identifying the attacker as a midget submarine, *Case* closed and rammed: fortunately for the US destroyer (see the fate of USS *Underhill,* page 248) the kaiten sank without detonating. At around the same time, a second kaiten ran on to the reef on the east of the lagoon and exploded. A third kaiten, probably Imanishi's weapon from *I-36,* was still outside the reef: obviously malfunctioning, it was spotted lying dead on the surface about five miles east of the atoll at around 0600, and was depthcharged and sunk by USMC aircraft.

Two kaiten had penetrated the anchorage—and at 0545 the suicide torpedoes claimed their first victim. This was the fleet oiler *Mississinewa* (11,300 tons), fully loaded with 405,000 gallons of aviation gasoline, 85,000 barrels of fuel oil and 9,000 barrels of diesel. Struck without warning by a kaiten (accepted by the Japanese as being that of Lt Nishina), the oiler blew up, sending a column of flame hundreds of feet into the air. The vessel was a total loss: 50 American officers and men were killed.

One kaiten remained. About 20 minutes after the destruction of *Mississinewa,* the light cruiser *Mobile* reported that a "torpedo" had narrowly missed her bow. The DEs *Rall, Weaver* and *Halloran* immediately began an anti-submarine search. The kaiten's periscope was spotted by *Rall* and shallow-set depthcharges from all three DEs tore the intruder apart. It was reported that two bodies had risen briefly to the surface directly after this action, leading the Americans to believe for a time that the attack had been made by two-man midget submarines: it was even suggested that these had lain concealed in the lagoon since the Japanese evacuation of Ulithi. Not until the wreckage of the kaiten that had run on to the reef was thoroughly examined did the US Navy realize the nature of Japan's new suicide weapon (although "Ultra"-derived intelligence at about the time of the Ulithi attack warned of Japanese deployment of a weapon of this kind).

The kaiten's first mission had, on balance, showed great promise. For the loss of five kaiten and their pilots at Ulithi (and, of course, *I-37*, her kaiten and all her crew at Kossol Passage), the Japanese had sunk a valuable auxiliary with heavy casualties and had dealt a shrewd blow to US morale. Admiral Sherman recorded that after the attack the ships' crews at Ulithi "felt as if we were sitting on a powder keg . . . far from enjoying a rest period, we felt we might be safer in the open sea". Japanese morale, albeit buoyed up by the exaggerated claims made on behalf of the Ulithi kaiten, was high.

The Kongo Group

Preparations began immediately for a second and more ambitious kaiten sortie. Five submarines, each carrying four kaiten, were to strike simultaneously at widely-separated targets. LtdCdr Teramoto was to make a second attack on Ulithi with *I-36*, while LtCdr Orita took *I-47* to strike at Hollandia, New Guinea. *I-53* (LtCdr Seihachi Toyomasu) would sortie to the Kossol Passage; *I-56* (LtCdr Masahiko Morinaga) to the Admiralty Islands; and *I-58* (LtCdr Mochitsura Hashimoto) to Apra Harbour, Guam. These attacks were scheduled for 11 January 1945. A sixth submarine, *I-48* (LtCdr Zenshin Toyama), was to make a follow-up attack with four kaiten on Ulithi on 20 January. Once more, the mission was given a name from the samurai past: the six submarines constituted the Kongo Group, named from the mountain stronghold of Masashige Kusunoki's warriors in the 14th century.

By striking at such widely dispersed targets, the Japanese Naval General Staff ostensibly hoped to throw their Allied opposite numbers off balance and halt their advance long enough to allow the IJN to prepare for the decisive battle in home waters that had long been the main feature of its overall war plan. In reality, the Japanese high command can have had little belief in this policy: early in 1945, following the disastrous battle of Leyte Gulf, the IJN's surface fleet was virtually non-existent and the surviving warships were crippled by the fuel shortage. It is broadly true to say that the Japanese were buying time, by the expenditure of suicide weapons, in the hope that the Allies would tire of attrition and, impressed by Japan's savage resistance, would be prepared to consider a negotiated peace rather than insisting on unconditional surrender.

And, in spite of the supposed successes of the Kikusui Group, the submarine skippers of the Kongo Group were apprehensive. Beyond the Inland Sea, the waters were dominated by Allied submarines, surface ships and aircraft. An improved Type 22 radar, giving warning of surface ships up to a range of 21.5nm (40km), now supplemented the Type 21 air/surface warning radar (detecting aircraft up to 32nm, 59km; surface warships up to 12.5nm, 23km) in most Japanese fleet

submarines but, according to the testimony of LtCdr Hashimoto of
I-58, the equipment was not very reliable.

Date: **12 January 1945**
Place: **Ulithi, Western Carolines**
Attack by: **Kaiten human torpedoes from I-36**
Target: **US warships at anchor**

The submarine skippers' fears proved well-founded: the only success
of the Kongo Group—and that a minor one—was scored by Teramoto
in *I-36*. Initially it seemed that his second sortie to Ulithi would be his
last, when, approaching the atoll on the surface at night, he ran
aground on a reef. Fortunately, the submarine was able to get clear by
first light, and launched all four kaiten off the US fleet anchorage at
c.0600 on 12 January.

At 0653, a lookout on the ammunition ship USS *Mazama* (5,450
tons) sighted a periscope off the starboard quarter. As the crew raced
to general quarters, the kaiten passed under *Mazama's* bow and
exploded about 40yds (37m) off the port side, holing the forward hold.
Although the ammunition ship's deadly cargo was not touched off,
one man was killed and 20 injured by the blast. With considerable
damage forward, *Mazama* was out of action for more than one month.
Fragments of conning tower found aboard *Mazama* made it possible to
identify the attacker as a kaiten.

Of *I-36's* three remaining kaiten, it is possible that one was
responsible for the destruction of the 246-ton infantry landing craft
LCI-600, which USN records attribute to "an underwater explosion of
undetermined origin". More underwater explosions were reported in
the lagoon at c.1200 hours and c.2045, but these, presumably
signalling the end of the two other kaiten, did no damage.

I-36 returned safely to Japan, where her kaiten were officially
credited with the destruction of a battleship, a fleet oiler and two
smaller ships. She left behind her at Ulithi a hornets' nest of
defensive air and surface patrols; but even so, *I-48*, making the
follow-up attack, was able to approach the atoll closely enough to
launch her kaiten on 20 January. One was piloted by Lt Kentaro
Yoshimoto, who had survived the Kikusui Group's attack on Ulithi, in
I-36, when his kaiten failed to start. There is no record of the fate
of *I-48's* kaiten—certainly they did no damage—but as the submarine
ran for home she was sighted by a patrolling aircraft which, after an
abortive attack, called up the hunter-killer escort groups. Located just
northeast of Yap on 23 January by the DEs *Corbesier, Raby* and
Conklin, I-48 was sunk by depthcharges.

Date: **12 January 1945**
Place: **Apra harbour, Guam**
Attack by: **Kaiten from I-58**
Target: **US warships at anchor**

LtCdr Hashimoto's *I-58*, flying beside its battle ensign a flag bearing
the (unintentionally ironic) legend "The Unpredictable Kaiten",
sortied from the Inland Sea on 29 December. On 1 January, Hashimoto,
his officers and the kaiten pilots—including two petty-officer pilots

who normally messed with the crew—celebrated the New Year in the wardroom by toasting the Emperor in *sake* (although the IJN, like the USN, was traditionally "dry" when at sea). Long periods of the voyage to Guam were spent submerged because the new radar installation proved unreliable. Hashimoto was impressed by the composure of the kaiten pilots, one of whom, Ensign Kudo, was making his second sortie, having failed to launch from *I-36* at Ulithi in November. The senior pilot, Lt Ishikawa, complained bitterly, however, of the shortcomings of Japanese reconnaissance: a spotter plane had reported some 60 transports in Apra Harbour on 9 January, but had given no indication of the state of the enemy's defences. In spite of his doubts, Ishikawa left with Hashimoto a poetically-worded final statement, reading in part:

"For the sake of our great country we have come to the place appointed . . . The meaning of life will be shown today . . . Thousands of young men will follow us as we lay down our lives for our country."

On the night of 11-12 January, Hashimoto made a submerged run into the launching area, having intercepted US radio traffic that suggested *I-58* had been sighted by patrol aircraft. At 0240 on 12 January, some two hours before dawn, he sent away the kaiten. The launch of one of the torpedoes was delayed because sea water had leaked into the engine: it got away at last—but an explosion a few minutes later marked a premature detonation. Forced to submerge by patrol planes, Hashimoto was unable to observe the explosions of the remaining kaiten—but on his return to Japan they were credited with sinking an escort carrier and two transports.

Like Hashimoto, LtCdr Toyomasu in *I-53* experienced malfunctioning kaiten. With considerable daring, he penetrated the intensely-patrolled Kossol Passage early on 12 January. His first kaiten refused to budge; the second, with a fractured fuel line, exploded almost immediately after leaving *I-53*. The remaining two were launched without difficulty—but, as US records show, without effect.

I-56, striking at Manus in the Admiralty Islands, had no chance even to launch kaiten. LtCdr Morinaga found the anchorage well-protected by anti-submarine netting and, after repeated attempts to penetrate the barriers—in which *I-56* became entangled for a short time—aborted the mission and headed homeward.

The last of the Kongo Group, *I-47*, succeeded in launching all four of her kaiten at Hollandia harbour, Humboldt Bay, New Guinea, evading patrolling destroyers and seaplanes on a daylight run-in on 11 January. After the launchings, at 0400-0430 on 12 January, LtCdr Orita reported four explosions from the anchorage within some 50 minutes. In fact, his kaiten came near to success: two kaiten exploded close aboard the "Liberty" ship *Pontus H. Ross*, which was slightly damaged. Running home, *I-47* picked up US signals from Hollandia which were thought to signify a successful submarine attack: on reaching Japan, Orita was credited with four large transports.

The "official" score of the kaiten after two missions stood at four aircraft carriers, three battleships, ten transports and one tanker. In fact, for the expenditure of 22 kaiten (not counting those which failed to launch) and the loss of two fleet submarines, the kaiten had sunk an oiler and (probably) an infantry landing craft and had damaged two transports. Some 210 Japanese sailors had died, as against 50-odd Americans. In spite of its inflated claims, the Japanese high command seems to have been fully aware that the price of attacking defended anchorages was too high—and was likely to become higher. The enemy was now on his guard and had a fair idea of the kaiten's capabilities and operational methods.

A Change in Doctrine
The Naval General Staff therefore decided on a shift in policy: attacks were henceforth to be mainly directed against ships in off-shore areas in invasion zones, rather than those in heavily-defended harbours. The zone around the island of Iwo Jima—bombarded by the Allies from 31 January 1945 onward, and invaded on 19 February—was to be a prime target. Technical improvements, as well as strategic and tactical considerations, had some bearing on this decision: fleet submarines had now been fitted to carry up to six kaiten each, with access hatches that would allow all the torpedoes to be manned while the parent craft was submerged.

"Type B3" submarine (**I-56** or **I-58**) carrying six **Kaiten**. Note the access hatches that allowed **Kaiten** pilots to enter their torpedoes for launching while the mother boat was submerged.

The Chihaya Group
Three submarines were grouped to carry kaiten to Iwo Jima: the fleet submarine *I-44* (Lt Cdr Genbei Kawaguchi), carrying four (possibly six) kaiten; and the much slower but longer-ranging transport submarines *I-368* (LtdCdr Mitsuteru Irisawa) and *I-370* (Lt Susumu Fujikawa), each carrying five kaiten. The senior kaiten pilot aboard *I-370* was Ensign Itaru Okayama, a strict but popular instructor from the kaiten training school at Hikari. Before leaving the school, he warned the trainees to continue to work hard—"or I shall return from Kudan [the abode of those deified at Yasukuni Shrine after death in battle] and beat you up again!"

The USN was prepared for such an attack. The concentration of bombardment, invasion and supply shipping off Iwo Jima—where there were no natural harbours or anchorages—obviously presented an excellent target for conventional submarines or kaiten. Before the bombardment began, two hunter-killer groups were formed specifically for anti-submarine duties: Capt G.C. Montgomery commanding the escort carrier *Anzio* (formerly *Coral Sea;* 28 aircraft) and up to nine DEs; Capt J.C. Cronin commanding the escort carrier *Tulagi* (28 aircraft) and up to nine DEs.

On 27 February, the *Anzio* group located *I-368:* the escort carrier's aircraft sank her with depth-bombs before she could launch her kaiten.

Although the Japanese were to claim that *I-370* loosed her kaiten at shipping off Iwo Jima, scoring hits, US records show no such attack. The submarine had, indeed, little time to make one: at 0555 on 26 February the radar of the DE *Finnegan,* on convoy escort some 100 miles (161km) south of Iwo Jima, recorded a surface contact about 7 miles (11km) distant. Closing in, *Finnegan* made sonar contact with the now-submerged submarine at 0630 and began a four-hour hunt with depthcharges and the "hedgehog" anti-submarine mortar. At 1034, an underwater detonation and an up-rush of debris signalled the destruction of *I-370.*

I-44 reached the Iwo Jima area after these sinkings, to find the defences fully alerted. Kawaguchi was unable to penetrate the web of patrol craft and planes surrounding the invasion shipping. Although never subjected to attack, he was forced to submerge repeatedly, on one occasion staying down for some 46 hours until his crew were on the verge of suffocation. With all aboard totally exhausted and demoralized, Kawaguchi abandoned his hopeless mission. He brought *I-44* safely home, her kaiten still on their chocks, on 9 March—only to be immediately relieved of his command by an angry Admiral Miwa.

The Kamitake Group

Even before the return of *I-44,* a second kaiten mission had been dispatched to Iwo Jima. The submarines of the Kamitake Group (also designated Shimpu Group, "God's Warriors") were veterans of kaiten operations—*I-36* (now commanded by LtCdr Tetsuaki Sugamasa) and LtCdr Hashimoto's *I-58*—each carrying six kaiten. Among the pilots

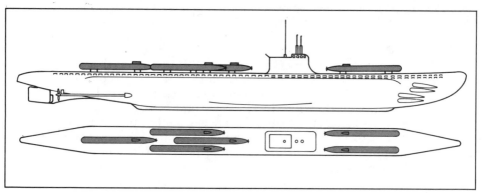

Final configuration of "Type B1" submarine **I-36**, early 1945. The seaplane hangar and catapult forward and the 5.5in (140mm) gun aft have been removed to allow the carriage of six **Kaiten**.

were four who had returned from *I-56's* abortive mission to the Admiralties with the Kongo Group.

Hashimoto sailed from Kure on 1 March, hoping to avoid US patrols off Iwo Jima by staying away from the convoy routes to the south and east and making his approach from the north. *I-36,* delayed by mechanical problems, did not sail until 2 March; then further engine trouble forced Sugamasa to abandon the mission and return to base on

9 March. Hashimoto brought *I-58* into the target area on 5 March, but US patrols kept him on the move, with little chance of breaking through to the off-shore shipping. At last, on the evening of 7 March, he decided to launch his kaiten to the northwest of Iwo Jima, early on the morning of the next day.

At c.0300 on 8 March, on his final run-in to the launching position, Hashimoto received a signal ordering him to abandon the kaiten mission and instead proceed to Okinawa for reconnaissance and radio-relay duties. Jettisoning his kaiten, he obeyed—but on his return to Kure on 16 March submitted a report critical of the standing order forbidding kaiten-carrying submarines to attack targets of opportunity with conventional torpedoes; he claimed that he had passed up an excellent target offered by a major warship on the evening of 6 March, only for this reason. The fact that his criticism was not ill-received was later apparent in one of the US Navy's greatest disasters—as will be seen.

Increasing the Suicide Effort

In Japan, production at a number of naval yards had now been re-scheduled to give priority to the construction of suicide weapons— kaiten, midget submarines and explosive boats—both for aggressive missions and for the defence of the home islands against invasion. It was planned to establish kaiten shore bases on the coast of Japan at the most likely locations for amphibious invasion. Japan's submarine arm was now so weakened that it was obvious that many trained kaiten pilots would never have the chance to sortie in the usual way; therefore, from April 1945 onward, many were assigned to bases from which they could be shore-launched against invasion shipping.

The suicide weapon programme was given added urgency when four submarines sent to make conventional torpedo attacks on US Task Force 58—now striking with carrier aircraft at airfields in the home islands—and on shipping off Okinawa were sunk within a three-week period. Because these submarines—*I-8*, *Ro-41*, *Ro-49* and *Ro-56*— sailed as a group on 18 March, and because one of them (*I-8*) had previously undergone conversion to carry kaiten, it has been suggested that this was a kaiten mission. This is incorrect: all were armed only with conventional torpedoes.

The Tatara Group

The next kaiten mission was not scheduled until 27 March—and its target was Okinawa, where a massive build-up of Allied shipping preceded the invasion of 1 April. The submarine skippers were specifically ordered to launch kaiten only at anchored major warships: the orders might be varied only if a large and vulnerable convoy was encountered. The parent submarines were the kaiten veterans *I-47* (LtCdr Orita), *I-44* (LtCdr Kyoshi Masuzawa, replacing the disgraced Kawaguchi), *I-56* (LtCdr Keiji Shoda) and *I-58* (LtCdr Hashimoto). Each carried six kaiten, and among the pilots were several survivors from aborted missions. To help avoid detection by Allied patrols, *I-47* (and probably others of the group) had received a coating of an "anti-radar" substance similar to the German *Alberich* "skin". The

Tatara Group took its name from the site of the destruction of a Mongol invasion force by a typhoon (*kamikaze*, "divine wind") and by the samurai of Tokimune Hojo in 1274.

The first of the Tatara Group to sortie, *I-47*, sailed from Hikari on 28 March. Next day, almost immediately after passing through Bungo Strait, she was forcibly reminded that the Allies now dominated the entire Pacific area, for a flight of US carrier aircraft forced Orita to make an emergency dive; some 30 depth-bombs were dropped, but *I-47* sustained no damage. Then, at c.0230 on 30 March, still running south on the surface, Orita sighted at c.6,000 yds (5,490m) two warships at first identified as cruisers. Submerging, with no time to ready his kaiten, Orita prepared for a conventional torpedo attack (the rule against such attacks having already been marginally relaxed). Almost too late, the targets were correctly identified as destroyers: making an emergency dive to below 200ft (61m), Orita awaited a depthcharge attack. For more than four hours, until the destroyers lost contact, *I-47* was hammered by repeated detonations. When Orita was at last able to surface to check the condition of his kaiten, he was picked up by the radar of US aircraft and bombed. Submerging again, he slipped away; but near-misses had left the submarine leaking oil and had rendered the kaiten inoperable. On 2 April, Orita brought his dejected kaiten pilots back to Hikari.

I-56 sailed from Otsujima on 31 March, followed by *I-44* on 3 April. The tightness of the Allied defensive screen at Okinawa, where the first "Kikusui" mass attack by suicide aircraft was made on 6-7 April (see page 171), was so effective that the submarines were forced to cruise for days, making repeated emergency dives, in the hope of reaching a position from which kaiten could be launched. Neither was successful—and both were at last sunk by US hunter-killer groups. On the morning of 18 April, *I-56* was lost 160nm (184 miles, 296km) east of Okinawa to a combined attack by five destroyers and aircraft from the small carrier *Bataan*. *I-44*, after surviving earlier depthcharge attacks by destroyers, was sunk by Wildcats from the escort carrier *Tulagi*, as she lay on the surface recharging her batteries on 29 April.

LtCdr Hashimoto's *I-58* sailed late on 2 April. It was a measure of the sorry state of Japan's defences that even while passing through Bungo Strait at night *I-58* was forced to keep a strict anti-submarine watch and that, during the first four days of her voyage, she was never able to surface for longer than four hours. Hashimoto decided to approach Okinawa from the west, and from 6 to 14 April made repeated attempts to penetrate the Allied screen, being constantly driven down by air and surface patrols. On 8 April, he was ordered by C-in-C Combined Fleet to "go in and fight to the death"—a signal probably provoked by the loss of the super-battleship *Yamato* on her suicide run to Okinawa (see page 116). Hashimoto judged it impossible to obey without sacrificing his boat uselessly—and since such an empty gesture would have contradicted the true samurai ethic, he felt able to retire without dishonour. He ran as far south as Formosa (Taiwan) in a hunt for targets before bringing back his kaiten un-launched to Japan on 29 April. Unlike Kawaguchi, whose treatment only a few weeks earlier is described above, Hashimoto escaped censure.

Attacks in the Open Sea

The losses and frustrations of the Tatara Group accentuated the error of the doctrine that limited kaiten to attacks on defended anchorages and off-shore warships in invasion zones. Nevertheless, an influential body of opinion on the Naval General Staff held that this policy should be maintained. The major opponent of this view was Cdr Tennosuke Torisu, a Sixth Fleet staff officer, who strongly advocated that kaiten attacks should be directed against the enemy's lines of communication, away from the main battle areas. The difficulty of operating kaiten in the open sea would, Torisu argued, be outweighed by the greater chance of hits if the targets were lightly-escorted supply ships and tankers. Further, he urged that attacks with conventional torpedoes on targets of opportunity should be sanctioned for kaiten-carrying submarines, at their commanders' discretion.

To the kaiten pilots, attacks on the lines suggested by Torisu presented formidable difficulties. Instead of running-in to a stationary target in a relatively calm anchorage, they must make contact with a moving vessel in a seaway. Much would depend on the accuracy with which the parent submarine's skipper could judge the target's course and speed, reporting these to the kaiten pilot immediately before launching. The pilot could not rely on his own periscope: to raise it for any length of time was to court discovery and destruction and it was, in any case, too small to be of much use in a choppy sea.

Although the kaiten's speed of up to 40kt (46mph, 74kmh) gave it a theoretical advantage in speed over most targets, its endurance (leaving navigational considerations aside) was limited. Running at c.10-20 knots (11.5-23mph, 18.5-37kmh) it had an endurance of about one hour before its oxygen fuel was exhausted. The torpedoes were equipped with a self-detonating device and some pilots hoped that, if their fuel ran out in a sea chase, leaving them helpless on the surface, the enemy would attempt to retrieve the kaiten, which could then be detonated by the pilot. In practice, surfaced kaiten were almost always blasted out of existence as quickly as possible by Allied surface fire or aircraft (but see the fate of USS *Underhill*, below).

Nevertheless, the skippers of Japan's few remaining operational submarines supported Cdr Torisu; and this wrung from the Naval General Staff the concession that two submarines might be dispatched on such a mission.

The Amatake (Tembu) Group

The two submarines of the Amatake Group (also called Tembu, "heavenly warriors")—Orita's *I-47* and LtCdr Tetsuaki Sugamasa's *I-36*—were ordered to strike at the supply routes between the US fleet base at Ulithi and Okinawa.

I-47 sailed on 12 April, carrying six kaiten. Reaching the convoy lanes, Orita made his first attack before dawn on 2 May, striking at a 12-ship convoy with conventional Type 95 torpedoes and claiming at least two hits. At 0930 the same morning, Orita sighted through his periscope a large transport escorted by two destroyers, proceeding at about 14kt (16mph, 26kmh), and sent his kaiten pilots to their weapons. Three kaiten were launched at a range of about 2nm (2.3

miles, 3.7km) and Orita later claimed three direct hits—but US records do not support him. Neither can his claim to have scored a kaiten hit on a target identified as a British cruiser, on 6 May, be substantiated. The two remaining kaiten, prepared for the latter attack, were not launched because a failure in the telephone link prevented Orita from giving them last-minute instructions. Immediately after reporting this attack, Orita was ordered by headquarters to bring *I-47* back to base.

Sailing from Japan on 20 April, *I-36* launched her kaiten on 27 April against an Okinawa-bound convoy. Because of mechanical failure, Sugamasa got only four kaiten away—later claiming to have sunk four ships. Some Allied sources credit one of Sugamasa's kaiten with the sinking of the ammunition transport *Canada Victory* in this attack—but USN records leave little doubt that she was the victim of a kamikaze aircraft attack later the same day. All that can be definitely said of Sugamasa's effort is that one kaiten was sunk by the gunfire of the destroyer *Ringgold*.

A Lone Sortie

Although both *I-47* and *I-36* returned safely—and were credited with destroying a light cruiser, two destroyers and five transports—the Amatake Group's mission had been yet another failure. At about the same time, a desperate attempt to set up a kaiten shore base in Japanese-held territory on Okinawa failed when a transport carrying eight kaiten, their pilots and maintenance personnel to the island was sunk by US aircraft.

Nor was a lone sortie to the Okinawa convoy routes by the converted transport submarine *I-367* (Lt Kunio Taketomi), with five kaiten, any more successful. Three of the kaiten could not be launched because of mechanical failure, but on 14 May Taketomi sent away one kaiten against ships of the USN's Logistic Support Group Servron 6, some 200nm (230 miles, 370km) south of Okinawa. The fleet tug *Sioux* intercepted and sank the human torpedo with 40mm fire. *I-367's* last kaiten was launched against a convoy on 28 May: brought under fire, it detonated prematurely, slightly damaging the DE *Gilligan*.

The Todoroki Group

By the time of *I-367's* return, yet another kaiten group was being formed for attack on the convoy routes. The makeup of the Todoroki ("sound of great cannon") Group reflected the decline of Sixth Fleet's strength: apart from LtCdr Sugamasa's fleet submarine *I-36*, with six kaiten, it comprised the converted transports *I-361* (Lt Masaharu Matsuura) and *I-363* (Lt Sakae Kihara), each with five kaiten, and the elderly (1932) *I-165*, adjudged unfit for active service and relegated to training duties in 1944, but now refitted to carry two kaiten. (The equally venerable *I-156*, *I-157*, *I-158*, *I-159* and *I-162* were similarly refitted at the same time.)

First to depart was *I-361*, sailing from Hikari on 23 May for a target area east of Okinawa. Failing to find targets, she made a long run south but, on 30 May, was located 400nm (460 miles, 740km) southeast of Okinawa and sunk by aircraft from a hunter-killer group based on USS *Anzio*. A similar fate awaited *I-165* (Lt Yasushi Ono), which did not sortie until 16 June: on 27 June, 450nm (517 miles, 832km) east of Saipan, she was sunk by USN aircraft. *I-363* sailed on 28 May and spent a fruitless month on the sea lanes between Ulithi and Okinawa, bringing her kaiten back to Japan unfired on 28 June.

I-36 left Hikari on 4 June and headed for the convoy routes east of Saipan. In contrast to earlier missions, when cheering crowds on small craft accompanied the kaiten-carrying submarines from the base, *I-36* moved away from a near-deserted dockside. Among her kaiten pilots was Lt Nobuo Ikebuchi who, during his pre-mission leave, had married in defiance of Special Attack Forces' regulations, spending only one night with his bride before returning to Hikari. The mechanical failures that had plagued earlier missions were soon in evidence. Two days out, all six kaiten were found to be inoperative — and only three could be repaired. Thus, when Sugamasa sighted a convoy on 22 June, he decided to attack with conventional torpedoes, slightly damaging the repair ship USS *Endymion*. On the evening of 23 June, near Saipan, Sugamasa sighted an unescorted tanker. He manoeuvred on the surface throughout the night in order to reach an attacking position at first light. Two kaiten were manned at 0400 — and both refused to start. Missing with conventional torpedoes, Sugamasa fled from the air patrols that his intended victim was sure to summon.

On 28 June, at 1100, Sugamasa made a periscope sighting on an unescorted transport moving at c.12kt (14mph, 22kmh). Lt Ikebuchi manned his kaiten and was launched at a range of about 3nm (3.5miles, 5.5km). Watching through his periscope, Sugamasa gave his crew a running account of the movement of the target (the 6,000-ton store ship *Antares*), which had spotted Ikebuchi's stubby periscope and was now taking evasive action while lobbing shells towards its attacker from its 5-inch and 3-inch guns. So engrossed was *I-36's* skipper in the sea chase that it was almost too late when, alerted by his sonar operator, he discovered two destroyers bearing down on the submarine. Narrowly avoiding a ramming attack, Sugamasa made an emergency dive as the first depthcharges thundered down. The destroyers subjected *I-36* to seven depthcharge runs in just over two hours until, with his boat damaged and down by 15 degrees at the stern, Sugamasa acceded to his kaiten pilots' frantic demands to be launched. At a depth of c.215ft (66m), very near their maximum tolerance, two kaiten were released.

The sacrificial gambit saved *I-36*. One kaiten detonated prematurely, but the destroyers, presumably following a sound contact with the survivor, moved away. Ikebuchi's kaiten had, meanwhile, detonated after narrowly missing *Antares*. The damaged submarine crept home, leaking oil that provided a marker for air attacks. Not until the evening of 29 June was Sugamasa able to surface and recharge his batteries — and then only after a plunge to 420ft (128m), some 95ft (30m) below the submarine's designed maximum diving depth, when an exhausted crewman, ordered to blow the main tanks, flooded them by mistake. *I-36's* miraculous escapes were not quite over: early on 6 July, only a few hours before docking at Hikari, she narrowly escaped a spread of four torpedoes fired by one of the US submarines that now roamed freely within Bungo Strait.

The Tamon Group

Early in July, Sixth Fleet decided to commit the last of Japan's operational submarine strength to battle with kaiten. It was, in the light of what had gone before, a hopeless gesture. Nevertheless, *I-47* (LtCdr Shokichi Suzuki), *I-53* (LtCdr Saichi Oba) and *I-58* (LtCdr Mochitsura Hashimoto), each with six kaiten, and the transports *I-363* (LtCdr Sakai Kihara), *I-366* (Lt Takami Tokioka) and *I-367* (Lt Kunio Taketomi), each with five kaiten, were formed into the Tamon Group (named for the Buddhist deity Tamon, traditionally the protector of Japan from foreign invasion).

First to leave Japan was *I-53*, sailing from Otsujima on 14 July to a target east of Okinawa. On 24 July she made contact with a convoy of seven LSTs and a transport, en route to Leyte from Okinawa, escorted by the DE *Underhill* (LtCdr R.M. Newcomb) and several PCs. According to US records, the convoy was shadowed by a Japanese aircraft which directed *I-53* to the area. At 1400, some 250nm (287 miles, 462km) east of Cape Engano, Luzon, *Underhill* made tentative sonar contact with the submarine and, preoccupied at that moment with a drifting mine in the convoy's path, sent *PC-804* to investigate. *I-53* had, in fact, by this time come undetected to within 1,000yds (914m) of the convoy and had launched at least two kaiten — and these were the subjects of the sonar contacts.

PC-804's depthcharges went down and a few moments later a periscope broke surface nearby. Aboard *Underhill*, Newcomb sent his men to general quarters and closed in, at first intending to ram and then deciding to drop more depthcharges. Rising debris after *Underhill's* first run signalled the end of one "midget submarine", as Newcomb identified his target. Almost immediately a second periscope was sighted some 700yds (640m) away: this time Newcomb set and held a ramming course. Whether *Underhill* finally rammed or was rammed by the kaiten is not known — for neither Newcomb nor any of the officers directly concerned in the attack lived to set the record straight. The impact with the kaiten triggered an explosion that tore off the DE's entire forepart as far back as her stack, killing 10 officers and 102 men. As the PCs closed in to take off survivors from the after section, which remained afloat until sunk by gunfire, they reported sighting and firing on at least one other kaiten. *I-53* remained at sea for a further three weeks, expending her remaining kaiten but scoring no more hits, before returning to Japan on 13 August.

The sinking of *Underhill* was a dramatic indication of continuing Japanese submarine activity in the Philippine Sea — and it was not the only such warning. On 21 July, *I-47* had attacked a convoy in the area, near-missing the attack transport *Marathon* with a kaiten that inflicted superficial damage. And although *I-363*, *I-366* and *I-367* of the Tamon Group returned to Japan without success, their movements were known to the Allied high command through "Ultra"-derived intelligence. Nevertheless, with victory in sight, the Allies were content to rely on routine patrol activity to counter the IJN's final efforts. This overconfidence led to one of the most tragic US naval losses of the war—inflicted by *I-58* of the Tamon Group.

The Sinking of USS Indianapolis

LtCdr Mochitsura Hashimoto's *I-58* sailed from Kure on 16 July, but was forced to return almost immediately when deep-diving trials revealed that the kaiten's periscopes were defective. By the evening of 18 July, Hashimoto was once again on his way to strike at the convoy routes east of the Philippines. At 1400 on 28 July, as *I-58* ran west on the Leyte-Guam route, Hashimoto made a periscope sighting which he identified as a large tanker (in fact, the cargo ship *Wild Hunter*) escorted by a destroyer. He launched two kaiten at long range, logging two explosions within the next hour and claiming two hits. The destroyer *Lowry* sustained moderate damage from one of these kaiten—and a report of the submarine's position was broadcast to Allied shipping.

A few hours before this attack, the heavy cruiser *Indianapolis* (Capt Charles B. McVay III) sailed from Guam for Leyte, where she was due at 1100 on 31 July. Only two days earlier she had completed a top-secret mission—delivering to Tinian vital components for the atomic bombs that B-29s were soon to drop on Hiroshima and Nagasaki. Because Allied knowledge of the Tamon Group's deployment derived from "Ultra" intercepts, it had not been circulated to the USN traffic controllers at Guam and Leyte; nor does it seem that Capt McVay received information of *I-58's* attack on *Wild Hunter* and *Lowry*, although he was warned that Japanese submarines were active in the area.

Thus, on the night of 29 July, *Indianapolis* was sailing unescorted; exercising his discretion, McVay was not zig-zagging as an anti-submarine measure and did not have the cruiser fully secured. At 2305, Hashimoto, then surfaced, sighted a ship some 5nm (5.75 miles, 9.25km) to the east. He immediately submerged to periscope depth, tracked his target, and ordered torpedo tubes readied. A few minutes later, fearing that the warship now heading towards him was a destroyer that had detected *I-58*, he ordered one kaiten pilot to his weapon and told another to stand by—obviously anticipating the need to launch kaiten and then make an emergency dive. When the target came within 4,000yds (3660m), the submarine skipper identified her as "an *Idaho*-class battleship" and decided on a conventional torpedo attack. Meanwhile, his kaiten pilots clamoured to be launched.

At 2332, Hashimoto fired a spread of six torpedoes at a range of 1,500yds (1370m), making two hits on *Indianapolis* forward and ripping away huge chunks of her starboard bow. Contrary to the assertions of some American writers, he did *not* launch any kaiten—although when *Indianapolis* failed to sink immediately his pilots begged to be allowed to administer the *coup de grace*. In fact, the heavy cruiser sank within 15 minutes: some 350 men died at once and, because details of the warship's ETA had been received in garbled form at Guam, some 500 more (the total death roll was 883) perished in the three days before rescue aircraft and ships were dispatched (Hashimoto's intercepted message to Tokyo claiming the sinking of a "battleship" having been at first dismissed by US codebreakers as yet another false Japanese claim). After the war, Hashimoto was flown to Washington to give evidence at the court martial of Capt McVay for hazarding his ship by failing to zig-zag: McVay was found guilty but the sentence was remitted.

Date: **10 August 1945**
Place: **Okinawa-Leyte convoy route**
Attack by: **Kaiten from I-58**
Target: **USS Johnnie Hutchins (DE 360)**

Hashimoto's eventful cruise was not yet over. On the morning of 10 August, hunting targets on the Okinawa-Leyte convoy lanes, he sighted what appeared to be a lone warship and ordered kaiten manned. After a delay when the engine of one kaiten proved faulty, a single human torpedo was launched at a range of about 7,000yds (6400m). The target was the DE *Johnnie Hutchins* (LtCdr H.M. Godsey), part of a hunter-killer group of five DEs. Her consorts were now sighted by Hashimoto, who launched a second kaiten before heading away on the surface at flank speed. He would later claim to have sunk two destroyers.

The kaiten launched at *Johnnie Hutchins*, perhaps malfunctioning, broke surface about 2,000yds (1830m) short of its target. The DE approached the surfaced "midget submarine" warily, opening fire at 1,500yds (1370m) without result and then closing to within 300yds (270m). Wisely, LtCdr Godsey did not shape a ramming course but instead circled to bring his portside guns to bear. Approaching to within 100yds (91m) he noted that, although travelling at no more than 2kt (2.3mph, 3.7kmh), the midget "appeared to be trying to keep its bow pointed towards the ship": obviously, the kaiten retained some power of manoeuvre and the pilot had not abandoned all hope of an attacking run. A 5-inch shell from *Hutchins* holed the kaiten, which sank without detonating—but moments later, sonar contact warned of a second submersible's approach, and a periscope was sighted 700yds (640m) to port. A depthcharge attack on this contact resulted in a claimed "kill"; but since a third contact was then reported (and Hashimoto had launched only two kaiten) it seems likely that the kaiten survived a little longer. *Hutchins's* third depthcharge pattern resulted in a 30-foot waterspout and an explosion felt more than 2,000yds (1830m) away, marking the destruction of the last kaiten; but *Hutchins*, now joined by a further eight DEs, spent 24 hours in a fruitless search for other "midget submarines" which were now believed to be in the vicinity.

Hashimoto still had one serviceable kaiten and, although *I-58* had picked up information from US broadcasts of the terrible destruction caused by the atomic bombs at Hiroshima and Nagasaki, the Japanese skipper was still full of fight. Late on the afternoon of 12 August, while running northward on the surface about 350nm (402 miles, 647km) southeast of Okinawa, he made visual contact with a target and at once submerged. Stalking his prey, which he identified as a "15,000-ton seaplane carrier" escorted by a destroyer, Hashimoto released his remaining kaiten, piloted by PO Yoshiaki Hayashi, and some 50 minutes later observed a large explosion, followed by the sounds of a depthcharge attack. After a brief prayer for the souls of his kaiten pilots, Hashimoto brought *I-58* to the surface and continued his run to the north, heading homeward to Japan.

The Last Kaiten

The target for Hashimoto's final attack—the last kaiten launch of the war—had been the 4,500-ton dock landing ship *Oak Hill*, escorted by the DE *Thomas F. Nickel* (LtCdr C.S. Farmer). At 1829, *Oak Hill* sighted a periscope; moments later, a kaiten broke surface in her wake and began to track her. *Oak Hill* zig-zagged, and the kaiten submerged as *Nickel* raced in. A few minutes later, the DE's crew had the startling experience of hearing the human torpedo scrape along *Nickel's* port side: it surfaced and exploded about 2,500yds (2290m) from the warship. Almost immediately, *Oak Hill* reported a second periscope approaching her (although *I-58* had launched only one kaiten). Cutting across the LSD's bow, *Nickel* disposed of the menace with a pattern of shallow-set depthcharges. LtCdr Farmer reported his belief that a parent submarine had been controlling the kaiten's movements from "beyond sonar range": in fact, beyond giving final course instructions over the telephone link immediately before launching, there was nothing the submarine's skipper could do to aid the kaiten.

Rear-Admiral J.B. Oldendorf, USN, commander of Task Force 95 at Okinawa, later commented that kaiten attacks "threatened to become of major importance had the war continued". Indeed, kaiten based in Japan (see Chapter 6) might have inflicted significant losses on an Allied invasion fleet. But overall the success rate of the kaiten was far below what may have been expected—and, it may be thought, far below what the dedication of the kaiten pilots deserved.

Four fleet submarines and four transport submarines were lost with all hands during kaiten missions. Of some 150 kaiten deployed operationally, only seven (or possibly eight) found targets, sinking a destroyer-escort and a fleet oiler (and possibly an infantry landing craft) and damaging a destroyer-escort and four transports. Eighty kaiten pilots were lost during operations and 15 more were killed in accidents that occurred during training.

GERMAN MANNED-TORPEDOES

Development of manned-torpedoes for use by the "Small Battle Units" of the German Navy was concurrent with that of midget submarines (see Chapter 2). However, the manned-torpedo, being simpler to produce and requiring less training to operate, was the first of the Kriegsmarine's "special attack" weapons to be operationally deployed.

The earliest of these weapons, designed in 1943-44, was the *Neger* ("Nigger"), so called from the name of its chief designer, the naval engineer Richard Mohr. (*Mohr* is the "polite" German word for "Negro"; thus, *Neger* is best translated as the pejorative "Nigger".) Mohr's brief was for a cheap, simple weapon that could be used in short-range operations against Allied shipping in the event of a cross-Channel invasion of Europe. Working at the torpedo-testing establishment at Eckenförde on the Baltic, near Kiel, the designer

GERMAN MANNED-TORPEDOES			
Type:	NEGER ("NIGGER")	MARDER ("PINE MARTEN")	HAI ("SHARK")
Length:	25ft (7.6m)	27.2ft (8.3m)	36.09ft (11m)
Beam:	1.6ft (0.5m)	1.6ft (0.5m)	1.6ft (0.5m)
Draught:	3.5ft (1.07m)	3.5ft (1.07m)	3.5ft (1.07m)
Displacement:	2.74 tons (2.78 tonnes)	2.95 tons (3 tonnes)	3.44 tons (3.5 tonnes)
Machinery:	1-shaft electric torpedo motor of 12hp	1-shaft electric torpedo motor of 12hp	1-shaft electric torpedo motor of 12hp
Range:	48nm @ 4kt on surface only	48nm @ 4kt with submergence to safe depth of c.100ft (30m)	30nm @ 5kt 63nm @ 3kt
Armament:	1 x 21in (533mm) G7e torpedo underslung	1 x 21in (533mm) G7e torpedo underslung	1 x 21in (533mm) G7e torpedo underslung or 1 mine
Crew:	1	1	1
Number completed:	c.200	c.300	Prototype only

produced the Neger, an easily-manufactured, one-man craft capable of carrying and launching a standard torpedo.

The "Neger" Manned-Torpedo

The Neger comprised two 21in (533mm) G7e electrically-propelled torpedoes, one clamped beneath the other with a clearance of no more than 3in (76mm). In the upper body, the 1,100lb (500kg) warhead was replaced by a tiny cockpit for the pilot, equipped with the most basic controls: start, stop, steer to port or starboard, and a trigger to start and release the lower torpedo. Overall, the weapon was 25ft (7.6m) long, with a mean draught of 3.5ft (1.07m), and displaced 2.74 tons (2.78 tonnes).

The single-shaft electric motor of the upper torpedo was theoretically capable of propelling the Neger at c.20kt (23mph, 37kmh)—the standard G7e being capable of 30kt (34.5mph, 55.5kmh) to a range of c.3.5nm (4 miles, 6.5km)—but because about 50 per cent of its battery capacity had to be removed to give the buoyancy necessary to support the lower torpedo, such a speed would have reduced its endurance to an unacceptably low level. The motor of the upper torpedo was therefore regulated to a maximum speed of no more than 10kt (11.5mph, 18.5kmh) and an endurance of some 48nm (55 miles, 89km) at 4kt (4.6mph, 7.4kmh).

The Neger had no submerged capability, operating only awash. Experiments with a flooding-tank proved unsuccessful: the added weight of a compressed-air "blower" dangerously compromised the craft's buoyancy and unacceptably reduced speed and range. The pilot, cramped in his cockpit with his head and shoulders no more than 18in (460mm) above the waterline, was protected by a plexiglass dome which, in earlier models, could not be opened from within. Although volunteers for Neger operations—a mixed bunch of soldiers and sailors; recruiting from the U-boat arm was forbidden by Grossadmiral Dönitz—were warned at the outset that they had no more than a 50 per cent chance of survival, the fact that the operator was literally imprisoned during his mission savoured too greatly of openly suicidal tactics. A cupola-release was fitted within the cockpit, although this led to losses when pilots opened-up for fresh air and were swamped. A self-contained Dräger breathing-apparatus with a face-mask, like those issued to aircrew, was provided, but cases of carbon-dioxide poisoning were not uncommon.

Although reliable figures are unobtainable, it is probable that more than half the operational losses of the Neger were caused by accident rather than enemy action. As well as the hazards already detailed, the Neger was highly unstable after its lower torpedo was fired—and there were occasions when the lower torpedo, once started, failed to separate from the carrier body and dragged the whole craft to destruction at high speed.

Even if the Neger pilot succeeded in approaching an enemy ship and lining it up in the rudimentary sights provided—a ring sight attached to the cockpit dome and a metal blade foresight on the casing forward—his chance of hitting a moving target from such a low-lying, unstable platform was small. If Negers had been employed more often against anchored transports, their success rate might have been greater: the German naval historian Cajus Bekker (who gives an overall loss rate of 60-80 per cent for German manned-torpedoes) states that Dönitz favoured limiting the craft to such employment but was overruled by Adolf Hitler, who wove fantasies of the "enormous strategical consequences" if Small Battle Units were to sink "six to eight battleships in the Seine estuary".

Date: **20-21 April 1944**
Place: **Allied beachhead at Anzio-Nettuno, Italy**
Attack by: **German "Neger" manned-torpedoes and EMBs**
Target: **Allied transports at anchor**

The possibility that the Führer displayed a personal interest in Germany's "special attack" craft is evident in the timing of the Negers' first mission. Before the manned-torpedoes could be properly evaluated, they were committed to action on 20 April 1944, Adolf Hitler's fiftyfifth birthday.

Some 40 Negers of K-Flotilla 175, commanded by Lt Hanno Krieg, were transported by road and rail, in extreme secrecy, to a base on the west coast of Italy south of Rome, not far north of the hard-held Allied beachhead at Anzio-Nettuno, into which men and material were being poured by sea in the build-up for the break-out in May. Here, transports anchored in inshore waters would provide an ideal target of considerable strategic importance for the Negers. (A simultaneous attack made by explosive motorboats is described in Chapter 3.)

The beach from which the Negers were launched, at Torre Vaianica some 15nm (17 miles, 28km) north of Anzio, shelved too gently to allow the craft to be lowered into the water by portable cranes. Instead, they had to be pushed out on wheeled trolleys (with 30 soldiers pressed into service on each trolley) until deep enough to float. Only 30 trolleys were available and of those 13 bogged down in soft sand before reaching the required depth. The 17 Negers able to sortie faced a long voyage under their own power in the dark of the moon, the only navigational aids being the pilots' wrist-compasses and beacons and starshell fired in pre-arranged positions by German units ashore. Somewhat surprisingly, all the Negers appear to have reached the target area—only to find, instead of anchored and vulnerable transports, patrolling submarine chasers of the US Navy at the ready with shallow-set depthcharges.

German and Allied sources are at variance in their accounts of the action. According to the US Navy's historian, the attackers were discovered at 0230 on 21 April, when *PC-591* made radar contact on an unseen intruder and claimed a depthcharge kill. One Neger was certainly destroyed later by US patrol craft: in the light of morning, at 0715, *PC-558* first spotted a small wake, then a glass cupola, made a depthcharge attack, and dragged from the water an uninjured Neger pilot. US sub-chasers claimed two more kills; all Allied accounts deny that any ships were torpedoed.

German accounts state that only four Negers were lost (all accidentally) and that two small Allied craft were sunk: by Midshipman Karlheinz Potthast, who penetrated Anzio harbour, and by Midshipman Voigt in Nettuno Bay. Of the surviving pilots, six scuttled their craft and made their way back to German lines through Allied-occupied country, while seven were able to beach in German-held territory. To preserve the weapon's secrecy, the returned Negers and those which had failed to launch were destroyed; but the Allies had captured an intact specimen, found drifting off Anzio with its pilot dead from carbon-dioxide poisoning.

Negers in the English Channel

In May 1944, with an Allied invasion of *Festung Europa* expected, the surviving Neger veterans were called back from Italy to train volunteers for manned-torpedo operations against invasion shipping. Operational losses began even before the new flotillas reached their bases on the French coast: their road convoys were strafed by fighter-bombers, Negers were destroyed or damaged, and personnel, including the commander Lt Krieg, were wounded or killed. But by the end of June 1944, a base under Kapitän-zur-See Böhme was established on the Seine Bay at Villers-sur-Mer, no more than 11nm (13 miles, 20km) from the eastern edge of the Allied invasion area. Two companies of a labour battalion constructed camouflaged runways along which the Negers' trolleys could be run out to deep water.

Date: **5-8 July 1944**
Place: **Off "Sword" and "Juno" beaches, Normandy**
Attack by: **German "Neger" manned-torpedoes**
Target: **Allied escorts on patrol**

At 2300 on the night of 5-6 July, the first occasion on which the weather favoured a sortie, 26 of the 40 Negers on hand at Villers were launched to run down on the ebb-tide for an attack on the invasion transports. The Allies were well-prepared—the transports were protected by the double line of escorts comprising the Support Squadron Eastern Flank (see page 126)—but since this was the first deployment of "special attack" craft in the Channel, some degree of surprise was achieved. The minesweeping sloops HMS *Cato* and *Magic* (both of 890 tons, 904 tonnes), anchored at the eastern extremity of the outer defence ring (the "Trout Line") were torpedoed and sunk, with a total of 51 dead. The Germans also claimed torpedo hits on a destroyer and an LCF (Landing Craft, Flak). Although Allied escorts claimed only four manned-torpedoes sunk and five "possibles", German accounts state that at least 12 Negers failed to return.

With a calm sea and a clear night of little moonlight again favouring them, 21 Negers were launched from Villers at c.2300 on 7 July. Again, their attack was made on the warships of the Trout Line, now fully alert and dropping depthcharges at regular intervals along their patrol routes, rather than on the attack transports. The leader of the sortie, the Anzio veteran Midshipman Potthast, evaded the escorts and reached the Orne estuary, where he torpedoed the old light cruiser *Dragon* (4,850 tons, 4928 tonnes), a former Royal Navy ship operated by the Free Polish Navy. According to Potthast's own account, he closed to within c.300yds (270m) before letting go his G7e torpedo at the slow-moving warship and blowing off its stern. (*Dragon,* too badly damaged to be worth repair, was scuttled to form part of a "Gooseberry" breakwater.) Potthast cleared the scene of his triumph but in daylight, at 0737, as he slumped exhausted in his cockpit, his Neger was spotted by the minesweeper HMS *Orestes* and taken under 20mm fire. Badly wounded, Potthast was taken as a prisoner from his sinking craft. Perhaps because of his capture, German propaganda at the time appears to have credited the sinking of *Dragon* to Cpl-Clerk Walter Gerhold, who was awarded the Knight's Cross.

The minesweeper HMS *Pylades* (890 tons, 904 tonnes) was sunk by a Neger on the same night, and two more minesweepers were damaged. A German source claims that *MTB-463* was also lost as the result of the explosion of a Neger that she was engaging at close range. These successes were achieved at heavy cost: only five of the 21 Negers committed returned to base. The Allies claimed only 12 certain kills during the night battle, but four more Negers—presumably stragglers drifting with dead pilots at the controls—were destroyed by Seafires of the Fleet Air Arm on 8-9 July.

Although the Negers had proved more effective than the Linsen EMBs deployed alongside them (see Chapter 3)—and far more effective than the Biber midget submarines that came into service in August 1944 (see Chapter 2)—a loss rate of 60 per cent in two sorties certainly established the slow, vulnerable manned-torpedo as a suicidal weapon. However, the fact that Neger operations were now phased out is probably due more to the increasing availability of an improved model (see below) than to any second thoughts on the part of the German authorities. Negers sortied again in the Seine Bay on the night of 19-20 July and claimed to have sunk the destroyer HMS *Isis* (1,370 tons, 1392 tonnes), although it seems more probable that this warship, destroyed by an explosion in which most of her crew perished, was lost on a mine. Most of the Negers deployed on that occasion failed to return, as did most of the craft committed in unfavourable weather off Honfleur on 15-16 August, the last sortie.

The "Marder" Manned-Torpedo

Developed from the Neger, the manned-torpedo named *Marder* ("Pine Marten") resembled it in every respect but one: it was "stretched", from 25ft (7.6m) to 27.2ft (8.3m), to allow the incorporation of a diving-tank and a compressed-air pump. This gave it the ability to submerge for a limited period to a safe depth of c.100ft (30m). However, since no navigational instruments other than a wrist-compass were provided, this ability was really only of use in evading attack and the Marder generally operated, like the Neger, while awash.

It is possible that the Marder was originally intended to be used in much the same way as the Italian Pig and British Chariot—submarine-launched for attacks on defended anchorages. At least one fleet submarine, *U.997*, was fitted with cradles on the casing aft to carry four Marders, and plans were made for an attack on Allied convoy shipping at Murmansk. The scheme appears to have been short-lived:

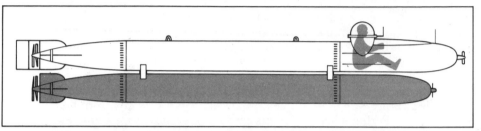

German **Neger** manned-torpedo; the **Marder** differed in appearance only in being 2.2ft (0.67m) longer. The upper, carrier body is a slightly "stretched" model of the lower G7e torpedo.

Marders were deployed in the Channel, replacing the Negers, and in the Mediterranean for shore-launched attacks on invasion shipping.

Marders in action off Normandy

The action off Courseulles-sur-Mer on 2-3 August 1944, when explosive motorboats and manned-torpedoes made a joint attack on Allied invasion shipping, is described in some detail on pages 126-128. In this, the Marders' first sortie, more than 50 manned-torpedoes and 24 EMBs sailed from Houlgate, some 15nm (17 miles, 28km) from the target area, at c.2300 on 2 August. An attack by Marders at the northern end of the Allied defence lines would, it was hoped, draw the attention of enough escort warships to allow the EMBs to break through in the centre and reach the soft-skinned transports.

The Allies' first indication of the Marders' assault came at c.0200, when a torpedo struck the blockship (ex-light cruiser) *Durban*, which formed part of a "Gooseberry" harbour. For a little over an hour, a fierce action was fought at the northern end of the Trout Line, as destroyers and smaller escorts manoeuvred at high speed to evade torpedoes, while cutting loose with automatic weapons and depth-charges at starshell-lit cupolas and moonlit wakes. If the British official figure of 40 Marders lost in the entire operation is accepted, then about half were sunk at this time—but not without cost to the Allies. The escort destroyer HMS *Quorn* (907 tons, 922 tonnes) took a torpedo at c.0250 and sank with heavy loss of life. (German claims notwithstanding, it is unlikely that this sinking should be credited to an EMB.)

Between 0350 and c.0600, the main thrust of the attack was made by

EMBs, but with the dawn the Marders closed in for a last desperate attempt to breach the Trout Line. Out from the shelter of a "Gooseberry" roared four British MTBs to join the fight: the .5in (12.7mm) machine guns of these 40kt (46mph, 74kmh) craft sent down five of the slow-moving Marders in quick time, while 10 more were claimed by other escorts. The destroyer HMS *Blencathra* was slightly damaged by a Marder which, abandoned by its pilot, self-destructed as efforts were made to winch it aboard. With the coming of full light, Spitfires of the 2nd TAF sank six more Marders, lying helpless on the surface, in low-level strafing runs.

Date: **16-17 August 1944**
Place: **Off the Normandy invasion beaches**
Attack by: **German "Marder" manned-torpedoes**
Target: **Allied warships and transports**

The second and last mass attack on the Allied defence line by what a British commander characterized as a "whimsical, though dangerous" weapon was made on the night of 16-17 August, when 42 Marders of K-Flotilla 363 sortied from Houlgate. A major objective of this attack was the old French battleship *Courbet* (23,189 tons, 23560 tonnes). Apparently riding at anchor just offshore, flying both the Tricolour and the Free French Croix de Lorraine flag, the battleship appeared to be in fighting condition; in fact, she was a mere hulk, resting on the bottom as part of a "Gooseberry" breakwater. Allied warships maintained the illusion of *Courbet's* continued activity by carrying out shore bombardments from her seaward side, and German shore batteries and aircraft had made several attempts to "sink" her. Now *Courbet* was struck twice by torpedoes from Marders and German propaganda claimed a famous victory. In fact, the only real success was the sinking of a 415-ton (422 tonne) LCF (Landing Craft, Flak).

This was achieved at great cost: 26 Marders were destroyed by escort warships and fighter-bombers. One was sighted on the surface at 0645 by the support landing craft *LCS(L)-251*, which opened with 6pdr fire at c.400yds (370m). The Marder submerged, then bobbed to the surface again much closer to the LCS. Fire from 20mm guns shattered its cupola and killed the pilot before he could launch his torpedo. Taken in tow, the Marder soon swamped and sank, but after a four-hour struggle with winches and hawsers—hidden from German shore batteries by smoke laid by another support craft—the LCS succeeded in lashing the manned-torpedo alongside and returning to port with its prize.

On the following night, the barrage balloon vessel HMS *Fratton* (757 tons, 769 tonnes; an ex-Channel rail ferry) was sunk by a torpedo believed to have been fired from a Marder. But thereafter, apart from sporadic and unsuccessful sorties in the Scheldt and Maas estuaries as late as October 1944, activity by Marders in the Channel area virtually ceased as winter weather set in.

Marders in the Mediterranean

In the late summer of 1944, following the Allied "Anvil"/"Dragoon" landings in the Toulon-Cannes area on 15 August, the focus of Marder

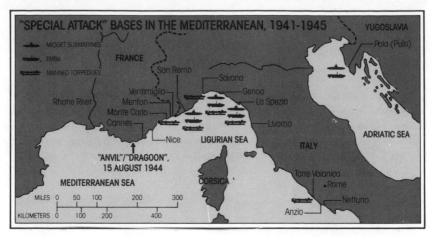

Mediterranean and Adriatic bases and launching points of **Neger** and **Marder** manned-torpedoes and **Linsen** explosive motorboats of the German Navy's "Small Battle Units", 1944-1945.

operations shifted to the Mediterranean, where a K-Force base was established at San Remo. Sorties were limited to small groups: at the beginning of September, only about 30 Marders were on hand in the launching areas near San Remo and Menton.

Date: **5 September 1944**
Place: **Off Monte Carlo, Monaco, Mediterranean Sea**
Attack by: **German "Marder" manned-torpedoes**
Target: **Franco-American bombardment force**

Early on the morning of 5 September 1944, five Marders slipped out from Menton to attack Allied destroyers which had been bombarding shore positions near Monte Carlo. The German pilots must have had navigational difficulties, for the attack was not made until full daylight, when the Free French destroyer *Le Malin* and the US destroyer *Ludlow,* awaiting a shore bombardment mission off Cap Ferrat at c.0810, sighted the Marders' cupolas glittering in morning sunlight. *Le Malin* opened fire, forcing the nearest Marder to submerge, and *Ludlow* raced in with depthcharges. At 0848 another Marder pilot abandoned his craft and surrendered as *Ludlow* bore down on him, and yet another pilot displayed a similar disinclination for a suicidal attack when he came under the US destroyer's guns at point-blank range. A fourth Marder was either destroyed by the Allied ships or lost on passage, for only one returned to Menton.

A second sortie against the bombardment force by 10 Marders launched near Ventimiglia on the morning of 10 September was no more successful—and again the German pilots, understandably enough, appeared to have little heart for pressing home completely suicidal daylight attacks on fast-moving warships. The US destroyers *Hilary P. Jones* and *Madison,* supported by two PT-boats, were firing off Menton at c.0715 when warning came from artillery spotters on land of small craft approaching the bombardment force from inshore. Guided by the shore observers, *Jones* dropped 5in (127mm) salvoes which forced a Marder to surface, where it was destroyed by direct fire.

Madison first sighted a tell-tale cupola at 0718: zig-zagging at high speed to avoid the expected torpedo, the destroyer and a PT-boat raked the Marder with 20mm and 40mm fire. The Marder submerged; its pilot alone surfaced to surrender. The presence of more Marders was now reported by a spotter aircraft and in a five-hour hunt *Madison* claimed at least four kills, while aircraft and PT-boats accounted for the remaining attackers. Having cleared the sea, the destroyers and the old Free French battleship *Lorraine* proceeded to bombard the Marders' launching area near Ventimiglia.

Similar bombardments of the main base at San Remo succeeded in disrupting the K-Force's efforts over the next few weeks. The final Marder sortie against the bombardment ships appears to have been made from Genoa on 25-26 September, when *Madison* and the Free French destroyer *Forbin* engaged and sank two manned-torpedoes. A handful of Marders based thereafter at Savona on the Gulf of Genoa appear never to have sortied. Nor do those few taken overland for service in the Adriatic early in 1945, after the last Marder sorties in the San Remo area, on 19 December 1944 and 1 January 1945, had resulted in almost 100 per cent losses with no success. Overall, the loss rate of the Marder appears to have exceeded that of the Neger, perhaps running as high as 80 per cent.

High-Speed Manned-Torpedo: "Hai"

Only one other attempt (excluding one aspect of the *Kleine Delphin*, described on page 72) was made to produce a manned-torpedo for the K-Force. In 1944-45, Versuchskommando 456 designed and built a super-Marder named *Hai* ("Shark"), in which the carrier body was stretched yet again, to 36.09ft (11m), to allow for extra battery capacity. This increased range to a maximum 63nm (72 miles, 117km) and, more importantly, gave a speed of c.20kt (23mph, 37kmh) for the final attacking run—provided the pilot did not give too much thought to husbanding power for a return to base. However, the craft proved to be so cranky in any seaway that only a single prototype was built.

Chapter Six

Banzai!

On 27 May 1943, the US 7th Infantry Division drove the Japanese from Fish Hook Ridge, their last stronghold on Attu island, Aleutians. The survivors of Col Yasuyo Yamasaki's garrison retreated into the hills around Chichagof Harbor, while in his HQ on Buffalo Ridge, overlooking the main US force, Yamasaki took stock. He had some 1,200 men, half of them wounded, left from an original c.2,600, with supplies for only two days. He faced some 11,000 Americans with strong air and naval support. He had no hope of reinforcement. Late on 28 May, after air-dropped US leaflets had called upon him to surrender, Yamasaki made his final radio contact with Tokyo: "I plan a successful annihilation of the enemy"!

Human Bullets: the Banzai Charge

Yamasaki's suicidal counter-offensive, the biggest of its kind to that date, was perhaps the best example of the "*Banzai* Charge", in which Japanese servicemen became *nikudan* ("human bullets"), intent on doing as much damage as possible to the enemy before dying in battle.

It is, however, important to note that the purpose of the banzai charge — so called because the slogan *Tenno heika banzai!* ("May the Emperor live 10,000 years!") was the last the soldier would utter — was not simply to die gloriously. Such purely death-seeking charges were made earlier in the war; but Imperial General HQ directed that banzai assaults should have at least some tactical aim and should be carefully planned for maximum effect. Only if facing inevitable capture should men attack recklessly — or die by their own hands.

Yamasaki's rationale was that his charge would be made at night against the weakest point in the US line. The impetus of the attack would take his men through the US infantry positions and up Engineer Hill, where artillery bunkers would be overrun and their 105mm howitzers captured and used to blast a way to the US supply base. Thus reprovisioned, he might hold out indefinitely in the southern mountains. Having established a tactical basis, Yamasaki took thought for the men too badly wounded to participate. Because it was unthinkable that they should be left to become prisoners, the comatose were saved from dishonour by lethal injections; the more active were given grenades, one to every three or four men, who would clasp each other in a last embrace before pulling the pin. The remainder of Yamasaki's men, some armed only with bayonets lashed to sticks, advanced silently into Chichagof Valley through pre-dawn fog on 29 May.

Yamasaki's plan nearly succeeded. Faced with the screaming, firing, slashing, stabbing human wave, the US infantrymen broke and fled. Sweeping down the valley, the Japanese overran two battalion command posts and a field hospital, where patients and doctors died in the frenzied killing. The charge reached Engineer Hill, surging upward in the light of dawn towards the vital guns — only to be halted by an improvised defence line of engineers, medics, cooks and HQ staff, commanded by BrigGen A.V. Arnold. A 37mm gun was dragged into action; grenades showered down; the assault wavered, halted, then came on once more. But in a hand-to-hand struggle on the hill-crest, Yamasaki's men were held and at last driven back.

Fighting continued throughout the day, but many Japanese had now lost heart for anything but death: it was estimated that more than half of Yamasaki's men deliberately blew themselves apart with their last grenades. Their colonel himself died sword in hand as he headed a final charge up Engineer Hill. When Attu was secured, only 28 Japanese survived as prisoners.

Saipan: "Seven Lives for My Country"

The *shinigurui* ("death frenzy") manifested by Yamasaki's men on Attu marked Japanese resistance on many islands. From Tarawa in the Gilberts, Tokyo received a last message on 22 November 1943: "All weapons destroyed . . . everyone is attempting a final charge . . . *Tenno heika banzai!*"; and of Rear-Admiral Keiji Shibasaki's 4,500-strong garrison, only 17 Japanese and 129 Korean auxiliaries survived as prisoners. At Kwajalein, in February 1944, 265 prisoners were taken from Rear-Admiral Akiyama's 8,700 men. At Eniwetok, a few days later, all but 64 of MajGen Nishida's 3,400 soldiers chose to die in battle. On Los Negros, Admiralties, bodies examined after a banzai charge revealed that the Japanese had bandaged pressure points on their bodies so that they might fight on briefly if an artery was cut.

What is usually said to be the biggest banzai charge of the war took place on Saipan, Marianas, after US forces had penned some 3,000 survivors of the garrison—originally of about 30,000 Army and Navy troops, jointly commanded by LtGen Yoshitsugo Saito and Vice-Admiral Chuichi Nagumo—at the island's northern extremity. On 6 July 1944, Gen Saito issued the order for a final assault: ". . . there is only death; but in death there is life. Take this chance to exalt true Japanese manhood". His men took as a battlecry *Shichi sho hokoku* ("Seven lives for my country"), based on the famous words of Masasue Kusunoki at Minatogawa in 1336. Immediately after drafting his order, Saito committed *seppuku*, facing towards the Imperial Palace and gashing his belly with his own sword before his adjutant administered the *coup de grâce* with a pistol. Admiral Nagumo, who had commanded the Pearl Harbor attack, followed Saito's example.

Between 1,500 and 3,000 Japanese concentrated at Makunsho on Tanapag Plain, late on 6 July. Although LtGen Holland M. ("Howlin' Mad") Smith, USMC, anticipated a banzai attack in this area and had ordered MajGen Ralph C. Smith, USA (subsequently removed from command by Holland Smith) to be prepared, the 105th RCT was taken by surprise by the mass assault at c.0500 on 7 July. Screaming their battlecry, the Japanese broke the 105th RCT's line and, despite point-blank fire, charged over their own heaped dead to overwhelm the twelve 105mm guns of 3rd Battalion, 10th Marines. But determined resistance by the Marine gunners, who had removed the locks from their heavy weapons, slowed the Japanese impetus while reinforcements were rushed forward and the guns retaken. After day-long mopping-up, US losses were 406 dead and many more wounded.

It was thought that Japanese resistance was at an end—but a few hundred survivors launched a final banzai in which many of the participants were walking wounded, cripples leading blind men, armed only with sticks, stones and broken bottles. Of this pathetic remnant, some 100 swam out to sea to drown when their comrades were cut down by machine gun fire. Three days later, US Marines watched as several hundred Japanese civilians, including small children, fell on grenades, impaled themselves on bayonets or threw themselves from the northern cliffs. Of the original garrison, 921 Japanese (including 17 officers) and 838 Koreans survived.

No significant decline in Japanese morale, as reflected in the number of surrenders, was apparent until the later stages of the Okinawa campaign, when large and well-organized parties sometimes surrendered. Even so, 107,549 Japanese died, as against 10,755 (including many Okinawan conscripts) taken prisoner. A more reliable guide to the savage resistance that the Allies might encounter in an invasion of Japan itself was provided at Iwo Jima and on Ie Shima.

Iwo Jima and Ie Shima: Civilians in Arms

LtGen Kuribayashi's standing order to his 23,000-strong garrison on Iwo Jima was starkly simple: "No man must die until he has killed ten of the enemy"! According to a staff officer who survived (Kuribayashi himself is said to have fallen in a banzai charge), the General issued special insignia to members of selected suicide squads and decreed that "each man must think of his defence position as his graveyard". That command was often obeyed literally: of the 20,703 Japanese killed, many were buried alive when US armoured bulldozers sealed them into their bunkers and caves.

At Okinawa, the offshore island of Ie Shima—where the US 77th Infantry Division took 1,120 casualties in an eight-day battle to secure a vital airfield, 16-24 April 1945—was defended by some 5,000 Japanese, of whom 4,706 died fighting. It was estimated that this total included c.1,500 civilians. In a banzai assault at Bloody Ridge on 21 April, women armed with bamboo spears, and some with babies strapped to their backs, formed an element of a 400-strong charge spear-headed by soldiers rigged as "human bombs", hung round with demolition charges. As the assault was made, Japanese mortars put down heavy fire on attackers and defenders alike. The final banzai on Ie Shima, early on 23 April, was made by a well-armed group consisting largely of civilians, again including many women.

Japanese Prisoners: Suicides at Cowra Camp

Inevitably, some Japanese were taken prisoner when wounded or insensible. Allied reports note that after a violent initial reaction, when many attempted suicide in any way possible, prisoners often became surprisingly tractable. Having received no instructions on how to behave—capture being unthinkable—prisoners would sometimes cooperate wholeheartedly with their captors, informing on the strengths and positions of their units and even volunteering as artillery spotters or ammunition carriers. But this was not always the case.

On 5 August 1944, some 1,100 Japanese PoWs held at Cowra Camp, New South Wales, Australia, staged a mass breakout, the purpose of which can only have been to seek honourable death in action. At c.0200 hours, prisoners armed with home-made knives and clubs stormed the wire fences at three points. One 400-strong group rushed a machine gun post and killed its crew. Although the Japanese failed to bring the MG into action, many prisoners were able to escape into the countryside, while those remaining set the camp buildings afire, burning to death twelve of their number in the process.

By the time the riot was quelled, 234 Japanese were dead. Many were shot by guards, but 31 had committed suicide and of the 108 wounded a further 16 were judged to be attempted suicides. The area was scoured for the escapees and all were recaptured; significantly, with little resistance: a lone police constable was able to arrest a group of eight fugitives. Some few, however, hanged themselves.

Suicidal Snipers and Anti-Tank Squads

As early as 1942, Australian troops advancing along the Kokoda Trail across the Owen Stanley Mountains, Papua-New Guinea, encountered suicide snipers: volunteer rearguards lashed into the treetops. Similar tactics were met with by US Marines on Tulagi and Guadalcanal in 1942. By the time of the US landings at Cape Torokina, Bougainville, in November 1943, a countermeasure had been found in the Doberman Pinschers of the 1st Marine Dog Platoon, 2nd Marine Raider Division. After several months' training, these canine auxiliaries proved able to "point" snipers concealed in trees or bush.

Suicidal weapons and tactics also played a significant part in Japanese anti-tank measures. Most island garrisons were short of heavy artillery or shells, especially anti-tank guns — since tanks were used in comparatively small numbers in most Pacific campaigns — and often resorted to grenades and mines of improvised types that called for self-sacrifice by their users. The IJA's Type 99 *Hakobakurai* grenade-mine could either be placed in advance as an anti-tank or -personnel trap or be thrown at an AFV, to adhere by means of four magnets set around its canvas cover. When thrown, however, it almost invariably bounced off, and many Japanese died in attempting to approach tanks closely enough to affix magnetic charges by hand.

By 1943, Japanese infantry trained as tank-hunters were often using either hollow-charge grenades effective only when thrown from c.10yds (9m), or "satchel charges", impact-fuzed explosives in a cloth bag (naval troops sometimes used small depthcharges in sacks) to be tossed on to or thrust beneath a tank. Soldiers often strapped the charges to their bodies and flung themselves beneath the tanks' tracks. On Okinawa, the US 193rd Tank Battalion assaulting the Shuri Line at Kakazu, 19 April 1945, lost 22 of the 30 tanks committed — six of them to the suicide assault squads of the IJA's 272nd Independent Infantry Battalion, who sacrificed themselves to place 22lb (10kg) satchel charges beneath the Shermans' bottom plates.

On Kwajalein, in February 1944, a US tank commander reported an attack by five Japanese armed only with swords, who beat furiously on the armour plating until all were shot down. Hardly more effective were the "human bombs" encountered by British armour during the advance into Burma in 1944-45. A Japanese soldier would crouch in a well-camouflaged fox-hole in a road or track, with an artillery shell or aircraft bomb with an exposed impact-fuze in its nose. He would attempt to detonate his charge with an improvised hammer as a tank or truck passed above him.

In 1945, anti-tank units were advised by an IJA manual to attack "with spiritual vigour and steel-piercing passion". The weapon provided was the "lunge mine", a conical grenade mounted on a 5ft (1.5m) pole (see Diagram). Approaching a tank, the soldier pulled out the safety pin separating the striker at the pole's end from the percussion cap. The pole was then wielded like a bayoneted rifle, thrust against the armour plating, where the rods projecting from the grenade's head ensured a "stand-off" effect. As well as destroying its user, the charge was claimed to penetrate up to 4-6in (100-150mm) armour at $0°$, but details of its effectiveness are scanty.

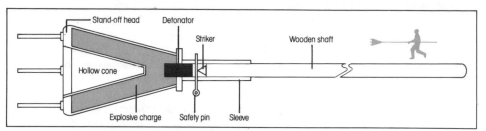

With the **"lunge mine"**, a conical shaped charge mounted on a 5ft (1.5m) pole, with protruding rods giving a "stand-off" effect, Japanese soldiers made suicidal attacks on Sherman tanks.

An odd "tank-busting" project of the IJNAF must be mentioned. Yokosuka planned to build, with the Mizumo company, a suicide weapon based on the small, experimental MXY5 assault glider of 1941-42. This unpowered aircraft would either make a rocket-assisted takeoff or, for longer-range missions, be towed aloft by a "Frances" bomber. Its pilot was expected to deliver an internally-mounted, impact-fuzed charge of c.220lb (100kg) with pin-point accuracy in a steep dive on an enemy AFV. Only one prototype of this *Shinryu* ("Divine Dragon") glider-bomb was completed.

"Giretsu" Airborne Operations

The IJA's paratroop forces were known as *teishin* ("raiding") units — and from late 1944 their operations, under the direction of LtGen Kyoji Tominaga, a prime mover in the formation of the Army's kamikaze aircraft units, increasingly relied on suicidal tactics. This was evident in a series of raids on US-held airstrips on Leyte, Philippines, in November-December 1944, aimed at interdicting Allied air activity while Japanese resupply convoys ran into Ormoc Bay.

As Japanese ground troops attempted to infiltrate the areas of the major airstrips — Dulag, Tacloban, Buri, San Pablo and Bayug — IJAAF transports flew from Luzon to para-drop troopers or crash-land with them on the airstrips. The main effort was made on the night of 6-7 December, when c.750 men of a *Teishin Rentai* ("Raiding Regiment") flew from Angeles, Luzon, in Mitsubishi Ki-57 ("Topsy") transports of the *1st Teishin Hikosentai* ("Raiding Flying Regiment"). Each aircraft carried some 13 fully-equipped paratroopers. Two plane-loads each were assigned to suicidal attacks on the Dulag and Tacloban airstrips, ordered to destroy as many US aircraft as possible and to hold their ground to the last man. The main objectives were Buri and

San Pablo where some 300 paratroopers hit the ground, holding the strips for a few hours but doing only limited damage. The shock troops sent to Dulag and Tacloban were even less successful. At Tacloban, where the "Topsys" approached with wheels and flaps down in an attempt to land, both aircraft were shot down by ground fire short of the strip. Both Dulag "Topsys" were also downed, one after dropping about five paratroopers who were speedily liquidated.

The most spectacular and successful suicidal airborne operation was launched against Yontan airfield, Okinawa, on the night of 24-25 May 1945, during the seventh kikusui offensive. Five Mitsubishi Ki-21-IIb ("Sally") bombers of the 3rd *Dokuritsu Hikotai* ("Independent Wing"), each carrying c.14 men of the *Giretsu* ("Heroic") Airborne Raiding Unit, arrived over Yontan at c.2230, in the wake of six waves of conventional bombers. Nine "Sallys" had taken off, but four had been shot down by US interceptors, and as the five remaining approached at low altitude, AA guns ringing Yontan brought down four. The survivor touched down with wheels up, skidding along the runway on its belly. From its nose and hatches, 10 Japanese armed with sub-machine guns tumbled out and rushed in among parked US aircraft, clamping on hakobakurai charges and hurling phosphorus grenades. Believing that the Japanese had landed in force, US pilots and groundcrew temporarily panicked, taking cover and firing wildly. By dawn, when Marines arrived to deal with the raiders, the Japanese had destroyed a fuel depot containing 70,000 US gallons (265 000 litres) of aviation gasoline and had completely wrecked 9 aircraft and damaged 26. Two Americans had been killed and 18 wounded.

The last and biggest suicide operation planned for airborne forces was frustrated by pre-emptive action on 9-10 August 1945. "Ultra" had alerted the Allies to Japanese aircraft concentrations at Misawa, northern Honshu, where the IJNAF had assembled about 200 transport planes to carry some 2,000 suicide commandos to crash-landings at the 21st Bomber Command's bases on Saipan, Tinian and Guam, whence the B-29s flew to destroy Japan's cities. In a series of low-level strikes from combined US and British carrier task groups, the Japanese air transport fleet, although carefully camouflaged in dispersed parking areas, was totally destroyed.

SUICIDE WEAPONS AND TACTICS IN THE FINAL DEFENCE OF JAPAN

As early as January 1945, the Imperial Japanese Army and Navy reached agreement (although their cooperation was, as always, limited by inter-service rivalry) on *Ketsu-Go* ("Operation Decision"): the final defence of the Japanese home islands against Allied invasion. A single phrase from the *Precepts Concerning the Decisive Battle* issued on 8 April 1945 by Gen Korechika Anami, Minister of War, will serve to illustrate these measures: all ranks were exhorted to "possess a deep-seated spirit of ramming". General Yoshijiro Umezu, Army Chief of Staff, emphasized that "the certain way to victory ... lies in making everything on Imperial soil contribute to the war effort ... combining the total material and spiritual strength of the nation ..." Servicemen and civilians alike were left in no doubt that the final defence would be to the death; that all available weapons would be used suicidally.

Meeting the Invasion Armada

Imperial General HQ believed (rightly) that an Allied invasion would be directed first against southern Kyushu and, once a beachhead was established there, against the Tokyo area, southeast Honshu.

Since the IJN was now almost bereft of surface striking units, the first line of defence against the invasion armada would be provided by the remaining aircraft for which pilots and fuel were available—some 10,700 according to USSBS figures—of the Army and Navy. Half of these, 2,700 of the IJN and 2,650 of the IJA, would be kamikaze.

Both the IJN and IJA sought to strengthen the kamikaze units and to impose some unity of aircraft types within them by producing purpose-designed suicide planes (see accompanying Table), of which the IJN's Yokosuka D4Y4 Model 43 and Aichi M6A1 are described in Chapter 4. The IJN's other major attempt at a "special attack" bomber, intended to be cheaply and quickly manufactured from non-strategic material, was the wooden-construction Yokosuka D3Y2-K (finally redesignated D5Y1), of which data are given in the Table. The programme was initiated in January 1945 and was aimed at a production target of 30 per month, but not even a prototype was completed.

JAPANESE "SPECIAL ATTACK" AIRCRAFT (PURPOSE-DESIGNED)				
Aircraft:	NAKAJIMA Ki-115a TSURUGI (SABRE)* Imperial Japanese Army	YOKOSUKA D4Y4 SUISEI (COMET) MODEL 43 ("JUDY") Imperial Japanese Navy	AICHI M6A1 SEIRAN (MOUNTAIN HAZE) Imperial Japanese Navy	YOKOSUKA D3Y2-K MYOJO KAI (VENUS MODIFIED) Imperial Japanese Navy
Type:	Single-engined special attack (suicide) aircraft	Single-engined special attack bomber	Single-engined, submarine-carried special attack bomber	Single-engined special attack bomber
Span:	28.2ft (8.6m)	37.73ft (11.5m)	40.23ft (12.26m)	45.93ft (14m)
Length:	28.05ft (8.55m)	33.53ft (10.22m)	38.19ft (11.64m)	37.78ft (11.52m)
Height:	10.8ft (3.3m) (jettisonable undercarriage)	12.27ft (3.74m)	15.03ft (4.58m) (detachable floats)	13.78ft (4.2m) (jettisonable undercarriage)
Loaded weight (normal):	5,688lb (2580kg)	10,013lb (4542kg)	8,907lb (4040kg)	10,207lb (4630kg)
Engine:	1 x Nakajima 23 air-cooled radial, take-off rating 1,130hp; attachment for 2 x RATOG rockets to boost terminal dive	1 x Mitsubishi Kinsei 62 air-cooled radial, take-off rating 1,560hp; 3 x RATOG rockets for short take-off or to boost terminal dive	1 x Aichi Atsuta 32 inverted-vee liquid-cooled, take-off rating 1,400hp	1 x Mitsubishi Kinsei 62 air-cooled radial, take-off rating 1,560hp
Maximum speed:	342mph (550kmh) @ 9,185ft (2800m)	350mph (563kmh) @ 19,355ft (5900m)	295mph (475kmh) @ 17,060ft (5200m)	292mph (470kmh) @ 16,405ft (5000m)
Service ceiling:	c.20,000ft (6100m)	27,725ft (8450m)	32,480ft (9900m)	30,350ft (9250m)
Normal range:	745 miles (1200km)	1,024 miles (1648km)	739 miles (1189km)	915 miles (1472km)
Armament:	Nil	2 x 7.7mm Type 97 MGs	1 x 13mm Type 2 MG	2 x 20mm Type 99 Mod 1 cannon
Bomb load:	1 x 551lb, 1,102lb or 1,764lb (250kg, 500kg or 800kg) bomb semi-recessed under fuselage	1 x 1,764lb (800kg) bomb semi-recessed under fuselage	2 x 551lb (250kg) bombs or 1 x 1,764-1,874lb (800-850kg) bomb	1 x 1,764lb (800kg) bomb
Crew:	1	1	2	1
Number built:	105 (including prototype)	296	28 (including prototypes)	Prototype incomplete
	*The Imperial Japanese Navy's projected **Toka** (Wistaria) special attacker closely resembled the Ki-115a. It was to be powered by any suitable reconditioned engines available.			

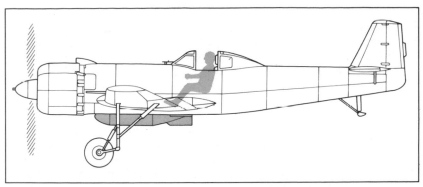

The IJA's Nakajima Ki-115 **Tsurugi** ("Sabre"); an open-cockpit aircraft for one-way missions.

The IJA had more success, in terms of production only, with its Nakajima Ki-115 *Tsurugi* ("Sabre"). This cheap and simply-produced suicide bomber was built largely of metal, with a wood-and-fabric tail assembly and, being intended only for one-way missions, with a jettisonable undercarriage. The open-cockpit aircraft was theoretically suitable to be flown by a pilot with only basic training, but not surprisingly in view of the speed of the development programme (design began on 20 January 1945; the prototype flew only seven weeks later) it proved a beast to handle, especially during takeoff on its unsprung undercarriage, which had to be modified. Of the 105 examples completed by the war's end, none was operational. No examples were completed of an improved model, the Nakajima Ki-230, or of the Showa *Toka* ("Wistaria"), a copy of the Ki-115 for the IJN.

Kamikaze and conventional air strikes, coordinated with suicidal attacks by the IJN's 45 remaining fleet submarines, would begin when the invasion armada was within c.180 miles (290km) of the Kyushu beaches. As the armada drew nearer, the rate of attack would increase, with troop transports the primary targets, until, off the beaches, all remaining aircraft would be committed to a non-stop mass suicide assault which, it was estimated, could be sustained for up to 10 days. At this time, the kamikaze would be supplemented by a "banzai charge" by the IJN's remaining surface units—only 2 cruisers and 23 destroyers remained fully operational in August 1945—midget submarines, human torpedoes and explosive motorboats.

Ambitious building programmes for small "special attack" craft were severely limited by material and power shortages caused by blockade and strategic bombing. Thus, by August 1945, there were available in the home islands only 100 *koryu* five-man submarines; 300 *kairyu* two-man submarines; 120 shore-based *kaiten* human-torpedoes; and about 4,000 *shinyo* and *maru-ni* EMBs. With the exception of the comparatively long-ranging koryu, these small suicide craft were deployed in well-concealed bases in southern and eastern Kyushu and southern Shikoku (see endpaper Map). The major locations were: in Kyushu, Kagoshima (20 kairyu, 500 shinyo), Aburatsu (20 kairyu, 34 kaiten, 125 shinyo), Hososhima (20 kairyu, 12 kaiten, 325 shinyo) and Saeki (20 kairyu); in Shikoku, Sukumo (12 kairyu, 14 kaiten, 50 shinyo) and Sunosaki (12 kairyu, 24 kaiten, 175 shinyo). The IJA's

EMBs were similarly but separately dispersed. In addition, 180 kairyu, 36 kaiten and 775 shinyo were deployed around Sagami Wan to defend the Tokyo area of Honshu. More shinyo and maru-ni (perhaps as many as 1,000 of each type) remained at bases in Korea, Formosa, Hainan Island, North Borneo, Hong Kong and Singapore.

"Fukuryu": the Suicide Frogmen

It was estimated that the mass onslaught would destroy some 35-50 per cent of the Allied armada *before* any troops could be put ashore. Offshore, a last line of maritime defence would be provided by the least-known of the "special attack" forces: the demolition frogmen called *fukuryu* ("crouching dragons").

Their training had begun at Kawatana in November 1944 (see page 105), although the IJN had employed teams of swimmers on hazardous missions since early in the war; notably at Hong Kong, where skin-divers defuzed Allied mines to prepare a way for landing craft. A Japanese prisoner taken at Peleliu, Palaus, late in 1944, claimed that he belonged to a 22-strong *Kaiyu* unit of swimmers trained to attack landing craft. Each swimmer was armed with three grenades, a knife and a simple demolition charge: a wooden box of c.160in^3 (2620cm^3) packed with trinitrophenol (Lyddite) with a fuze cut to the required length. But the kaiyu units, credited with damaging an LCI in the Palaus and a DE and an attack transport at Okinawa, were surface swimmers rather than frogmen.

The fukuryu appear never to have been deployed outside the home islands. Their role in the final defence would have been suicidal—as

Above left: Fukuryu ("crouching dragon") frogman of the IJN, armed with a "lunge mine".
Allied landing craft approaching the beaches of Japan **(Above right)** would face command-detonated mines; **fukuryu** attacking from underwater bunkers **(Below)**; magnetic mines; and beach mines.

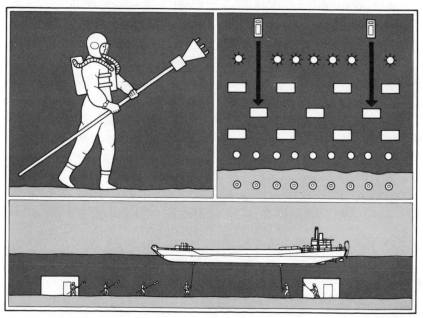

was, to some extent, their training. Their equipment—a loosely-fitting wet suit; a clumsy helmet not unlike that of a deep-sea diver; bulky air circulation and purification tanks strapped to chest and back and linked by a tangle of hoses—was most unsatisfactory. "There were very many [fatal] accidents during the training of fukuryu", a Japanese veteran told me, "because the twin-tank oxygen re-breathing equipment was no good—but nothing better was available". Nevertheless, some 1,200 fukuryu graduated from Kawatana and Yokosuka Mine School by the war's end, when 2,800 were still in training.

To destroy inshore landing craft, each fukuryu was armed with a 22lb (10kg) impact-fuzed charge, incorporating a flotation tank, mounted on a stout pole (much like the anti-tank "lunge mine" described above). *If* his equipment functioned perfectly, the frogman could stay at an optimum depth of 50ft (15m) for up to 10 hours, sustained by a container of liquid food. Construction was begun of underwater pillboxes, concrete with steel doors, in which fukuryu would shelter from a pre-landing bombardment while awaiting their opportunity to sally forth and thrust their explosive lances against the bottoms of landing craft.

As the accompanying diagram shows, the fukuryu would form part of a network of beach defence. Farthest from the beach were moored mines, electrically detonated from ashore; then three lines of fukuryu deployed so that each man guarded an area of c.470sq yds (390sq m); then lines of magnetic mines; and finally beach mines. Capt K. Shintani, commanding the fukuryu, was somewhat optimistic in hoping that his men might "cause as much damage as the kamikaze aircraft".

"Special Motorboats": Amphibious Tanks

Attacks by fukuryu on landing craft might have been supported by the few completed *Toku 4-Shiki Naikatei* ("Type 4 Special Motorboat"; called the *katsu*) which, in spite of its designation, was an amphibious AFV. Originally designed by Mitsubishi for the IJN as a troop, weapon or freight carrier with a capacity of c.10 tons, the katsu was adapted early in 1944 to serve as a coast defence craft. Only 18 examples of this tracked amphibian were built.

The katsu's 240bhp diesel engine gave a maximum land speed of c.15mph (24kmh) or, driving retractable twin propellers, a water speed of c.4.5kt (5mph, 9kmh). The craft displaced c.20 tons (20.3

Katsu "special motorboat": a tracked amphibian with two 13mm MGs and two torpedoes on drop racks.

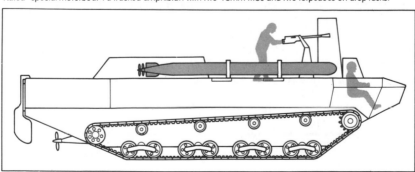

tonnes) and was 36ft (11m) long overall, 10.8ft (3.3m) in beam, and of 7.5ft (2.3m) draught from track-base to deck-level. It mounted two 13mm MGs in shielded positions forward and carried two 17.7in (450mm) torpedoes in launching racks to port and starboard at deck level. The engine was within a pressurized compartment so that the katsu might be carried on the casing of a submerged submarine; but a wild scheme—*Tatsumaki-Go* ("Operation Tornado")—to transport katsu in this way to Bougainville, in mid-1944, for an attack on offshore shipping, was abandoned, as were plans for their deployment at Peleliu and Saipan. They were held at Kure for possible employment in the final defence. They were slow, noisy and unhandy.

"Operation Olympic": the Invasion of Kyushu

Operations "Olympic" (later re-named "Majestic", but rarely known thus), the invasion of southern Kyushu scheduled to begin on 1 November 1945, and "Coronet", the Honshu landings planned for 1 March 1946, would have been the largest amphibious operations of all time. The US 3rd Fleet (covering force) and 5th Fleet (amphibious force) would employ more than 3,000 warships and attack transports, *excluding* inshore landing boats. Anglo-American naval strength in the Pacific in August 1945 included approximately 30 fleet carriers, 78 escort carriers, 29 battleships, more than 50 cruisers and 300 destroyers, and close on 3,000 large landing craft.

Landings on Kyushu would be made by LtGen Walter Krueger's 6th Army, of three Marine divisions, one armoured division and nine infantry divisions. And although General Marshall, US Army Chief of Staff, feared that "Downfall" (ie, both "Olympic" and "Coronet") would cost at least 250,000 US casualties, a US War Department study of June 1945 predicted that the initial, critical, 30-day phase of "Olympic" should involve only c.30-35,000 casualties.

The Japanese hoped to destroy up to 50 per cent of the invasion force before it hit the beaches. And whatever proportion succeeded in landing would be opposed *à outrance* at the water's edge. Imperial General HQ reasoned that only if the *first* of the amphibious assaults was bloodily repulsed might the Allies be brought to moderate their demand for unconditional surrender. All Japan's limited resources must be devoted to this "decisive battle", with little or nothing in reserve to counter later landings. Field-Marshal Hajime Sugiyama, overall commander of the final defence, 1st General Army HQ, Tokyo, decreed in mid-July: "The key to final victory lies in destroying the enemy at the water's edge, while his landings are still in progress".

In the summer of 1945, Japan had about 6 million men under arms, of whom some two-thirds were in isolated island garrisons, in Korea, or with the Kwantung Army in China-Manchuria, where a Soviet offensive might be expected. Regular Army forces in the home islands totalled c.2,350,000, with about 3 million Army and Navy auxiliaries (labour battalions and the like). FM Shunroku Hata's 2nd General Army, with its HQ at Hiroshima, was responsible for *Ketsu-Go* Area No 6, embracing Kyushu, Shikoku and west Honshu; within this zone, the vital area of southern Kyushu was covered by the 14 infantry divisions and two armoured brigades (their AFVs near-immobilized by lack of fuel) of LtGen Isamu Yokoyama's 16th Area Army.

Every man of military capability had now been drafted, but many newly-raised units consisted of ill-trained troops without adequate armament and sometimes even without full personal kit and uniforms. Transport was severely limited by a shortage of fuel, vehicles, mechanics, and even draught animals; communications were disrupted nationwide by the P 29 raids; and the paucity of adequate construction materials meant that beach defence works remained incomplete.

"One Hundred Million Will Die ...!"

As early as 1944, Imperial General HQ had begun constructing a vast underground complex in the mountainous region of Matsushiro, central Honshu, with a similar refuge for Emperor Hirohito at nearby Nagano. While the great ones resisted to the last in this Japanese equivalent of Hitler's mythical "Alpine Redoubt", the ordinary civilians must emulate the aspirations (but not the almost non-existent exploits) of the German "Werwolf" guerrillas.

In November 1944, on pain of imprisonment in default, all Japanese male civilians between the ages of 14 and 61 and all unmarried females of 17-41 were ordered to register for national service as required. From this register, in June 1945, was drawn the *Kokumin Giyu Sento-Tai* ("National Volunteer Combat Force"), officially some 28 million strong. Cadres from Tokyo's *Nakano Gakko* ("Army Intelligence School") were sent throughout Japan—especially to Kyushu—to instruct this militia in the techniques of beach defence and guerrilla resistance, as laid down in the *People's Handbook of Resistance Combat*.

Sustained by an individual ration of less than 1,300 calories daily— rice being often bulked out with sawdust or replaced by acorn flour— the unpaid militia, without uniforms but with armbands denoting combatant status, drilled with ancient rifles (one to every ten men); swords and bamboo spears; axes, sickles and other agricultural implements; and even long-bows, "effective at 50yds (45m)" according to the instruction manual. Empty bottles were collected to make "Molotov cocktails" and "poison grenades" filled with hydrocyanic acid; local craftsmen manufactured "lunge mines", "satchel charges" and wooden, one-shot, black-powder mortars; and small-arms workshops, their labour forces decimated by dietary deficiency diseases, produced single-shot, smooth-bore muskets and crude pistols firing steel rods.

Those who lacked arms of any kind were told to cultivate the martial arts, judo and karate. Women were advised, with the endorsement of Empress Nagako, to wear *mompei* (the loosely-fitting pantaloons traditionally worn only by peasants working their fields), and were instructed on the efficacy of a kick to the testicles.

Thus, inspired by the spirit of the Special Attack Corps, the entire population of Japan stood ready to fight to the death. The slogan was displayed everywhere: "One Hundred Million Will Die for Emperor and Nation!"

The Last Kamikaze Hits

While most of Japan's aircraft were reserved for use against an invasion fleet, a few kamikaze sorties continued to be made against Allied shipping in the Ryukyus. Most were flown by *Shiragiku* ("White Crysanthemum") units, so called because they were composed largely of venerable training aircraft; notably a purpose-modified kamikaze version of the IJN's Kyushu K11W1/2 *Shiragiku* (see Data Table, page 161). IJA trainers such as the Kokusai Ki-86 (Allied codename "Cypress"), and Tachikawa Ki-9 ("Spruce") and Ki-17 ("Cedar"), all three biplanes, took part in similar operations.

The last Allied warship sunk by a kamikaze aircraft fell victim to one of these veterans. From USN reports, which describe the attacker as a twin-float biplane of wood and fabric construction—and thus immune to proximity-fuzed shells—the aircraft that fell out of the sky over Okinawa at 0041 on 29 July 1945 to strike USS *Callaghan* was probably a Yokosuka K5Y2 ("Willow"). This flimsy machine, capable of only 132mph (212kmh) with a maximum bombload of 132lb (60kg), struck a ready-ammunition locker and triggered a chain of explosions and fires that sank the big destroyer, with 47 dead and 73 wounded, within 90 minutes. In a similar attack on the following night, another "sticks-and-string" kamikaze badly damaged USS *Cassin Young*.

It is generally accepted that the last Allied ship struck by a kamikaze aircraft was USS *Borie* (DD 704), damaged by the crash-dive of a lone "Val" while on radar picket duty for TF 38, as the carriers' aircraft were launched off Honshu on 9 August. However, Inoguchi and Nakajima (see Bibliography) state that the attack transport USS *La Grange* was damaged by a kamikaze off Okinawa on 13 August. Also, it is possible that the Russian minesweeper *T-152* (215 tons, 218 tonnes) was sunk by a kamikaze during Soviet landings on the northern Kuriles on 18-19 August, when a few suicide sorties are believed to have been flown by IJA aircraft from Shimushu Island.

"Body-Crashing": the Ramming Interceptors

On 14 June 1944, Boeing B-29 Superfortresses struck for the first time at the Japanese home islands. Most early raids were made at high level (above c.30,000ft, 9150m), but although Japan's air defence was deficient in both AA guns and aircraft with the speed and combat ceiling successfully to intercept the Superfortresses—of 414 B-29s lost, only 147 fell to Japanese interceptors or AA fire—it was felt that the results of such operations did not justify even the lowest loss rate.

Early in 1945, MajGen Curtis LeMay took over the Marianas-based 21st Bomber Command from BrigGen Haywood Hansell, adopting a policy of low-level incendiary raids at c.5-6,000ft (1500-1800m) by B-29s virtually unarmed for extra speed. By August, LeMay could claim that fire raids had completely shattered some 58 major cities and that by bombing alone Japan would soon be "beaten back into the dark ages". Fire raids indeed caused far greater material and moral damage than the two atomic bombs: on 9-10 March, in a raid by 325 B-29s, 15.8 sq miles (41 sq km) of Tokyo were gutted and c.84,000 killed and more than 100,000 injured (compared to c.78,000 dead and 68,000 injured in the atomic blast at Hiroshima). In a fire raid on Toyama on 1-2 August, no less than 99.5 per cent of the city was devastated. And when Prince Konoye told the USSBS that the major factor in Japan's decision to surrender was "fundamentally . . . the prolonged bombing by the B-29s", he was speaking of the fire raids. One Japanese statesman, however, referred to the atomic destruction as "the big kamikaze that saved Japan"; meaning that the terrible civilian casualties sustained in just these two strikes afforded a decisive argument to the peace faction.

With fuel stocks low, factories and repair facilities dislocated, and many aircraft lacking trained pilots or held in reserve for the final kamikaze onslaught, the Japanese air arms proved unable to deal effectively with the low-level raiders and thus increasingly resorted to suicidal aerial ramming interceptions. Isolated instances had occurred earlier in the war. On 4 July 1942, Lt Mitsuo Suitsu, enraged when his naval air squadron's field at Lae, New Guinea, was badly damaged by US bombers, fulfilled a vow of vengeance by destroying a Martin B-26 Marauder in a head-on collision with his Zero. The first Army pilot credited with such self-sacrifice was Sgt Oda who, also flying from New Guinea and unable to maintain the altitude conventionally to engage a B-17 that was "snooping" a Japanese supply convoy, brought down the Fortress by ramming with his Nakajima Ki-43 "Oscar".

Tai-atari ("body-crashing") tactics were not invariably fatal: a few US bombers were destroyed by Soviet-style *Taran* attacks (see page 196), their tail assemblies chewed away by fighters with armoured propellers. USAAF personnel reported the first cases of what they judged to be deliberate ramming during a raid on the steel works at Yawata, Kyushu, on 20 August 1944. Of four bombers lost over the target area, one fell to AA, one to aerial gunfire, and two to a single Kawasaki Ki-45 *Toryu* (Dragon Killer; "Nick"): the "Nick" rammed one B-29 and the debris of the two aircraft brought down another.

In February 1945, an IJA manual stated that against B-29s (and the expected B-32 Dominators, of which only a handful became operational) "we can demand nothing better than crash tactics, ensuring the destruction of an enemy aircraft at one fell swoop . . . striking terror into his heart and rendering his powerfully armed planes valueless by the sacrifice of one of our fighters". The manual noted that only partly-trained pilots need be used and recommended as rammers the Nakajima Ki-44 *Shoki* (Demon; "Tojo") and Kawasaki Ki-61 *Hien* (Swallow; "Tony"), on the dubious grounds that their designs gave the pilot a faint chance of baling out immediately before impact.

Earlier than this, in November 1944, the 2nd Air Army's 47th *Sentai* formed the volunteer *Shinten Sekutai* squadron, dedicated to ramming attacks in "Tojos". Their successes included the destruction of a B-29 over Sasebo on 21 November by Lt Mikihiko Sakamoto; another B-29 on 24 November (one of only two Superfortresses brought down in a 111-strong raid); and two B-29s (out of only six lost from a 172-strong force over Tokyo) on 25 February 1945. Fighters of the Kwantung Army also adopted ramming tactics, bringing down two B-29s over the Mukden aircraft works on 7 December 1944 and another on 21 December. On both occasions, Japanese aircraft also attempted air-to-air bombing, releasing time-fuzed phosphorus bombs above the US formations. At least one B-29 was destroyed by this method, which was also used in the defence of the homeland.

A less extreme measure than ramming was the formation at Matsuyama NAFB, Shikoku, in January 1945 of a fighter wing led by Capt Minoru Genda and including Saburo Sakai and other "aces". Flying the Kawanishi N1K2-J *Shiden* (Violet Lightning: "George")—probably Japan's best interceptor; only c.350 were built—they achieved especially good results against Allied carrier strikes. On 16 February, WO Kinsuke Muto was credited with engaging single-handed 12 F6F Hellcats from USS *Bennington* over Atsugi, Tokyo, shooting down four and driving off the rest.

Attempted Aid from Germany

Unable to produce in sufficient quantity such advanced interceptors as the Kawasaki Ki-100 (396 of all models built), the Kawasaki Ki-102 ("Randy"; 238 built) and the Mitsubishi A7M3-J *Reppu* (Hurricane; "Sam"; prototype only), or to bring to operational status the *Funryu* ("Raging Dragon") surface-to-air guided missiles, Japan sought German aid. Plans, and in some cases completed models, were acquired of the Bachem *Natter* (see pages 194-195), the *Reichenberg* piloted-bomb (pages 191-193; built as the *Baika*, see page 189), and the Messerschmitt Me 262 twin-engined jet fighter-bomber. A prototype based on the latter, the IJN's Nakajima *Kikka* ("Orange Blossom"), flew on 7 August 1945; if production had been attained it was to have been deployed in concealed revetements as a "special attack" bomber.

A major effort at a point-defence interceptor was the joint IJN/IJA project for the Mitsubishi J8M1 (Navy) or Ki-200/202 (Army) *Shusui* ("Swinging Sword"), a near-identical version of the Luftwaffe's Messerschmitt Me 163 *Komet*. Rights to produce a version of the Komet's airframe and Walter HWK 509A bi-propellant (*T-Stoff* and *C-Stoff*, see page 195, which the Japanese called *Ko* and *Otsu* liquids respectively) rocket engine, with a completed example of the aircraft itself, were purchased as early as March 1944; but only one Walter unit and an incomplete set of blueprints reached Japan. Germany's final effort to provide her ally with more material on the Komet and other "special weapons" was made on 2 May 1945, when *U.234* (Cdr Johann Fehler) sailed from Norway for Japan with high-ranking Luftwaffe officers, technicians, and two Japanese scientists aboard. En route, Fehler received the news of Germany's collapse and, as he headed for the USA to surrender his boat, both Japanese committed *seppuku*.

In Japan, training with the Komet-replica MXY8 *Akigusa* ("Autumn Grass") glider began in December 1944. The first powered flight was attempted on 7 July 1945 at Yokoku airfield, Yokosuka. Successfully jettisoning the takeoff trolley, LtCdr Toyohiko Inuzuka had reached c.1,300ft (400m) when, probably because of a fuel line blockage caused by the steep climb, the engine flamed out and the Shusui stalled and crashed, mortally injuring Inuzuka. Later that month, an explosion of the volatile fuel mixture during ground testing killed another of the project's officers. Many similar fatalities—especially during the hard skid-landings that often brought the liquid propellants violently together—had occurred in Germany, where the "Devil's Egg" was regarded by many Luftwaffe personnel as semi-suicidal at best.

The Japanese rocket interceptor differed little from its German pattern. The J8M1 had a span of 31.2ft (9.5m), a length of 19.86ft

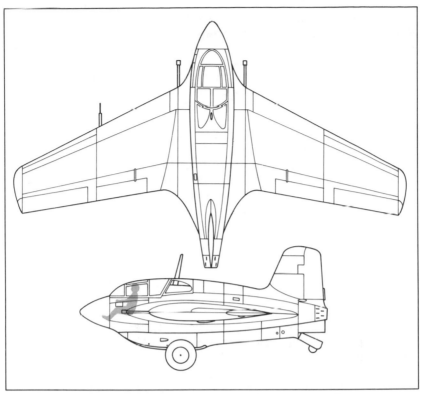

Mitsubishi J8M1/Ki-200 **Shusui** rocket interceptor; based on the Messerschmitt Me 163 **Komet**.

(6.05m) and a height on its jettisonable trolley of 8.86ft (2.7m). Powered by a Toko Ro.2 motor giving 3,307lb (1500kg) thrust for up to c.5.3 minutes, it was estimated to be capable of a maximum 559mph (900kmh) at 32,810ft (10 000m); thus probably having a range at optimum flight profile of less than 60 miles (96km). Its armament was to be two wing-mounted 30mm cannon—although if the planned production of more than 1,000 examples by August 1945 had been achieved, it is likely that many would have been expended in ramming attacks after exhausting their ammunition of 50 rounds per gun. In the event, only seven Shusui, which were to have been operated by the 312th Naval Air Group, were completed by the war's end.

Seeking Death: Surrender and its Aftermath

At 0700 on 15 August, the day of Emperor Hirohito's surrender broadcast, Fleet Admiral Nimitz ordered an end to all offensive action. But Admiral Halsey, commanding 3rd Fleet while TF 38 (including British and Commonwealth units) launched strikes against the Tokyo area, nevertheless strengthened his CAPs and gave instructions that all "snoopers" should be shot down "in a friendly sort of way". This was wise, for a few Japanese pilots, unwilling to accept even an Imperial directive, were determined to die in delivering a last blow.

Some sought to combine the dictates both of obedience and honour simply by taking off and crash-diving into the sea when within striking

277

distance of Allied ships: a CAP pilot reported to the battleship HMS *King George V* that he had witnessed a group of more than 40 aircraft self-destructing in this way. A more serious threat was made at c.1120, when a single "Judy" evaded CAPs and came over HMS *Indefatigable*, scoring two near-misses with bombs before attempting a low-level kamikaze run. Only c.100yds (90m) short of the carrier, it was hacked down by a Corsair from USS *Shangri-La* (CV 38).

It has been suggested that this aircraft carried Vice-Admiral Matome Ugaki; but although the commander of the Kyushu-based 5th Air Fleet had decided that he must end as a samurai, his sortie was not made until later in the day. Stripping off his badges of rank, but carrying a short sword that had been a personal gift from Admiral Yamamoto, Ugaki came to the runway at Oita AFB at c.1700—to find 11 two-seat D4Y2 "Judy" divebombers ready for takeoff. "I must have a place to die", he had told his aircrews: the place he had chosen was Okinawa, whither he had dispatched so many kamikaze of his command, of whom 22 more were now determined to die with him.

Ugaki took off in the observer's seat of the "Judy" piloted by Lt Tatsuo Nakatsura; the original observer, WO Akiyoshi Endo, insisted on crowding in beside the Admiral. Four of the 11 aircraft had to turn back, but Ugaki and the remainder flew on until, at c.1925, a last radio message reported that they were diving on the enemy. Since there are no Allied records of this action, it may be that Ugaki, wishing to die as a kamikaze but not to disobey an Imperial command, deliberately led his flight into an empty expanse of ocean. These were probably the last of the kamikaze pilots to die in action: the total, according to a Japanese estimate, being 4,615 (2,409 of the IJN; 2,206 of the IJA).

Early on the morning of the next day, Vice-Admiral Onishi, "father of the kamikaze", who as recently-appointed Vice Chief of Naval General Staff had desperately opposed the surrender, also chose his place to die. Alone in his study, Onishi—perhaps in the spirit of *setsujoku*, to avoid the dishonour of surrender; but more probably as *kanshi*, in protest against those senior officers who would not support his irredentism—cut open his belly in the ancient tradition. He completed the ritual by stabbing himself in the throat but, probably deliberately, wishing to make his death agony the more prolonged and exemplary, did not strike deeply. Found by his aides, he refused either medical attention or honourable decapitation, conversing with restraint and dignity until he expired after some 15 hours. His last testimony praised the kamikaze and called upon Japan's youth to strive for their country's good "with all the fervour of spirit of the special attackers". Whatever Onishi's faults, few men have died so nobly: "*Ubi saeva indignatio ulterius cor lacerare nequit*".

Among the war leaders who anticipated Onishi's action or followed his example were Gen Korechika Anami, Minister of War; Gen Seiichi Tanaka, commanding in the Tokyo area; FM Hajime Sugiyama, commanding 1st General Army, whose wife died with him; Gen Shigeru Honjo of the Kwantung Army; and Prince Fumimaro Konoye, Prime Minister in the immediate pre-war period. Gen Hideki Tojo, Japan's supremo from October 1941 to July 1944, attempted suicide but survived to be executed as a so-called "war criminal". Japan's finest general (in my opinion, the greatest commander of World War II), Gen Tomoyuki Yamashita, deliberately refrained from *seppuku* in the hope, probably justified, that his judicial murder by the Allies would serve to moderate the western mob's clamour for the trial and degradation of Emperor Hirohito. "The world I knew is now a shameful place", commented Yamashita shortly before his death by hanging.

A few officers, most of junior rank, opposed the surrender with violence. Resistance among IJN pilots centred on Atsugi AFB near Tokyo, whence a number of kamikaze flew to drop anti-surrender leaflets over the capital on 16 August. There was bloody fighting between the hot-headed airmen and Army units loyal to the Imperial command, but tempers were cooled by the personal intervention of the Emperor's brother, Prince Takamatsu; although some pilots committed suicide when their efforts failed to inflame the mass of the populace.

A group of Army officers led by Major Kenji Hatanaka had raided the Imperial Palace on the night of 14-15 August in what they saw as an attempt to liberate the Emperor from the influence of treacherous, peace-seeking advisers. The ill-planned coup was a fiasco: Hatanaka blew out his brains with his service pistol, as did some of his followers. A few civilians, mostly students belonging to nationalistic societies, occupied Atago Hill, Tokyo, and declared that they would resist to the death. Most commited suicide with hand grenades, locked in a fraternal embrace, when their position was surrounded by civilian police.

The Last of the Human Torpedoes
When LtGen Richard K. Sutherland, USA, MacArthur's Chief of Staff, met Japanese delegates at the surrender negotiations in Manila, among his first questions was: "Are the kaiten still at sea?"; showing how seriously the Allies regarded the threat of this weapon in spite of its limited success in combat. He was assured that all units at sea had been ordered to surrender and that the kaiten deployed for shore-launching against an invasion, under the overall command of Rear-Admiral Mitsuru Nagai, would not be used.

In the home islands, however, there were some defiant gestures; largely instigated by LtCdr Genbei Kawaguchi who, having been somewhat unfairly dishonoured when removed from command of the kaiten-carrier *I-44* (see page 242), perhaps sought to redeem himself by making a fiery speech advocating further resistance to the human-torpedo crews at Otake, Hiroshima Bay. Some influence was also exerted by anti-surrender leaflets dropped by would-be kamikaze fliers from the nearby Iwakuni NAFB.

As well as some acts of *seppuku*, the most notable result of these patriotic but in the circumstances misguided activities was the last of the kaiten sorties. On 16 August, Lt Takesuke Takeyama sailed from Hirao, near Tokuyama, in the old training submarine *I-59*, carrying two kaiten. But perhaps Takeyama or his kaiten volunteers, Ens Masashi Saito and PO Shinizo Imada, both on their first missions, had second thoughs on disobeying an Imperial command, for two days later *I-59* brought back her kaiten intact.

Having sunk USS *Indianapolis* on his last cruise (see page 249), and himself despondent yet obedient to the surrender order, LtCdr Hashi-

279

moto brought *I-58* into Bungo Suido on 18 August. He now encountered six "Type SS" transport submarines of the *Ha 101* class, whose skippers proclaimed that they were sailing out from Kure to "fight to the death". The gesture was purely symbolic: these small (429 tons, 435 tonnes, surfaced displacement) boats had no torpedo tubes and mounted only one 25mm gun. Perhaps influenced by the prestige of the "ace" submariner Hashimoto, the would-be suicide attackers followed him back to Kure, where a stern harangue from Admiral Nagai on 20 August calmed down other irreconcilables.

The sortie of the "Type SS" boats would have been more serious in intent, and in possible consequences, if made by some of the ten completed "Type STS" submarines of the slightly larger *Ha 201* class. These streamlined, high-speed "Guppy" boats were powered when submerged by single-shaft electric motors of 1,250shp, giving a maximum 13kt (15mph, 24kmh). Short-ranging, they were specifically intended for coastal defence, mounting two 21in (533mm) torpedo tubes and one 7.7mm MG, and would probably have been suicidally deployed in the final defence.

The Shinyo Squadrons: Tragedy and Hope

The shinyo explosive motorboat squadrons were involved in two tragically unnecessary actions following the surrender. On 16 August, a rumour spread at Shinyo Squadron No 128's base in southern Shikoku that an Allied task force was approaching Tosa Wan, apparently to invade in spite of the surrender decision. In a frantic scramble to prepare the EMBs for action, engine fires broke out and a chain of warhead explosions killed 111 of SS 128's personnel.

Similarly, some Allied commanders feared that the "fanatics" of the "special attack" forces would not observe the ceasefire. This led to a massacre at Hong Kong after the arrival of the British and Commonwealth Task Group 111.2 (Rear-Admiral C.H.J. Harcourt) on 29 August. Harcourt had been warned of a shinyo base on Lamma Island, and when his strong force steamed into the channel leading to the naval dockyard at 1200 on 30 August, his ships' companies were at action stations.

As the Allied force approached, SubLt Awamura of SS 35 set out across the channel with a message to Japanese naval HQ. "All the warheads had been removed from our boats", a Japanese veteran told me, "and the Allies knew this. A shinyo was sent on the errand only because nothing else was available". But the British (whose official historian claims that "three . . . suicide craft were seen to leave their moorings") immediately launched air strikes from HMS *Indomitable* and *Venerable*. Hellcats and Avengers swarmed over the defenceless Japanese, bombing and strafing the EMBs and many of their crews out of existence.

Lt Hideo Aita, commanding the isolated SS 6 at Sandakan, North Borneo, gave me a detailed account of his reaction to the surrender:

"SS 6 was the only naval unit at Sandakan. All of us were sick: of the 300 men I had brought to Borneo in October 1944, just over 100 were still alive. Most were victims of malaria and malnutrition; less than 30 had fallen to the enemy's fire. I felt that my responsibility was to see that not one more man died, to take them safely back to Japan—after protecting them from the hardships of life as PoWs (which I thought might continue for many years). Only I, the squadron's only regular officer, could do this—it was *my* responsibility—and so I abandoned my first idea of suicide in the honourable fighting man's way because of my failure in my duty to protect the Empire. *The idea of dying in the explosion of a "special attack" boat never frightened me; but the thought of death in the present circumstances did.* [My italics.] "My men kept perfectly calm and there was no breach of discipline . . . we were disarmed by Australian troops and put into a camp at Labuan . . . I myself was arrested as a suspected war criminal . . ."

Since it is difficult to imagine what "war crimes" Lt Aita could have committed in his isolated base, and since he was released without charges being brought after some 16 months, it seems to me probable that the Allies had marked down officers of the "special attack" units as potential trouble-makers and chose to isolate them from their men by this method. I consulted Japanese veterans who were inclined to agree with this view. And Allied records show that savage treatment was sometimes accorded to Japanese prisoners: only a few hundred of the 21,000 Japanese who surrendered to Australian troops in North Borneo survived a "death march" to Beaufort on the west coast.

In describing to me his actions at the time of surrender and subsequently, the commander of a shinyo squadron then based on Hainan Island, Kwangtung, China, provided a suitable end to this book. I have italicized certain key passages.

"There was no special reaction to the surrender in my unit other than sadness . . . and when I saw this, I ordered training to carry on as usual. I believe that this sustained my men's morale.

"At last I called them all together to discuss, as equals, what we might do. I said that we had three choices: we could fight on, thus disobeying an Imperial command; we could all commit suicide; or *we could choose to live on and work for Japan in such a way that the sacrifice of our comrades in other "special attack" units would not have been in vain.* As I hoped, the men agreed on the third choice—and it is my firm belief that the dedication of men like these did much to aid Japan's post-war recovery.

"The chance of making a successful attack in a shinyo was slight, but some succeeded—and I believe that the attacks made by our tiny craft were more effective than, for example, the *Yamato* Force's suicide sortie at Okinawa; *because the individual gesture made by the "special attack" pilot was of greater significance than the sacrifice of major warships.*

"My men were not 'war machines': they were young, they loved their country, and they took no thought for themselves. The spirit that inspired them stems from the warrior tradition of Japan; but, really, men of all nations are capable of summoning up a similar spirit. It isn't something that belongs to Japan alone.

"The reason for Japan's great recovery since the war is, I believe, that these many human sacrifices brought good fortune to the homeland."

Select Bibliography

A. Adams (ed), **The Cherry Blossom Squadrons: Born to Die** (Ohara, Tokyo 1973)

R.E. Appleman (et al), **US Army in World War II—Okinawa; The Last Battle** (Washington DC, 1948)

Asahi Shimbun, **28 Years in the Guam Jungle: Sgt Yokoi Home from World War II** (Tokyo, 1972)

E. Bagnasco, **Submarines of World War II** (Arms & Armour Press, 1977)

H.W. Baldwin, **Battles Lost and Won: Great Campaigns of World War II** (Hodder & Stoughton, 1967)

A.J. Barker, **Suicide Weapon** (Pan/Ballantine, 1972)

C. Bekker, **K-Men** (George Mann, 1973)

D. Bergamini, **Japan's Imperial Conspiracy** (Panther, 1972)

C. Berger, **B-29: The Superfortress** (Macdonald, 1971)

J.V. Borghese, **Sea Devils** (Andrew Melrose, 1954)

M.A. Bragadin, **The Italian Navy in World War II** (US Naval Institute, Annapolis, 1957)

D. Brown, **Carrier Fighters 1939-1945** (Purnell Book Services, 1975)

R.J. Bulkley Jr, **At Close Quarters; PT Boats in the United States Navy** (Washington DC, 1962)

M. Caidin, **Zero Fighter** (Macdonald, 1970)

M.H. Cannon, **US Army in World War II—Leyte: The Return to the Philippines** (Washington DC, 1954)

W.R. Carter, **Beans, Bullets, and Black Oil: Fleet Logistics in the Pacific** (Washington DC, 1953)

W.S. Chalmers, **Max Horton and the Western Approaches** (Hodder & Stoughton, 1957)

E.K. Chatterton, **Gallant Gentlemen** (Hurst & Blackett, 1931)

M. Chihaya & Y. Abe, **IJN Yukikaze/Destroyer/1939-1970** (Profile Publications, 1972)

M. Chihaya, **IJN Yamato and Musashi** (Profile Publications, 1974)

W. Churchill, **The Second World War** (6 vols; Reprint Society, 1950)

CinCPac-CinCPOA Bulletin 126-45 of 28 May 1945, **Suicide Weapons and Tactics, "Know Your Enemy!"**

S. Conn (et al), **US Army in World War II—Guarding the United States** (Washington DC, 1964)

P.G. Cooksley, **Flying Bomb** (Robert Hale, 1979)

A.D. Coox, **Japan: The Final Agony** (Macdonald, 1970)

W. Craig, **The Fall of Japan** (Pan Books, 1970)

W.F. Craven & J.L. Cate (ed), **The Army Air Forces in World War II—The Pacific: Guadalcanal to Saipan/Matterhorn to Nagasaki** (Vols IV & V, University of Chicago Press, 1950, 1953)

P.A. Crowl, **US Army in World War II—Campaign in the Marianas** (Washington DC, 1960)

US Army in World War II—Gilberts and Marshalls (Washington DC, 1960)

A.B. Cunningham, Viscount Hyndhope, **A Sailor's Odyssey** (Hutchinson, 1951)

K. Edwards, **Operation Neptune** (Collins, 1946)

F.D. Fane & D. Moore, **The Naked Warriors** (Appleton-Century-Crofts, NY, 1956)

W.R. Fell, **The Sea Our Shield** (Cassell, 1966)

B.J. Ford, **German Secret Weapons: Blueprint for Mars** (Pan/Ballantine, 1972)

A. Fraccaroli, **Italian Warships of World War II** (Ian Allan, 1974)

R.J. Francillon, **Japanese Aircraft of the Pacific War** (Putman, 1970)

B.M. Frank, **Okinawa: Touchstone to Victory** (Macdonald, 1970)

W. Frank, **The Sea Wolves** (World Distributors, 1957)

G. Frere-Cook, **The Attacks on the Tirpitz** (Ian Allan, 1973)

M. Fuchida & M. Okumiya, **Midway: The Battle that Doomed Japan** (Ballantine Books, NY, 1974)

S. Fukui, **The Japanese Navy at the End of World War II** (WE Inc, Conn., undated)

A. Galland, **The First and the Last** (Fontana Books, 1975)

B. Garfield, **The Thousand-Mile War: Alaska and the Aleutians** (Ballantine Books, NY, 1973)

W. Gerbig, **Six Months to Oblivion: The Eclipse of the Luftwaffe Fighter Force** (Ian Allan, 1975)

G.H. Gill, **Royal Australian Navy 1942-1945** (Australian War Memorial, Canberra, 1968)

W. Green, **Rocket Fighter** (Macdonald, 1971)

Famous Fighters of the Second World War (Macdonald & Jane's, 1975)

Warplanes of the Third Reich (Macdonald & Jane's, 1976)

B. Gunston, **Submarines in Colour** (Blandford Press, 1976)

Combat Aircraft of World War II (Salamander Books, 1978)

Rockets and Missiles (Salamander Books, 1979)

W.F. Halsey & J. Bryan, **Admiral Halsey's Story** (McGraw-Hill, NY, 1947)

A.C. Hampshire, **The Secret Navies** (William Kimber, 1978)

T. Hara, **Japanese Destroyer Captain** (Ballantine Books, NY, 1972)

M. Hashimoto, **Sunk: The Story of the Japanese Submarine Fleet 1942-1945** (Cassell, 1954)

S. Hayashi, **Kogun: The Japanese Army in the Pacific War** (Marine Corps Association, Va., 1959)

C. Hocking, **Dictionary of Disasters at Sea** (2 vols, Lloyd's Register of Shipping, 1969)

C.W. Hoffman, **Saipan: The Beginning of the End** (Washington DC, 1950)

R. Inoguchi & T. Nakajima, **The Divine Wind** (Ballantine Books, NY, 1972)

J.A. Isely & P.A. Crowl, **The US Marines and Amphibious War** (Princeton University Press, 1951)

M. Ito & R. Pineau, **The End of the Imperial Japanese Navy** (Weidenfeld & Nicolson, 1962)

H. Jentschura (et al), **Warships of the Imperial Japanese Navy** (Arms & Armour Press, 1977)

W. Karig (et al), **Battle Report** (Vols I, III, IV, V, Rinehart, NY, 1944-1949)

E.J. King, **US Navy at War 1941-1945** (Washington DC, 1946)

J.D. Ladd, **Assault from the Sea** (David & Charles, 1976)

 Commandos and Rangers of World War II (Macdonald & Jane's, 1978)

J. Larteguy, **The Sun Goes Down** (New English Library, 1975)

H.T. Lenton, **American Battleships, Carriers and Cruisers** (Macdonald, 1968)

 German Submarines (2 vols, Macdonald, 1968)

 American Fleet and Escort Destroyers (2 vols, Macdonald, 1971)

 British Submarines (Macdonald, 1972)

W. Lord, **Day of Infamy** (Corgi Books, 1971)

A.S. Lott & R.F. Sumrall, **Pearl Harbor Attack** (Leeward Publications, N.J., 1974)

J.P. Mallman Showell, **U-Boats Under the Swastika** (Ian Allan, 1974)

S.L. Mayer (ed), **The Japanese War Machine** (Bison Books, 1976)

B. Millot, **Divine Thunder** (Macdonald, 1971)

 The Battle of the Coral Sea (Ian Allan, 1974)

Y. Mishima, **Yukio Mishima on Hagakure: The Samurai Ethic and Modern Japan** (Condor Books, 1977)

S.E. Morison, **History of the United States Naval Operations in World War II** (15 vols, Little, Brown & Company, Boston, 1947-1962)

I. Morris, **The Nobility of Failure: Tragic Heroes in the History of Japan** (Secker & Warburg, 1975)

R. Nagatsuka, **I Was a Kamikaze** (New English Library, 1974)

C.S. Nichols & H.I. Shaw, **Okinawa: Victory in the Pacific** (Washington DC, 1955)

Z. Orita, **I-Boat Captain** (Major Books, Calif., 1976)

K. Phelan & M.H. Brice, **Fast Attack Craft** (Macdonald & Jane's, 1977)

N. Polmar, **Aircraft Carriers** (Macdonald, 1969)

A. Price, **Aircraft versus Submarine** (William Kimber, 1973)

A. Raven & J. Roberts, **British Battleships of World War Two** (Arms & Armour Press, 1976)

J. Rohwer & G. Hummelchen, **Chronology of the War at Sea 1939-1945** (2 vols, Ian Allan, 1972)

T. Roscoe, **United States Destroyer Operations in World War II** (Annapolis, 1953)

S.W. Roskill, **The War at Sea 1939-45** (3 vols, in 4, HMSO 1954-1961)

S. Sakai, **Samurai** (New English Library, 1974)

L.A. Sawyer & W.H. Mitchell, **The Liberty Ships** (David & Charles, 1973)

 Victory Ships and Tankers (David & Charles, 1974)

G.F. Scheer & H.F. Rankin, **Rebels and Redcoats** (Mentor Books, 1975)

E.F. Sieche, **German Human Torpedoes & Midget Submarines** (``Warship'' No 14, April 1980)

P.H. Silverstone, **US Warships of World War II** (Ian Allan, 1971)

O. Skorzeny, **Special Mission** (Futura, 1974)

J.R. Smith & A.L. Kay, **German Aircraft of the Second World War** (Putnam, 1975)

P. Smith, **Task Force 57: The British Pacific Fleet 1944-1945** (William Kimber, 1969)

R.R. Smith, **Triumph in the Philippines** (Washington DC, 1963)

E.P. Stafford, **The Big E: The Story of the USS Enterprise** (Ballantine Books, NY, 1974)

W.H. Tantum & E.J. Hoffschmidt, **The Rise and Fall of the German Air Force** (WE Inc, Conn., 1969)

J.C. Taylor, **German Warships of World War II** (Ian Allan, 1971)

B. Tillman, **Hellcat: the F6F in World War II** (Patrick Stephens, 1979)

J. Toland, **The Rising Sun** (Bantam Books, NY, 1971)

H.R. Trevor-Roper (ed), **The Goebbels Diaries** (Book Club Associates, 1978)

Ufficio Storico Della Marina Militare, **La Marina Italiana Nella Seconda Guerra Mondiale, Vol XIV, I Mezzi D'Assalto** (Rome 1972)

United States Naval History Division, **Naval Chronology, World War II** (Washington DC, 1955)

United States Naval Institute, **Sneak Craft Attack in the Pacific** (Proceedings, March 1947)

 Kamikazes and the Okinawa Campaign (Proceedings, May 1954)

C.E.T. Warren & J. Benson, **The Midget Raiders** (Ballantine Books, NY, 1973)

A.J. Watts & B.G. Gordon, **The Imperial Japanese Navy** (Macdonald, 1971)

J. Weeks, **Men Against Tanks: A History of Anti-Tank Warfare** (Purnell Book Services, undated)

J. Winton, **The Forgotten Fleet** (Michael Joseph, 1969)

T. Wood & B. Gunston, **Hitler's Luftwaffe** (Salamander Books, 1977)

S. Woodburn-Kirby, **The War Against Japan** (5 vols, HMSO, 1957-1969)

Y. Yokota, **Suicide Submarine: the Kaiten Weapon** (Ballantine Books, NY, 1973)

J.L. Zimmerman, **The Guadalcanal Campaign** (US Marine Corps, Washington DC, 1949)

Glossary

Note that many of the items in the Glossary are more fully described within the main text. Reference should be made to the Index.

ABDACOM: American, British, Dutch and Australian Command; unified Allied command in the Pacific theatre under Gen Sir Archibald Wavell, in existence only from 28 December 1941 to 25 February 1942.

A-Hyoteki: "A-Target": Japanese cover-name for Type A midget sub.

A-Kanamono: "Type A Metal Fittings"; also cover--name for Type A midget.

Akigusa: "Autumn Grass": popular name for Yokosuka MXY8 glider-trainer.

"Alpine Redoubt": Mountainous area, covering southern Bavaria/western Austria/north Italy, where Allies believed Nazi fanatics would make a last-ditch stand. It was a myth.

Baika: "Plum Blossom": popular name for the IJA's Kawanishi piloted bomb based on the German Reichenberg.

Baka: "foolish; idiotic": a name probably originating with Nisei (qv) personnel, given by the Allies to the IJN's Ohka piloted bomb.

Bakufu: "tent government": the central authority under the Shogun.

Bakugeki-Hyoteki: "Anti-Submarine Bombing Target": another cover-name for the Type A midget submarine.

Banzai Charge: the final, death-seeking assault made by Japanese warriors facing certain defeat.

"Base P": training centre for kaiten human-torpedoes at Otsujima, Tokuyama Bay, southwest Honshu.

"Betty": Allied codename for IJN's Mitsubishi G4M twin-engined bomber; also nicknamed "one-shot lighter" or "flying lighter" because of the vulnerability of its fuel tanks.

Biber: "Beaver": German one-man midget submarine.

"Big Blue Blanket": US carrier aircraft (dark-blue livery), launched en masse to interdict Japanese land-based air power in the Philippines.

"Blowtorch & Corkscrew": US tank-infantry teams, including flame-throwing AFVs with strong artillery support, employed to blast out defenders on the Shuri Line, Okinawa.

"Bugs": small "limpet" type demolition charges used by Italian "frogmen".

Bushido: "the way of the warrior"; the code governing the behaviour of the samurai.

CAP: Combat Air Patrol: defensive air cover over a naval unit; notably a carrier task force or group.

"Cargo Pipes" (Toku-gata Unka-To): unarmed submersibles somewhat like the Type A midget, launched from IJN fleet submarines for short-range supply missions to island garrisons.

"Cedar": Allied codename for IJA's Tachikawa Ki-17 biplane trainer.

Chariot: British version of Italian Maiale ("Pig") manned-torpedo.

Chu: loyalty owed by individual Japanese to the Emperor; emphasized in "Imperial Rescripts" of 1882 and 1890 as above all other duties.

C-Stoff: liquid fuel (hydrazine hydrate/methanol/water) acting as catalyst in Walter rocket motor of Natter and Komet. Japanese name, for proposed use in Shusui, was "Otsu" liquid. (See T-Stoff).

"Cypress": Allied codename for IJN's Kyushu K9W Momiji (Maple) and IJA's Kokusai Ki-86 biplane trainers.

Dackel: "Dachshund": German long-range, pattern-running torpedo.

Dai-hatsu: "large-engined craft": landing craft/transport barge of various sizes used by IJA and IJN.

Daimyo: "great name": a feudal lord, ruler of a province or territory.

Dai Nippon: "Greater Japan": a term especially used in the 20th century to express "manifest destiny"

Delphin: "Dolphin": series of German experimental midget submarines.

"Dinah": Allied codename for IJA's Mitsubishi Ki-46 twin-engined reconnaissance plane/interceptor.

EMB: Explosive motorboat.

"Frances": Allied codename for IJN's Yokosuka P1Y Ginga (Milky Way) twin-engined medium bomber, night-fighter or (P1Y3 Model 33) planned carrier of Ohka piloted bomb.

"Fritz-X": German codename for a radio-guided air-to-surface bomb.

Fu-Go: Japanese layered-paper, hydrogen-filled balloon of c.35ft (10.7m) diameter, carrying small anti-personnel bomb and incendiaries.

Fukuryu: "crouching dragon" or "crawling dragon": IJN "frogman" equipped for suicidal attack on inshore landing craft.

Fundoshi (or Fundiyoshi): cotton breech-clout; a Japanese undergarment.

Funryu: "Raging Dragon": experimental series of air-to-air guided missiles of IJN. None became operational.

"Gamma Group": Italian "frogmen", often operating in conjunction with Maiale manned-torpedoes.

"George": Allied codename for IJN's Kawanishi N1K1-J Shiden (Violet

Lightning) single-engined, single-seat, land- or carrier-based fighter.

Giretsu: "Heroic": Special Airborne Raiding Unit of IJA.

Giri: duty of a samurai to fulfil all moral obligations; notably on, the duty owed to his lord. Lesser obligations, ninjo, concerning human sentiments were subservient to giri, and chu (qv) was later stressed as superior to all other obligations.

"Glen": Allied codename for IJN's Yokosuka E14Y submarine-borne reconnaissance seaplane.

"Gooseberry": breakwater formed by a sunken ship (both expendable transports and badly-damaged warships) as part of a "Mulberry" artificial harbour to protect Normandy invasion shipping, June 1944 onward.

"Great Marianas Turkey Shoot": US Navy's nickname for the Battle of the Philippine Sea, 19-20 June 1944, in which the IJN's carrier-borne air strength was shattered.

Grillo: "Cricket": Italian experimental EMB-type craft of World War I.

Hachimaki: head-band traditionally worn by samurai when going into battle to keep hair and sweat from obstructing their vision. As a symbol of do-or-die determination, hachimaki were often worn by "special attack" (qv) personnel.

Hagakure: "Hidden Among the Leaves": the most famous codification of bushido, compiled by a disciple from the teachings of the samurai-monk Jocho Yamamoto (1659-1719), but not widely published until the era of nationalism beginning with the Meiji Restoration of 1867-68.

Hai: "Shark": German manned-torpedo, planned as an improvement on the Neger (qv) and Marder (qv) but reaching prototype stage only.

Hayabusa: "Peregrine Falcon": name given by IJN to class of 59ft (18m) MTBs. (Note that one British "Official History" confuses Hayabusa with shinyo suicidal EMBs). The name was also given to one of the eight "Ootori" class torpedo boats of 840 tons (853 tonnes) completed in 1936-37. (see also "Oscar".)

Hecht: "Pike": German Type XXVIIA U-boat; a three-man midget submarine.

"Hedgehog": US Navy anti-submarine weapon, throwing ahead a set pattern of 24 x 7.2in (183mm) depthcharges.

"Helen": Allied codename for IJA's Nakajima Ki-49 Donryu (Storm Dragon) twin-engined heavy bomber; purpose-adapted for suicide attack as the Ki-49-II.

Hitlerjugend: "Hitler Youth": the all-embracing German youth movement which, it was hoped, would produce the future Nazi elite. Boys of the Hitlerjugend were put into the fighting line for the final defence of Berlin, and were to pilot the Volksjäger (qv).

H-Kanamono: "Type H Metal Fittings": Japanese cover-name for Type A midget.

IFF: "Identification, Friend or Foe": fitted to Allied aircraft, an electronic device that automatically responded to a radar pulse from a ship or shore identification station.

IJAAF/IJNAF: Japan had no independent air force in the sense of the RAF or USAAF. Within the main text, I have sometimes used the above acronyms to refer to the air arms of the IJA and IJN respectively.

Ji-jin: seppuku (qv) decreed as a punishment for a samurai.

"Jill": Allied codename for IJN's Nakajima B6N Tenzan (Heavenly Mountain) single-engined, three-seat, carrier-borne torpedo-bomber.

Jinrai Butai: "Divine Thunderbolt Corps": the 721st Kokutai, IJNAF, formed to operate the Ohka (qv).

"Judy": Allied codename for IJN's Yokosuka D4Y Suisei (Comet) single-engined, carrier- or land-based divebomber/reconnaissance plane/night fighter. The D4Y4 Model 43 was purpose-adapted for kamikaze missions with RATOG (qv).

Junshi: seppuku as a mark of respect and transcendental loyalty on the death of one's lord or Emperor.

Kairyu: "Sea Dragon": Japanese two-man midget submarine; armed either with torpedoes or with warhead for suicidal ramming attack.

Kaiten: "turn towards heaven" or "make a tremendous change" (a single dramatic action is implied); the IJN's suicidal human torpedo.

Kamikaze: "Divine Wind": originally the typhoons which destroyed Mongol invasion forces in the 13th century. Name popularly applied (in the West, rather than in Japan) to the aerial suicide squadrons of World War II.

Kanshi: seppuku as a protest against unjust or dishonourable action by a superior, to bring shame on him.

K-Gata-Tei: smaller version of IJA's Maru-ni (qv) EMB.

"K-Gun": US Navy's Depthcharge Projector Mk 6 Mod 1, a mortar-type weapon of up to c.150yds (140m) range depending on d/c type.

Kikka: "Orange Blossom": Japanese popular name for IJN's twin-jet attack bomber based on the German Messerschmitt Me 262.

Kikusui: "floating crysanthemum";

originally the emblem of the great warrior Masashige Kusunoki (1294-1336). Adopted as emblem by several "special attack" units in World War II, and taken as overall operational name for a series of mass suicide attacks on Allied ships off Okinawa.

Kleinkampfverbände: "Small Battle Units" or "K-Force": the "special attack" command of the German Navy (Kriegsmarine), formed 1943-44, to operate midget submarines, EMBs and manned-torpedoes.

Kokumin Giyu Sento-Tai: "National Volunteer Combat Force": ill-armed civilian militia conscripted for last-ditch defence of Japan, 1945.

Kokutai (i): "national polity": a phrase with semi-mystical implications, denoting those qualities felt by Japanese to make them unique among the nations of the Earth.

Kokutai (ii): "Naval Air Corps": the basic IJNAF unit with a full strength of c.150 aircraft (but usually fewer). Because of these widely varying strengths, I have not always been consistent in my designation of Japanese air units as "Groups", "Corps", "Wings" etc.

Komet: "Comet": Messerschmitt Me 163 rocket-propelled point-defence interceptor. (See also Shusui.)

Koryu: "Scaly Dragon": five-man, Type D midget submarine of IJN.

Kwantung Army: more than 700,000 strong by 1945, the IJA's Kwantung Army established a semi-autonomous military state in Manchuria, called Manchukuo, from c.1931 onward.

"Lily": Allied codename for IJA's Kawasaki Ki-48 twin-engined light bomber (purpose-adapted for kamikaze missions as the Ki-48-II KAI).

Linse: "Lentil": German EMB, radio-controlled; sometimes used suicidally.

"Long Lance": Popular name for IJN's Type 93 oxygen torpedo, largest and most powerful of World War II; the basis of the kaiten human torpedo.

Maiale: "Pig": Italian manned-torpedo with detachable warhead; two-man crew.

Manta: "Manta-ray": projected German high-speed midget submarine/surface skimmer to be powered by closed-circuit Walter turbine.

Marder: "Pine Marten": German manned-torpedo.

Maru-ni: "capacious boat", also called renraku-tei (Re-boat; communications boat): one- or two-man EMB of IJA, usually armed with depthcharges in dropping gear, and used both suicidally and non-suicidally.

Maru-Se: "SE-boat": experimental high-speed midget submarine of IJA.

MAS (Motoscafi Anti-Siluranti): MTBs of various types of Royal Italian Navy.

Meiji Restoration: period of swift modernization and growing nationalism in Japan following the fall of the Shogunate (qv) and accession of Emperor Meiji (reigned 1867-1912).

Mignatta: "Leech": Italian manned-torpedo ot World War I.

M-Kanamono: "Type M Metal Fittings": Japanese cover-name for projected mine-laying variant of Type C midget.

Molch: "Salamander": German one-man midget submarine; an improved Biber.

"Molotov Cocktail": improvised hand grenade, usually a petrol-filled bottle with a rag wick.

MTM (Motoscafi da Turismo modificati): "modified tourist motorboat": major Italian EMB of World War II.

MTR: smaller version of MTM (see above), to be carried in metal cylinder on casing of submarine.

MTSM: Italian motorboat armed with a torpedo and two small depthcharges.

Myojo-Kai: "Venus Modified": Japanese popular name for planned kamikaze variant of IJN's Yokosuka D3Y Myojo (Venus) single-engined bomber trainer.

"Myrt": Allied codename for IJN's Nakajima C6N Saiun (Painted Cloud) single-engined, carrier- or land-based recce aircraft/night fighter.

Napalm: thickened gasoline (and the metallic salts used as thickener) used in incendiary bombs.

Natter: "Adder" or "Viper": German Bachem Ba 349 rocket-propelled, point-defence interceptor.

Neger: "Nigger": German manned-torpedo, similar to Marder (qv).

"Nick": Allied codename for IJA's Kawasaki Ki-45 Toryu (Dragon Killer) twin-engined heavy fighter/night fighter/ground-attack aircraft.

Nisei: American-born citizens of Japanese descent, serving in non-combatant roles with Allies (eg, interpreters) in the Pacific theatre.

Ohka: "cherry blossom": piloted bomb of IJN. (See also Baka.)

"Oscar": Allied codename for IJA's Nakajima Ki-43 Hayabusa (Peregrine Falcon) single-engined fighter.

"Peggy": Allied codename for IJA's Mitsubishi Ki-67 Hiryu (Flying Dragon) twin-engined heavy bomber (purpose-modified for kamikaze as Ki-67-I KAI).

"Pig": see Maiale.

Rammjägers: "Battering Rams": heavily-armoured interceptors of the Luftwaffe's Sturmstaffeln (qv).

"Randy": Allied codename for IJA's Kawasaki Ki-102 twin-engined, high-altitude night fighter or ground-attack aircraft.

RATOG: Rocket Assisted Take Off Gear: auxiliary rockets fitted to

Glossary

reduce take-off length of aircraft or – as in Yokosuka D4Y4 "Judy" (**qv**) – to boost terminal diving speed.

Reichenberg: piloted version of German Fieseler Fi 103 (FZG 76) "flying bomb" ("V-1").

"Rita": Allied codename for IJN's Nakajima G8N Renzan (Mountain Range) four-engined bomber. Four only were completed: the G8N1 was intended to carry and launch the Ohka Model 43.

Sake: fermented rice wine, traditionally served hot by Japanese. Sake issued for final toast by "special attack" personnel was often announced as the gift of a senior officer or of the Emperor. Properly, the farewell toast was water, as a symbol of purity.

"Sally": Allied codename for IJA's Mitsubishi Ki-21 twin-engined heavy bomber/transport. Originally named "Jane" after Gen Douglas MacArthur's wife: the General objected! Sometimes also called "Gwen" (Ki-21-IIb); properly, "Sally 3").

"Sam": Allied codename for IJN's Mitsubishi A7M Reppu (Hurricane) single-engined, carrier- or land-based fighter/interceptor.

Samurai: "one who is a servant"; ie, the retainer of a feudal lord; hence the name given to the traditional warrior caste of Japan.

SCAP: Supreme Commander of Allied Powers in Japan (ie, the occupation force, from August 1945); a post occupied, as dictator in all but name, by Gen Douglas MacArthur, USA.

Schlitten: "Sledge": German experimental EMB of catamaran design.

Schwertal: "Grampus": projected German "underwater fighter aircraft" a super-manoeuvrable, high-speed midget submersible, Walter-powered.

Seehund: "Seal": German Type XXVIIB U-boat; a two-man midget submarine.

Seeteufel: "Sea Devil": German experimental "special attack" amphibious craft.

Sentai: "Air Group": basic IJAAF unit with an average strength of c.40 aircraft in three Chutai ("squadrons") (See **Kokutai (ii)**.)

Seppuku: ritual suicide, known less elegantly as **hara-kiri** ("belly-slitting"), by disembowellment.

Shimbu Tokubetsu Kogekitai: official designation of suicide units of IJA; **shimbu** may be translated as "band of heroic warriors" or "brandishing the sword". (See **Shimpu**; **Kamikaze**.)

Shimpu Tokubetsu Kogekitai: "Divine Wind Special Attack Force"; official name of suicide units of IJN, often abbreviated to **Tokko-Tai**. (**Kamikaze** and **Shimpu** are alternative readings of the Sino-Japanese characters for "Divine Wind".)

Shinkai: "Sea Vibrator": experimental two-man midget submersible of IJN.

Shinryu: "Divine Dragon": experimental piloted glider-bomb of IJN.

Shinto: "The Way of the Gods": the indigenous, animistic, non-exclusive religion of Japan. During the 20th century, "State Shinto" became the vehicle of ultra-nationalism.

Shinyo: "Ocean-shaker" or "Sea-quake" boat: one- or two-man EMB, usually with bow-mounted impact-fuzed charge, employed suicidally by IJN.

Shiragiku Units: Among the last kamikaze strikes were those made by Shiragiku ("White Crysanthemum") units; so called because they were composed largely of venerable training aircraft such as the IJN's Kyushu K11W Shiragiku and the IJA's "Cypress" (**qv**), "Spruce" (**qv**) and "Cedar" (**qv**).

Shogun: "great general"; originally **Seii Taishogun**, "Barbarian-quelling commander". The Shogunate estab-lished in 1192 by Yoritomo Minamoto set a pattern for the military govern-ment of Japan, theoretically on behalf of the God-Emperor, until the Meiji Restoration (**qv**).

Shusui: "Swinging Sword": popular name for the Mitsubishi J8M1 (IJN) or Ki-200/202 (IJA), a Japanese copy of the German Komet (**qv**).

"Special Attack": throughout the main text I have used this translation of the Japanese phrase Tokko-Tai (see **Shimpu**) as a convenient way of referring to suicidal units and weapons of all arms and nations.

"Spruce": Allied codename for IJA's Tachikawa Ki-9 biplane trainer.

Sturmstaffeln: "Assault Squadrons" of the Luftwaffe, formed for close-in – sometimes ramming – attacks on Allied heavy bomber formations.

Tai-atari: "body-crashing"; a euphemism for kamikaze tactics.

Taran: Soviet-pioneered aerial "special attack" method: a fighter with an armoured propeller closed in astern of a bomber and attempted to "buzz-saw" its tail assembly.

Tatsumaki Butai: "Tornado Corps": 722nd Kokutai, IJNAF, formed to operate the Ohka, but was not operational.

Teishin Hikosentai: "Raiding Flying Regiment"; transport unit of c.35 aircraft of IJAAF, principally for paratroop unit operations.

Teishin Rentai: "Raiding Regiment": paratroop unit, c.700 strong, of IJA.

"Tojo": Allied codename for IJA's Nakajima Ki-44 Shoki (Demon) single-engined, single-seat fighter.

Toka: "Wistaria": Japanese popular name for IJN's projected copy of IJA's Nakajima Ki-115 Tsurugi (**qv**).

"Tony": Allied codename for IJA's Kawasaki Ki-61 Hien (Swallow)

single-engined, single-seat fighter.

"Topsy": Allied codename for IJA's Mitsubishi Ki-57 transport.

Tornado: German experimental high-speed EMB powered by Argus pulse-jet.

T-Stoff: liquid fuel (hydrogen peroxide/water) for Walter rocket motor. Japanese name was "Ko" (See **C-Stoff**.)

Tsurugi: "Sabre": Japanese popular name for IJA's Nakajima Ki-115 utility "special attack" bomber.

UDT: Underwater Demolition Team, USN, of "frogmen" and swimmers for pre-landing beach reconnaissance and demolition of beach obstacles.

U-Kanamono: "U-Type Metal Fittings" Japanese cover-name for torpedo-armed awash-boat for coast defence.

"Ultra"/"Magic": major code-breaking operations of British and American intelligence respectively.

USSBS: United States Strategic Bombing Survey: major investigation into all aspects of (primarily) aerial operations in World War II by teams of special interrogators. Many of its findings have been disputed, but it remains a vital reference source.

"Val": Allied codename for IJN's Aichi D3A single-engined, carrier- or land-based divebomber.

Volksjäger: "People's Fighter": the Luftwaffe's Heinkel He 162 (unofficially called "Salamander") jet-propelled, utility interceptor.

"Weasel": name originally given by Allies to German "special attack" craft at time of Normandy landings.

Wilde Sau: "Wild Boar": Luftwaffe night-fighter tactic – freelance interceptors operating against Allied bombers in brilliantly-illuminated flak-free areas over the Reich.

"Willow": Allied codename for IJN's Yokosuka K5Y land-based or float-plane biplane trainer.

"Window": anti-radar device: strips of metal foil cut to lengths of radar frequencies and air-dropped to cause excessive "clutter".

X- and XE-craft: British midget submarines armed with detachable side-charges: X-craft used in European theatre; XE-craft in Far East.

"Zeke": Allied codename for IJN's Mitsubishi A6M Reisen (Zero Fighter); probably best-known to all, however, as the "Zero". Codenames "Ray" "Ben", "Hap" and "Hamp" (the two latter for the A6M3 Model 32; later "Zeke 32") were also given to this famous aircraft at various times and places.

Zero: see "Zeke", above.

Index

Index

EXPLOSIVE MOTORBOATS
Austrian
British
German
Italian
Japanese (Army)
Japanese (Navy)

"FROGMEN" & SWIMMERS
American
German
Italian
Italo-British
Japanese

HUMAN TORPEDOES & MANNED TORPEDOES
British
German
Italian
Italo-British
Japanese

KAMIKAZE AIRCRAFT (JAPANESE)
(see also individual types, units and operations)

MIDGET SUBMARINES
American
British
German

Index

291

Index

Index

295

Index

Picture Credits

The author and publisher wish to thank the individuals and organizations who have supplied illustrations, here credited by page number and indicated by caption directs where necessary. The following abbreviations have been used: AWM, Australian War Memorial, Canberra; DM, Deutsches Museum, Munich; UFF, Fujifotos, Tokyo; IWM, Imperial War Museum, London; MARS, Military Archive & Research Services, London; UFF, Ufficio Storico Marina Militare Italiana, Rome; USA, US Army; USAF, US Air Force; USCG, US Coast Guard; USMC, US Marine Corps; USN, US Navy; USNA, US National Archives.

25: IWM (3); 26: Above & Bottom, USNA/Below, Capt Masayuki Koyama, JMSDF; 27: Left, USN/Below, USNA; 28-29: Top & Above, AWM (Neg nos 12427, 12723)/Left, IWM; 30-31: Above left & Left, IWM/Above centre, USN/Above, USNA/Below, USNA(MARS); 32-33: IWM (5); 34-35: IWM (4); 36: Above & Right, DM/Below, IWM; 85: UFF (3); 86-87: UFF (2); 88-89: Above & Below, USNA/Far left, USA/Left, USMC; 90-91: Right & Far right, USNA/Below, IWM; 92-93: Above left & centre, IWM/Above & Left, Bundesarchiv, Koblenz/Below, Signal; 94-95: USN (7); 96: USN (4); 145: Above, USN/Left, USNA (2); 146: Right, USN/Below, USNA; 147: Top, IWM (2)/Below, USN; 148-149: USN (3); 150-151: Above & Far right, USN/Right, USAF/Below, IWM; 152-153: Far left & Left, USN/Above, IWM/Below, USAF; 154-155: IWM (4); 156: Above (upper), IWM/Above (lower), Bundesarchiv, Koblenz/Right, USAF; 205: Above, Museo Navale, La Spezia/Left, IWM/Below, UFF; 206-207: Above, Science Museum, London (MARS)/Right & Far right, IWM/Below, Keystone; 208-209: Above left, Above & Left, FUJ(MARS)/Below, IWM; 210-211: Above & Left, IWM/Far left & Below, USNA/Bottom left, USN/Centre left, USA(MARS); 212-213: above & Right, MARS/Below right & centre, IWM (4)/Below, DM; 214: Above, IWM(MARS)/Above right, USA/Below, IWM (2); 215: Above left, USCG/Above & Below, IWM/Left, USA; 216: Above, AWM (Neg nos 13966/68/69/70)/Left, USNA/Below, AWM (Neg no 73484).

Jacket (Front): Left & Centre, USN/Right, DM; Jacket (Back): Top, UFF/Centre, USN/Bottom, Jennifer Moore Personality Picture Library, London; Jacket (Back Flap): Mark Holt (Courtesy of IWM).

PRINTED IN BELGIUM BY

INTERNATIONAL BOOK PRODUCTION

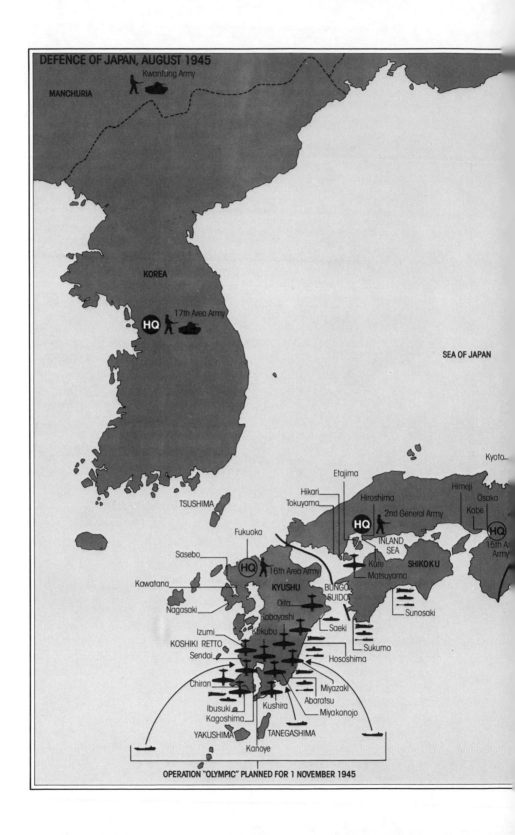

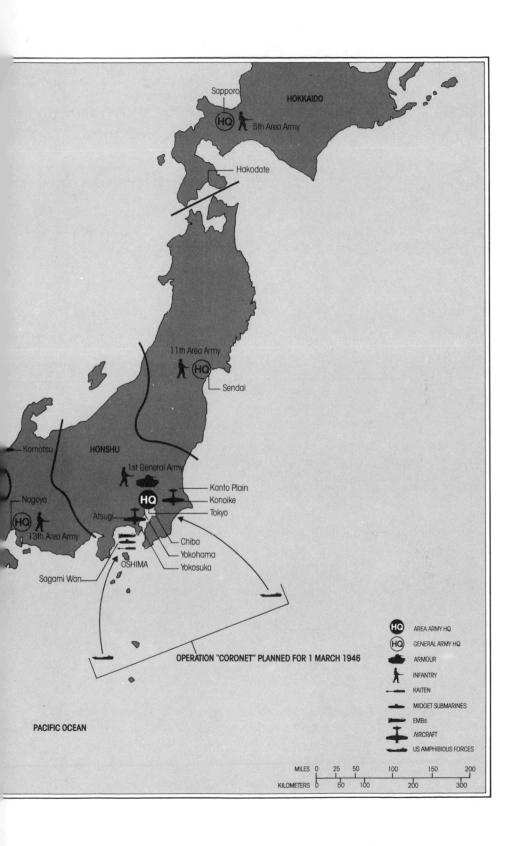

HOKKAIDO

Sapporo
HQ 5th Area Army

Hakodate

11th Area Army
HQ
Sendai

Komatsu

HONSHU

1st General Army

HQ
Kanto Plain
Konoike
Atsugi
Tokyo

Nagoya

HQ
13th Area Army

Chiba
Yokohama
Yokosuka

OSHIMA

Sagami Wan

OPERATION "CORONET" PLANNED FOR 1 MARCH 1946

PACIFIC OCEAN

HQ AREA ARMY HQ
HQ GENERAL ARMY HQ
ARMOUR
INFANTRY
KAITEN
MIDGET SUBMARINES
EMBs
AIRCRAFT
US AMPHIBIOUS FORCES

MILES   0   25   50   100   150   200
KILOMETERS 0   50   100   200   300

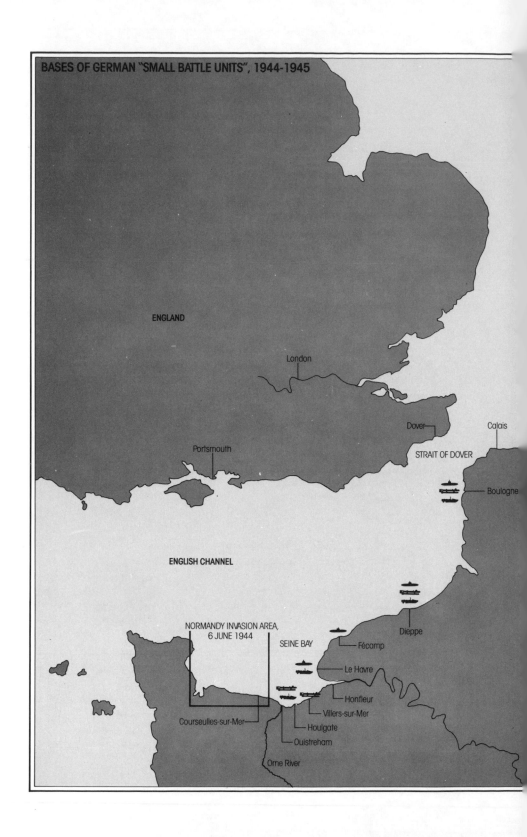

BASES OF GERMAN "SMALL BATTLE UNITS", 1944-1945

ENGLAND

London

Dover

Calais

STRAIT OF DOVER

Portsmouth

Boulogne

ENGLISH CHANNEL

Dieppe

NORMANDY INVASION AREA,
6 JUNE 1944

SEINE BAY

Fécamp

Le Havre

Honfleur

Villers-sur-Mer

Courseulles-sur-Mer

Houlgate

Ouistreham

Orne River

IJSSELMEER

HOLLAND

Ijmuiden

Amsterdam

Nijmegen

NORTH SEA

Waal River

Emmerich

Rotterdam

Maas River

SCHELDT ESTUARY

Hollandschdiep

Vlissingen

Walcheren

Rhine River

Dunkirk

Antwerp

BELGIUM

GERMANY

FRANCE

LUXEMBOURG

MIDGET SUBMARINES

EMBs

MANNED TORPEDOES

MILES 0 10 20 30 40 50 60

KILOMETERS 0 20 40 60 80